Song of the North Country

For

my student, Sandy Fuhr (1947–2008)
my colleague, Bill Holm (1943–2009)
my father, Donald Pichaske (1916–2009)

Song of the North Country

A Midwest Framework to the Songs of Bob Dylan

David Pichaske

continuum

2010

The Continuum International Publishing Group Inc
80 Maiden Lane, New York, NY 10038

The Continuum International Publishing Group Ltd
The Tower Building, 11 York Road, London SE1 7NX

www.continuumbooks.com

Library of Congress Cataloging-in-Publication Data
Pichaske, David R.
  Song of the North Country: a Midwest framework to the songs of Bob Dylan / by David
Pichaske.
    p. cm.
Includes bibliographical references and index.
ISBN-13: 978-1-4411-4232-0 (hardcover: alk. paper)
ISBN-10: 1-4411-4232-0 (hardcover: alk. paper)
ISBN-13: 978-1-4411-9766-5 (pbk.: alk. paper)
ISBN-10: 1-4411-9766-4 (pbk.: alk. paper) 1. Dylan, Bob, 1941—Criticism and
interpretation. 2. Middle West—Civilization. I. Title.

ML420.D98P46 2010
782.42164092—dc22
                            2009042863

ISBN 978-1-4411-9766-5 (paperback)
ISBN 978-1-4411-4232-0 (hardcover)

Typeset by Pindar NZ, Auckland, New Zealand
Printed in the United States of America

Contents

Acknowledgments

Like most serious writing projects, this book has been in process for a long time. A letter to my father of 20 years ago reads, "began work on the Dylan book last week," but that particular start became, as I recall, an article for the *Telegraph*. Under various titles in numerous journal articles *Song of the North Country* shaped itself, its focus shifting as I moved from one geography to another and from one academic interest to another. Routinely, I gathered my energies, and routinely "the Dylan book" got put on hold while I assembled the anthology *Late Harvest: Recent Rural American Writing* or wandered off to Poland, Latvija, and Mongolia on Fulbright fellowships. And again while I worked on *Rooted: Seven Midwest Writers of Place*. But all of those detours, including the stints abroad, altered my perceptions of life, America, and Bob Dylan. In its final form, *Song of the North Country* combines two of my main career interests — sixties rock and Midwest literature — and reflects as well experiences abroad. Insofar as I'm returning now to a subject on which I wrote early in my career, this book represents one of those coming-back-after-going-out journeys I discuss in Chapter 4.

"Did you interview Dylan?" people ask whenever I mention this project. No, I did not. He told me not to bother: no sense talkin' to him, it's the same as talkin' to myself. I listened to Dylan, I read Dylan, and, as should be obvious, I read the many interviews of people who have talked to Dylan. To them, and to the others on whose books and essays this work builds, my thanks. This book is almost as referential and allusive as Dylan's songs. Especially among them I want to thank John Bauldie, editor of the *Telegraph* and *Wanted Man*; Andrew Muir, editor of *Judas!*; Gary Burns, editor of *Popular Music and Society*; and Terry Kelly, editor of the *Bridge*. This book draws on material in articles published in those magazines. My thanks also to Michael Gray, who visited us in Minnesota during the flood of April, 2001; to Ken Stuart, my editor at Schirmer Books and Paragon House, who signed *A Generation in Motion* and was "interested in" a Dylan book way back in 1986; to Joe Amato, who invented the Rural and Regional Studies Center at Southwest State which supported my work in Midwest Literature for so many years; to Hibbing High School Assistant Principal Jac Fleming, who dredged up old high school newspapers for me to read; to Carolyn Kangas, who talked at length about Hibbing High School in the fifties; to the Minnesota Historical Society Library for access to its collection of Bob Dylan materials; to the Iron Range Research Center research library in Chisholm for access to their collection; to Marek Jedlinski and Krzysytof Majer in Łódź, Poland, who share my interest in Dylan and provided ideas and insights; to individuals who fed me ideas at conferences in Sioux Falls, Manchester, Minneapolis, and Łódź; to Brian O'Flaherty, Sandy Mosch, Lorien Downing, and Ashley Hoyme for proofreading and advice; to Sandy Zeug, who helped create search-and-find electronic text files for this project; to Hugh Curtler, Dana Yost, Barton Sutter, David Lanegran, and Ben Erickson who read all or parts of this manuscript in early draft and offered valuable suggestions. And to my wife, Michelle, and other close friends, from whom I've been a bit absent lately this past year. I can change, I swear . . .

COPYRIGHT ACKNOWLEDGMENTS: DYLAN MATERIAL

Special thanks to Bob Dylan for permission to reprint lyrics, liner notes, fiction, and other prose, and to Jeff Rosen and Callie Gladman in the offices of the Bob Dylan Music Company.

"Well, I'm from the Midwest. Boy, that's two different worlds."

— *Rolling Stone*, November 29, 1969

Introduction: Bob Dylan and the Midwest

"May you have a strong foundation
When the winds of changes shift"

— "Forever Young"

In an essay titled "Tradition and the Individual Talent," published in 1919, T. S. Eliot wrestles with the relationship between the individual artist and the tradition within which he works. Defining this tradition was problematic for Eliot the expat, born and raised in St. Louis, educated out East at Harvard, self-exiled to the other side of the Atlantic like too many members of the Lost Generation, married to a British girl, working in a British bank. Also Eliot — a classicist of the highest order — was one of the founders of literary modernism, and a chum of that other expat modernist poet Ezra "Make It New" Pound. Of what use is tradition to a modernist? Eliot admits in his opening sentences that tradition has a bum rap: "You can hardly make the word agreeable to English ears without [some] comfortable reference to the reassuring science of archaeology" (47). Poets strive to be innovative, because we value them for how they are different from their predecessors — how they find their own material and their own voice, and speak to the present generation. We have a "tendency to insist, when we praise a poet, upon those aspects of his work in which he least resembles anyone else. . . . We dwell with satisfaction on the poet's difference from his predecessors, especially from his immediate predecessors" (47).

Popular culture was not unknown when Eliot wrote, and even then the music biz was an important part of the popular culture machine. And while the rock-'n'-roll, folk, and rock music scenes with which Dylan grew up and which he helped to shape were far in the future, one cannot help reading Eliot's remarks on poetry as an interesting commentary on American pop culture. Even in Dylan's youth, the pop music machine valued sounds it could promote as new, even if they were a cover version of "Hound Dog" which paled in comparison to Mama Thornton's original, a sanitized version of "Irene, Good Night" which changes "get you in my dreams" to "see you in my dreams," and a smooth-as-silk Peter, Paul and Mary version of "Blowin' in the Wind." Certainly, the criticism most leveled at late fifties rock-'n'-roll — by Dylan, by the Beatles, by a sixties generation still in high school — was that it had retreated from the innovations of Little Richard, Chuck Berry, Jerry Lee Lewis into the tired and timid formulae of Top 40 AM radio. And as the fifties melted into the sixties, that generation continued to value innovative over traditional, alternative over mainstream.

Conversely, the bedrock principle of the "folk revival" which welcomed Dylan to Greenwich Village in 1961 was a reassertion of Tradition with a capital T: no new songs, no commercial songs, no new styles or instruments, and especially no electric guitars. The invention of the generation ahead of the sixties crowd, this revival nevertheless presented enough of an alternative to Your Hit Parade schlock to briefly catch the youngsters' fancy until it proved too dogmatic, too conservative, too tradition-bound to advance. The youth moved to rock, and the folk revival stagnated. Innovation won out over Tradition.

This is not exactly the direction in which Eliot heads in his essay. Eliot, who quotes from and alludes to others almost as much as Dylan, takes a position which turns out to be very Dylanesque, especially in light of recent Dylan material: if we approach a poet's work without our prejudice against Tradition, Eliot argues, "We shall often find that not only the best, but the most individual parts of his work may be those in which the dead poets, his ancestors, assert their immortality most vigorously" (48). The artist should not be a cult or a personality; historical sense is essential to anyone who would continue to be a poet beyond his twenty-fifth year. However, the proper use of tradition is not "following the ways of the immediate generation before us in a blind or timid adherence to its successes" (48), which was the position of the Greenwich Village folk purists; the individual talent borrows from and is defined by tradition, but it also reshapes, builds upon, and redefines that tradition. The present is "directed" by the past, but the present alters the past. The poet must be conscious of "the main current," but he must also understand "the obvious fact that art never improves," because development is not necessarily improve-ment; development is mostly — and this is brilliantly prescient on Eliot's part — "based on a complication in economics and machinery" (52). The role of the true poet — can we read "rock poet" here? — is impersonal: "the mind of the mature poet differs from that of the immature one not precisely in any valuation of 'personality,' not being necessarily more interesting, or having 'more to say,' but rather by being a more finely perfected medium in which special, or very varied, feelings are at liberty to enter into new combinations. . . . The poet's mind is in fact a receptacle for seizing and storing up numberless feelings, phrases, images, which remain there until all the particles which can unite to form a new compound are present together" (53, 55). "What is to be insisted upon," Eliot concludes, "is that the poet must develop or procure the consciousness of the past and that he should continue to develop this consciousness throughout his career" (52).

Much has been written in the last 40 years about Dylan's mind and art, but Eliot hit the nail right on the head two decades before Dylan was even born.

We need not, however, accept Eliot's interpretation of the relationship between tradition and the individual talent, or even his definition of what that tradition is, to agree that, yes, every artist operates within a tradition, and that Dylan has always seemed conscious of his place within a tradition and of the need of every artist to sustain the tradition and "take it that step further," as he put it toward the end of the Westwood One Radio interview. Discussions of Dylan's art typically have focused on identifying sources and allusions, defining the tradition(s) within which Dylan works, and — in an age highly sensitive to "intellectual property rights" and obsessed with individuality — arguing the fine distinctions between alluding-sampling-expanding and copying-plagiarizing. Many Dylan songs from the high sixties to the present are dense tapestries referencing an amazingly wide range of American and world culture. Thus a hefty tonnage of printed material already tracks the musical, literary, philosophical, religious, and aesthetic traditions within which Dylan's work operates. This work is especially valuable and convincing when it references Dylan interviews, biographies, and autobiographies, showing us what Dylan actually heard, read, knew, borrowed, or breathed in the air around him . . . when it describes a tradition, and places Dylan's talent within that tradition.

For Eliot, tradition was culture in the broadest sense: art, history, language, philosophy, and most especially literature — "the whole of the literature of Europe from Homer and within it the whole of the literature of his own country" (49) and much of the rest of the world. Eliot was a book man, who mostly read and quoted. Sometimes he visited and listened, and wrote what he saw and heard. We get occasional autobiographical references, and some readers have found vestiges of Eliot's childhood place, St. Louis (especially the Mississippi River), but for Eliot tradition came mostly secondhand, through cultural artifacts. For Dylan, tradition is also mostly cultural: the primary tradition is music, but also important are literary and religious traditions, and the traditions of graphic and cinematic art. However, even when being derivative or imaginative, Dylan offers a stronger sense of experience-in-place than Eliot. This book argues that first impressions being the most lasting, Dylan's Minnesota place offers an important framework — not, certainly, the only framework — for considering his work. It suggests that the traditions of the Midwest, the Upper Midwest, and the Minnesota Iron Range offer a useful context within which to assess Dylan's individual talent and interpret his work. It argues, to be upfront about things, that Dylan's experiences growing up in Minnesota shaped, and thus explain, much of his work, from actual subject matter through speech and style to conscious and unconscious habits of thought and perception. In a nutshell, I argue that for all his explorations of the Other, Dylan's Minnesota Self made him what he is. "You create out of your own experiences," Dylan once told Robert Hilburn of the *L.A. Times* (Diddle: 30).

This book, then, belongs to what has been called "bioregionalism": a focus in American Studies on regional units "bringing together literature, the visual arts and historical accounts in terms of 'regional images'" (Bradshaw: 3), including a basic understanding of "the ways in which geographical space affects social practice and acts as an essential medium for it" (Bradshaw: 172). While this complex, multi-disciplinary "science" is barely off the academic drawing boards, hard-core bioregionalists make claims for the relationship between place and personality almost as strong as those some geneticists make for the cause–effect relationship of genes and behavior (namely that chromosomes determine everything you do, from the time you wake up in the morning, to the meal you order at the restaurant, to your reaction to opportunity, adversity, and crisis). Before turning our attention in subsequent chapters to the connection between Dylan's work and his Minnesota roots, we should examine those arguments in a general sense and take a broad look at the way place impacts art.

Bioregionalism is nothing new. Geography has always ranked high among the many ways we describe human beings; it is as commonly used as class, gender, ethnicity, and religion. We group people this way because these categories help define us. Insofar as we are Lutheran, Catholic, Jewish, or Buddhist, we worship in separate places led by clergy who studied distinct theologies in separate seminaries . . . so we develop unique, shared experiences and distinct ways of looking at the world. We belong to a distinct group of people. Sometimes we identify ourselves or others by gender — and thus programs in Women's Studies (if not Men's Studies), on the assumption that all women share some commonalities which separate them from all men, making "women" a distinct group worthy of analysis. We identify people as Asian, African, Afro-American, or Hispanic . . . not without justification do colleges offer what they call Asian Studies, Afro-American Studies, Latino/Latina Studies. We talk about country yokels, suburbanites, and "city types." Urban studies programs are common at colleges throughout the country, although they are not as popular as Gender Studies or ethnic studies; our college has its Rural and Regional Studies Program; Augustana College in Sioux Falls, South Dakota, has its Western American Studies Center. We may be rich, we may be poor, and in some respects rich and poor share a common experience no matter what their race or gender (and let us be honest: race, ethnicity, and gender are not much of an issue until belonging to a particular race, ethnicity, or gender consigns an individual to a lower class). Thus F. Scott Fitzgerald writes in his short story, "Let me tell you about the very rich. They are different from you and me" ("The Rich Boy": 152). We understand what he's talking about because we've read our Thorstein Veblen. We collectivize other groups, for the purpose of analysis and discussion: "senior citizens," adolescents, toddlers, special needs students, "the Greatest Generation," "sixties types," members of a Generation X, Y, or Z.

We often attach a behavior or manner of thinking to a geography. We title a textbook *The American Tradition in Literature*, as if America — a place — is also an identifiable aesthetic. On the assumption that a particular place defines a special content, we offer courses in *British* constitutional law, *Minnesota* history, *Western American* literature. Someone is a Yankee, a Midwesterner, a Southerner, a Hoosier, or a Texan. Even within states, we differentiate outstate Minnesota from the Twin Cities, "downstate" Illinois from Chicago, and — this is true — "West River" South Dakotans from the wimps who live "East River." "She's from California," says a friend, assessing a colleague's work ethic: "demands a lot, delivers very little." "Talks like a Southerner," says somebody else, implying much more than speech patterns. "Iowa farm girl," says somebody approvingly. "East Coast arrogant," says somebody else, less approvingly. We all know and use stereotypes based on place, and we all know — even if it's not acceptable to say so — that stereotypes are stereotypes because they are mostly true.

Place is as important as religion, wealth, experience, education, training, and occupation, because place sets parameters, or at least proclivities, on all of these. In *An American Childhood*, Annie Dillard writes, "When everything else has gone from my brain . . . when all has dissolved, what will be left, I believe, is topology: the dreaming memory of the land as it lay this way and that" (3). Place determines whether we live among pines or palms, cacti or cement walls; whether we surf or ice fish; whether we fear tornadoes, hurricanes, floods, or terrorist attacks; whether we imagine ourselves a writer, a farmer, or a commodities broker. Especially in America, still the land of recent immigrants, place often correlates with ethnicity and ethnic cultures, so that the strong Italian Catholic, Finnish Lutheran, Eastern European Jewish belief systems of particular places seep into the brains and daily habits of everyone in the area, regardless of personal ethnicities and religions. Even in this homogenized global economy, place influences the food we eat, the alcohol we drink, and thus our very lives: health studies correlate geography with incidences of cancer and heart disease, advising us to "drink more red wine, like the French; eat less red meat, like the Chinese." Place influences the books we read in school, the music we hear, even to an extent the television and films we watch. "What I learned in college," a graduate once told me, "is how much of what I believe is a result of having lived in a certain place at a certain time."

Beyond the subtleties of everything associated with ethnicity, simple density of population affects our experience and thinking. Population density makes a tremendous difference in the experiences of rural and urban kids, because it circumscribes the available options. Wallace Stegner points this out in his reminiscence of growing up in a Great Plains town ironically named White Mud:

> Once, in a self-pitying frame of mind, I was comparing my background with that of an English novelist friend. Where he had been brought up in London, taken from the age of four onward to the Tate and the National Gallery, sent traveling on the Continent in every school holiday, taught French and German and Italian, given access to bookstores, libraries, and British Museums, made familiar from infancy on with the conversation of the eloquent and the great, I had grown up in this dung-heeled sagebrush town on the disappearing edge of nowhere, utterly without painting, without sculpture, without architecture, almost without music or theater, without conversation or language or travel or stimulating instruction, without libraries or museums or bookstores, almost without books. . . . How, I asked this Englishman, could anyone from so deprived a background ever catch up? How was one expected to compete, as a cultivated man, with people like himself? He looked at me and said dryly, "Perhaps you got something else in place of all that."
>
> He meant, I suppose, that there are certain advantages to growing up a sensuous little savage, and to tell the truth I am not sure I would trade my childhood of freedom and the outdoors and the senses for a childhood of being led by the hand past all the Turners in the National Gallery. (*Wolf Willow*: 24–5)

Looking back at his own youth, Dylan — who certainly did not grow up "a sensuous little savage" — said something very similar in the *Spin* interview of 1985:

If I had any advantage over anybody at all, it's the advantage that I was all alone and could think and do what I wanted to. Looking back at it, it probably has a lot to do with growing up in northern Minnesota. I don't know what I would have been if I was growing up in the Bronx or Ethiopia or South America or even California. I think everybody's environment affects him in that way. (Engel: 80)

To quote Wallace Stegner again, "Expose a child to a particular environment at his susceptible time and he will perceive in the shapes of that environment until he dies" (*Wolf Willow*: 5).

Population density may explain some of our most fundamental character traits. In sparsely populated areas, everyone knows everyone else, everyone depends on everyone else, and the community needs all the help it can get; there is of necessity a higher tolerance for individual quirks, and a tendency to privilege people less because of what they are than for what they bring to the table beyond attitude and appetite. While the local support-training system will not carry a kid far in any musical or artistic direction, the need for participants in school organizations offers almost infinite opportunity to try everything. Nebraska State Poet William Kloefkorn recalls playing the snare drum "in my football uniform at halftime because I was the only drummer in our band" (54). You will not feel ignored on the Great Plains, Wallace Stegner says, although you might feel puny. And perhaps feeling puny builds character: screened from the actual processes of industrial and agricultural production, and living in an essentially service economy, a city kid just might get the idea that the world exists to make him comfortable. Or he might delude himself into thinking, like Robin Haynes, that "what matters is not objective reality, but how it is perceived" (1). Those who live in the country (or in New Orleans) understand that people must adjust themselves to accommodate environmental realities. Nature is large, powerful, ragged in tooth and claw, largely indifferent to you and me, and unlikely to change any time soon. As South Dakota poet Linda Hasselstrom points out, a blizzard can kill you. Blizzards and tornadoes aside, you had better get those crops planted in the spring, cultivated in the summer, and harvested before the first snow, or you won't have much to eat this winter. "You're pretty much ruled by nature up there," Dylan told Kurt Loder in 1984, referring to the Iron Range; "You have to sort of fall into line with that, regardless of how you're feeling that day or what you might want to do with your life or what you think about" (Cott: 293).

A long winter might give northerners Seasonal Affective Disorder (SAD). In cold climates, people might feel cosy or claustrophobic, depending on point of view, in buildings that reduce heating costs with lower ceilings, thick walls, and smaller windows. In warmer climates, high ceilings were mandatory in the days before air-conditioning, and the distinction between indoors and outdoors is more blurred. You get a different type of person in each place. Traveling Europe, I could not help noticing that the differences between Scandinavian and Mediterranean parallel those between American Yankees and Southerners, and I came to suspect that social differences reflected climatic differences. A year in Outer Mongolia had me speculating that living life so very much at the mercy of weather makes Mongolians better at thinking and acting reactively, less adept at long-range planning. In *Chronicles*, Dylan plays a similar game: "Northerners think abstract," he says; "I think abstract, too" (194).

Even if we live lives largely insulated from nature, looking out the window as it were, place has its impact upon us. The fundamentally horizontal or vertical nature of our place — high sky versus high-rises — turns our thinking horizontal or vertical and colors everything from our brains to our feelings to our writing style. This is Minnesota writer Bill Holm's take in the essay "Horizontal Grandeur":

> There are two eyes in the human head — the eye of mystery, and the eye of harsh truth — the hidden and the open — the woods eye and the prairie eye. The prairie eye looks for distance, clarity, and light; the woods eye for closeness, complexity, and darkness. The prairie eye looks for usefulness and plainness in art and architecture; the woods eye for the baroque and ornamental. Dark old brownstones on Summit Avenue were created by a woods eye; the square white farmhouse and red barn are prairie eye's work. Sherwood Anderson wrote his stories with a prairie eye, plain and awkward, told in the voice of a man almost embarrassed to be telling them, but bullheadedly persistent to get at the meaning of the events; Faulkner, whose endless complications of motive and language take the reader miles behind the simple facts of an event, sees the world with a woods eye. One eye is not superior to the other, but they are different. To some degree, like male and female, darkness and light, they exist in all human heads, but one or the other seems dominant. The Manicheans were not entirely wrong. (*Music*: 17–18)

This particular passage has been often quoted by Minnesota writers, who realize that the difference between a woods eye and a prairie eye is a big difference indeed. Gertrude Stein once wrote, "After all, anybody is as their land and air is. It is that which makes them and the arts and the work they do and the way they eat and the way they drink and the way they learn and everything" (Spitz: 9). Bob Spitz uses this quotation to open his biography of Bob Dylan, but he might just as well have quoted his subject, who announced in the famous *Playboy* interview of 1966, "if I was born and raised in New York or Kansas City, I'm sure everything would have turned out different . . . but I'm *not* a New Yorker. I'm North Dakota-Minnesota-Midwestern. . . . My brains and feelings have come from there" (Cott: 109).

We can pursue the influence of place on thought even further. Long ago linguists Edward Sapir and Benjamin Lee Whorf suggested that language sets parameters that circumscribe our perception of the world. If we don't have the word, we don't think the thought, because we think in terms of the denotative and connotative meanings of the words we know. Where a variety of words for colors or weather phenomena allow subtle distinctions, they are made; where the words do not exist, those distinctions are overlooked. Thus philosopher William Gass, born in North Dakota, writes, "Words are properties of thoughts and thoughts cannot be thought without them" (*On Being Blue*: 21), and my own philosopher friend Hugh Curtler worries that the limited vocabulary of many modern students handicaps them with a restricted range of thought. The by-now-familiar strategy of attempting to excise sexist and racist attitudes by banning the use of sexist and racist words (gone over-the-top when David Howard, an aide to Washington mayor Anthony Williams, was made to resign in 1999 for saying, "I will have to be niggardly with this fund because it's not going to be a lot of money") is an example of the Sapir–Whorf hypothesis in action. So is the feminist argument that "sexual harassment" was not recognized before somebody coined a word for it, and the male counterargument that the absence in English of a female equivalent for "misogynist" makes it impossible to acknowledge some women's hatred of men.

While language comes first from our parents and later from our peers, the language of both parents and peers has been shaped by place: subjects discussed, words used in discussion, attitudes carried by those words. Live in one place and you grow up thinking about hockey, Christmas, and *Little House on the Prairie*; live somewhere else and you grow up thinking about Ramadan, stock car races, and *Little Women*. And talking in the voice of *Little House on the Prairie* or *Little Women*, and thinking in the mindset of *Little House on the Prairie* or *Little Women*. Thus studies of regional dialects regularly examine not only vocabulary, idiom, pronunciation, and grammar, but also values, perceptions, and attitudes.

But, someone objects, we now live in a global village that is no longer a village. Internet and cable television annihilate space and place, and our educational agenda homogenizes even while preaching diversity. Ours is an age of *USA Today*, Fox TV, MSN online news, and increasingly powerful national media with little sense of Hibbing, Minnesota. Even smart people trying to escape Fox News do so by reading the *New York Times* online. Local newspapers are dead or dying. TV gives us New York, Miami, Las Vegas, Hollywood — or the remote corners of Asia and Africa — but rarely our own place. Kathleen Parker headlines her October 16, 2008 column (dateline, ironically, New York), "Mainstream Media Need to Get Outside Their Bubble."

This mostly commercial agenda shapes our language and our thinking, right down to the songs we sing and the art we see. "Mobility and the profit motive blunt our sense of place, allowing the land to be bulldozed into a vast commercial way station," write Wayne Franklin and Michael Steiner (7); "Surveying the forlorn stretches of Holiday Inns and Wal-Marts and McDonald's, or Levittown, Las Vegas, and much of Los Angeles, Doloren Hayden has concluded that 'despair about placelessness is as much a part of American experience as pleasure in the sense of place.'" "Contemporary evocations of place in America," Michael Kowalewski writes,

> often seem embattled, unsettled, and besieged: at odds — often overwhelming odds — with attitudes and economic, technological, and social forces that threaten the local distinctiveness of the American landscape, both rural and urban. . . . The spiritual as well as physical "macadamization" of contemporary America has eroded the distinctiveness of individual places and preemptively discouraged people from caring about them. (12)

In 1977 Wendell Berry published his famous *The Unsettling of America*. In 1985, Joshua Meyrowitz published a book titled *No Sense of Place*. In 1993 James Kunstler published a book titled *The Geography of Nowhere*.

These books were written after Dylan grew up, American place has had a significant technological component for at least a century now, and technology usually works against the natural environment to buffer and homogenize place. In his interview with Kurt Loder, Dylan made a little joke about growing up with no television (Cott: 302), but even Dylan knew *The Lone Ranger* and *I Love Lucy*, the eviscerated rock-'n'-roll of fifties commercial radio, Hibbing High School textbooks that were pretty much nationally standardized. Even the radio, records, and films that offered connections to more interesting alternative geographies and cultures — *Blackboard Jungle* and *Rebel Without a Cause*, Gatemouth Page's *No-Name Jive* show out of Shreveport, Louisiana — were seen and heard all around America, including suburban Philadelphia where I grew up. The same "parallel universe," as Dylan terms it in *Chronicles*, which helped Dylan escape Main Street, Hibbing, allowed me to escape Springfield High School. But — and here is the crucial point — Dylan also admits that his preferences among the various media-disseminated alternatives he found as a kid in Hibbing, and later in Minneapolis, were influenced by his own experience. The counter-identity to the "three-buttoned-suit post-war generation of America" which attracted him was not urban jazz or European high culture; it was music and cinema which reflected his origins in a place where that counter-identity could still be found: "What I was most interested in twenty-four hours a day was the rural music" (Cott: 425).

This last remark raises the $64,000 question: when push comes to shove, how much do we really invent? How much do we absorb from media? Do we ever fully adjust to a new place? Is it true that "you can take the boy out of the country, but you can never take the country out of the boy"? Granted, our shared human DNA allows us to recognize, understand, and absorb material from places, cultures, traditions not our own. Granted that some people are very good actors, even in the particularizing details of speech and gesture. Granted even that Robert Frost, preeminent spokesman for New England, and Dave Etter, poet of the Midwest village, were both born in California. Still, can we finally become what we were not to begin with? In the final analysis, I think we can — but not without the soul connection that Dylan felt for the foreign influences that most influenced him, the connection that gives the white, Irish musicians of *The Commitments* the right to play Wilson Pickett: "You're workin' class, right? . . . We're gonna be playin' Dublin soul." Without that fundamental connection, artifice remains unconvincing.

And if the Other we explore and absorb is just a disguised version of the Self, have we ever really gone out?

Chapter 4 of this book will argue that there is in fact a long-standing rural paradigm of going out, of seeking the Other, of breaking the roots, of escaping rural place for the University of Minnesota, New York, London, and gay Paree. Perhaps that is a human paradigm: perhaps we all need to rebel against our parents in adolescence and go somewhere else, be somebody — often the exact opposite of what they hoped we would be; break away from our same-sex group of friends and connect with a sexual Other; throw away the old culture and "Make It New." Departure is an exciting time of life. However, it often produces more turbulence than great art, and Minnesota poet Robert Bly once told an audience at Knox College, "You can't write great poetry in your youth because you're too neurotic in your twenties; your job in your twenties is to go out into the world, make connections with the world. The time for poetry is later."

Implicit in that remark is the suggestion that what seeks those connections is a kind of adolescent neurosis, enhanced by the technologies which form the basis (I nearly said bedrock, but that would have been a contradiction in terms) of postmodern life. So we reach out for everything, make all kinds of connections. But unless they are soul connections, they do not satisfy us. We feel uneasy, uncomfortable, alienated. We do not know who we are.[1] We're living in a foreign country, as Dylan says, and ultimately we will seek "Shelter from the Storm." In "Abandoned Love," after pointing out that "Everybody's wearing a disguise," Dylan admits, significantly, "I can't cover what I am." We tire of disguises, and as we grow older we understand that "I" is ultimately *not* Other. Dylan told Rosenbaum in 1978 that one thing life on the road had taught him was, "if you try to be anyone but yourself, you will fail; if you are not true to your own heart, you will fail" (Cott: 218). That, according to Dylan, is the point of the film *Renaldo and Clara*: being untrue to the Self is a kind of death. There is no Dylan in *Renaldo and Clara*.

If we're looking for a cure for our age of anxiety, then recovering a sense of place might be the appropriate starting point. Many have argued that America, culturally, has engaged in a four-century-long postmodern experiment in going out, and an almost equally long search for some long-lost home. "Return" is the second half of that long-standing rural paradigm. One way to look at Dylan's career is that it is a long series of alternating bouts of frantic going out and laid-back returning home. He blew out of backwoods Minnesota for New York City, then in an attempt to go home retreated to Woodstock, New York, where he could ride a motorcycle around the back-country roads as he had done in Hibbing (and with the same disastrous results). Dylan exploded into the nervous, urban sound of rock and then retreated in time and tempo to the country sound of albums *John Wesley Harding* and *New Morning*. He then returned to New York, moved to California . . . and bought a farm back in Minnesota. He experimented with new age ideas and songs, then wrote nursery rhymes and blues and forties-era blues and waltzes. You can always go back, Dylan told us, even if you can't go back all the way. We reminisce in photographs and stories and songs. "Time it was, I have a photograph," sang Paul Simon. "All I've got is a photograph," sang Ringo Starr.[2]

It is not only rural Midwesterners who depart and return, and not only Bob Dylan. American literature and literary analysis seem to follow this pattern, and many see a new valuation of the home place in academic disciplines like environmental studies and some recent American writing. Leo Marx notes that after a long period of very careful attention to details of place, American literature moved after World War II "toward abstraction, away from the specification of social actualities, and away, above all, from that preoccupation with those subtle relations of property, class, and status that form the substance of the great

Victorian novel . . . into an abstract realm of morality and metaphysics" (342). (I suspect that writers were just too lazy to pay close attention to details.) During that period, literary criticism also moved away from regionalism; Franklin and Steiner quote postmodernist Kenneth O. Hanson as saying regionalism was "as dead as the carrier pigeon" (8). (They add with a wry grin that Hanson probably meant "passenger pigeon," not "carrier pigeon," although he was too removed from objective facts to know that it was the passenger pigeon, not the carrier, which once filled North American skies in flocks of up to 2 million birds, which was hunted to extinction early in the twentieth century.) In a book titled *Knowing Your Place* (1997), Barbara Ching and Gerald Creed go so far as to say, "In much postmodern social theory, the country as a vital place simply doesn't exist" (7) because "many intellectuals seem hesitant to pursue identities grounded in the rural/urban distinction because 'real' places seem antithetical to constructionist thought" (12). Possibly because bad ideas eventually implode, possibly because of our nervous exhaustion, possibly because everything runs its course in time, possibly because critics go out and come back like everyone else, the past decade has brought increased attention to place as a significant component of art, although the American Heartland has not been one of the favored places. This book is part of that move in the direction of recovered place . . . as are many Dylan songs.

So we return to analyzing renderings of place in faithful reconstructions like *Lake Wobegon Days*, and dishonest constructions like *The Horse Whisperer* and *Brokeback Mountain*. We can analyze place in the songs of Dylan: his stories, references, markers in both his natural and performed voice, paying attention to the old self that intrudes when he is trying hard to be somebody else. Even when performing on stage or at work, people inadvertently revert to their natural selves — especially in moments of crisis or stress — and we can look for those moments. Especially we can examine Dylan's semi-conscious or subconscious habits of thought which seem peculiarly Midwestern, Minnesotan, Iron Range. A good artist expands through experience and study and practice, and gradually an artist can become quite adroit in manipulating icons of place and voice — but it's hard to manipulate habits of thought. These are the most subtle, interesting, and important impressions left on our character by our early environment, and I don't think we ever outgrow them.

This book devotes most of its time to those larger patterns of thought: the sensitivity to the natural landscape that one acquires growing up in a low-population-density environment, the introversion and internal search for meaning one develops in a Minnesota winter, and the awareness of devastation and restoration one finds in nature; the habit of working your ass off, knowing that your life is utterly at the mercy of larger natural forces which you can do nothing to control (see Martin Van Hees's essay "The Free Will in Bob Dylan"); the generally leftist politics of the Minnesota Iron Range, with its legacy of socialist immigrants and history of labor–management struggles, yoked with the Midwest tradition of individualism and self-reliance; the wealth of cranks and curmudgeons one finds below the bland, Republican surface of any Midwestern town; the need of small-town youth to escape their heritage early in life, and to reclaim later in life a heritage they have pretty much carried with them. This is the true legacy of Dylan's youth, and Harvey Abrams was 100 percent wrong when he told Robert Shelton that Dylan's true nature had been covered up for 18 years by living in Hibbing (*Home*: 75). And Shelton is wrong in thinking Dylan's whole life was just a performance (*Home*: 13).

Of course conclusions are provisional. There are places within the places that influence our character: are you lake country Minnesotan, prairie Minnesotan, Iron Range Minnesotan? Town or farm? '50s Minnesotan or '80s Minnesotan? How has the influence of place been reshaped by other determinants of character: religion, race, ethnicity, sex, sexual preference, class, education, talent, looks (there's something for you to think about), age.

And then there's the matter of Dylan himself. Toward the beginning of *Song & Dance Man III*, Michael Gray observes that Dylan does not offer a sustained, cohesive philosophy of life, "intellectually considered and checked for contradictions" (2). Like America and Walt Whitman, he is large; he contains multitudes. His old affection for the American West, his years in New York and California, his relatively recent interest in the American South, and the studied postmodernism he picked up from writers like Rimbaud, artists like Warhol and Raeben and Red Grooms, collaborators like Jacques Levy, friends like Bobby Neuwirth all took him away from his Midwest home . . . or allowed him to see it in a different light. The postmodernism especially has proven attractive to listeners and critics, particularly British and academic audiences.[3] Dylan was good enough at this act, as anyone who has seen the films knows, for Joan Baez to describe him in her autobiography *Daybreak* as "The Dada King," although one way of interpreting the conclusion of "Black Diamond Bay" is that Dylan tosses a whole postmodern canvas in the trash as he turns off the TV and reaches for another beer.

But Dylan's films are not his successes, are they? Dylan may be as obsessed with identity as anyone in this disconnected, abstract, postmodern world, but it is inaccurate to say, as Sam Shepard and so many others have said, that Dylan "made himself up from scratch" (100). It makes no sense to spend a book examining Dylan's quest for identity (I am thinking here of Aidan Day's

Jokerman, but there are others) without some grounding in Dylan's biography and place.[4] Dylan is grounded beyond almost any of us in the culture of his country, which he himself designates as the source of his material (Cott: 425), and a significant part of that America is his old Midwest home, as he says in "11 Outlined Epitaphs": "the town I grew up in is the one / that has left me with my legacy visions." The acorn which takes root beneath the parent tree dies for lack of sun and nourishment, a geneticist once told me, but even though it must root some distance away from the parent to find room to grow, it thrives in soil like the soil which nurtured its parent, in a climate like the climate which formed its parent . . . and it becomes not a pine or a cactus, but another oak. Did not Dylan wish for us all a strong foundation against the winds of change? Indeed he did.

This book examines the Midwestern, Minnesotan, Iron Range tradition as it exists in life and in representative works of literature, past and present. That tradition, presented in some detail at the beginning of each chapter, becomes a context for examining Dylan's work. I argue that Bob Dylan's language and character reflect the rural Midwest and Minnesota, a place where — as Dylan himself understands — America's myths and strengths are less extinct than they might be elsewhere in the country. That is the tradition to which Muir's Professor Lott refers when he says, "Dylan knows how embedded in his culture he is" (*Troubadour*: 270). That is the truth Mark Polizzotti tells at the end of his introduction to his *Highway 61 Revisited*, when he recognizes that Dylan's very need to discover new selves is "a feeling any Midwestern (or suburban) boy knows in his bones" (24). That is the truth to which John Herdman attests when he says, "when all is said and done it is the stuff of life which influences an artist most" (11); "realities give rise to feelings, which in their turn engender ideas" (123).

That is the truth Dylan spoke in the Rosenbaum *Playboy* interview of 1978: "It is going to make you a certain type of person if you stay 20 years in a place" (Cott: 211). Case closed.

Chapter 1

Dylan's Songs of the North Country

"That's where I feel rooted, you know. I feel more familiar with the landscape, the people and the . . . earth, I think. . . . I feel more at home there. I feel Minnesota more than I feel New York or L.A. . . . My work reflects the thoughts I had as a little kid that have become superdeveloped."

— Minneapolis *Star*, October 27, 1978

Hibbing High School and Times Square, New York, are a lot further apart than the 1,337 miles MapQuest estimates. They're worlds apart, even today, with plenty of ignorance on both ends of the line, a degree of defensive hostility at one end, occasional ignorant curiosity at the other. It's been that way for a long time now. In 1976, journalist Harrison Salisbury, born and raised in Minnesota, described his own youthful experience:

When you got to New York and someone asked you where you were from, you said Minnesota and more than once their faces remained blank and you knew they simply had no idea of where Minnesota might be or whether it was a state or a city or what. . . . New Yorkers didn't seem to understand the difference between Minneapolis and Indianapolis. And even when I explained, they didn't seem to think it really made a difference. I knew that New Yorkers were very sophisticated people. In fact, I was ashamed of coming from a place way out west where, as I understood the New York view, no one really lived and certainly no one from New York ever ventured. I felt very gawky, very provincial. . . . That was the way New York was then — and still is. (70–1)

Arriving in New York in 1961 from someplace called the Iron Range, Dylan lacked the easy cachet that someone from the East would have found in the Midwest or West.[1] Despite the fact that Dwight Eisenhower was from Kansas, Adlai Stevenson was from Illinois, and Barry Goldwater was from Arizona, everything west of the Appalachians melted together in an East Coast mind into what Fitzgerald described in *The Great Gatsby* as "ragged edge of the universe," what we now call "fly-over country." From the perspective of Long Island, where *The Great Gatsby* takes place, Minnesota was "the West." I know. I lived there for a time.

Dylan picked up on Manhattanites' naiveté very quickly, turning it into the joke which concludes "Talkin' New York":

> So one mornin' when the sun was warm
> I rambled out of New York town
> Pulled my cap down over my eyes
> And headed out for the western skies
> So long, New York
> Howdy, East Orange

In truth, Dylan was visiting Woody Guthrie (on leave from Greystone Park Psychiatric Hospital) at the East Orange home of Bob and Sidsel Gleason, but the point of "Talkin' New York," like the point of Woody Guthrie's "Talkin' Subway" on which it is based, is Manhattanites' provinciality: East Orange, ten miles out of town; Indianapolis, 710 miles out; Minneapolis, 1,210 miles out — they're all out there somewhere in the West.

On the other hand, Dylan's particular corner of Manhattan was Greenwich Village, where in 1961 he encountered a folk revival which, while insulated and arrogant, was sympathetic to the proletarians, laborers, and backwoods types which populated the songs of Harry Smith's *Anthology of American Folk Music*, Lomax's *Folk Songs of North America*, and Carl Sandburg's *The American Songbag*. These people, like Dylan, were looking for an alternative to the American mainstream, and where Dylan hoped to find it in New York, they sought it in folk songs of distant eras and geographies from Appalachia to "the West." Sam Shepard calls this "a giant communications gap between the stolid intellectual East Coast and the wide-open mysteries of the West. The East was intrigued and curious about all these dudes, and the West was more than willing to supply them with all the fancy embroidered 'facts' of their heroism" (76). Dylan could play to this curiosity, and he did with tales of life west of the Hudson River. We now know that he had actually had some experience in

Fargo, Denver, and Central City, Colorado (as well as Minneapolis, Chicago, and Madison, Wisconsin), but most of the stories he spun in New York were fiction — like the stories he spun in Minneapolis, Chicago, and Madison, and like the tales I told as a college freshman when I arrived at a school 500 miles from my home. The persona Dylan pitched to the East Coast crowd was as much a character out of a folk song as a reincarnation of Woody Guthrie: the singer, while not Hollis Brown or Rambling, Gambling Willie in the flesh, was at least an interesting young dude who had rambled out of the wild West, leaving the towns he loved best, in an empty boxcar, or as Dylan claimed in "My Life in a Stolen Moment," a four-door Pontiac with five people. Interesting, very interesting.

In "Long Time Gone," Dylan claimed, "My mind got mixed with ramblin' / When I was all so young, / And I left my home the first time / When I was twelve and one." Talking to Oscar Brand on WNYC before his first concert at Carnegie Hall, he claimed to have been raised in Gallup, New Mexico, and to have picked up some of his songs while traveling with a carnival at the age of thirteen.[2] He told Dave Van Ronk that he was part Sioux Indian (Sounes: 85). Neither Brand nor Van Ronk bought the stories, nor did Dylan's New York girlfriend Suze Rotolo believe him when he claimed to have been abandoned at a young age in New Mexico and lived with a traveling circus (Rotolo: 95). In the film *No Direction Home*, Izzy Young looks over his old notes on young Dylan, reflects for a moment and admits, "I should have figured out he was bullshitting me. . . . I was a set-up." Fictional biography appears in songs like "Talkin' New York" and "Dusty Old Fairgrounds," in interviews, and in his 1963 Kerouacian poem "My Life in a Stolen Moment," in which he claims to have run away from Hibbing when he was 10, 12, 13, 15, 15½, 17, and 18. In the poem, Dylan claims to have traveled from Minneapolis to Galveston, Texas, to California, Washington, New Mexico (Indian festivals), Louisiana (Mardi Gras), and up and down routes 61, 51, 75, 169, 37, 66, and 22. "Got jailed for suspicion of armed robbery," he writes; "Got held four hours on a murder rap / Got busted for looking like I do." "An' I never done none a them things," Dylan adds ambiguously (*Lyrics, 1962–1985*: 71). Like he never done that trip to Galveston, and he never actually done the poem's last Dean Moriarty adventure out of New York through Florida, Cincinnati, South Dakota, Kansas, Iowa, Minnesota, looking up old pals and girlfriends before returning to New York and Twenty-eighth Street.

Far from disqualifying him for a coffeehouse gig, being from out there (and "sounding like a hillbilly") helped to credential him with both recording companies and the Village folkniks who preferred Cisco Houston and Leadbelly to groups like the Kingston Trio, the Chad Mitchell Trio, The Brothers Four, and, to an extent, Peter, Paul and Mary, who sounded a little too polished, a little too pop. Dylan's tales of life as a carnie traveling from Fargo to Aberdeen to the Black Hills ("Dusty Old Fairgrounds" and "Long Time Gone"), of having picked up songs from Mance Lipscomb, Arvella Gray, "a lady named Dink" (who had given "Dink's Song" to Alan Lomax back in 1904), and Big Joe Williams, whom he'd met when he ran away from home at age ten (Spitz: 156) — these were part of a persona, part of that sell.

MARKETING MINNESOTA

Amid the fiction, however, is some legitimate autobiography and much that reflects Dylan's youth in . . . not Gallup or Galveston, but Hibbing, Minnesota. Several early songs are specifically about the North Country, including "Ballad for a Friend" (originally titled "Reminiscence Blues"), recorded in January 1962 on a demo tape for Leeds Music. The song, which was too prosaic to go anywhere beyond the pages of Dylan's printed lyrics, is an elegy for a friend purportedly killed in Utah by a diesel truck and brought back to his hometown for burial. No specific friend has ever been identified, although Heylin notes that Dylan's friend Larry Kegan was paralyzed in a wheelchair accident shortly after Dylan left Hibbing and might be a general model (*Revolution*: 65). The song's third verse does localize the story in the North Country with "lakes and streams and mines so free." Years before the accident, according to the song, Dylan and he had hung around together, watching trains roll through town. Then some unidentified break sent one friend in one direction, the other in another. The two lost contact, and now the dead friend is headed home on another train, graveyard bound. Built on four Midwest images (train, smokestack, diesel truck, and bells), "Ballad for a Friend" was probably too mundane to interest a New York crowd — and to be honest, watching trains does not exactly fire the imagination, even though it's what folks did in Hibbing on Saturday nights.

"Dusty Old Fairgrounds," Dylan's fictional autobiography of life on the carnival circuit, is a little more up-tempo and exotic. There is intrinsic appeal in a tale of adventure on the carnival route from Florida through Michigan and Minnesota, to the Dakotas and Montana. In 1958, Dylan's high school band had actually played the St. Louis County Fair, and toward the beginning of *No Direction Home*, Dylan reminisces about the carnival he saw in his youth, an annual escape from relentlessly bright-side Main Street into dark-side surrealism which prefigures "Desolation Row": all the human perversities (sexual and otherwise) denied by church and school and Rotary Club. In a prose poem titled "Circus and Transformation," John Caddy recalls the circus' stand in his own Iron Range town:

We crane our necks, see everything: cooktent, performers,
Instant clothesline full of wash, midgets, cages, sideshow tents,
Maybe Clyde Beatty himself in trademark boots and jodhpurs.

That night, the bigtop: whipcracks and hoops of fire,
Three-ringed tightrope and spangles and big cats.
After the show, we sneak under canvas into the only place
We have no pass for, the back end of the freakshow.
We watch a lady with a little pot and big tits dance naked. . . .

(*Color.* 61)

To this day, little Minnesota towns celebrating midsummer "Bird Island Wing Ding Days" or "Wood Lake World's Fair Days" import carnivals with spinning caterpillars and low-altitude Ferris wheels (no gambling shows behind and no dancing girls out front, but one year a couple of Vikings cheerleaders showed up to sign autographs and flash cleavage, titillating the teenaged boys and challenging the small-town girls). Years ago, on *A Prairie Home Companion*, Garrison Keillor spun a tale of the Beeler kids feeding peanuts to Mazumbo at the Nobles & Norman Circus in Lake Wobegon, and in the July 2009 *National Geographic* he was promoting the "Top Ten State Fair Joys."

Dylan's song is a reasonably accurate description of Midwest carnivals, circa 1960: the trucks and trailers that transport Ferris wheel and caterpillar rides from one clear country lake village or cow country town to the next, the carnies with their come-ons and cons, the posters, the circus tents themselves (now mostly gone), the lure of the exotic and unfamiliar, the shot of high-octane hustle into a mundane existence, the pepped-up kids with their chatter and smiles. Still, this is an Upper Midwest song, from the country fairs themselves, to the geography (Fargo, Aberdeen, Montana), to the language: "git" for "get," long "o" in "Minnesota," and "Wisconsin" accented on the first syllable, and everything "ol'", from "dusty ol' fairgrounds" to "ol' music box" to "ol' Black Hills." Carnivals will get you only so far, however, even in the Midwest. Early in Jack Kerouac's *On the Road*, Sal Paradise is offered work at "a little carnival that's pitched a few miles down the road" by a guy who is "looking for some boys willing to work and make a buck for themselves" (22). If he takes that job then *On the Road* sells maybe a thousand books.

While "Girl of the North Country" ("Girl *from* the North Country" on the album jacket and bobdylan.com) lacks travel adventures, it does have a lost love — and American pop songs about lost love outnumber songs about deceased friends and county fairs at least 50:1. "Girl of the North Country" is also a fine song. Its sparse imagery and harsh weather are perfect for a frozen relationship; the quiet, understated melody speaks "loss" better than anything in Dylan until *Blood on the Tracks*. He feels a loss, but just what did he lose? The befuddlement of "I'm a-wonderin' if she remembers me at all" suggests the relationship was no affair to remember, if they ever, like, really connected. The song's retro-gazing coulda, shoulda, woulda, dinna raises the question, how much of this love, and this loss, is in the singer's mind?

Or is this song, like "Bob Dylan's Dream" and so many other songs and poems popular in the sixties, more about a lost time or place than about a lost love, and thus part of Dylan's pastoral vision? Or is the song really about that old Midwest don't-want-to-jump-to-any-conclusions indeterminacy? One thing for sure: it is filled with Upper Midwest nature: falling snowflakes, howling winds, frozen rivers, a summer that ends somewhere in early August. (Interestingly, Dylan's North Country is fairest not in springtime or summer, but in late autumn and early winter.) So firmly is the song planted in Dylan's personal history that all biographers seek the woman behind the song. Toby Thompson was convinced that he'd found her in Echo Star Helstrom, Dylan's high school girlfriend, and Robert Shelton mentions that seeing the porch swing, "heavily rusted and weather-beaten" at the Helstrom house in 1968, made him feel "the swing was 'Rosebud,' the reporter's long-sought clue to lost childhood in *Citizen Kane*" (*Home*: 49). Howard Sounes leans toward Bonnie Beecher, the actress girl who kneed Dylan in the gut when he dated her in Minneapolis ("My Life in a Stolen Moment"). The hair hanging long may favor Beecher over Helstrom: Echo's class photo shows her with short hair, but a classmate remembers her hair as streaming out behind her. Beecher also remembers a coat with a fur collar that she wore when dating Dylan. But Beecher clearly remembered Dylan — she visited him in New York early in the spring of 1961, when she "anxiously sought Bob out" (Sounes: 81). But when Dylan returned to Minneapolis in mid-May (planning, incidentally, not to return to New York City), Beecher was already seeing somebody else — thus, perhaps, the line borrowed from "Scarborough Fair," "she once was a true love of mine," which hints at infidelity. About that time, Dylan recorded a throwaway song "Bonnie, Why'd You Cut My Hair?" and on a subsequent visit in December, Dylan wrote a "Song to Bonnie," based on "Song to Woody," reproduced in manuscript in the *Telegraph* (Heylin, *Stolen Moments*: 25).

Echo Helstrom was not only seeing somebody else when Dylan returned to Hibbing, she was a married mom. But Echo claims that she and Dylan met during the December 1961 visit, when Dylan was playing a concert at the University of Minnesota, and "we both got pretty tipsy and later when we were alone he got very sentimental and asked me to come back to New York with him" (Thompson: 76). The long story short is that Dylan encouraged both Beecher and Helstrom to imagine themselves as the girl in this song, at a time when they were both long gone and he was seeing Joan Baez and Suze Rotolo. Clinton Heylin reports that in 1978 Dylan dedicated the song to both Echo and Bonnie at separate concerts in Oakland (*Revolution*: 120). Heylin himself adds Gretel Hoffman as a third candidate, but sees Suze as the girl "by proxy." Suze as the lost love? Andy Gill claims that immediately after Suze Rotolo left for Italy, June 8, 1962, Dylan took off again for Minneapolis; a few days later Dave Van Ronk got a phone call from Dylan, "who was standing in a Minneapolis phone box in sub-zero temperatures, crying for Suze" (27). Even Minneapolis doesn't get this cold in June, so perhaps we discount Van Ronk's story and all autobiographical interpretations of this song, and go with the pastoral interpretation — what Dylan misses is not so much the home girl as the home place.

In "Ballad of Hollis Brown," "North Country Blues," and "The Walls of Red Wing," Dylan found North Country material that he could market in the Greenwich Village of the early sixties.[3] "North Country Blues" uses material closest to home: a first-person narrator recounts life on the Iron Range as the mines that had provided the ore for World Wars I and II stumbled in the late fifties. This was the story of Dylan's youth: declining demand, declining production, strikes, and closings. In the early years of the twentieth century, mining money had made the Iron Range rich, but by the end of the fifties, Hibbing was the dying town Dylan describes in "11 Outlined Epitaphs."

Actually, Hibbing had already died once, due to an accident of history ... or geography. Old Hibbing was a thriving mining community of 10,000 people in the early twentieth century, with an elegant Carnegie Library, paved streets, courthouse, fairgrounds, streetcars, and as many as 60 saloons before liquor sales in America stopped in 1915. But the city rested atop some of the richest iron ore on the Range (itself the largest source of high-grade hematite ore in the world), and citizens of Iron Range towns did not own mineral rights to the earth below their own homes. In 1919 the Oliver Mining Company began buying surface rights from owners for what would total $2.5 million, according to the possibly suspect *Hibbing Minnesota 1893–1968 Diamond Jubilee Days* booklet. Then it offered 80 acres in Central Addition, south of Old Hibbing, as the site of a new town. Once the land had been "condemned," the North Hibbing homeowners could buy their homes for $1 and have them "relocated" for an average cost of $4,500. Dylan mentions the process in "11 Outlined Epitaphs":

a train line cuts the ground
showin where the fathers an mothers
of me an my friends had picked
up an moved from
north Hibbing
t south Hibbing.

Between 1919 and 1923 the L. J. Pocket Company of Mountain Iron, Minnesota, moved 185 dwellings, 12 frame businesses, and eight brick buildings (including hospitals, churches, and the Colonia Hotel, but not the Sellers Hotel, which fell off the skids and crumbled to rubble) from Old Hibbing to New Hibbing. For a time during the Depression, buildings were wrecked rather than moved (to create more jobs for construction workers), but with the labor shortages of World War II the moving resumed, continuing into the 1950s. Shovels the size of a small hotel dug a pit four miles long and a mile across that Bob Dylan describes as "that great ugly hole in the ground" (Shelton, *Home*: 16) and Robin Morris describes as "a gigantic vagina" (168). More earth was moved out of Old Hibbing than was excavated for the Panama Canal. In 1957, according to a story in the Hibbing High School newspaper, a 1,200-ton dragline was brought in to demolish the already abandoned courthouse, Carnegie Library, and Lincoln High School, which Dylan's mother had attended. A celebration to close the school, then used as a junior high, was scheduled for May 31, 1957. Dylan remembers:

old north Hibbing . . .
deserted
already dead
with it's [sic] old stone courthouse
decayin in the wind
long abandoned
windows crashed out
the breath of it's [sic] broken walls
being smothered in clingin moss . . .
an there was no sound except for the wind
blowin thru the high grass
an the bricks that fell back
t the dirt from a slight stab
of the breeze . . . it was as tho

the rains of wartime had
left the land bombed-out an shattered

("11 Outlined Epitaphs")

Stephen Scobie opens his book *Alias: Bob Dylan Revisited* with a long description of Hibbing, imagining the young Bobby Zimmerman exploring the ghost
of the old town, finding in its displaced center a reflection of himself.

But hematite rebuilt what hematite destroyed: a new city hall, a new library,
a new main street (Howard Street was virtually complete by June 1921), and
a new high school. With a post-World War II average income well above the
national average, New Hibbing prospered into the early 1950s, supporting,
among other enterprises, the corner bars with polka bands that Dylan mentions
in "My Life in a Stolen Moment," Micka Electric (owned by Dylan's uncles and
which employed Dylan's father), a dozen hotels, over a dozen churches, two golf
courses, a municipal airport, and four movie theaters owned by the Edelstein
Amusement Company . . . Bob Dylan's great-grandmother.

Then supplies of high-grade and easily mined hematite ore (60 percent iron)
failed even as demand nose-dived and competition from mines in Venezuela
increased. The taconite ore which remained (only 20–25 percent iron) had to be
blasted from its beds, increasing mining, shipping, and smelting costs. Mesabi
iron ore production remained steady through 1953, then dropped. Iron Range
employment dropped from 18,000 in 1958 to 14,000 in 1964, rebounded in
the sixties and seventies with the help of a taconite-pellet process developed
by the University of Minnesota's Edward Davis, then dropped again in the
Reagan Depression, recovered in the 1990s, declined again at the turn of the
twenty-first century. At one point unemployment in St. Louis County outside
of the city of Duluth — the Iron Range area — hit 27 percent. People left. The
eyesore open pit, and the mountains of tailing remained. Today Hibbing is a
quiet place indeed, and the area around it is mostly small engine repair shops,
abandoned houses and schools, cemeteries without churches, empty barns,
buildings for rent, gun and ammunition and quilt shops, biker bars on back-
country roads.

Some towns disappeared entirely: Genoa, Sparta, Leonidas, Mahoning, and
Elcor, where officials of Picklands, Mather and Company announced, after
closing the Corsica Mine in 1955, that they were "reclaiming" the land and
Elcor's citizens would have to move. Today the ghost towns are barely recognizable, like many other spots in the Upper Midwest, where a railroad siding or
a small graveyard is often the only indication that here, once upon a time, was
a functioning rural community with homes, village store, church, and school.

This Iron Range economic history, but not the environmental degradation, is encapsulated in Dylan's song "North Country Blues," a tale which begins in the days when the red iron ore pits ran plenty, and ends with the whole town empty. Remarkably for Dylan and the early 1960s, the story is told by a woman: a woman who worked herself; a woman who stayed behind as the males in her life died in mining disasters or departed — father, brother, husband, children. The song may owe something to the experience of Dylan's high school pal John Bucklen. When Bucklen's father was injured in a mine accident, there was neither welfare nor insurance coverage; his mother went into business as a seamstress, and Dylan's mother Beatty brought her work (Engel: 88). The song is the story of success-turned-failure: in its larger details of humming draglines turned to old men on benches, in subtle details like the move during prosperous times from the wrong side of town (the south side, where the speaker was born, and where Echo lived) to the more upscale north end of town (where the Zimmermans lived), and with its look toward a future of house empty of husband and family. Little details are brilliant: "lunch bucket filled every season" suggests the miners' modest aspirations; the heavy smell of drinking reflects Old Hibbing with its 60-plus saloons; the "silence of tongues" certainly reflects the brooding isolation of North Country males. The phrase "with no reason" expresses the Iron Range detestation of callous management, which in the fifties cut work to half a day's shift, which today cuts the 40-hour workweek to whatever level allows them to avoid paying benefits. When Number Eleven closes for good, it is just "a man" who makes the announcement; he is the always absent, anonymous "they" who make the decisions that sacrifice local communities to global economics. Eastern mine owners, Dylan writes in *Chronicles*, were more hated in Hibbing than Russian communists (271).

While localized in the specifics of Iron Range Minnesota, including language like "I was raised up" and "a man come to speak," the song reaches upward and outward to half a dozen larger concerns. One, of course, is the situation of women in American society. In *A Freewheelin' Time*, Suze Rotolo is critical of sixties males in general, and Bob Dylan in particular, but in this song he is clearly sensitive to, and supportive of, the situation of a woman subject to the whims of men (who are themselves subject to capricious outside forces). Part of this story is the male–female disconnect of no dialogue, no consultation, no joint planning, no long-term commitment, which Dylan understands perfectly. Another, larger context is the age-old plight of small-town Midwestern adolescents: the song's closing line — "there ain't nothing here now to hold them" — is Dylan's own take on Hibbing, and the take of small-town Midwestern children today. "North Country Blues" also embodies labor–management tensions everywhere, and the cardboard-filled windows (these days it's plywood-covered windows) and stores folding one by one can be found in the work of any writer describing the demise of towns all over the Midwest.[4]

"Ballad of Hollis Brown," set in the state next door to Minnesota, tells another story of Midwest economic collapse, this one agricultural. While influenced by Steinbeck's *The Grapes of Wrath*, the song is generally true to the Midwest rural reality of the early 1960s. Dylan's coyotes in the wilderness might sound western, but East River, South Dakota (like western Minnesota) has its share of coyotes and wilderness, as small farms fail and are assimilated into larger "farming operations" or turned into grasslands under the Conservation Reserve Program.

The demise of the small farm is particularly noticeable in the Minnesota-South Dakota-Iowa region, possibly because of the settlement pattern there: under the Homestead Act of 1862, settlers received 160 acres free and clear if they lived on, and cultivated, it for a period of five years; they could claim an additional 160 acres as a "timber claim" if they planted 40 of those arces in timber. The result was a grid pattern of one-mile roads, each enclosing four 160-acre tracts — with four (perhaps three) farmsteads per square mile, each with its own house, barn, and grove of trees. To buy produce (cheap) and to sell equipment and other necessities (dear) to farmers whose transportation was a horse-drawn wagon, railroad companies planted towns every seven miles or so along their tracks. So each little railroad village served about 50 square miles of farms, and with three or four seven-to-ten-member families per square mile, 50 square miles per town made a good population base for stores, schools, and churches. For a shining moment around the turn of the century, before the invention of the tractor, the American pastoral idyll seemed realized: the villages and the farmers who lived around them did very well, helped by high commodity prices during World War I. Then came mechanization and consolidation: the tractor was as responsible as the Dust Bowl drought for kicking the Joads off their farm in *The Grapes of Wrath*. (It now appears that by facilitating deep tillage of Great Plains soil that should not have been deep-tilled, mechanization was responsible for the Dust Bowl as well.) To make matters worse, commodity prices dropped when World War I ended, and for Midwest agriculture, the Great Depression began in the early 1920s. With the crash of 1929, the Great Depression began in earnest. When the market bottomed out in 1932, corn was selling for 10 cents a bushel, hogs were bringing 3 cents a pound, and cattle 5 cents a pound. "Farmers burned corn for fuel and cattle sent to market did not even bring the cost of transportation," writes David Nass (xi). World War II brought a temporary recovery,[5] but as technology developed and opportunities off the farm beckoned, Midwest agriculture went through a series of consolidations and depopulations which left barns, farm houses, and small towns abandoned. These "adjustments" seem to occur every other decade: the '60s, the '80s, and the beginning of the present century. Wendell Berry calls the process *The Unsettling of America*.

Of course the more expensive the technology, the larger the mortgage, and the more colossal the failure during a lean cycle. The 1980s were especially rough: a summary of 20,000 responses to the 1985 *Minnesota Farm Financial Survey*, released by the Minnesota Department of Agriculture on February 3, 1986, reported a one-year net equity decrease of 31.3 percent, with 23 percent of respondents "highly leveraged," 17 percent "very high leveraged," and 13 percent "technically insolvent." Over half of the respondents under the age of 35 were, like Hollis Brown, either highly leveraged or technically insolvent. It was to these farmers that Dylan alluded in his remark at Live Aid on July 13, 1985, after performing "Hollis Brown": "I'd just like to say I hope that some of the money that's raised for the people in Africa, maybe they could just take a little bit of it — maybe one or two million maybe — and use it, say, to pay the mortgages on some of the farms." However, the farmers of 1985 received about as much sympathy as Andy Gill gives Hollis Brown: "though the South Dakota farmer may have had a run of bad luck, it's ultimately hard to feel that much sympathy for someone reckless enough to have five children — one, we learn, a baby — which he clearly cannot support" (43).

Hollis Brown is caught in one of these cycles — not necessarily the 1930s, as Stephen Scobie has it ("Interview": 53) — squeezed by technology, economics, nature, and bad luck. Published in *Broadside* magazine for February 1963, "The Ballad of Hollis Brown" carried a subtitle: "A True Story." Well — true in the general sense. Brown is no homesteader, and he has probably seen better, maybe even flush times that would have supported five kids. For example, in the North Country the word "cabin" does not necessarily refer to a pioneer's log structure, especially in the eastern Dakotas, where trees were scarce. Nor is it synonymous with the "one-room country shack" Dylan mentions in "Dirt Road Blues." A cabin "may be a very simple structure without indoor plumbing, or it may be a five-bedroom, three-bath house," notes David Lanegran (*Minnesota*: 88); "No matter; it is still 'the cabin.'" *The Cabins of Minnesota*, a photo-text book published by the Minnesota Historical Society Press in 2007, shows up-scale modern structures and older buildings like the "Greek Revival house (circa 1890)" on Bay Lake, Crow Wing County (Holm and Ohman 2007: 67), where Dylan later bought property. A timber-frame farm house with lathe-and-plaster walls and normal glass windows, erected in the twentieth century (perhaps a kit bought from Sears), would qualify as "a cabin" . . . like the cabin in "On a Night Like This." These buildings are civilized, if Spartan: usually two rooms down and one long bedroom upstairs, with an additional room and indoor plumbing added in the late forties, early 1950s. Next time you're in Granite Falls, stop by and I'll point out the ghost of just such a "cabin" where, friends assure me, not half a century ago, a farmer lived with his wife and "five or six kids." This is Brown's "cabin" — not the shack most people would imagine. Nor is it any sign of indigence that even in the fifties, Brown relied on well water (my own rural Minnesota home still uses well water), and had a horse (but I have no horse). It is quite probable that he — and his wife — sought employment in town, and it is not unthinkable that a farmer facing difficulties should consider shotgun shells. Poet Leo Dangel, raised on a farm in East River, South Dakota, writes about just such a farmer in a poem titled "What Milo Saw": "After the hail pounded his corn crop / into the ground, Milo said / he would shoot himself. . . . Milo's wife hid the shotgun in the cellar / on a shelf, behind the pickle jars." Dangel also mentions Milo's "six runny-nosed kids."

So Dylan's song spins toward its inevitable conclusion, from one detail to another and from one feature of rural Midwestern life to another: natural disaster, social disaster, economic disaster. Hollis Brown exhibits the same North Country male introversion we just saw in "North Country Blues": a refusal to communicate with wife or family, a withdrawal into the self as he contemplates diminishing options, a growing anger, possibly some alcohol . . . and finally, after long silence, violence. The song's final lines offer only the terrible promise of continuing cycles: Great Plains fecundity (seven more children being born) promising little more than another disaster in the next swing of an apparently unbreakable cycle, bringing Dylan, in 2006, to the farmer in "Workingman's Blues #2": "The place I love best is a sweet memory" because "They burned my barn, they stole my horse." *They* being, as always, the class of people who never worked a day in their life and don't even know what work means.

"The Walls of Red Wing," while set squarely in the picturesque Mississippi River town of Red Wing, Minnesota, is more ideology than reality, but it is an ideology more marketable in early sixties America than a displaced farmer or even an out-of-work miner: the misunderstood juvenile delinquent. Although Dylan backed off this song early on, Joan Baez, perhaps unaware of the poetic license Dylan had taken with his material, recorded it on *Any Day Now* (1968), her two-record collection of songs by Bob Dylan. Clinton Heylin reports that Larry Haugen claimed he and Dylan spent time in Red Wing in the summer of 1958 — a story Heylin dismisses as unlikely (*Revolution*: 131). Heylin himself suggests that the "strict regime" of "Walls of Red Wing" reflects Dylan's brief stay at Deveraux, a boarding school in Pennsylvania, to which young Bob Zimmerman was sent by his parents, in 1958 or 1959, to straighten him out

(*Stolen Moments*: 7). Probably the song owes more to films like *Rebel Without a Cause* than to Dylan's personal experiences. Of course it is no more necessary for Dylan to have spent time in Red Wing than it is for the singers of any ballad to actually *be* the first-person narrator of their song; the problem here is that Dylan's song invents not only the speaker's experience — something we rather expect and accept from writers — but details of the setting. The inaccuracies — a good indication Dylan had never seen the place, and probably the result of Red Wing being a good 150 miles from Hibbing, and nearly 50 from Minneapolis — have troubled Dylan fans and commentators for some time.

The Minnesota Correctional Facility at Red Wing was founded in 1867 as a House of Refuge for juvenile delinquents. Located at what is now Concordia College in St. Paul, it became the Minnesota State Reform School in 1879, and in 1890 moved to its present site in Red Wing. Early on, the facility housed girls as well as boys, orphans as well as young criminals; fast-forwarding to Dylan songs to the far end of his career, it would have been a good orphanage from which to recruit "some tough sons of bitches." "Inmates" have always been housed in cottages, which might reasonably be called "bunkhouses," but the word "dungeons" strains the imagination, and early photos show no crossbars on the windows. Today's barbed wire fence "with the 'lectricity sting" was added only in the 1990s. Corporal punishment was outlawed in 1947, and by the time Dylan wrote his song, a progressive program of "Guided Group Action" had been initiated. There are no dungeons, no boardwalk, no screen, and no cast-iron gates. In a 2003 article on "The Walls of Red Wing" for CityPages.com, Brad Zeller quotes Eddie Sharkey, who did two stints at Red Wing in the 1950s:

> "In those days we weren't stabbing and shooting each other like they are today," Sharkey recalls. "I was just a dumb kid and a general screw-off, but compared with some of the other guys I guess I was a pretty rough character. They had kids from small towns who were in there for skipping school."
>
> Sharkey sounds almost sheepish when he admits that he enjoyed his time in Red Wing. "People see that big old evil-looking place up there and get all sorts of ideas in their heads," he says. "But it was like a military school more than anything else. I mean, hell yes, it was a rough-and-tumble place, and they worked the shit out of you. You were always doing something. But it was a pretty good education, the best I ever got anywhere, and I made a lot of good friends down there, guys I still keep in touch with."

Dylan's song does not really want Red Wing to educate juvenile delinquents; it sees Red Wing as producing future inmates of St. Cloud Prison and other evil characters, including lawyers. The notion that there is not much difference between the criminals inside and the lawyers outside of Red Wing and St. Cloud Prison will be developed more fully in the judges of "Hattie Carroll," "Percy's Song," and "Hurricane," and in an oft-quoted line in another song: "to live outside the law, you must be honest." "The Walls of Red Wing" closes with the point toward which Dylan has shaped his material: "some of us'll stand up / To meet you on your crossroads." Dylan does not go so far as to make the outlaw a hero, and the sheriff the crook — he'll do this in later songs — but he humanizes the inmates by exaggerating the harshness of his Red Wing environment, and softening the persona with innocuous concerns like hometown memories and songs in the night.

Neither "The Walls of Red Wing" nor "North Country Blues" appeared in Agnes "Sis" Cunningham's *Broadside*, the Village magazine devoted to publishing topical protest songs associated with "Ban the Bomb," civil rights, and other allied causes, and apparently "Ballad of Hollis Brown" got a less-than-enthusiastic reception from British folk purists Peggy Seeger and Ewan MacColl when Dylan performed it in London, December 22, 1962 (Heylin, *Stolen Moments*: 36). However, between February of 1962 and March 10, 1965, *Broadside* did publish nearly two dozen Dylan compositions not set in Minnesota: "Blowin' in the Wind," "Masters of War," "Who Killed Davey Moore?" In writing these topical protest songs, Dylan drew more on newspapers and matters current in Greenwich Village than on Minnesota memories.

Another early song which certainly suggests the North Country is "Bob Dylan's Dream." Robert Shelton locates the song in Minnesota: "Dylan reflects during a return to Minnesota, how simple the answers seemed during adolescence. John Bucklen believed the song directly related to the times he and Bob spent in Hibbing with Echo and John's sister. It could as easily refer to days at Minneapolis with Tony Glover or Bonny" (*Home*: 156). The song has the generally ramshackle feel which fills Upper Midwest writing of the late twentieth century. Howard Sounes suggests that the setting was the apartment of Wavy Gravy, where Dylan hung out "over the Gaslight, sitting around an old wood-burning stove" (93); in *Chronicles*, Dylan mentions that Izzy Young "had a back room with a potbellied wood-burning stove" (19). I was not there, of course, but a functioning wood-burning stove in Lower Manhattan, 1961, sounds more than a little far-fetched, and the song itself sounds more Hibbing than New York. But even if the wood stove is in Manhattan, Dylan is interested in it because it recalls Minnesota. Andy Gill writes, "Dylan's several return journeys to Minnesota, both before and after the release of his first album, undoubtedly helped crystallize the theme of the song, as he realized the disparate paths taken by himself and his old friends from Hibbing and the Dinkytown campus neighbor-hood of Minneapolis" (31). His theory is that — chided by Minneapolis friends like Tony Glover, "Spider" John Koerner, and Jim Pankake for his politically active protest songs — "Dylan clearly felt his Minnesota friends were being left behind" (32), which is what's happened in this song. Talking to Studs Terkel on WFMT radio in May, 1963, Dylan drifted onto the subject of his old friends:

> I can tell you about people I growed up with, that I knowed since I been four and five. . . . Little small-town people. This was in Hibbing. . . . These people were my friends . . . and you know, either me or them has changed. . . . I'm not putting them down. It's just my road and theirs, it's different. . . . They're not thinking about the same things I'm thinking about. (Cott: 8, 9)

"Bob Dylan's Dream" is based on "Lord Franklin," a nineteenth century British ballad about the disappearance of captain and crew in a failed attempt to discover the Northwest Passage, but the borrowings — "I dreamed a dream," and "ten thousand guineas I would freely give" — have nothing to do with place, and Dylan's song is about memory tied to place: the memory of good, simple times lost in the complexities of postmodern adult life. Honest poverty is worth more than money — more than ten thousand dollars.[6] The song is romantic in the extreme, and slightly posturing for a singer who in 1963 had neither age nor wealth. In fact, the entire song is contrived, but the manner of its contrivance suggests that even early in his New York period, Dylan was romantically nostalgic about his Minnesota roots. In the song he is on a train "goin' west" toward Indianapolis, Minneapolis, or Denverapolis — he is not specific — so the dream itself, though not specifically located west of Hudson, absorbs North Country mystique by association. That mystique is enhanced by the old stove (a wood-burning stove, we hope, not the "wooden stove" Dylan mentions), the hats (we imagine not cowboy hats or seed corn caps, but woolen sock caps or hunter's caps, with earflaps), and a (snow?) storm raging outside. Like so many of Dylan's storms, this one is a metaphor for everything outside of the room: age, complexity, time, disagreement. The song draws a simple dichotomy: inside the North Country cabin are youth, humor, joy, harmony, unity, true friendship, a certain naiveté, and, more than anything else, satisfac-tion. Outside of the room? Nothing but trouble. What is most disconcerting: the unpredictability of gambles, the disappearance of friends, the passage of time, or the loss of certainty that comes with knowing almost nothing in life is black and white? The song was a way for Dylan to sell his roots to an audience that was as predisposed in the turbulent sixties to romanticize "The Simple Life" as were twenty-first century viewers of Paris Hilton and Nicole Richie's TV show.

"Motorpsycho Nightmare," a talkin' blues in the Guthrie tradition, opens with a twisted version of the ubiquitous traveling salesman joke which Leo Dangel incorporates into "Old Man Brunner and the Traveling Salesman" (53):

> One stormy night a traveling salesman's car breaks down right by Old Man Brunner's driveway. The traveling salesman knocks on his door and asks for a place to sleep. Old Man Brunner is surprised and happy to find himself in a joke that he has told many times. "You're welcome to stay the night," he says, "but we're short on beds — you'll have to sleep with my daughter."
>
> The traveling salesman hesitates. He is actually thinking it over. Finally he says, "Oh, I can sleep in the car."
>
> "Don't you want to see what she looks like?"
>
> "I'll sleep in the car."
>
> "It's all right," says Old Man Brunner. "She's out in the barn finishing chores."
>
> He takes the arm of the traveling salesman and guides him to the barn. Old Man Brunner opens the door and switches on the light. "There she is," he says, pointing to a heifer in a pen.

In Dylan's song, the farmer stipulates "don't touch my daughter / And in the morning, milk the cow," but come midnight, daughter Rita is inviting Dylan to a shower right out of *Psycho*. Dylan's farmer is less Old Man Brunner than a stereotypical gun-totin', commie-hating, *Reader's Digest*-reading, North Country conservative, but both Dangel and Dylan end with the visitors avoiding trouble by hitting the road — young Dylan pursued by Echo Helstrom's dad.

REFLECTIONS, ECHOES, AND ALLUSIONS

One finds fewer reflections of Hibbing, Minnesota, in the cosmopolitan landscape of Dylan's middle sixties albums. One rather remarkable, specific reference is the first line of "Desolation Row": "They're selling postcards of the hanging." In 1920, three black hands from the John Robinson Show Circus were arrested in Hibbing for raping a white girl while her boyfriend was made to watch. On June 15 they were lynched at the corner of First Street and Second Avenue; postcards of a photo of the scene circulated for years in the city (Polizzotti: 135).

Another North Country reference, of course, is *Highway 61 Revisited*. Dylan's title is a direct reference to an old blues song, "Highway 61" or "Highway 61 Blues," recorded by many bluesmen dating back to 1932. In the days before the interstate system, U.S. Highway 61 was a major north–south artery, linking Thunder Bay, Canada, with New Orleans, Mississippi, via Duluth, St. Paul (home of F. Scott Fitzgerald), and Red Wing, then south through musical and literary history: Hannibal, Missouri (Mark Twain); East St. Louis (Chuck Berry); Dyess, Arkansas (Johnny Cash); Memphis, Tennessee (Elvis Presley); Meridian, Mississippi (Jimmie Rodgers); and Clarksdale, Mississippi (where Bessie Smith died). Lacking publicists such as Steinbeck and Kerouac, Route 61 looms not as large in the American imagination as Route 66, but it was as historically important. Some have argued that Route 66 was a white highway, and Highway 61 a black highway, thus reading the American preference for 66 as unconscious racism.[7]

Route 61 has strong personal associations for Dylan: Highway 61 offered a road of sorts from Duluth, where he was born (and lived the first five years of his life, and visited frequently with family and friends for the next 13 years of his life), to the world beyond Minnesota. Dylan traveled Highway 61 when he went to see Buddy Holly perform on January 31, 1959, just before Holly died in the famous plane crash, and Highway 61 took Dylan to the University of Minnesota. Dylan's remarks in *Chronicles* suggest that it was a road away from home that was comfortable enough to be a road back to home:

> I always felt like I'd started on it, always had been on it and could go anywhere from it, even down into the deep Delta country. It was the same road, full of the same contradictions, the same one-horse towns, the same spiritual ancestors. The Mississippi River, the bloodstream of the blues, also starts up from my neck of the woods. I was never too far away from any of it. It was my place in the universe, always felt like it was in my blood. (241)

However, the lyrics for "Highway 61 Revisited" contain no markers of place, accurate or invented, personal or communal-cultural, local or distant. It is also possible that Dylan's opening line — "Oh God said to Abraham, 'Kill me a son,'" — is a conscious or subconscious reference to his own father (as Freudians have it), Abe Zimmerman, but in the song the highway's significance is entirely metaphoric. Ed Vulliamy, in an essay titled "Highway 61 Revisited" (*Guardian*, 10 September 1988), offers this interpretation:

> It seems reasonably safe to say that Highway 61 was chosen for the sacrifice of Isaac, the dumping of "a thousand telephones that don't ring," and eventually the "promotion" of World War III by a "rovin' gambler," because it is such a quintessential slice of the American Midwest along which life was stable and looked unlikely to change

much — even as recently as 1965–66. Twenty-three years later, driving off the old Highway at Hinckley and up to the thundering clamour of the Interstate, it felt as though that slice of America had been — perhaps mercifully — left behind. And it is the same all over Middle America — the deserted town centres with their gracious, quirky wooden buildings on Main Street; and then the bright lights on the four-lane strips, never asleep, and always looking exactly the same — the motels, new Tobie's and the rest. (Thomson and Gutman: 101)

Generally speaking, however, Dylan thinks within a pastoral tradition that locates insanity in the city and finds restoration in nature. Given the relatively rural character of Highway 61 in the mid-1960s — Michael Gray notes that for large portions of Minnesota, this highway is reduced "to the status of a country road" (*Song*: 296), which is what parts of it were in the 1950s — it's an odd site for an existentialist confrontation with absurdity. Mack the Finger, Louie the King, Georgia Sam, the rovin' gambler are not characters you'd expect to meet in Duluth, Red Wing, or even Minneapolis; they sound more like Memphis or New Orleans. As Mike Marqusee points out, "Highway 61 links the land of 'North Country Blues' to the setting of 'Only a Pawn in Their Game'" (181). Or these characters might be viewed as grotesque distortions of the materialistic, antipastoral side of Main Street which Dylan always abhorred: make money no matter what the moral or ethical costs. Dylan is less interested here in pinning the next world war on any particular region than he is in expanding the insanity of the song and album all across the United States, far north to far south. America, Dylan is saying, has a problem on both ends of Highway 61.

Fourth Street is an even more elusive reference. Echo Helstrom thought "Positively 4th Street" was about Hibbing: "I remember when it came out I said to myself, Bob wrote that song about Hibbing. For all those people who used to boo him when he played, and who probably now couldn't be nicer or more polite when they see him" (Thompson: 72). When Ellen Baker was hosting Toby Thompson in Minneapolis, she took him down to the University of Minnesota and told him,

"This is Fourth Street. . . . Whether or not this Fourth Street is 'positively' the one, who can say but Bob? Everyone here in Dinkytown always thought their main drag was the one Bob sings about, though. It makes sense. Dinkytown is the student neighborhood where not just Bob lived, but everyone he hung around with. The Scholar and Bastille coffee houses were in Dinkytown. And as you can see, now that we're on it, Fourth Street would represent all of that to Bob, the social scene, the university crud . . . the old folk people." (Thompson: 120–1)

The New York crowd was convinced Dylan meant Fourth Street, Manhattan, and the song was about his acquaintances there. "'Positively 4th Street' was Bob Dylan's valedictory to the Greenwich Village scene," writes David Hajdu (279) in a book titled *Positively 4th Street*. Izzy Young was personally offended: "I don't know if it was [about me], but it was unfair. . . . Dylan comes in and takes from us, uses my resources, then he leaves and *he* gets bitter?" (90). Dave Van Ronk, who also thought this was Fourth Street, Manhattan, defended Dylan: "I think that 'Positively 4th Street' is a great song. It was high time that Bobby turned around and said something to Irwin Silber and all those Jewish mothers" (Shelton, *Home*: 99). Or perhaps Dylan meant Fourth Street in Marshall, Minnesota, where a couple of my colleagues live.

Dylan makes few references to his (limited) experiences at the University of Minnesota, but as "Positively 4th Street" may reflect the Dinkytown crowd, "Ballad of a Thin Man" may reflect U. of M. intellectuals. Mr. Jones could be any befuddled intellectual anywhere, and half a dozen individuals have been proposed for "Mr. Jones," including a student journalist at the 1965 Newport Folk Festival who claims Dylan taunted him there with "Getting' it all down, Mr. Jones?" However, connections among the lumberjacks as well as the lawyers and crooks, and a general familiarity with the books of Minnesotan F. Scott Fitzgerald, give a University of Minnesota flavor to this particular thin man.[8]

Dylan's revenge on Sigma Alpha Mu fraternity had come in a line of "Last Thoughts on Woody Guthrie." Dylan had lived his first semester at the "Sammy" house, the most prestigious of four University of Minnesota Jewish frats, in part because his cousin, a law student, already belonged and convinced Dylan's father that the fraternity would give him direction and connections. Dylan left — or was kicked out — at the end of his first semester. The Sammies appreciated Dylan about as much as Bonnie Beecher's sorority sisters, who also asked her to leave the house after they started seeing too much of Dylan at their sorority house. One theory on Dylan and the frat is that Dylan was interested more in Dinkytown folkies than in the future MBAs of fraternity row. Another theory is that Dylan was trying hard to not be Jewish. "The truth was the Sammies simply did not like Bob," writes Howard Sounes. "He kept strange hours and did not join in their activities or share their interests, and his introverted nature made him seem aloof" (51). Bob, Abe Zimmerman told Dylan biographer Robert Shelton, considered the frat rats "phonies, just spoiled kids with whom he didn't have much in common" (65). Apparently, a group of upper classmen was selected to "shape Zimmerman up," which meant "helping him make better grades, wear the right clothes, and fit in." They were not successful (Bauldie: 16). In "Last Thoughts on Woody Guthrie," delivered at the Town Hall Concert of April 12, 1963, Dylan inventories places where salvation for a rotting culture can *not* be found: a dollar bill, Macy's windowsill, Hollywood wheat germ, half-wit comedians, yacht clubs, golf courses . . . and "no fat kid's fraternity house."

This is all we find of the North Country in Dylan's electric songs, unless you want to count the barbed wire of "Sitting on a Barbed-Wire Fence" (barbed wire fences are common in the Upper Midwest and West, rarer elsewhere, where one finds fences of stone or wood). However, Dylan later returned to the Midwest landscape and affection for remembered roots. We might localize the album *John Wesley Harding* in the Upper Midwest, based on the offer in "As I Went Out One Morning" to "fly south" together, Judas spreading his roll of tens on a footstool "above the plotted plain" ("plotted" being a reference to the Midwest grid system of roads), and the steamboat whistle of "Dear Landlord." Writes Nick Hawthorne, "Images of the North Country and Dylan's youth started to work their way into a couple of songs on *New Morning*, and would fully manifest themselves on *Planet Waves*. It was clearly influencing Dylan greatly at this time" (33).

One of these songs, "Never Say Goodbye," was written in 1973 but anticipates marital problems later in the decade. (In this regard, the song foreshadows *Blood on the Tracks*.) While the song appears to be an offer to Sara — "Time is all I have to give / You can have it if you choose" — this woman, like most of Dylan's good women, embodies a certain pastoral comfort which Dylan contrasts to his own dreams of "iron and steel" (an Iron Range image if ever there was one). What is unclear, or contradictory, is the landscape: a frozen landscape with footprints on the snow and the north wind breaking in the first stanza, then "crashing waves" in the fifth stanza. Well, the lakes of the North Country are not always frozen over, and Duluth does sit on the shores of the largest of the Great Lakes. Even if "Never Say Goodbye" is not addressed to the Girl of the North Country, it is apparently addressed to a woman who, in Dylan's mind, had become associated with the landscape of his youth.

The city of Dylan's birth, Duluth, crops up in "Something There Is About You," written in 1973. This is one of Dylan's many love songs to the right kind of girl; a girl with style and grace and "the soul of many things," including Dylan's lost youth — rainy days on the Great Lakes and "the hills of old Duluth." As far as I know, no specific woman has been identified or proposed, but here, as in "Girl of the North Country" and "Winterlude" (another song about the right kind of woman, set in a region of corn in the field, snowflakes and skating rinks), identification is largely irrelevant. In the song Dylan struggles to join an idealized and very remote past with a comparatively chaotic present. Duluth represents something distant, "from another century," a combination of wonder and phantoms of youth which, John Hinchey notes, "seem to emerge directly from the womb of the Great Lakes landscape" ("Planet Waves": 20). "Phantoms" is an interesting word — it carries slightly negative connotations of delusion and fear — but the memories, the girl, the phantoms represent a long-forgotten truth now pleasurably recovered which has brought Dylan out of the whirlwind he was in. The song — if not the situation — foreshadows the 1990 song "Born in Time," in which Dylan recalls another woman, the same place, and a moment before Technicolor when both were still in the process of becoming, and all the world lay ahead of them like a book opened to page one. This woman too — probably Sara, although I'd like to think Echo — is associated with "hills of mystery" (an echo of "the hills of old Duluth"?), and with snow and rain (more reflections of the North Country). Dylan, as usual in songs of the 1990s, is wrecked, but the fire is still smoking (not flaming, just smoldering). The point is, again, that a remote and vaguely idealized place past is contrasted with a harder place present, personified in a woman. In both songs, Duluth, as much as love, seems to offer salvation.

Over the rest of his career, Dylan has occasionally used Minnesotan and Midwestern material. Often these are general references, like "piney woods" ("I'll Remember You"), "the cold in the North" ("Isis"), "the great north woods" ("Tangled Up in Blue"), the bursting grain elevators of "Slow Train," the woodshed and sauna of "I Shall Be Free." Trev Gibb goes so far as to imagine the doorway in "Standing in the Doorway," written in 1997, as "some broken down shack in the Midwest" (6). Sometimes Dylan's reference is merely an image (black crows in a meadow in "Black Crow Blues"), a simile ("walk like a duck and stomp like a skunk" in "I Shall Be Free"), or an idea ("I'm used to four seasons / California's got but one" in "California"). Sometimes it's an unconscious pattern of selection, like the Upper Midwestern animals in "Man Gave Names to All the Animals" — bear, cow, bull, pig, sheep . . . as opposed to gorillas, alligators, or Gila monsters. The Midwest references diminish in the eighties and nineties, when Dylan waxes (at various points) allegorical, abstract, biblical, new age and slightly preachy. Although the Iron Range would have been a gold mine (or an iron mine) of material for "Union Sundown," Kansas is as close to home as Dylan comes in the song. He did, however, link the song to Iron Range in his 1984 *Rolling Stone* interview with Kurt Loder: "ninety percent of the iron for the Second World War came out of those mines up where I'm from. And eventually they said, 'Listen, this is costing too much money to get this out. We must be able to get it someplace else.' Now the same thing is happening, I guess, with other products" (Cott: 293).

But there are always a few reflections of Minnesota and the Upper Midwest.

Aidan Day reads the wind which excites the furnace of "Caribbean Wind" as an echo of "the winds of the / north" mentioned in "11 Outlined Epitaphs" ("Judgment": 100). The Black Hills of South Dakota show up at the end of "Day of the Locusts" as a place to which Dylan can escape the East Coast pretension of Princeton University. Several details in *New Morning* songs sound Minnesotan — snow, country streams, corn, groundhogs and rabbits in the woods, daisies, apples, Main Street, a country mile or two, and of course "that little Minnesota town," for whatever it's worth. Not much, thinks Michael Gray. He reads the final lines of "Went to See the Gypsy" as non sequitur bordering on self-parody, and certainly the town — whatever town it is — plays no role in the song. Similarly, because there is no intersection of Fifty-sixth and Wabasha Avenue, it is difficult to find significance to the mention of this downtown St. Paul avenue in "Meet Me in the Morning" (written the year after "Something There Is About You").

The Greyhound buses in "Last Thoughts on Woody Guthrie" and "Get Your Rocks Off" are another passing reference of no major consequence: the Greyhound Bus Company was founded in Hibbing, which today contains a Greyhound Museum. However, his use of Red Wing's St. James Hotel in "Blind Willie McTell" is brilliant, and oddly timely: when Red Wing was designated one of the 2008 Dozen Distinctive Destinations in America by the National Trust for Historic Preservation, the honor was celebrated with a banquet on February 7 in . . . the St. James Hotel. A stone's throw from the train depot and Mississippi River, the hotel is a well-preserved, four-story Victorian Italianate masterpiece, designed by E. P. Bassford of Minneapolis and built in 1874–75 at a cost of $60,000. In the 1850s, Lake Pepin — just below Red Wing on the Mississippi River — was alive with lumberjacks assembling millions of logs from the Upper Mississippi and St. Croix Rivers into enormous rafts to be floated down the Mississippi; a few decades later, Red Wing was the largest wheat-trading city in the world, shipping almost 2.5 million bushels a year. After a period of decline, a major renovation in 1977 (adding banquet rooms and shopping mall space, decorating with antiques and period reproductions, converting the bank vault into a wine cellar) made the St. James Hotel a plush tourist destination . . . the kind of place that wins awards from the National Trust for Historic Preservation.

Michael Gray reads "St. James Hotel" as coming from "St. James Infirmary," and Greil Marcus suggests "James Alley Blues," which Dylan sings on the "Minneapolis Party Tape" made by Bonnie Beecher at her apartment in May of 1961, but Dylan's North Country roots suggest Red Wing as a conscious allusion. The hotel is famous throughout the state, and its ties to local and national politics, suggestions of the age of wheat and timber barons, up-scale Victorian and neo-Victorian elegance, and the vaguely upper-class British sound of the name St. James all work perfectly in Dylan's song: a bill of particulars on American corruption from then to now. Along with the carnival tents being taken down in stanza two (echoes of "Dusty Old Fairgrounds"?), the hotel functions as a northern terminus to balance East Texas, and the plantations, cracking whips, slave ships, and whiskey-sipping squires we'd find in the South. America's problems today are not a case of bad rebel South and virtuous Yankee North, Dylan tells us: this land is condemned "all the way from New Orleans to Jerusalem." His portrait of America in this song is not too far from his portrait in "Highway 61 Revisited," with the Mississippi River opening the scope of this song as Highway 61 gave scope to that song.

No geographical markers of place locate "Tweedle Dee & Tweedle Dum" in North Country Minnesota, or "Under the Red Sky" in a small Midwestern town, but circumstantial evidence is strong. The language of "Tweedle Dee & Tweedle Dum" suggests a certain northern backwoods type: "one day older and a dollar short," "lying low and they're makin' hay," and "noses to the grindstones" all sound like Minnesota, especially given the long "o" in "grindstones" (see Chapter 2). Speaking of the state's wealth of writers, humorist Howard Mohr notes, "Nearly two-thirds of all Minnesotans put their nose to the grindstone and do a little scribbling" (68). Also vaguely North Country is the silent antagonism between friends, the desire for things they are too cheap to buy — Cheryl Temple Herr calls this Midwest "parsimony on principle" (106) — the back-stabbing and the isolation. The Brick and Tile Company is compatible with the Upper Midwest: one of the more noticeable features of Howard Street in Hibbing — of many buildings in Hibbing actually — is the amount of brick and tile used in construction.

Dylan told Don Was that "Under the Red Sky" is "about people who got trapped in his hometown. I think it's about Hibbing and about people who never left" (Gray, *Song*: 692–3), and Dylan's references to wind, rivers, and horses suggest something rural and Midwestern. The song itself is a sad tale of promise buried by small-town smallness, "baked in a pie," led around by a blind horse until vision dries up and escape becomes impossible.

Late in his career, Midwest idioms and specific references to North Country places increase in Dylan's songs, including small references like the wolves in "Trust Yourself" and "Cat's in the Well," the hills and fog of "Born in Time," the dirt road and hail of "Dirt Road Blues," the winding stream of "When the Deal Goes Down," and perhaps the "peaceful sacred fields" and barn and horse of "Workingman's Blues #2." Although the specific reference is Chicago, "Cold Irons Bound" suggest Duluth in winter — hillsides are in short supply 20 miles outside of Chicago. The strong north wind of "Thunder on the Mountain" is picking up speed in Granite Falls, Minnesota, as I write this paragraph, although we're not yet in planting season or in twister season. The house on a hill with hogs lying around of "Summer Days" sounds familiar, especially with the souped-up cars and the thick fog; so do the barren fields, woods, mill, and washed-out roads of "Lonesome Day Blues." Very old-time Minnesota-Dakota. Although Dylan's country landscapes are increasingly southern Midlands, Appalachian, or even Southern in the songs of *Love and Theft*, the features on which he focuses reflect what one sees on the outskirts of Hibbing and other more northern rural towns. This is especially the case in "Floater (Too Much to Ask)": while the references to "tobacco leaves" and the Cumberland and Tennessee Rivers localize the song in Appalachia, back alleys, bullheads, a grove of trees, and wood ducks would work in the Midwest.

Then there's "Red River Shore." The song, which dates to 1997, is one of *Tell Tale Signs'* recovered gems. The accordion and steel guitar of this performance suggest the Red River of the South, which forms the Texas–Oklahoma border, an identification perhaps strengthened by Dylan's echoes of the cowboy love song known to us as kids as "Red River Valley" (the song's line "come and sit by my side if you love me" becomes Dylan's "I sat by her side"). Another Red River exists, however, and evidence — which Dylan may or may not know — suggests that "Red River Valley" is about the Red River of the North, which marks the Minnesota–North Dakota border, flowing north to Lake Winnipeg in Canada. "Red River Valley" was known in Canada before the turn of the century and had been composed around the time of the Wolseley Expedition of 1870 into Canada. If we take Dylan's Red River to be the Red River of the North, Dylan's "Red River Shore" takes on an interesting autobiographical meaning, supported by his reference to "cabins" and lines like "I been to the east and I been to the west and I been out where the black winds roar." Dylan went East, and he went West, and he long ago sang about the North Country, where the wind hits heavy on the borderline. The song becomes a rather heartrending hymn to the memory of the Girl of the North Country, who suggested that he just "Go home and lead a quiet life." Folks in Hibbing still tell the story of Dylan returning to Hibbing in April 1984 "to see about it once," standing in the street staring at his old house lost in the foggy ruins of time (have not all of us over the age of 50 found ourselves in a similar position?), tangled up perhaps with Echo Helstrom, the only one who ever really saw him at all. Recalling for Anthony Scaduto a hurried visit in 1966, Echo Helstrom said, "I told him something like: 'The happiest people are those that are married and live an ordinary life and have the sense to appreciate what they do have,' and he said: 'Yeah, I've always felt that's true'" (234). This interview, incidentally, took place long before Dylan composed "Red River Shore." Echo is not dealing herself into Dylan's song.

The geography of "Highlands" is fuzzier even than that of "Red River Shore." The landscape appears to be United Kingdom, with the allusion to Burns and the Inn of the Black Swan in Penrith, on the northern edge of England's Lake District, but there are other possibilities. As Muir points out, in Scotland the Borders are down south, not "up in the border country" as in Dylan's song (*Troubadour*: 244). In Minnesota the border country is up, and there's plenty of honeysuckle . . . but no bluebells. Gray points out that there are Aberdeens in Mississippi, Idaho, and Washington (*Song*: 820). Or maybe we're in neither Scotland nor Minnesota: Ohio, after all, is the Buckeye State.

Dylan wrote "Tell Ol' Bill" for Niki Caro's film about a sexual harassment case brought in 1984 by Lois Jenson, who worked in the iron mine in Eveleth, Minnesota, near Hibbing. The film was shot in Eveleth, Virginia, and Chisholm, and Dylan's song is naturally full of Iron Range markers of place (dark woods, bleak rocks, bare trees, lakes, streams, hills, clouds, wind, blasted trees, snow-flakes) and idiom ("hardly a penny to my name," "tell me straight out," "I lay awake at night," "they'll drag you down," "plain as day"). The song leaves much left unspoken — "secret thoughts are hard to bear," "emotions we can never share" — a reticence which reflects the temper of local citizens. In "North Country Blues" it was the male miner who buried his problems in alcohol and silence; 30 years later a female miner turns inward upon herself, walking the countryside alone and lying in bed with troubled mind.

AS THE TWIG IS BENT . . .

Beyond specific stories, people, and references, Dylan's Iron Range-Midwest roots are reflected in the broad patterns of speech, thought, and behavior which are the subjects of subsequent chapters and in several general ideas and behavioral patterns, like his work ethic, and his preference for things rough, unpolished, down-to-earth, and even unprofessional over things finely crafted, carefully polished, overly refined. I would even suggest that Dylan's tendency to play East and West as contrasting opposites (as in "Day of the Locusts") and connect the western parts of the Upper Midwest with the more western side of the South (as in "Highway 61 Revisited") reflects the Minnesota side of a fundamental split in American cultural thinking: what we call the East has a Revolutionary War *and* a Civil War history and a consciousness of that history; the eastern and central Midwest and South have little Revolutionary War history or consciousness, but a profound lingering sense of the Civil War; the West begins at the north–south line — roughly the Mississippi River — where the Civil War counts for little, if anything, in the daily imagination of the populace, and people west of that line — north and south — think alike.

Another large idea, attached in "With God on Our Side" to Dylan's home place, is his suspicion of what Shelton calls mainstream Midwest "provincialism, isolation, back-water Babbittry, and conservatism" (*Home*: 24). This is the middle-class belief system promoted by the Republican Party and satirized in Garrison Keillor's Lake Wobegon stories. Promoted in church, school, and local newspaper, it has largely (but not entirely) supplanted the older, leftist, immigrant tradition which Dylan also knows and we will examine later on. As we shall see, this is the Midwest small-town Dylan rebelled against early, the Gopher Prairie of Lewis's *Main Street*, the "B, Indiana" of William Gass's "In the Heart of the Heart of the Country":

> Sports, politics, and religion are the three passions of the badly educated. They are the Midwest's open sores. Ugly to see, a source of constant discontent, they sap the body's strength. Appalling quantities of money, time, and energy are wasted on them. The rural mind is narrow, passionate, and reckless on these matters. Greed, however shortsighted and direct, will not alone account for it. I have known men, for instance, who for years have voted squarely against their interests. Nor have I ever noticed that their surly Christian views prevented them from urging forward the smithereening, say, of Russia, China, Cuba, or Korea. And they tend to back their country like they back their local team: they have a fanatical desire to win; yelling is their forte; and if things go badly, they are inclined to sack the coach. (197)

This is the mentality Dylan attacks in "With God on Our Side." Proclaiming his Midwest origins in his second line, Dylan recalls that, as a good Midwestern boy, he has been taught to live by the laws because America has God on its side. His picture of rural Minnesota in this song sounds like something out of William Gass . . . or, better yet, out of *Letters from the Country* by Carol Bly, right down to her focus on the key word "they": "Most people in rural Minnesota seem to face evil seldom, inaccurately, and slothfully," Bly writes. "Our usual procedure is to point to the fantasy enemy '*they*'" (69). "They" in Dylan's "With God on Our Side" are the Indians, the Confederates, the Spanish, the Germans, and in the 1950s and '60s, the Russians. "They" equals bad, "us" equals good.[9] We good guys kill them bad guys, and we do not ask questions or count the dead. We memorize heroes and learn to hate everybody else.

Carol Bly's perspective on this feature of Midwest culture is especially relevant when we realize that this critic of small-town Midwestern Babbittry was born in Duluth and, at the time she wrote the *Letters*, lived with her husband Robert Bly (equally critical, cantankerous, and native) in the small Midwestern town of Madison, Minnesota. This critique *of* the Midwest country mentality comes *from* the country. So too Duluth-Hibbing's Bob Dylan — critical of what he's been taught and the way he's been taught to behave — thinks his own way, through many a dark hour, out of black/white dichotomies and Midwest complacency.[10] We could argue that both sides of "With God on Our Side" have roots in Dylan's hometown, Hibbing. .

A second reflection of Dylan's Hibbing background is his somewhat unusual position on the nuclear arms race. On the matter of war, of course, Dylan is very much Iron Range; even while providing ore for the steel which went into ships and tanks, the blue-collar workers of the Iron Range have consistently opposed wars, starting with World War I, continuing through World War II and Vietnam and Iraq.[11] In several songs, however, Dylan goes off on an apparent tangent: fallout shelters. The early 1960s were full of antinuclear songs and protests, but few people did "Ban the Fallout Shelter" protests. In *Chronicles*, Dylan explains that "Let Me Die in My Footsteps" was inspired by the fallout shelter craze that had blossomed out of the Cold War, but in Hibbing, fallout shelters "did not catch" because there was no paranoia about communism. On the Iron Range, stores did not sell fallout shelters, and peddlers selling them were turned away. Besides, Dylan explains, having something your neighbor did not have might lead to class consciousness, and in an actual war, bomb shelters "could turn neighbor against neighbor and friend against friend," divide families, and create mutiny (271). Dylan devotes a good two pages in *Chronicles* to the subject of bomb shelters, and his position is typically Midwestern: it's bad form to stand too far apart from your fellow citizens, especially in material possessions.

Dylan devoted at least three songs in whole or in part to Cold War paranoia and fallout shelters. The longest is "Let Me Die in My Footsteps," a screed against fear which has become eerily relevant in an age eager to sacrifice privacy, freedom, and money to protection from unlikely, if not entirely imaginary, attacks by foreign and domestic terrorists. The immediate inspiration for the song, according to Dylan on the jacket of *The Freewheelin' Bob Dylan*, was a shelter being constructed outside of Phillipsburg or Marysville, in Kansas; the immediate terrorist threat at that time was Cuba. Early in the Kennedy administration, the U.S. had helped to plan and underwrite the ill-fated Bay of Pigs Invasion designed to replace communist leader Fidel Castro with a regime more favorable to the United States. A year and a half later, on October 15, 1962, U-2 reconnaissance flights over Cuba brought home photographs that appeared to show the construction of missile bases — not the actual presence of missiles — in Cuba. Seven days later, President Kennedy addressed America and the world, asserting that Cuba was within the sphere of American safety and interest, and demanding that Russia halt "the missile build-up" there. He also announced that ships of any nation headed toward Cuba would be intercepted, and ordered the American armed forces to "prepare for any eventuality." It was a grim moment indeed, although probably less so for Iron Range Minnesotans (who lived 1,750 miles away from Cuba) than for New Yorkers, a mere 1,300 miles from the Havana terrorists. In less than a week the crisis had been resolved with a U.S.–U.S.S.R. agreement negotiated by U.N. Secretary U Thant, whereby Russia agreed to dismantle its missile sites in Cuba and America agreed to remove missiles from Turkey.

Still, Cold War angst ruled for years thereafter (as it was probably intended to do), and it is to the timid and the terrified that Dylan sings. Those in control have always found fear useful, he points out; Cold War politicians have been talking of the war now for many long years. What's new? Besides, what are you gonna do? If the war comes and death is everywhere, we are all toast. You might as well die in your footsteps. Dylan also suggests the possibility of a con job: Get 'em good and scared, and sell 'em protection in the form of fallout shelters — or Homeland Security — suspend habeas corpus and other constitutionally guaranteed freedoms, bring in the parking lot cameras and airport security checks. Of course, if terrorist-inspired fear makes America spend bundles of money and energy on phantom defenses, the terrorists and their leaders have won. If Americans allow their government to use magnified threats of terrorism to turn them into a nation of sheep, then our leaders have won, which is just about as bad. Dylan's most compelling argument in this song, and one which anticipates the closing stanza of "A Hard Rain's A-Gonna Fall," is the old argument that the best defense America has against terrorists abroad and obtrusive government at home is an independent citizenry these days. Instead of learning to live, Americans are learning to die, he points out. What kind of a life is that? A guy with a ton of money might buy up all the munitions and then destroy them, but a poor man's best response is to stand tall and speak out. In this song Dylan is not quite ready to stand on a mountain so all souls can see him, but he is resolved to die in his footsteps before ducking underground like a coward. (Interestingly, the steps lead to mountain streams, meadows, wildflowers, and grassy leaves . . . to the restoration in nature which is an important component of the pastoral tradition.)

The fallout shelters unpopular in Minnesota crop up elsewhere in Dylan's early songs. "Talkin' World War III Blues" is a satirical critique of America clearly set in New York, with Dylan driving down Forty-second Street in his Cadillac and failing to pay his Con Ed bill. The dream which he recounts begins with Dylan surviving the nuclear attack in the sewer, a poor man's fallout shelter, where he's making out with his girlfriend. Walking through the empty city, Dylan happens upon an actual fallout shelter, and encounters the kind of citizen-against-citizen situation he described in *Chronicles*: "I rung the fallout shelter bell / And I leaned my head and I gave a yell / . . . A shotgun fired and away I ran." As this song is more humorous than its predecessor, and its subject is broader than that of its predecessor, its conclusion is more communal than individualistic: "I'll let you be in my dreams if I can be in yours." Terrorism and cold wars end when we cut that deal.

Then there is the controversial "Talkin' John Birch Paranoid Blues," which Dylan was asked, during rehearsals, to not perform on *The Ed Sullivan Show* of May 12, 1963, leading to Dylan not performing any songs on the program, leading to a major blowup in the newspapers which made Dylan a hero and Ed Sullivan a coward. Although the song was also excised from Dylan's second album, he performed the song at his October 26 Carnegie Hall concert, introducing it with the remark, "There ain't nothin' wrong with this song." While the song does not mention fallout shelters, it does satirize the Cold War paranoia used to sell shelters. Here that paranoia is embodied in the speaker, who, fearing Reds in every television and toilet, joins the John Birch Society and begins investigating everyone everywhere: under his bed, in the sink, behind the door, in the car's glove compartment. In Northern Minnesota, Dylan observes when talking about fallout shelters in *Chronicles*, "As far as communists went, there wasn't any paranoia about them. People weren't scared of them, seemed to be a big to-do over nothing" (271).

Another reflection of Dylan's childhood experience in Duluth and Hibbing is his fixation on bells and trains. "The railroad imagery is of course one of Dylan's staple recourses," observes John Herdman (45); Herdman even points out three uses of "slow trains coming" on the jacket notes of *Highway 61 Revisited*, written long before the *Slow Train Coming* album (111). Whence, really, come all these trains (and bells) in Dylan?

In New York, Dylan enjoyed his freedom, of course, and the possibility of doing something remarkable and revolutionary in music, but his descriptions of the city itself are generally negative. Oddly, the things he genuinely liked about the city itself were things which reminded him of Minnesota. One was the companionship of a whole bunch of people from the other side of the American tracks; another was the apartment of Chloe Kiel and Ray Gooch ("a character from out of some of the songs I'd been singing" [*Chronicles*: 26]), with its floor-to-ceiling bookcases . . . and the sounds of trains and bells. In *Chronicles*, Dylan recalls listening to trains at their apartment in the Village:

> I'd seen and heard trains from my earliest childhood days and the sight and sound of them always made me feel secure. The big boxcars, the iron ore cars, freight cars, passenger trains, Pullman cars. There was no place you could go in my hometown without at least some part of the day having to stop at intersections and wait for the long trains to pass. Tracks crossed the rural roads and ran alongside them as well. The sound of trains off in the distance more or less made me feel at home, like nothing was missing, like I was at some level place, never in any significant danger and that everything was fitting together. (31)

Trains, in other words, connected Dylan to Hibbing and Duluth. Much later, looking out the window of a bus while talking to Jonathan Cott in 1978, Dylan drew the same connection. Pointing to two kids playing by the train tracks, Dylan observed, "They remind me of myself."[12] In Hibbing, Dylan lived five blocks from the train tracks, which ran just north of Howard Street, and those trains are most likely the source of Dylan's trains and, more important, the way Dylan uses trains in his songs.[13] The train tracks are silent these days, and the station is now an antique shop, but that was not the case in the 1950s. Running right through town as they did, each train would have blown its whistle long and loud — sounds which carry farther than the ringing of bells in a cold winter night. (Perhaps if Dylan had lived closer to the Hibbing airport, his songs would be filled with references to airplanes instead of trains.)

Trains, a long tradition in American culture and song, are useful metaphors for escape, for sex, and for the company of the elect on their way to Glory: "This Train Don't Carry No Gamblers," "People Get Ready ("Train A-Comin')," "Get on Board, Little Children." The train in "A Man of Constant Sorrow," which Dylan sings on the *Little White Wonder* bootlegs, is both escape from a hard life and a vehicle to "God's golden shore," where he'll be reunited with his darlin'. Dylan's *Slow Train Coming* has obvious gospel significance. Dylan uses trains to represent sex in "Honey, just allow me one more chance / To ride your passenger train" ("Honey, Just Allow Me One More Chance") and "your railroad gate, you know I just can't jump it" ("Absolutely Sweet Marie"). And Dylan uses the train to represent travel or escape, as in "Hey, stop you ol' train / Let a poor boy ride" ("Poor Boy Blues"), or the long-distance train that's rolling through the rain in "Where Are You Tonight? (Journey Through Dark Heat)." Hank Williams was Dylan's first idol because he sang about the railroad lines and the iron bars and rattling wheels, Dylan claimed in the liner notes to *Joan*

Baez in Concert, Part 2. In the poem, the train works as an obvious symbol of escape, a counter to the grass, which is symbolically place, which young Dylan is symbolically tearing up by its roots.

But Dylan's trains do not usually represent an attractive escape. In fact, in "I'll Keep It with Mine," the train as escape is specifically discarded: forget the train, Dylan suggests; why search for what's not lost? Dylan's trains generally represent some kind of hardness, threat, or disaster. Dylan may consciously or unconsciously see in trains a reminder of the day he was riding his motorcycle and stopped at a crossing while a train passed, gunned his engine as soon as the last car passed, and started to take off, only to discover a track behind the track in front of him, with a second train bearing down on him, coming from the opposite direction of the one he had seen. Or the day Leroy Hoikkala likes to recall, when Dylan decided he'd race across the tracks by the power plant north of Howard Street just ahead of a coal train, and almost did not make it (A. Brown: 215). Train-as-death trumps train-as-sex or train-as-escape, and darkens the metaphor. In Woody Guthrie's song "Little Black Train," the train symbolizes death and judgment, a significance Dylan would borrow for *Slow Train Coming.* Early on, Dylan gives us the iron train of hatred ("Train A-Travelin'"); somewhat later, in the obscure song "Trouble," an ear to the train tracks brings in the sound of trouble, nothing but trouble. In "John Brown," the train brings a mother's son home from the war so mutilated she can hardly recognize him. "[T]he railroad lines were not beautiful," Dylan recalls in *Joan Baez in Concert, Part 2*; "They were smoky black an gutter colored / An filled with stink an soot an dust" [sic]. What they taught him was ugliness. The train line "cuts the ground" in "11 Outlined Epitaphs." "It Takes a Lot to Laugh, It Takes a Train to Cry," Dylan titles one of his high sixties rock songs. In "Only a Pawn in Their Game," the train represents the racist system, with Medgar Evers's killer and his ilk riding the caboose. Maybe this is the same trainload of fools that travels the rails again in "Señor (Tales of Yankee Power)." In "Simple Twist of Fate" the night hits Dylan like a freight train. In "When the Deal Goes Down," Dylan looks forward to a midnight rain (grace) which "follows the train" (disaster). In "Marchin' to the City," the train that keeps rolling all night long is associated not with Dylan who is *marching* toward the New Jerusalem, as with the sexy babe who done him wrong and is not coming with him. In "Can't Escape from You," the train is death: "The dead bells are ringing / My train is overdue."

Then there is that scene in *dont look back*, where an obviously wrecked Dylan rides the train to Manchester.

Then there's "When I Paint My Masterpiece." Over years of performance, John Hinchley notes, the "plane ride" from Rome to Brussels in the last verse mutated into a train ride, and, with the 1975 Rolling Thunder Revue, "into 'train wrecks,' in which form it has since remained" ("New Morning": 15). Not without warning does Mona in "Stuck Inside of Mobile" warn, "Stay away from the train line."

We would expect a train to move vision forward, but the connection of trains with childhood means that for Dylan, the symbol of escape, whether it's in Minnesota or New York, carries an echo of the past. That was its value in the early *Joan Baez in Concert, Part 2* poem, and in "Bob Dylan's Dream" ("While riding on a train goin' west. . .") and in "Something's Burning, Baby": "Please don't fade away on me, baby, like the midnight train." That's the train's value in the recent "Nettie Moore," where Dylan opens with an echo of Little Bobby sitting by the Hibbing railroad track: "Lost John sitting by the railroad track." That's the function of the train in "Brownsville Girl," where memory calls like a train. People waiting for the trains remind Dylan of his lost love in "Tryin' to Get to Heaven." Perhaps the smartest thing to do is never leave in the first place: throw your ticket and suitcase and troubles out the window and stay put, as Dylan does in the beatific "Tonight I'll Be Staying Here with You," from his country period.

Another sound that Dylan claims made him feel comfortable in Ray and Chloe's apartment was the ringing of bells:

> Across the street from where I stood looking out the window was a church with a bell tower. The ringing of bells made me feel at home, too. I'd always heard and listened to the bells. Iron, Brass, silver bells — the bells sang. On Sundays, for services, on holidays. . . . Any special occasion would make the bells ring. You had a pleasant feeling when you heard the bells. (*Chronicles*: 31)

The Zimmerman house at 2425 Seventh Avenue East was exactly one block from the huge Blessed Sacrament Roman Catholic Church; Dylan passed it twice daily walking the two blocks to school, and any time he walked to Howard Street. Also within hearing distance were St. James Episcopal Church, Our Savior's Lutheran Church (built in 1952), First Presbyterian, First Lutheran, Wesley Methodist, and Holy Trinity Lutheran. The county courthouse bell rang on the hour and half hour. Here was a cacophony of bells, richer perhaps than your average European cathedral city, and a more likely source for the many bells in Dylan's songs than the bell-like chords of Blind Lemon Jefferson's guitar on "See That My Grave Is Kept Clean," or Allen Ginsberg, or William Blake. The bells ring in Dylan songs from the early "Chimes of Freedom" to the later "Standing in the Doorway." Railroad tracks and church bells defined the North

Country back in "Ballad for a Friend," where the train represents death and the bells represent memory. Trains and bells have the same relative associations in "Standing in the Doorway," where Dylan weighs the pros and cons of returning to a dead love. On the one hand there's the midnight train (departure); on the other hand are the "church bells ringing in the yard."

While there's a ringing bell on the last fire truck from hell in "Shooting Star," bells in Dylan are a better deal than trains. In the unreleased and relatively obscure "Nobody 'Cept You," which dates to the *Planet Waves* period, Dylan hears in his woman the "old familiar chime" of "a hymn I used to hear / In the churches all the time / Make me feel so good inside." The sound of bells calls Dylan from urban nightmare (machine guns, time bombs, flying rocks) to countryside quiet in "Farewell Angelina." Cathedral bells and chimes restore a frazzled and cynical Dylan in *Joan Baez in Concert, Part 2*, and the chimes of dawn close "11 Outlined Epitaphs," their music ending that poem with a note of resurrection and salvation. Mission bells might have saved Frankie Lee in "The Ballad of Frankie Lee and Judas Priest," and bells ring again in the first line of "Call Letter Blues" (recorded for *Blood on the Tracks*, released finally in *Bootleg Series I–III*). Bells ring more recently in "Beyond the Horizon": "The Bells of St. Mary, how sweetly they chime." The bells of evening ring most recently in "'Cross the Green Mountain," where they honor the Union's great captain Abraham Lincoln.

Most interesting in this regard is the song "Ring Them Bells," which follows the lament "Everything is Broken" on *Oh Mercy*. In a manner that anticipates the connection between "Thunder on the Mountain" and "Spirit on the Water" in *Modern Times*, the second song here acts to redeem the world of the first. Dylan's scope is broad indeed in "Broken World": everything is busted, in both city *and* countryside (in the alternate version released on *Tell Tale Signs*, Dylan adds broken leaves and broken trees to the broken beds, broken gates, broken laws, broken treaties, broken bones, broken hearts, and broken people). Then comes the ecumenical "Ring Them Bells": some bells rung by heathen and from a city that dreams, others rung from a fortress and a room, yet others rung from the sanctuaries St. Peter's Church and St. Catherine's Church . . . all ringing their call of mixed admonition and reconciliation across a pastoral landscape: valleys and streams and pastures full of lost sheep and sleeping shepherds. The bells bring healing to a world knocked on its side by preaching that God is one (this is a late Dylan song), breaking down distinctions between right and wrong. The bells of "Ring Them Bells" thus echo those of "Chimes of Freedom" on *Another Side of Bob Dylan*, where wedding bells dissolve into the bells of lightning and celebrate Dylan's transformation from protest singer to symbolist poet, movement spokesperson to individual, and from us/them dichotomies to an egalitarian acceptance of rebels and rakes, mothers and prostitutes, outlaws and warriors, and underdogs, all "the countless confused, accused, misused, strung-out ones an' worse / An' for every hung-up person in the whole wide universe."

Another reflection of Dylan's experiences in Hibbing, according to many people, is the strong presence of death in many of Dylan's songs, particularly on his early albums. Andy Gill writes, "One notable aspect of the material chosen for his debut [album] is the pervasive presence of death in many of the songs, particularly for such a young man" (12). Bob Dylan had been preoccupied by death — obsessed, some say — since his youth. In 2009, Christie's Auction House sold a transcription of Hank Snow's "Little Buddy" that Dylan had passed around summer camp at age 15, about a blue-eyed kid whose pet dog was beaten to death by a drunk for barking too enthusiastically. In New York, several friends, including Suze Rotolo, perceived an undertow of pessimistic despair beneath Dylan's comic exterior. Joan Baez mentions Dylan being on a death trip (Scaduto: 209), and Gretel Whitaker told Robert Shelton, "We never really expected Bobby to live past twenty-one" (*Home*: 54). Dylan himself admitted to Robert Shelton in 1966, "I have a death thing — I have a suicidal thing" and "I've seen so many people die" (Cott: 81, 84). "[James] Dean was the first cat I ever met with that kind of thing, the magnetism and the feeling he was running too fast and was going to get himself killed because he was running too fast. And Bob was the second I ever met," recalled Jack Elliott (Scaduto: 59). Toward the end of the *Biograph* booklet, an older Dylan tells Cameron Crowe, "Actually I'm amazed that I've been around this long, never thought I would be" (33). Dylan mentions a fear of "getting killed on motorcycles" in his *Planet Waves* reminiscence of Hibbing, but Bobby Zimmerman, the high school rebel with a cause was not killed by that coal train. He merely picked himself up, rode off with his friend Leroy Hoikkala, sold his Harley, bought another bike in Woodstock, and had himself a real motorcycle accident on July 29, 1966.

The title of Dylan's poem "11 Outlined Epitaphs" probably owes less to Masters's *Spoon River Anthology* than it does to Dylan's morbid fascination with dying young, to the deaths of friends and Buddy Holly (whom Dylan saw perform only three days before his death), and to the people he might have killed in accidents, especially the three-year-old kid who darted out from between two cars just as Dylan passed on his motorcycle in another Hibbing near-miss.

It owes something to the 1958 diving accident which left his summer-camp pal Larry Kegan paralyzed. "For Bob, the fact that a contemporary — a healthy boy who was as ambitious about music as Bob himself was — could have his life frozen by a freak accident remained a sobering lesson" (Sounes: 28). Perhaps Dylan's sense of imminent death is related to the foghorns of Duluth: in *Chronicles*, remembering the attraction of Bertholt Brecht's song "Pirate Jenny," which he heard in a theatre production Suze Rotollo was involved with, Dylan writes, what drew him in at first was the refrain line about the freighter, with his heavy foghorn reminiscent of Duluth:

> Foghorns sounded like great announcements. The big boats came and went, iron monsters from the deep — ships to wipe out all spectacles. As a child, slight, introverted and asthma stricken, the sound was so loud, so enveloping, I could feel it in my whole body and it made me feel hollow. Something out there could swallow me up. (273–4)

Then again, one thing living in the Midwest does teach is the brevity of summer — and of life — and the dark, absolute chill of winter. Death is an annual event of considerable duration. Willa Cather opened part III of her novel *O Pioneers!* with a set description of winter and death:

> Winter has settled down over the Divide again; the season in which Nature recuperates, in which she sinks to sleep between the fruitfulness of autumn and the passion of spring. The birds have gone. The teeming life that goes on down in the long grass is exterminated. The prairie-dog keeps his hole. The rabbits run shivering from one frozen garden patch to another and are hard put to it to find frost-bitten cabbage-stalks. At night the coyotes roam the wintry waste, howling for food. The variegated fields are all one color now; the pastures, the stubble, the roads, the sky are the same leaden gray. The hedgerows and trees are scarcely perceptible against the bare earth, whose slaty hue they have taken on. The ground is frozen so hard that it bruises the foot to walk in the roads or in the ploughed fields. It is like an iron country, and the spirit is oppressed by its rigor and melancholy. One could easily believe that in that dead landscape the germs of life and fruitfulness were extinct forever. (187)

Dave Engel writes of winter in Duluth,

> In winter, [Lake Superior is] all frozen. Residents, when they must leave superheated rooms, rush from door to doorway between piles of snow, while trying not to slip on the icy slopes of every east-west thoroughfare, breathing great clouds of frost, wondering when, if ever, it will end. But truth to tell, it doesn't end. Any day of the year can be winter cold, wind whipping flags and jangling ghostly chains. (39)

"January and February are the dead season," Minnesota's Senator Eugene McCarthy once told me, "a time to do nothing at all. Lyndon [Johnson] went into Vietnam in January." Having grown up in close contact with nature and the annual cycle of birth and death, Dylan might be more sensitive to death than his more insulated and comfortable urban countrymen . . . especially with the ghost of North Hibbing a short hike away.

On that first album, "Fixin' to Die," "In My Time of Dyin'," and "See That My Grave Is Kept Clean" are borrowed and fatalistic takes on the subject of death, reflecting, perhaps, Dylan's background among people who live hard and often die hard . . . and anonymously. To that time also date songs like "Ballad for a Friend," "Man on the Street" and "Only a Hobo" (the last two songs are meditations on the corpse of an unidentified man lying dead and ignored on the pavement — scenes right out of *Midnight Cowboy*), "Let Me Die in My Footsteps," and "Percy's Song," about a friend convicted of vehicular homicide. Suze Rotolo mentions a letter from Dylan about the time of the Cuban Missile Crisis: "He wrote that in the time leading up to the face-off between the United States and the Soviet Union, he felt that: 'the maniacs were really going to do it this time,' and he recounted his passive acceptance of the inevitability of dying. He only hoped that he would 'die quick and not have to put up with radiation'" (194). "Standing on the Highway" (1962) offers two roads, one to the bright lights, the other "goin' down to my grave."

Dylan's own anxiety about an obscure death may be reflected early in the song title "The *Lonesome* Death of Hattie Carroll," later in Rosemary's resolve "to do just one good deed before she died," and in the even later assurance that, for a Christian, "Death Is Not the End." (This life in the Upper Midwest also teaches us: after winter comes spring, and then summer . . . and then autumn and winter again. It's a wonderful system, and quite reliable.) After his Christian period, Dylan returned to a more pessimistic view and obsession with death, including "I'm walking through streets that are dead" ("Love Sick" on *Time Out of Mind*) and the bleak observation, "Beyond Here Lies Nothin'."

School was a larger component of Dylan's life in Hibbing than trains, bells, and death combined. His experience there was certainly troubled, although Dylan did return to Hibbing for his tenth class reunion. "We were in a box," recalls Carolyn Kangas, who was a year or two behind Dylan at Hibbing High School, "and he was out of the box." Very astute observation.

Hibbing High School, which can be seen briefly in the film *No Direction Home*, is one of the seven man-made wonders of Minnesota — and not just its auditorium — perhaps what Dylan had in mind with his remark about Miss Lonely having gone to the finest school, all right. Begun in 1920, completed in 1923, the school cost nearly $4 million. Paid for by the mining companies, its classy red brick, trimmed with Bedford stone, is a monument to elegance and opulence. It was once the third largest high school in the country, with an 1,800-seat auditorium which Dylan describes in *Chronicles, Volume One* as "no small music box theater but a professional concert hall like Carnegie Hall built with East Coast mining money, with curtains and props, trapdoors and orchestra pit" (125). "Every stage that Bob Dylan has played on over the forty-plus years since has been, after the Hibbing High School auditorium, an anticlimax," writes Scobie (*Alias*: 18). Three custodians were assigned to care for the auditorium's four crystal chandeliers, its 40-by-60-foot stage, 45 stage backdrops for class plays and other events, nine single dressing rooms, private boxes, and a 1,900-pipe Barton organ. Outside the auditorium, the school is rich in classy decoration, with art nouveau leaded glass, intricately tiled entrance, and plenty of original art — most famously a series of six paintings by David Ericson by the stairs of the main entrance (lumbering, fur trading, and immigrants swearing the oath of citizenship, on one side; on the other, Columbus landing in America, the signing of the Declaration of Independence, and an ox cart with pioneers). In the library, which purportedly contained 20,000 books in Dylan's day, a mural by David Tice Workman depicting Iron Range steel production — and the many ethnic groups involved — is flanked by two quotations in large, ornate letters: "They force the blunt and yet unbloodied steel to do their will" (Cowper), and "Lifting the hidden iron that glimpses in labored mines undrainable of ore" (Tennyson). The school had its own doctor and dentist, even its own monogrammed dinner plates: HHS. The building certainly gives students the impression that they are important — an impression underscored by one story, perhaps apocryphal, of girls showering after gym in individual marble showers, and drying themselves when finished with towels handed to them by shower attendants.

But education in Hibbing — like the newspaper, mainstream cultural institutions, police and fire departments, and city hall — was underwritten by Main Street for the benefit of Main Street. If mine management poured money into building schools, it did so in the belief that education for Hibbing's youth and adults (the high school was originally K-12 plus adult education) would temper, if not eradicate, the leftist-to-communist proclivities of their immigrant laborers just off the boat. "In school and in church," writes Garrison Keillor of his fictional Lake Wobegon High, perhaps 150 miles southwest of Hibbing, "we were called to high ideals such as truth and honor by someone perched on truth and hollering for us to come on up" (6). That was the box of which Carolyn Kangas spoke, and it was a box which did not interest Bob Zimmerman.[14]

On the one hand, Hibbing embodied a functioning fraternity of workers of all ethnicities living in a mixed settlement of modest middle-class houses — plenty of brick and stucco and wood, no ghettos or slums. In the 1950s, the high school celebrated diversity in forms ranging from the mural of iron workers, to Civic Music Programs celebrating "A World of Dance" (November 8, 1957: Spain, Scotland, Portugal, Japan, Cuba, Java, and Bavaria), to a developing foreign student exchange program, to editorials promoting tolerance like the one printed in the March 20, 1959 student newspaper:

> Now before we go any further, we should like to state that it is not our intention to protect anti-Semitism, racism, and evils of that magnitude. We students of Hibbing High School are fortunate to have few people in our midst who comply with the aforementioned bigotries, and those few who do are more to be pitied than expostulated with.

On the other hand, the student newspaper was not in the slightest bit dark-side-diverse,[15] nor were high school assemblies which, during Dylan's sophomore, junior, and senior years, featured things like girls modeling Herberger's fashions, movies like *Crosby Sings* and *Around the World in 80 Days*, Jose Silva and his banjo, bagpipe imitations with toy balloons and a bicycle horn sonata, and on January 24, 1958, a trained bear. Twice in Dylan's high school years the school prom had a French theme: *Les Nuits de Fantasie*. His junior year the prom theme was "Bewitched, Bothered, and Bewildered." The student newspaper enthused:

> Tonight will be a time for all dreams to come true. Thrilled juniors and seniors will dance the evening away in a blind daze of happiness. The rose pink of Gail Stevens' dress will match the flesh colorings in her cheeks as she and her date, Larry Seger, survey the "bewitched" gym. Her dress is sheer nylon over net and satin with a full skirt falling in tiers to a ballerina length. Enchantment will fill Larry Fabro as he dances with Nancy Aanes beneath the crepe-paper ceiling. . .

Bob Zimmerman and Echo Helstrom went to the prom. Outsiders, they left early, skipping the post-prom supper dance at the Moose Lodge.

A Student Council Talent Show raising funds for the American Field Service exchange in 1958 featured "jazz combo, soft shoe, girls' specialty dance act, duets, instrumental solos, and comedy skits and routines." A Girls' League, to which every girl in the school belonged, gave annual Christmas teas, very formal and proper, where they all dressed up and hosted equally dolled up parents. (Did this include Echo Helstrom?) "Dean Quigley believed in manners,"

Carolyn Kangas recalls. In December 1957, the Girls' League committee presented Hibbing High School with a new silver tea service.

Movies like *Rebel Without a Cause* and *Jail House Rock* did not play in Hibbing High School assemblies, although they played in Hibbing movie theaters. In fact, the Hibbing High School powers were not particularly keen on Elvis Presley. The editorial page of the November 30, 1956 student newspaper says it all: above a cartoon captioned "Out of This World," a Martian with a guitar sings, "You Ain't Nothin but a Hound Dog." Below the cartoon, an article by Mariana Manthey is headlined "Achieving Well-Groomed Look Takes Extra Time, Little Money." In another editorial in the October 4, 1957 newspaper headlined "Calypso, Presley Style to Wane as Pop Melodies, Jazz Increase," Susan Beasy assures readers, "Pop melody will dominate the channels on television this season. Ballads (the few that are left), rock 'n roll, country and hillbilly music, jazz, and the slightly modified classical will find their place, but the emphasis will be on pop. Competition will be keen between the Pat Boone and Elvis Presley type of song. Critics say the year will see a sharp rise in the popularity of the Pat Boone style, and a practically extinct Presley."[16] When Dylan gave them his impression of Little Richard in February of 1958, the students booed ("He didn't sit at the piano properly," Carolyn Kangas recalls; "maybe that was the reason"), Dylan broke the pedal on the piano, and principal Kenneth Pederson pulled the mike plug . . . and then dropped the curtain. The student newspaper reported only, "A local rock 'n roll instrumental group entertained, and several vocal selections were also presented." The paper for the following year makes no mention of any local rock 'n' roll group, although Dylan purportedly performed at the January 9 Jacket Jamboree with a new band, The Rockets.

Dave Engel reports that Hibbing High School Principal Kenneth Pederson told him the school had no dress code in the 1950s: "Slacks and levis have not been school garb for more than 10 years. But we have no ban. We have used a positive plan of encouragement. If a girl wears slacks to school, the next time she wears a dress the teacher will comment 'how nice you look today'" (167). Either that plan did not work, or somebody took the liberty of BS-ing: the October 17, 1958 *Hibbing Hi-Times* contained an article headlined, "Student Council Outlines New Dress Code for Students." The code outlawed "improperly fitting clothing, unbuttoned or not tucked in shirts, and turned up collars. A belt which properly supports the trousers, and avoidance of unduly long hair are prerequisites of good grooming for boys." For girls, no slacks or jeans. The girls' dress code stipulated two inches below the knees. "And Quigly would measure," recalls Carolyn Kangas. Arguments supporting the dress code were based on good taste and the need to avoid distractions. An April 10, 1959, editorial pointed out that since "school policy is for the maximum benefit of all concerned . . . most students do not object to it."

Thus says the Hibbing High School student newspaper. But Kangas also recalls that boys started wearing jeans in the late fifties, and she tells an intriguing story of the time, shortly after Dylan graduated, that three female teachers — not without terrific anxiety and trepidation — came to school one Friday in slacks. Nothing was said, and the following Friday a few more women wore slacks, and the battle was won. And in the summer of 1959, Dean of Girls, Miss Quigley herself, toured Europe . . . including Moscow, Leningrad, and Kiev.

In any case, Hibbing High School in the fifties valued manners over passion, sports over art, convention over exploration, conformity over dissent. This was not Bobby Zimmerman, so the school did not reward him with the attention that it showered on its athletes, club members, newspaper writers, or 4.0 scholars. Not a mention in any issue of the *Hibbing Hi-Times*, which made an obsession out of naming everybody who coughed or sneezed:

> Tonight at 8 p.m. high school students will present a variety show sponsored by the student council. The hour-and-a-half performance will include an assortment of student talent with John Borovac as master of ceremonies.
>
> A group led by Jean Edelstein will present its version of Arthur Murray's Dancing Party. These actors are Joe Sacco, Peggy Demgen, Darlene Ranta, Mary McGraw, Judy Musech, Bill Greniuk, Mike Hines, Gail Passeri, and Roger Goman.
>
> Lending their musical talents to the show, Barbara Benchina and Sam Lukens will sing, and Marlana Manthey and Roger Drong will play piano solos. A vocal quartet composed of Mike Milinovich, Larry Fabbro, Loren Chiodi, and John Milinovich will also entertain. Marvin Imbertson will afford amusement with his accordian.
>
> Jeff Kangas, Ray Reid, and John Popovich will give pantomimes, while Evelyn Anderson will offer a humorous reading.
>
> HHS Mandrake the Magician, Joe Brekke, will perform one of his magic acts. Music for the show will include a pit band under the direction of Clyde Hill. . . .

No mention of Bobby Zimmerman. To Dylan standing outside the box, Hibbing High School was a veritable "Maggie's Farm." In his senior year, Scaduto reports, he circulated a petition to "impeach" an English teacher who had failed him (25). Introducing "Blowin' in the Wind" at Carnegie Hall, Dylan said, "Met a teacher who said he didn't understand what *Blowin' In The Wind* means. . . . Told him there was nothin' to understand, it was just blowin' in the wind. If he didn't feel it in the wind, he'd never know. And he ain't never gonna know, I guess. *Teachers*" (Scaduto: 157). Behind everything Dylan would write about

American education lie his experiences at Hibbing High, and looking carefully at the record, at what Hibbing High was in the fifties and what Dylan was then and what he became, one is forced to conclude that from his high school Dylan took absolutely nothing except alienation, and possibly his familiarity with John Steinbeck.[17]

Dylan took one other thing from his adolescence in Hibbing which shows up in his songs and writing: a glimpse of what I'll call in Chapter 5 "the other side of Main Street," the world of Echo Helstrom and her father. "Hibbing was like, well, when I was a little girl it was a happy place to be," Echo recalled, adding, perhaps with a reference to Dr. Seuss's story "The Sneetches,"

> but when I grew up it was like having fancy goldfish and plain goldfish in one bowl, and the plain goldfish would just kill the fancy for being fancy. That's what Hibbing was like. If you were different they would pick you to pieces. Bob rebelled against it. . . . And he planned on breaking out, getting away from there. (Scaduto: 5)

Echo herself came from a predominantly Finnish area south of Hibbing called Maple Hill. These people were mostly farmers — a Maple Hill Farmers Club had been chartered in 1922, and as late as 1959 Maple Hill had its own school and 4-H Club — but they were still Finns, and far left of (and therefore below) the Main Street crowd, especially in the eyes of the Main Street crowd. Echo wore a motorcycle jacket and jeans, listened to blues records, and jimmied the door of the Moose Lodge (or was with Dylan when he jimmied the door) so that Dylan could play boogie piano for her (Sounes: 32; Shelton, *Home*: 47; Scaduto: 14). A high school acquaintance, Linda Fidler, told Anthony Scaduto,

> Bob was considered part of the tough motorcycle crowd. Always with the black leather jacket, the cigarette in the corner of his mouth, rather hoody. And Echo with her bleached hair and a vacant look; that's mostly how I first noticed him, running around with this freaky girl hanging on the back of his motorcycle with her frizzy white hair flying and her false eyelashes. It was shocking to me. I tried not to be narrow-minded, but I thought that crowd was a bunch of creeps. (Scaduto: 20)

Dylan no more belonged to the greaser crowd than he belonged to the jocks or student government types, but with his friends, he discovered "a new Iron Range that his family scarcely knew" (Shelton, *Home*: 46). At Whitaker's he posed for photos that made him look like Marlon Brando or James Dean, movie stars from the other side of the tracks. Dylan reaches into that side of Hibbing on the liner to *Planet Waves*. While the crazy scene filled with whacko characters recalls the grotesque figures of his middle sixties songs (as well as Kerouac–Ginsberg free-flow prose poems), we are actually in Hibbing, Minnesota and

> Back to the starting point! The kickoff, Hebrew letters on the wall, Victor Hugo's house in Paris, NYC in early autumn, leaves flying in the park, the clock strikes eight. Bong — I dropped a double brandy & tried to recall the events . . . beer halls & pin balls, polka bands, barbwire & thrashing clowns, objects, headwinds & snowstorms, family outing with strangers — Furious gals with garters & smeared lips on bar stools that stank from sweating pussy — doin' the hula — perfect priests in overhauls, glassy eyed, Insomnia! Space guys off duty with big dicks & ducktails all wired up & voting for Eisenhower, waving flags & jumping off of fire engines, getting killed on motorcycles whatever — we sensed each other beneath the MASK, pitched a tent in the Street & joined the traveling circus. Love at first sight! History became a lie! The sideshow took over — what a sight . . . the threshold of the Modern Bomb, Temples of the Pawnee, the Cowboy saint, the Arapahoe, Snapshots of — Apache poets searching through the ruins for a glimpse of Buddah — I lit out for parts unknown, found Jacob's Ladder up against my adobe wall & bought a serpent from a passing angel — Yeah the ole days are gone forever and the new ones aint far behind, the laughter is fading away, echoes of a star, & Energy Vampires in the Gone World going Wild! Drinking the blood of innocent people, Innocent lambs! The Wretched of the Earth, My brothers of the flood, Cities of the flesh — Milwaukee, Ann Arbor, Chicago, Bismark, South Dakota, Duluth! Duluth — where Baudelaire lived & Goya cashed in his Chips, where Joshua brought the house down! From there it was straight up — a little jolt of Mexico and some good LUCK, a Little power over the Grave, some more brandy & the teeth of a Lion & a Compass.

It is tempting to say that Dylan severed whatever hometown habits might have accompanied him to New York with his shift in the mid-sixties from acoustic to electric and from ballad-like narratives to surrealistic imagistic poems, but as we've just seen, that is not the case. The standard read is less influence of folk music (especially Guthrie), more influence of the urban, postmodern literary tradition (especially Rimbaud, and the Beats). Dylan becomes the ultimate New York hipster. It is true that Dylan mined North Country people and places less often, and that the most visible influences on him were not those of the Midwest he had known in the 1950s. Dylan himself said around this time, "it's easier to be disconnected than to be connected" (Gill: 83). And even if he did not cut those roots in New York, Dylan must surely have lost them when he bought the house in Malibu, California . . . or certainly when he took to gallivanting literally all around the globe in the 1980s and 1990s.

But we know this is not true biographically, artistically, or mentally. Dylan returned frequently to Minnesota, to Hibbing, and to his farm on the Crow River. Besides, old habits die hard, and even those of us who are not neurotic have a repetition compulsion. We now know that in "going electric" in the middle sixties, Dylan was not striking out in a new direction; he was reverting to the guitar he'd played in high school. If Dylan found himself attracted to the random, dada style of American Beats, perhaps the aesthetic legitimatized some experience in his past: Robert Shelton reports a conversation with Dylan's "best buddy" in Hibbing, in which John Bucklen recalls ad-libbing verses on tape: "We'd get a guitar and sing verses we made up as we went along. It came out strange and weird. We thought we'd send them in somewhere, but we never did" (*Home*: 46). (Dylan just saved them for 1967, for a spring and summer of improv with The Band in the basement of a house called Big Pink in Woodstock, New York.) Perhaps abstract expressionism attracted Dylan because the North Country becomes, especially in winter, a bit abstract. Perhaps imagism attracted Dylan because the sparse north woods environment — especially in winter — highlights the individual image: a bright red stop sign in a whole windshield full of white snow; a single wedge of geese against a gray sky; the call of the coyote or the train whistle's moan in a large, still, empty night. If surrealism made sense to Dylan, perhaps that is because he had always found his North Country landscape surreal. If Dylan was — or tried to be — a good father in the conventional sense, perhaps that is because, as Howard Sounes suggests, "something of [Dylan's] father's Midwestern values always remained with him" (22). If Dylan drifted into various spiritualisms, perhaps they called to something in his youth.[18] If Dylan converted — for a time at least — to Christianity, perhaps it's because he got so much of it in Hibbing. It is possible that the tremendous sense of loss Dylan has felt and expressed throughout his career ("Bob Dylan's Dream" in 1963, "It's All Over Now, Baby Blue" in 1965, "I Threw It All Away" in 1969, "If You See Her, Say Hello" in 1974, "Señor [Tales of Yankee Power]" in 1978, "Blind Willie McTell" in 1983, "Death Is Not the End" in 1988, "Born in Time" in 1990, "Love Sick" in 1997, "Summer Days" in 2001, "Nettie Moore in 2006) . . . the enervating emptiness that is so prominent in Dylan has its origins in the long-abandoned ghost towns of the Iron Range, in the empty farm houses lurking in dark groves along gravel roads throughout Minnesota, in the shrinking villages of the Upper Midwest with their boarded-up grocery stores and abandoned schools, in the country cemeteries that have lost their churches, in the shredded fence lines that keep nothing in and nothing out, in the losses of Hibbing itself, the ghosts of Old Hibbing, the train station, the graveyard, the high school but a shadow, really, of its former self . . . or on the absolute loss of frozen winter that reduces the entire landscape to a few brushstrokes of black and white. "Each male here wants life to be / a silent Arctic waste, one / black heroic dot trudging into / endless white," writes John Caddy (*Color*: 55).

Dylan's mental and spiritual connections to his Upper Midwest upbringing are more difficult to identify than geographical references, because they involve defining and tracking an overall mindset. I have already suggested a few; in subsequent chapters, we turn our attention to more of those large influences: language, pastoralism, that old trope of going out and coming back, politics, and that sense of mission and moral conscience that makes American Jeremiahs out of so many Midwesterners. And it is always when we go big-picture that things get really interesting.

Chapter 2

"And the Language That He Used"

"I'm North Dakota-Minnesota-Midwestern. . . . I'm that color. I speak that way."

— *Playboy,* 1966

THE MATTER OF VOICE

History and Structure of the English Language is probably the most feared English course offered at my little college on the prairie, required of English Education and Professional Writing majors alike. Although I'm a literature person, I teach History and Structure because I'm the only person in the department who can read and understand Anglo-Saxon . . . or, for that matter, some dialects of Middle English. (If we keep hiring postmodernist fiction writers and gender theory experts, I'll soon be the only person who can read Chaucer, Milton, and Alexander Pope.) I'd rather teach a section of rural-regional literature, but explaining the evolution of English allows me to bootleg into History and Structure bits of *Beowulf, The Canterbury Tales,* and *Gawain and the Green Knight.* And truth to tell, after a couple decades with the class, I now almost enjoy charting the alphabet's development, identifying dialects British and American, and tracking changes in English pronunciation, spelling, grammar, and usage. Counting, sorting, and tabulating linguistic minutiae — although tedious — brings high-flying intellectuals back to earth, and grounds ideas in facts.

Students at first resist the class because it involves rote memory and weekly exams — the Achilles' heel of today's youth — but once they know enough

63

to play the game, they also enjoy it. They look at a name like Bret Favre, and say, "His last name is a good example of metathesis." They point to a poster announcing a committee to study "why students attrit" and ask, "How's that for a back-formation, Pichaske?" They tell a friend, "You know, in Old English times, a thousand years ago, they used to say 'hwat' instead of 'what' . . . just the way you do." They run around talking like Yorkshire men, New Yawkahs, or Brits. Sometimes they parody their own Minnesota accents.

We watch several videos in that class — the strength of today's student — including the award-winning *American Tongues*, put together in 1987 by Louis Alvarez and Andrew Kolker for the Center for New American Media. A series of amusing and outrageous interviews samples a wide range of American accents, and professional linguists provide an overview of the processes of linguistic change and the values we place on one accent or another. The film also sets up the course's only paper: an analysis of one contemporary English dialect — American, British, or other — using researched linguistic materials (dialect maps, surveys, theory) and examples of written and spoken English.

Although I'm still no Professor Henry Higgins, teaching History and Structure has given me a better ear for speech than I once had, a certain self-consciousness about my own speech patterns, an appreciation for Midwest and Minnesota dialect in writers like Garrison (*A Prairie Home Companion*) Keillor and Howard (*How to Talk Minnesotan*) Mohr, and a consciousness attuned to the idioms and speech of Minnesotans, Iron Rangers, and Bob Dylan.

When it comes to speech, almost all of us speak in at least two voices: our natural or private voice, and our public or performance voice. One voice for home, one voice at work. Writers especially develop a performance voice, sometimes several voices, whether they write poems, stories, or books like this one. Writers who perform their work in public — I am thinking of Mark Twain, Vachel Lindsay, T. S. Eliot, Robert Frost, Allen Ginsberg — become even more sensitive to their performing voices, and actors and singers have even more cause than the rest of us to develop their performing voices, especially if they sing a lot of blues. The more varied their repertoire, the more flexible that performance voice becomes, until — theoretically at least — really good performers can do any voice they choose, modulating from one to another as the occasion or song requires. Or even, for the sake of adding a little variety to repeated ballad stanzas or blues lines, changing voice within a single song. Dylan is this kind of poet-performer.

The performance voice is consciously created from many sources, and over a writer's or singer's career it may change or "develop." Almost any art-ist goes through an early period of borrowing and imitation, when his art is "multi-vocalic" or "derivative," depending on your point of view. Eliot subtitled the original *The Waste Land*, "He Do the Police in Different Voices," and across his career, Dylan certainly did the populace in different voices, starting early with Elvis Presley, Hank Williams, Little Richard, Robert Johnson, Woody Guthrie, and the sounds of country and blues singers he picked up on late-night radio shows from Little Rock, Arkansas, and Shreveport, Louisiana . . . and from the records he bought after hearing them advertised by Gatemouth Page, received as a graduation present from his uncle, borrowed from girlfriends like Ellen Baker, or kiped from acquaintances. We can eavesdrop on the early stages of this process in the Little White Wonder bootlegs and the first disc of the officially released Bootleg Series, with Dylan sounding consciously black ("No More Auction Block," "Worried Blues"), Guthrie ("Bear Mountain," "Talkin' John Birch"), Williams ("Kingston Town"), or just plain hillbilly ("Moonshiner"). Developing a performance voice, or "learning the trade," is usually a conscious process, and you know it don't come easy. Brooklyn-born Jack Elliott needed a lifetime, Robert Shelton thought, to perfect his performing voice, but he finally did it: "He had so good an ear for the speech, song, and wit of the American plains that he wasn't a citybilly anymore" (*Home*: 102).[1]

So difficult it is to sound like someone else. And, in most cases, "sounding like someone else" is not what finally happens. For all their multivocality, Eliot and Shakespeare remain recognizably Eliot and Shakespeare. After all the experiments and borrowings and influences, Dylan sounds recognizably Dylan. Some Dylan is indeed borrowed: any great writer consciously *selects* a unique set of native and *borrowed* linguistic features from which to create his voice; in Dylan's case, at least three prominent features of both his performance and personal dialect are *not* characteristic of his native Upper Midwest: the missing "r" in words like "poor" and "farmer,"[2] the pronunciation of "I" as "ah" instead of "eye," and the a- prefix on the present participle of verbs, which is something Dylan and fellow folksinger Phil "I Ain't A-Marchin' Any More" Ochs picked up mostly from Woody Guthrie.[3]

However, it is not accurate to attribute all of Dylan's odd or idiosyncratic pronunciations and emphases to secondary influences. Old habits are hard to break, especially in unguarded moments, and most of us never really escape the language we learned at home. Despite the overlays he so quickly and constantly assimilated, Dylan's language, as he himself pointed out, is "North Dakota-Minnesota-Midwestern."[4] "Sitting across from Bob Dylan on this afternoon, one could see his influences very clearly," writes Cameron Crowe in the *Biograph* booklet; "His speech sometimes flecked with the country-isms of his youth, the leather jacket draped on his shoulders, a sharp gesture with a cigarette barely holding its ash . . . for all the years of who-is-Bob-Dylan analysis, the answer seemed obvious" (31).

The Iron Range dialect can be defined using three tools. The first is linguistic studies that identify features of the dialect in terms of vocabulary, idioms, grammar, and pronunciation: Harold Byron Allen's *The Linguistic Atlas of the Upper Midwest*, Lewis and Marguerite Herman's *American Dialects*, Frederick Cassidy's *Dictionary of American Regional English*, Craig Carver's *American Regional Dialects*, Timothy Frazer's *"Heartland" English*, and Gary Underwood's *The Dialect of the Mesabi Range*. The second is writers who seem to have that idiom down pretty well, like Howard Mohr and Garrison Keillor. The third, as a check on the theorists and in the faith that dialect does not change dramatically in 50 years, is careful attention to the voices of the Midwestern radio and television, and listening attentively to the voices in Hibbing streets and restaurants. Meanwhile, Dylan's performance voices are there in the albums, officially released bootlegs, and bootlegged bootlegs. His natural voice is there in taped interviews and documentary films. His words are there — printed lyrics, album sleeve, interviews. These words can be counted, tabulated, sorted, analyzed. So we can identify Upper Midwest and Upper Minnesota usages, and then we can watch those preferences play out in Dylan's words. For this chapter — admittedly a brief look at a mountain of material — I have used sound recordings, taped interviews, and printed collections of Dylan's own words, including *Lyrics: 1962–2001*, *Chronicles*, *Tarantula*, and the online Dylan concordance available at bobdylan.com.

Before the results, several upfront caveats. First, except in rare cases, when we talk about a specific dialect we are not looking at things that are unique to a region; we are looking at a recognizable set of traits, many of which may be shared with other English dialects. *What is unique is the set, not the individual traits.* Because of immigration patterns, the Northern Midland dialect shares more general language features with the New York State dialect than do most other American dialects. We must also recognize that the Midwestern-Northern American dialect has, until recently, been the broadcast standard, an American equivalent of Britain's "Received Pronunciation" (RP) learned in U.K. schools and preferred by the BBC. It is therefore not as easily recognized as an accent as would be a Boston, New Jersey, Tangier Island, or Louisiana dialect. "More Americans use the Middle Western dialect speech, or a modification of it, than any other speech in America," observe Lewis and Margurite Herman (297), who tracks this dialect from the western side of the Appalachians to the Pacific coast of Washington and Oregon. It is, however, a dialect. When I presented these ideas at a Bob Dylan symposium in Minneapolis, and someone reacted, "Well,

Dave, everyone talks that way," a Scot in the audience objected immediately: "Nay, laddie. Donna ya be believin' all native speakers talk like you folks!"

The second caveat is that the Mesabi Range is something of a demographic, and therefore linguistic, abnormality in that until 1890 — when Minnesota's population had reached 1.3 million people — the Range was virtually uninhabited (standing water made it unattractive to loggers; the shelf of rock six inches below the soil surface made it poor farming land). Then the discovery of iron ore brought a flood of people, 57 percent of whom in 1905 were foreign born, with Finland, Austria, Sweden, Canada, and Norway heading the list (Underwood: 7). Immigrants from 18 other countries would soon follow. Of course the foreign-born population learned their English at school more than at home, but the sound of their English retained some of the coloring of the native tongues. The Iron Range dialect is therefore in some features distinct from Minnesotan or Upper Midwest English.

The third caveat, of course, is that people's language reflects their education. Linguistic studies often differentiate the speech of people with "a seventh or eighth grade education" from those who finished high school (Underwood: 13).

The fourth caveat is that in a song, vocabulary choices may be dictated or influenced by rhyme, alliteration, and meter; and pronunciation may be altered by awareness of how things will sound on record, or a heightened consciousness of recording studio technology, or even the tempo of the line in which it appears. Although Suze Rotolo says that John Hammond did not interfere with Bob's process but watched and listened, letting Bob do as he wished (159), other evidence indicates that Dylan received and accepted considerable direction, especially early in his career, and especially on the explosive sound of the letter "p" (Shelton, *Home*: 117). On early albums, Dylan appears to try to articulate carefully in front of the studio mike. To offer but one example, in the lyrics of "It's Alright, Ma" printed in *Writings and Drawings*, the word "forget" is actually printed "fergit" (it rhymes in the song with "lit," "fit," "quit," and "it") . . . but despite the rhymes and the printed spelling, and despite the fact that even highly educated Midwesterners often say "git," Dylan actually sings "get."

For all the multivocality, the caveats, and the complexities, however, we discern an identifiable pattern of vocabulary and pronunciation preferences in Dylan's performance voices and his personal voice.

VOCABULARY

The Linguistic Atlas of the Upper Midwest records the vocabulary preferences of more than 400 Midwesterners among clusters of synonyms. For the purposes of comparison, the editors chose clusters used in an earlier study, *A Word Geography of the Eastern United States.* Thus the vocabulary reflects America's agrarian past, some of it even more remote than Dylan's early songs, and some of it lost even in 1960. Words in some clusters — like *bin* or *granary; loft, bent, bay,* or *mow;* coal *hod* or coal *scuttle;* and *privy, outhouse, crapper, water closet, biffy, shit house* — are no longer commonly used, no longer a useful measure of dialect. However, the *Atlas* and Underwood's study of the Mesabi Range dialect list many important vocabulary options for things still discussed every day.[5] Some preferences are peculiar to the Upper Midwest, and some are unique to Minnesota-North Dakota. Here are some interesting clusters of synonyms from the *Atlas*, with Dylan's preferences in songs and speech and writings:

Cluster 1: what the sun or moon does in the morning and evening
Eighty percent of Upper Midwesterners use "rise"/"set," while only 20 percent use "come up" and "go down," but "came up" and "went down" are more common in Minnesota and North Dakota than elsewhere in the region. In Dylan's songs, we find seven instances of "rise"/"set," and three uses of "come up"/"go down":

"Spanish moon is rising on the hill" ("Abandoned Love")
"I watched that sun come rising" ("Went to See the Gypsy")
"If you wanna see the sun rise" ("Leopard-Skin Pill-Box Hat")
"free to drink martinis and watch the sun rise" ("Hurricane")
"Where the sun never set" ("In the Summertime")
"When the shadowy sun sets on the one" ("Only a Pawn in Their Game")
"Saw the rising sun return" ("Rollin' and Tumblin'")

"sun comes up" ("Where Teardrops Fall")
"sun was coming up" ("Motorpsycho Nightmare")
"sun is going down" ("Ring Them Bells")

Cluster 2: the noun form of the setting of the sun
According to the *Atlas* (1: 152) the word "sundown" dominates in northern Minnesota (and in Canada, home of Gordon Lightfoot, who had the hit song "Sundown"), while the word "sunset" is not used. Dylan does not use the word "sunset," but he uses "sundown" six times, early and late:

"candles of sundown" ("11 Outlined Epitaphs")
"sundown, yellow moon" ("If You See Her, Say Hello")
"it's sundown on the union" ("Union Sundown")
"left here after sundown" ("Sweetheart Like You")
"between sundown's finish" ("Chimes of Freedom")
"at sundown" ("Last Thoughts on Woody Guthrie")

Cluster 3: the noun form of the rising of the sun

The *Atlas* found a 77 percent preference in the Upper Midwest for "sunrise" over "sunup." Only seven of 437 people interviewed used the word "dawn" . . . but those seven included the ones from the Iron Range. Dylan's Iron Range roots are very evident in his preference: he uses "sunup" not at all, "sunrise" once, and "dawn" nearly two dozen times in songs and poems from all points in his career (and not always for the sake of rhyme):

"There's beauty in the sunrise in the sky" ("Tomorrow Is a Long Time")

"against the drums of dawn" ("Lay Down Your Weary Tune")
"I left town at dawn" (Where Are You Tonight?")
"right before the dawn" ("Meet Me in the Morning")
"It was nearly dawn" ("Went to See the Gypsy")
"when the dawn is nearing" ("I Believe in You")
"at the break of dawn" ("Don't Think Twice," "Joey," "Highlands")
"somebody's eyes must meet the dawn" ("Restless Farewell")
"up past the dawn" ("Visions of Johanna")
"Titanic sails at dawn" ("Desolation Row")
"dawn came over the river bridge" ("Up to Me")
"at dawn my lover comes to me" ("Gates of Eden")
"travelin' through the dawn of day" ("Spirit on the Water")
"I get up in the dawn" ("Rollin' and Tumblin'")
"As each new season's dawn awaits" ("Tell Ol' Bill")
"the surprises of dawn" ("'Cross the Green Mountain")

Cluster 4: a paved road surface

Residents of the Upper Midwest use "pavement" (37 percent), "concrete" (24 percent) and "cement" (12 percent) almost interchangeably. So does Dylan: "I'm on the pavement" ("Subterranean Homesick Blues"), "In this concrete world full of souls" ("Three Angels"), and "with my face in the cement" ("The Groom's Still Waiting at the Altar").

Cluster 5: to remove dirt or debris from a room

Upper Midwesterners prefer "clean up" (36 percent) and "straighten" (30 percent) to "tidy up" which, Duluth poet Barton Sutter wrote in the margin of a draft of this manuscript, "sounds sissy Eastern to me." "Straighten," the *Atlas* notes, "has a more northern correlation" (1: 172). Dylan uses "clean up," "pick up," and "straighten," but he does not once use the sissy Eastern "tidy up":

> "cleaned up all the food from the table" ("The Lonesome Death of Hattie Carroll")
> "poor boy, pickin' up sticks" ("Po' Boy")
> "was all but straightened out" ("John Wesley Harding")
> "quit your mess and straighten out" ("Slow Train")

Cluster 6: to close or shut the door

Upper Midwesterners use both "shut" and "close." So does Dylan:

> "shut all the doors" ("Clothes Line Saga")
> "tryin' to get to heaven before they shut the door" ("Tryin' to Get to Heaven")

> "close the door" ("I'll Be Your Baby Tonight")
> "closed the door behind him" ("George Jackson")
> "you forgot to close the garage door" ("Leopard-Skin Pill-Box Hat")

Cluster 7: large open metal vessel for water, milk, beer, etc.

In the Upper Midwest people use either "pail" or "bucket," although "pail" is preferred in Minnesota. Dylan uses both — in the same song in one instance:

> "wiggle like a pail of milk" ("Wiggle, Wiggle")
> "playin' with their pails in the sand" ("Sara")

> "with their buckets to fill" ("Sara")
> "buckets of rain" ("Buckets of Rain")

Cluster 8: a container for dry goods

Upper Minnesota and North Dakota are alone among Upper Midwest states in preferring "bag" over "sack." "Infrequent on the Range is (PAPER) SACK, a common term with other Minnesota informants," writes Underwood (25). Dylan's preference is 3:1 for "bag":

"a bag full of sorrow" ("Handy Dandy")
"my detective bag" ("Talkin' John Birch Paranoid Blues")
"two big bags of dead man's bones" ("Tweedle Dee & Tweedle Dum")

"put 'em in a sack" ("Someday Baby")

Cluster 9: a window cover

Midwesterners prefer "shade" (85 percent) to "blind" (18 percent), but "Mesabi informants have as another frequent variant the Midlands BLINDS, which is infrequently used by other Minnesota informants," writes Underwood (19). Dylan uses "shade" four times, "blinds" three times:

"shut the shade" ("I'll Be Your Baby Tonight")
"light burst through a beat-up shade" ("Simple Twist of Fate")
"he raised the shade" ("Foot of Pride")
"doctor who pulls down the shade" ("Tombstone Blues")

"through the blinds" ("Floater [Too Much to Ask]")
"through my blinds" ("Ragged and Dirty")
"blinds pulled down" ("Step It Up and Go")

Cluster 10: a male's outer garment, with legs and a zipper

The overwhelming choice of Midwesterners is "pants" (85 percent). Nobody there uses "slacks" or "trousers." We find seven instances of "pants" in Dylan's songs, but no "trousers" or "slacks":

"short pants, romance" ("Subterranean Homesick Blues")
"with the drumstick in his pants" ("Don't Fall Apart on Me Tonight")
"the other is in his pants" ("Desolation Row")
"as I pulled down my pants" ("Bob Dylan's 115th Dream")
"pants and shirts" ("Lenny Bruce")
"a couple pairs of pants" ("Clothes Line Saga")
"tear your pants" ("Nettie Moore")

Cluster 11: wet ground with a small stream running through it

The overwhelming choice of Upper Midwesterners is "swamp" (74 percent). Settlers in Garrison Keillor's Lake Wobegon "sat in a swamp from April until June" (37), because Minnesotans do not say "marsh" or "slough." Dylan uses "swamp" several times but never "marsh" or "slough":

"across the swamp of time" ("If Dogs Run Free")
"swamp's a-gonna rise" ("Down in the Flood")
"I might be in the swamp" ("Motorpsycho Nightmare")

Cluster 12: running fresh water

According to the *Atlas*, "creek" is the "common designation in the Upper Midwest," but the words "brook" and "stream," though not used elsewhere in Upper Midwest, are heard in most of Minnesota (1: 236). "Brook" and "stream" were used by ten of Underwood's 17 Mesabi Range informants (29). Dylan uses all three, but his preference is "stream":

"where the creek used to rise" ("Isis")
"by the edge of a creek" ("Workingman's Blues #2")
"suckling brook" ("Apple Suckling Tree")

"Father who turneth the rivers and streams" ("Father of Night")
"lakes and streams and mines so free" ("Ballad for a Friend")
"fishes that float through the stream" ("Time Passes Slowly")
"country stream" ("New Morning")
"where the mountain streams flood" ("Let Me Die in My Footsteps")
"who wrote psalms beside moonlit streams" ("I and I")
"'cross the valleys and streams" ("Ring Them Bells")
"Mr. Hudson come a-sailin' down the stream" ("Hard Times in New York Town")
"where the trout streams flow" ("Hurricane")
"followed a singing stream" ("When the Deal Goes Down")

Cluster 13: maternal parent

Perhaps the most interesting cluster of options is the term we use for our maternal parent. Only 8 percent of Minnesotans use the term "mom," and only 9 percent use "maw," while 25 percent use "ma," 42 percent use "mama," and 58 percent use "mother." Dylan's uses reflect his Minnesota roots: no examples of "mom," one use of "maw," ten uses of "ma," 28 uses of "mama," and 27 uses of "mother" — too many to quote here.

There are other preferences among other clusters of synonyms, and other odd Iron Range options. In the Upper Midwest, the *Atlas* informs us, you don't *take* sick, you *get* sick (as in "Get sick, get well, hang around the ink well"). You are

"AND THE LANGUAGE THAT HE USED"   73

more likely to be buried in a *casket* than a *coffin* (Dylan is 3:1 casket). You are *tired*, not *bushed, pooped, tuckered,* or *done in* (Dylan's statistical preference is for "tired"). You are more likely to be *raised up* than *brought up*, and dontcha know, Dylan uses "raised up" three times and "brought up" only twice, even though "raised up" sounds odd to most Americans. If you're looking for them gol-darned Reds in Minnesota, you look up your *chimney hole*, not your *flue* or *stovepipe*. The sign is on the *porch*, not the *stoop, foyer, entrance,* or *entry* ("Sign on the Window"). And that's "a new *grove* of trees on the outskirts of town" ("Floater [Too Much to Ask]"), not a *thicket* or a *copse* or a *clump* or *stand*. Howard Mohr devotes a couple pages in *How to Talk Minnesotan* to explaining Minnesota groves: "A grove is the stand of trees planted north and northwest of the farm house and farm buildings. Its purpose is to protect the owners from the north wind in the winter, and to capture the snow" (171).

Gary Underwood's study of the Mesabi Range dialect notes that five of 17 respondents offered "parlor" as an option for "living room" (18), as does Dylan in "Tryin' to Get to Heaven" and throughout *Chronicles*. Underwood notes that while "mantel" is the usual word in Minnesota and on the Iron Range, "the Southern SHELF, which is infrequent with other Minnesota informants (6/49) is frequent among Iron Range informants" (19); Dylan uses "mantel" in "Ballad in Plain D" and in *Chronicles*, but he uses "shelf," in the sense of "mantel," in "Lily, Rosemary and the Jack of Hearts" and arguably in a couple other songs (although "shelf" is always a rhyme word). Underwood notes that while Iron Range informants prefer the simple "owl" to "screech owl," five of 17 offered "hoot owl," which is "unusual with other Minnesota informants" (36). In "Blind Willie McTell," it's the hoot owl singing.

According to the *Atlas*, the word "boat" is an Upper Midwest synonym for "ship" (as in "steamboat"), and such big boats are common in Dylan songs: "Rambling, Gambling Willie," "When the Ship Comes In," "Apple Suckling Tree," "Dignity," "Floater (Too Much to Ask)," "My Back Pages," "Quinn the Eskimo," and "Talkin' Bear Mountain Picnic Massacre Blues": "That big old boat started t'sink."

In Northern and Midlands English, the long green vegetable was a string bean until the days — after Dylan's youth — when commercial canners began marketing the product as "green beans" (Underwood: 35); Dylan's early and memorable line in "Talkin' World War III Blues" is indeed "Give me a string bean, I'm a hungry man."

American Regional Dialects reports an idiomatic use of "heave" to mean "throw," and we find Dylan right on the Upper Midwest norm with "the puppets heave rocks" ("Farewell Angelina") and "your advisors heave their plastic" ("Queen Jane Approximately"). Underwood reports a preference for the verb "haul" over "tote" (26), which is Dylan's choice in songs and *Chronicles*. He also reports "clear across" to be the Iron Range choice over "all the way," "straight," and "right," a preference reflected in Dylan's "clear through Tennessee" ("Thunder on the Mountain").

Familiar words and phrases often have idiomatic variants. Iron Range Minnesotans are more likely than most Americans to add an "s" to "way" and "where," to form things like "somewheres in the distance" ("Ballad of Hollis Brown"), "a mighty long ways to the Golden Gate" ("Hard Times in New York Town"), "somewheres back I took the time" ("My Life in a Stolen Moment"), and "the ways of the flesh" ("Solid Rock"). "All of the Mesabi informants responding say WAYS, which is usual in the rest of Minnesota," reports Gary Underwood (32). On the other hand, Minnesotans are *less* likely to add a "t" to words like "across," which picks up a final "t" below the Minnesota-Iowa line (Allen 3: 16). Dylan sings "across" without the "t": "across that lonesome ocean" ("Boots of Spanish Leather"), "lay across my big brass bed" ("Lay, Lady, Lay"), "Look out across the fields" ("When the Night Comes Falling from the Sky"). Dylan sings "across" even when the word is rhymed with "frost" in the line "could not get across" ("It Takes a Lot to Laugh"). Dylan's "amongst" in "I Dreamed I Saw St. Augustine" sounds a little odd to the Midwest ear, a little archaic, as it was perhaps intended to be: this is also the song in which Dylan violates Midwest preference, and his own habit, by using the grammatically incorrect "whom": "whom already had been sold."

The "of" in the phrase "a couple of" has a habit of disappearing in the Midwest — some of the time, not all of the time. In *How to Talk Minnesotan*, Howard Mohr writes, "a couple more days" (73), "a couple times a year" (147), and "a couple more times" (201); in *Lake Wobegon Days*, Garrison Keillor writes "a couple years" (16) and his Prairie Home Companion website for November 22, 2008, notes, "a couple listeners wrote in." Customers in Hibbing restaurants order "a couple eggs, a couple pieces of toast." In his book *Overburden: Modern Life on the Iron Range*, Aaron Brown writes, "only a couple dozen copies of his [Dylan's] book were sold in our town" (103). In his book on Bob Dylan, Minnesotan Dave Engel writes, "Bobby's personal blackboard jungle has been located a couple blocks from his house" (121). My daughter Kristin writes in an e-mail from Chicago, "a couple other things." Iowa writer Jim Heynen seems to take great care with this expression: his characters say "a couple"; Heynen as author uses "a couple of." Dylan sings "a couple pairs of pants" ("Clothes Line Saga"), and Cameron Crowe's note to "I Don't Believe You" on the *Biograph* album quotes Dylan as saying, "There's a couple things that people don't realize."

In a transcribed conversation with Sam Shepard published in *Esquire*, 1987, Dylan says, "I just gotta make a couple phone calls" (Cott: 348), and in his 2001 *Rolling Stone* interview, Dylan says, "I thought, 'I'll make a couple more records...'" (Cott: 419).

To these preferences, we might add some other Midwestern-Minnesotan expressions, idioms, and usages — Cameron Crowe's country-isms of Dylan's youth. Usually, Dylan avoids over-the-top, *Fargo*-type Minnesotan idiom — "Oh, for stupid," "doncha know," "yah, you betcha" — but a few expressions leap out as strikingly rural Minnesotan:

> "holy moly" (used by "an uncle" talking to a farmer friend, *Tarantula*: 20)
> "holy mackerel" ("Alternatives to College," *Writings and Drawings*: 214)
> "I can see / When someone is pullin' the wool over me" ("Let Me Die in My Footsteps")
> "froze to the bone" (in both "Talkin' New York" and *Joan Baez in Concert, Part 2*)
> "you're a pumpkin" (a term of Minnesota endearment, *Tarantula*: 66)
> "water under the bridge" ("Things Have Changed")
> "anyone with any sense" ("Lily, Rosemary, and the Jack of Hearts")
> "paint myself into a corner" ("Mississippi")
> "one day late and a dollar short" ("Tweedle Dee & Tweedle Dum")

Chronicles is full of rural Midwestern speech: "hunky-dory" (14), "seeing that" (42), "the boonies" (39), "quite a character" (40, 89), "was really something" (44), "kick your silly ass" (91), "scared the lights out of me" (91), "the whole shebang" (109), "couldn't make hide nor hair of it" (130), "a cold, frozen fact" (193), "run of the mill stuff" (226). "You'll go right off your nut" (*Tarantula*: 94) echoes an expression found in Illinois poet Dave Etter's "Boomboom on B Street": "I tell you I must have been off my nut, / about good and ready for a rubber room." "Oh, sweet Jesus!" (*Chronicles*: 133) sounds like something right out of Nebraska state poet Bill Kloefkorn.

Dylan's use of the word "deal" may reflect his North County roots. Howard Mohr devotes half a chapter to this cornerstone of the Minnesota Language System (in Minnesota it's usually "heckofa deal"), and uses the word himself in expressions like "a pretty good deal" (ix) and "a pretty sad deal" (128). In Dylan's songs it's "my last deal gone down" ("Changing of the Guards"), "When the Deal Goes Down," and in *Chronicles*, "a big deal" (28, 70). Of course "deal" is a common Americanism, as in "Let's Make a Deal" and "Deal or No Deal?" Julia Roberts uses the word "deal" in her documentary film on Mongolia, and she's from Georgia. But wait a minute — Julia Roberts's mother came from Minneapolis. . . .

The affectionate use of "old," sometimes reduced to "ol'," as a filler adjective in front of nouns which are not necessarily old is quite common in the Midwest: in Mohr's *How to Talk Minnesotan*, "Ol' Daryl caught a walleye" (23); in Dylan, "Hibbing's a good ol' town" ("My Life in a Stolen Moment"), "friendly old town" ("Hard Times in New York Town"), "big old boat" ("Talking Bear Mountain"), "old smokestack" ("Ballad for a Friend"), "some old businessman" ("Summer Days"), "same old page" ("Highlands"), "dusty old fairgrounds" ("Dusty Old Fairgrounds"), "dirty old mess hall" ("Walls of Red Wing"), "that old sign on the cross" ("Sign on the Cross"), "hills of old Duluth" ("Something There Is About You"), "the old Northwest" ("Ballad of Donald White"), "old Honolulu" ("You're Gonna Make Me Lonesome"), and "old Cheyenne" ("Gypsy Lou").

The verb in "bum a ride" ("Standing on the Highway") and "bummed a cigarette" ("Desolation Row") is often heard in Minnesota, although it too is not exclusively Midwestern. Double negatives are certainly not exclusive to the Midwest, and a case might be made for this linguistic feature going from Woody "I Ain't Got No Home" Guthrie to Bob "You Ain't Goin' Nowhere" Dylan to Bruce "Ain't Got Nowhere to Go" Springsteen. Still, double negatives are very common on the Iron Range, as they were in the speech of Abe Zimmerman (Shelton, *Home*: 33), and in Dylan's songs. Listening to one old guy taunt one of his dice-rolling buddies in a Hibbing café with "you ain't got nothin', buddy," you think you're listening to Bob Dylan: "When you ain't got nothin', you got nothin' to lose." Dylan even manages a triple negative in "Union Sundown": "they don't make nothin' here no more."

In referring to people, Midwesterners prefer "that" to "who" (Mark Twain's story is titled "The Man that Corrupted Hadleyburg"), probably because they have trouble choosing between "who" and "whom." And when they do opt for "who" or "whom," Minnesotans tend to use "who" even where "whom" is grammatically correct. Dylan's preference for "that" shows up early in "Song to Woody" ("not many men that done the things that you've done") and it continues late with "Red River Shore" ("the one that I'll always adore"). A search through the online concordance of Dylan's lyrics produces only nine instances of "whom" in all Dylan, at least one of them ungrammatical: "that man whom with his fingers cheats" ("I Pity the Poor Immigrant"). He also fumbles his grammar in his fable of the Three Kings and Frank on *John Wesley Harding*: "Frank, whom for all this time had been reclining with his eyes closed." The search produces 118 examples of "who," some of them ungrammatical: "for who He died" ("When You Gonna Wake Up?") and "who should I tell" ("Apple

Suckling Tree"). The total uses of "that" is too high to tabulate, although not all of them, of course, are pronouns referring to human beings.

Similarly, the differences between "sit" and "set" are lost on most Minnesotans, as they are on many Americans: "Mr. Rockefeller sets up as high as a bird" ("Hard Times in New York Town") and "you set back and watch" ("Masters of War"). The verbs "lie" and "lay" have troubled Midwesterners since *The Adventures of Huckleberry Finn*: "It was kind of solemn, drifting down the big still river, laying on our backs" (55). In Dylan,

"I'd lay awake all night" ("If Not for You")
"lay down and die" ("Neighborhood Bully")
"feel like laying down" ("Spirit on the Water")
"go down and lay in the shade" ("Rollin' and Tumblin'")
"I lay awake at night" ("Tell Ol' Bill")
"I'm laying in the sand" ("Huck's Tune")
"I lay awake and listen to the sound of pain" ("Forgetful Heart")

"What is Bob Dylan's problem with the grammatical distinction between 'lie' and 'lay'?" asks Stephen Scobie in a review of *Chronicles, Volume One* ("Always": 43). I began tracking examples of the "lie"/"lay" confusion in that book ("There were other things laying around," "I'd lay in the green grass," "He had had a lot of guns laying around," "everything laying around on all the tables"), but I quit after page 61 . . . *Chronicles* was sounding too much like my freshman composition papers.

In *How to Talk Minnesotan*, Howard Mohr writes, "in the grammar business, of course, we've all been told that it's bad to have dangling participles, and I believe it, though I have never understood exactly what they are. . . . To me, danglers are words and phrases that are glued on to sentences — they may seem to have no more purpose or meaning than a floating cylindrical article in a bucket of milk, but they are part of what distinguishes a native speaker from an outsider. *Though* is in that category" (169). He offers a few examples: "He's a good guy, though"; "I've never seen any of his paintings, though"; "I haven't actually started writing things down on paper, though." Mohr might just as well have quoted Dylan lines, early or late:

"Quite lucky to be alive, though." ("Talkin' Bear Mountain Picnic Massacre Blues")
"I wouldn't worry 'bout it none, though" ("Talkin' World War III Blues")
"I don't blame him too much, though" ("Talkin' World War III Blues")

"Thought of, though, somehow" ("My Back Pages")
"But I did, though" ("I Want You")
"And with all of them ladies, though" ("Minstrel Boy")
"This ol' river keeps on rollin', though" ("Watching the River Flow")
"Something about that movie, though" ("Brownsville Girl")

Dylan's verb usage also reflects Iron Range preferences. "Ain't" is common enough in English that even Frederick James Furnival, an early editor of the *Oxford English Dictionary* and co-founder of the Early English Text Society, is reported to have used the word habitually (Jesperson 5: 434), but "ain't" is more common in Minnesota than elsewhere (a 39 percent acceptance rate, as against a 29 percent acceptance rate in the general Upper Midwest, with Underwood reporting 27 of 49 informants using the word). Counting refrain lines only once, the word appears about 130 times in Dylan's songs.

Dylan's preference for particle verbs (phrasal verbs containing adverbs), especially those involving "up," is characteristically Minnesotan. Examples in Howard Mohr's *How to Talk Minnesotan* include "Ralph cranked it up," "Let's settle up," "when you show up," "money he saved up," "lined up for everybody to see," and "anything happen you wanted to bring up?" Keillor also uses simple Anglo-Saxon "up" particle verbs rather than Latinate polysyllabic synonyms: "it cheers me up" (23), "all used up" (26), "the whole town was churned up" (38). In Dylan, it's "hold up" ("Standing on the Highway"), "seal up" ("Tryin' to Get to Heaven"), "messed up" ("I Wanna Be Your Lover"), "tear up" ("Blind Willie McTell"), "strangle up" ("Stuck Inside of Mobile"), and "wind up," "stand up," and "end up" ("Walls of Red Wing").

On the subject of particle verbs involving "up," both the *Atlas* and the Hermans report a Midwest preference for "wake up" over "arise" or "awake," a preference shared by Dylan. Despite the intentionally biblical "arise, arise" in "I Dreamed I Saw St. Augustine," Dylan's overall preference is "wake up"/"woke up" (16 usages) over "arise"/"arose" (four usages), "awake"/"awoke" (three usages), or the simple "wake"/"woke" (four usages). Note also in passing the expression "get up"/"got up," as in Dylan's "wishin' I'd never got up that morn" ("Talking Bear Mountain Picnic Massacre Blues"), "whenever I get up" ("Goin' to Acapulco"), "I get up in the dawn" ("Rollin' and Tumblin'").

Another common Midwest particle verb is "head out," as in Howard Mohr's "We better head out" and Bob Dylan's "heading out for the East Coast" ("Tangled Up in Blue").

Minnesota usage prefers several *standard* past tense forms over nonstandard forms common elsewhere in the U.S.: "dreamed" over "dreamt," as in "I Dreamed

I Saw St. Augustine" and "I dreamed a dream that made me sad" ("Bob Dylan's Dream") and "after my dreams have been dreamed out" ("All Over You"). (In "Talkin' World War III Blues," set in New York, Dylan goes with "dreamt.") Minnesotans prefer "blew" (nine usages in Dylan) over "blowed" (three usages); "climbed" (two usages in Dylan) over "clumb" (no usages); "drank" (three usages in Dylan) over "drunk" (no usages); "grew" (three usages) over "growed" (no usages); "brought" (ten usages) over "brung" (no usages); and "threw" (ten usages) over "throwed" (no usages, but note "knowed" in the Guthrie-influenced "Talkin' John Birch Paranoid Blues" and in "Don't Think Twice").

Minnesotans prefer several *standard* participle forms over nonstandard forms used elsewhere in the United States: "had written" (five usages in Dylan) over "had wrote" (no usages), "had taken" (ten usages) over "had took" (no usages), "had eaten" (one usage) over "had ate" (no usages), and "had torn" (11 usages) over "had tore" (no usages).

However, Minnesota idiom admits a couple of *nonstandard* past participles, including "laid" for "lain," as in "Where my love and I had laid" ("One Too Many Mornings"). A computer search of lyrics and *Chronicles* turns up not a single instance of a grammatically correct *lain* in Dylan's writing.

While Dylan's use of "knowed" and "growed" in his 1963 radio interview with Studs Terkel was Dylan speaking in his Woody Guthrie performance voice, 40–50 percent of Minnesotans use the following *nonstandard* past tense verb forms, which can easily be found in Dylan's songs: "come" for "came," "done" for "did," "run" for "ran," "give" for "gave," and "seen" for "saw." To cull but a few examples from Dylan,

"don't even know why we come" ("Oxford Town")
"I know what you come here for" ("New Pony")
"You that never done nothing" ("Masters of War")
"what I done before" ("Most Likely You Go Your Way")
"I run down most hurriedly" ("Talkin' John Birch Paranoid Blues")
"it give me a chill" ("Day of the Locusts")
"I give her my heart" ("Don't Think Twice, It's All Right")
"I never seen him before" ("Leopard-Skin Pill-Box Hat")
"Seen the arrow on the doorpost" ("Blind Willie McTell")
"seen the rising sun return" ("Rollin' and Tumblin'")

Interestingly, Dylan opens the song "Brownsville Girl" with "movie I seen one time," but later in the same song passes on the opportunity to use "they was" or "every time money come up."

According to the *Atlas*, 30 percent of Minnesotans use "we was" ("We was layin' down around Mink Muscle Creek" in "Get Your Rocks Off!"); 27 percent use "you was" ("you wasn't there" in "John Brown"); 35 percent use "they was" ("our hats was," "our chances really was" in "Bob Dylan's Dream"); 45 percent use "he don't" ("if he don't expect to be caught housin' flushes" in "Open the Door, Homer"). Also common is "me" as half of a compound subject, as in "me and Delores were about to leave" in *Chronicles* (69). Again, while these usages are not exclusively Minnesotan, they are unusually common in this neck of the woods.

PRONUNCIATION

Let us turn our attention to Dylan's pronunciation. Now anybody who has ever visited Minnesooota or watched the film *Fargooo* knoooz where I'm goooin' here, but Dylan avoids the extreme pronunciation found in the movie. He can be very funny, and his early performances in the Village were successful as much for his comedy as for his guitar work, but Dylan is a singer, not a stand-up dialect comic. And, again, Dylan is a singer with many voices: he did a good Guthrie, and he can sing blues like Blind Willie McTell. Dueting early with Joan Baez on songs like "Lost Highway" and "So Lonesome I Could Cry," he sounds more country than he'd sound on *John Wesley Harding*. Dueting late with Ralph Stanley on "The Lonesome River," he sounds so bluegrass you can't believe it's him. Listening to Dylan on interviews and on film, you realize the difference between his performance voices and his natural voice, and listening carefully to records, you realize that Dylan's pronunciation of simple words like "the," "you," "of," and "to" varies within a single song: it's "tu" make you feel my love in one stanza, "ta" make you feel my love in another. When he's not using a recognizably Oakie or blues performance voice, Dylan even seems to hypercorrect out of his native Midwest dialect . . . at least until he forgets he's supposed to be hypercorrecting. Early in "Blowin' in the Wind," for example, he seems unnaturally careful with "to" and "just" (not "ta" or "gist"), and he has the Minnesota long "o" under control in words like "roads" and "knows," almost as if he is consciously clipping them — but then things come unglued and the "u" and "e" of "too many people" sound like something out of Old Hibbing, 1918.

While Dylan's pronunciation is complex, that bedrock Minnesota sound is there early and late, as Dylan himself knows. In the 1978 *Playboy* interview with Ron Rosenbaum he described the sound of *Highway 61 Revisited* as the sound of "twilight" and "the street" with the sun shining down and a particular type of people walking on a particular type of street. When asked when he first heard that sound, or felt it, Dylan answered, "way back when I was growing up."

Playboy:	*Not in New York?*
Dylan:	Well, I took it to New York. I wasn't born in New York. I was given some direction there, but I took it, too. I don't think I could ever have done it in New York. I would have been too beaten down.
Playboy:	*It was formed by the sounds back in the ore country of Minnesota?*
Dylan:	Or the lack of sound. In the city, there is nowhere you can go where you don't hear sound . . . but I got something different in my soul. (Cott: 210)

In another *Rolling Stone* interview later that year, with Jonathan Cott, he repeated himself: "I've had this sound ever since I was a kid" (Cott: 267). For Dylan, sound came before words . . . and it came from Minnesota when he was growing up.

The two most prominent features of Dylan's speech are definitely Minnesotan: his elongated vowels and his nasality (which must be central and back, as David Alan Stern warns aspiring actors, in contrast to a New York City high or frontal nasality). Both are components of what Bob Spitz, in his biography, unkindly calls "a dopey Midwestern twang" (74). The most famous sounds in Minnesota English are the elongated vowels, especially the "e" and "o". In a detective novel titled *Yellow Medicine*, author Anthony Neil Smith tracks a Yellow Medicine County sheriff's deputy (who coincidentally lives in a house I own, which Smith rented for half a year) as he pursues a group of terrorist methamphetamine dealers all across the state. At one point Smith — himself a recent immigrant from New Orleans — describes the local conversation: "When he spoke, it was the soundtrack of Minnesota, heavy on the vowels" (103). Smith means the "e" and the "o".

In most of the Midwest, the elongated "e" is slightly diphthongized to something like "e-uh," with a weak offglide, like the "steal" at the end of the third stanza of "Like a Rolling Stone," or "what did you hear" in "A Hard Rain's A-Gonna Fall." Northern Midwestern dialect is an exception to this pattern, in that while the "e" is long in duration, it is usually pure (Allen, *Atlas* 3: 21). This sound appears in the voice of Hibbing High School Assistant Principal Jac Fleming talking about "students' neeeds," and in Dylan lines like "geeez, I can't find my kneees" ("Visions of Johanna") and "Kneeeling 'neeeath your ceeeiling" ("Temporary Like Achilles"). A nice string of Iron Range long e's can be found in "Absolutely Sweet Marie": "You seee, you forgot to leeeave me with the keeey / Oh, where are you tonight, sweeet Marieee?"[6]

The long "o" is another hallmark of Minnesotan dialect. It is lowered like a foghorn and usually elongated like a Minnesota winter: the lips are rounded slightly while the sound is pushed back (not forward) in the throat. The vowel comes out straight, with no diphthong and plenty of resonance. The word "oh" sounds like the word "owe." The sound, almost an unconscious self-parody, is especially prominent in words like "know," "don't," "go," "home," "so," and of course "Minnesota." In the "weather" broadcast of Theme Time Radio Hour, Dylan gave his audience an exaggerated parody of the Minnesotan "Minnesooota" when early on he mentioned "Rochester, Minnesota," and a straight but clearly recognizably Minnesotan version of the word when he said "she's from Minnesota." Sitting around Zimmy's Restaurant and Pub in Hibbing, one hears locals talking about the need to "gooo see the ooold folk ooover there" and "a whooole lot of thoooose things goooin' on."

Dylan appears to go out of his way to avoid this sound, but it slips in all over the place: in his introduction to "Pretty Peggy-O" ("I been around this *whooole* country, but I never yet found Fennari*ooo*"); in "I *froooze* right to the *boooone*" ("Talkin' New York"); in "she gave me a rainbow" ("A Hard Rain's A-Gonna Fall"); in "my children will *gooo* as soon as they *groooow*" ("North Country Blues"); in "I believe I'll *gooo* see her again" ("Just Like a Woman"); in "shot it full of *hooooles*" ("Stuck Inside of Mobile"). The fully developed Minnesota long "o" can be heard in the sequence of rhyming last words of the second stanza of "Highway 61 Revisited": "nose," "clothes," "go," "know." In "no direction home" and "like a rolling stone," Dylan rides that "o" for a long time.

As we might expect, the Minnesota "o" is especially prominent in the early '60s songs of the first disc on the Bootleg Series, especially in the demo tapes when Dylan was not using his performance voice,[7] but it crops up later as well.[8]

That Upper Midwest long "o" makes a different sound when it appears in a final unaccented position, and is represented by the letters "ow," as in the words "fellow," "yellow," and "window." In these cases, like other unaccented vowel sounds, it often deteriorates to the "uh" sound: "fellow" becomes "fella," "yellow" becomes "yella," "window" becomes "winda." This is the pronunciation one hears in the Hibbing shops, in the interviews of the television special (produced by Barbara Wiener) *The Iron Range: A People's History*, in "crosses the yella dog" ("Nettie Moore"), in "a fella callin' you" ("The Ballad of Frankie Lee and Judas Priest"). "Fellow" does not pick up an "r", as it does in some areas of the West, to become "feller." Reflecting the Iron Range pronunciation of "fellow," Dylan actually writes "fella" in "Bob Dylan's New Orleans Rag," "Open the Door, Homer," "Too Much of Nothing," and "Three Angels." The fable "Three Kings," on the back of the *John Wesley Harding* album, also prints "these three fellas." Dylan waffles between "window" and "winda," but he never uses "winder."[9]

In the North Country, the long "u" is elongated, but, as is the case elsewhere in the Upper Midwest, it does not usually pick up the glide that slips in else-where in the United States, so does not produce a diphthong . . . except in the words "you" and "humor," which tend to become "yeou" and "heumor." The two "u" sounds in "the carpet *too* is moving under *you*" ("It's All Over Now, Baby Blue") provide a good example of the glide which intrudes in "you" but not in other words with this vowel sound. In fact, the elongated "u" of "school," "two"/"too," "tooth," "shoe," etc., is clearly "stronger in Northern speech terri-tory" (Allen 3: 22) than elsewhere in the United States. Listen to the sequence of 'u' sounds in the next-to-last verse of "Oxford Town": "Oxford Town in the after*noon* / Ev'rybody singin' a sorrowful *tune* / Two men died 'neath the Mississippi *moon* / Somebody better investigate *soon.*"

In the words "root" and "roof," however, Minnesotans often sound the "u" like the "u" in "put" and "soot," not like the "u" in "toot" or "suit." Likewise "creek" often rhymes with "thick," not "cheek." Dylan is usually busy rhyming "root" with "fruit" and "shoot," "roof" with "bulletproof," and "creek" with "week" and "weak," so it's hard to tell where he stands with these words.

The Minnesota long "a" is relatively pure, with the tongue always forward and toward the roof of the mouth, especially in a final position or before a voiced consonant (Herman: 300). Sometimes the elongation involves a subtle but recognizable additional "e", turning the sound into a diphthong in a word like "may" or "say": "mae" and "sae." Two such instances in Dylan are the "a" in "lady" in the refrain of "Sad-Eyed Lady of the Lowlands," and the "a" of "say" in "say, 'Jeeze / I can't find my knees'" ("Visions of Johanna").[10] Generally, however, Dylan does not diphthongize "a", and even the final "a" of "I Threw It All Away," where the vowel is sustained in several lines for a half note, the "a" remains pure.

In the Midwest, the American long "i" sound — actually a diphthong writ-ten phonetically as [aI] — is sometimes elongated enough to pick up a short additional [ə] glide to produce a combination of three vowels, like [aIə] at the beginning of "aisle." However, the *Atlas* notes, in Minnesota "the offglide is generally short and weak" and this vowel is relatively pure (3: 15). "That [aI] is gonna be there," David Alan Stern warns aspiring actors, but don't drop in an additional "uh." "Keep the tongue movin', so you get the full diphthong" (14). The pure [aI] sounds in "for others to fire" in "Masters of War," where the note is held long enough to use a glide; the long "i" sounds in "Mr. Tambourine Man" are pure — "rhyme," "time," "behind," "mind." The words "tired," "wired," and "child" in the more recent song "Love Sick" have, although elongated, only the slightest of glides. Minnesotans have a *slight* tendency to reduce the first-person pronoun *I* to "ah," especially in an unaccented situation, but this reduction is not nearly so pronounced as it is in Bob Dylan, whose "I" almost always comes out "ah," and whose "my" always comes out "mah." This pronunciation shows up early in both his performance and personal voices. Possibly it is a western borrowing, but I notice that many singers of all denominations avoid that [aI], perhaps because they are consciously or unconsciously aware of how unpleasant a prolonged "aIIIIII" would sound in anything but "My, my, my, my, my Sharona."

Although Minnesota vowels are relatively pure, as we have noted, a slight "uh" sound, or "schwa," or [ə] sometimes slips into specific words, especially "four," "there," "prowl," "sour," "assure," and any word ending in the letter "l". Like other Midwesterners, Dylan is inconsistent. Note the glides in "growəl" and "howəl" in both "Man Gave Names to All the Animals" and "All Along the Watchtower." The glide is not usually apparent in Dylan's "four" — "twenty-*four* years" ("Lonesome Death of Hattie Carroll") — but it can be heard in "on a paəle afternoon" ("Masters of War"), in "faiəl to understand" ("Drifter's Escape"), in "too personal a taəle" ("Chimes of Freedom").[11]

Not much needs to be said about short vowels, except that in the Midwest they tend to deteriorate to the [ə] sound. While not unique to the Midwest, this reduction is especially strong in the area. "One of the most characteristic speech habits of the Middle Westerner is his reduction of most of the unstressed vowel sounds to 'UH,' particularly in informal speech," warn the Hermans (300). Especially the vowel sounds in unaccented "to," "you," and "of" deteriorate. Sometimes *Writings and Drawings* and *Lyrics* print that sound as an "a": "the rest a the stuff" and "side a them" in "11 Outlined Epitaphs." In other printed poems and stories of the 1960s, Dylan signals the lost vowel with an apostrophe, spelling *to* as *t'*, as in "t' reshape them an' restring them / t' protect my own world" in "11 Outlined Epitaphs." In several typed stories and letters of this period cited by Clinton Heylen, manuscripts reproduced in facsimile in *Bob Dylan: Lyrics: 1962–2001*, and poems on the sleeves of *The Times They Are A-Changin'* and *Another Side of Bob Dylan*, "to" is typed as the letter t: "tells them not t answer phone no matter what, then goes out t phone booth and calls herself" (*Rain Unravelled Tales*: 19), "I'll come an be cryin t you" (*Lyrics, 1962–1985*: 140), "she wants me / t say what she wants me t say" ("Some Other Kinds of Songs"). Either spelling would reflect the Midwest speech reduction of "to" to "tuh." *Joan Baez in Concert, Part 2* prints "you" as "yuh" in "yuh won't fool me anymore," and as late as "Disease of Conceit" (1989) Dylan writes "ya" for "you." In most manuscripts, Dylan uses standard spelling, an indication that the abnormalities I've just cited are indeed a conscious attempt to reflect spoken dialect.

Like many Americans but not all native English speakers, Dylan often contracts "of," "to," and "have" to produce "kinda" (ten different songs in the online lyrics contain lines in which "kind of" is printed "kinda," the spelling Dylan uses in *Tarantula*); "outa" ("out of" is printed "outa" in the lyrics of "Where Are You Tonight?" in *Lyrics: 1962–2001* and "get outa here" in *Tarantula* [33]); "lota" ("lot of" is printed "lotta" in "Positively 4th Street" in *Lyrics: 1962–2001*; printed "a lot of" but actually sung "a lota" in "If You See Her, Say Hello"), "gotta" ("Gotta Serve Somebody"), "herda" (*Tarantula*: 113), "gonna" ("When You Gonna Wake Up?"), "wanna" (see especially "Do Right to Me Baby"), "coulda" (printed "could have done better" but sung "coulda done better"), and "shoulda" (printed "he should-a stayed" in "Where Are You Tonight?"). In the printed lyrics of "Bob Dylan's Blues," we get "Somebody musta tol' 'em," and in *Tarantula* Dylan prints "musta drunk too much" (14) and "you oughta see his foot" (91).[12] A few years ago a German friend visiting me in Minnesota amused himself by greeting everyone he met with "Hi. I em Wolfgang Bleich. I em vrom Berlin. Whatcha gonna gimme?"[13]

Of course the Beatles' first big hit was "I Wanna Hold Your Hand." Very good ears, those lads from Liverpool.

Talking with Carolyn Kangas at Hibbing High, I could not help noticing "your" turning into "yer," and "for" into "fur." Dylan's language demonstrates this tendency in examples too numerous to cite, including "Talking Bear Mountain Picnic Massacre Blues," where "for" is actually spelled "f'r," and "Last Thoughts on Woody Guthrie," where "your" is always spelled "yer."[14] Minnesota dialect is more responsible than Howlin' Wolf for Dylan's ability to rhyme "hers" with "yours" in "I Wanna Be Your Lover."

In the Upper Midwest, as in many other parts of America, "get" often becomes "git." Thus we are advised to "furgive and furgit." Although he prints "get" as "git" in *Tarantula* to reflect its sound in his own private spoken English, the pronunciation of "get" is one thing Dylan seems consciously to correct, with limited success, in his performance voice. In his recorded version of "Highway 51 Blues," it's "git" in "get the gal I'm lovin'," but it's "get" in the last stanza. It's "get" in "I never did get" ("With God on Our Side"), but it's "git" in "To get him to feel more assured" ("Desolation Row"), and "get it together" ("What Was It You Wanted?"). It's "fergit" in "don't forget to flash" ("Million Dollar Bash"), but "forget" in "True Love Tends to Forget."

A similar vowel change often occurs in the word "just," which is often pronounced like the word "gist." Dylan uses this pronunciation several times in the Bootleg Series recording of "Talkin' Bear Mountain Picnic Massacre Blues," in "I just thought you might like something fine" ("Boots of Spanish Leather"), in "If I just turned away" ("What Good Am I?"), and in the *No Direction Home* performance of "Leopard-Skin Pill-Box Hat" (Dylan at his most urban East Coast) in "just like a bottle of wine." But in "Honey, Just Allow Me One More

Chance," "just" is just "just." In "The Death of Emmett Till," Dylan sings "just" in the third stanza ("just for the fun of killing him") but "gist" in the last stanza ("just a reminder").

Some fine features of consonant pronunciation are worth mentioning. In speech, "d" and "t" are close enough that "learned" can become "learnt." In the Lower Midwest "learned" does become "learnt," but "learned" is Northern Midwest (Allen 3: 16), and Dylan uses "learned": "I learned from my friend Mouse" ("Open the Door, Homer"), "I've learned to hate the Russians" ("With God on Our Side"), "I've just learned to turn it off" ("If You See Her, Say Hello").

Like "d" and "t", the sounds "s" and "z" are related, but there is a subtle difference between them: "z" is "voiced" or buzzed (the speaker is making some noise as the consonant is pronounced), and the "s" is "unvoiced"; it comes with a hiss but no buzz. The sound at the end of plurals like the word "dogs" and "years," and the word "was" is represented by the letter "s" but it's actually the voiced "z" sound . . . except in the Upper Midwest, where you often hear the unvoiced "s". "A frequent Range variant [of the word "Missis"] is the Northern /mIsIs/," notes Gary Underwood (63) — that's with an "s" at the end, not a "z". That unvoiced "s" plural can be heard daily in the restaurants and streets of Hibbing, and in the words "ears" and "years" in Dylan's most famous song, "Blowin' in the Wind."

In some situations other consonants morph. For example, "d" or "t" followed by "y" sometimes turns into a "j" or a "ch": listen carefully to "made your mind up" ("Make You Feel My Love"), or "don't you just come out once and scream it" ("Positively 4th Street"). Dylan is singing "madjer" and "donchu." Note also the t+y = ch in "ask about you" ("Million Miles"), and "What was it you wanted?" in the song of that title, and "*wonchu* come see me Queen Jane?" "11 Outlined Epitaphs" actually prints "doncha know" — Dylan's single usage of this quintessentially Minnesota expression.

Seventy-eight percent of Minnesotans drop a final "g" in words ending with "ing." This feature of pronunciation would appear to be beyond mentioning, but in coaching aspiring actors on the Midwest accent, David Alan Stern makes a point of reminding them to drop that "g". And whether you write it "goin'" or "going," the word is still going to be pronounced "goin'."[15] Minnesotans, as we have noted, do not preface the "goin'" with "a-," to produce "a-goin'."[16]

Iron Rangers, like other Americans, often drop a final dental or labial — b, d, p, t, or th — in front of a word beginning with one of those same letters, or a nasal (m or n). In writing, the missing sound shows up in inadvertent misspellings like "prejudice person" or "I happen to." Dylan gives us intentional misspellings like "the nex time I looked" ("11 Outlined Epitaphs") and unintentional misspellings like "Got ice water in my veins" ("Standing in the Doorway"). Singing, Dylan is careful with these sounds, but d's and t's sometimes disappear: the lost "d" in "use[d] to it" ("Like a Rolling Stone" and "If You See Her, Say Hello"), the lost final "t" in "disconnec[t] these cables" ("Señor"). "There's a bran[d] new gimmick every day" in "Talking Bear Mountain Picnic Massacre Blues."

One of the more interesting consonant aberrations of the Upper Midwest involves the letter "h" and the breath it represents. Midwesterners sometimes reverse the "w" and "h" in words like "where" and "what," to make "h-wen" and "h-wat" (T. Frazer: 128). Or an "h" breath sneaks ahead of the "w" in "way" to produce "h-way." As I noted in opening this chapter, King Alfred the Great would have said not "what," but "hwæt," so perhaps Minnesotans are throw backs to the Anglo-Saxons. I first noticed this little breath in my wife's speech, then in the speech of some of my Minnesota students, then in the shops and streets of Hibbing: "Hwat did yer mom hwant?" yells a kid on a bike. "No hway!" shouts an excited 18-year-old girl at the Chinese buffet. In the voice of a middle-aged man in Zimmy's Restaurant, there is just a hint of "h" in "anyhway." Marjorie Guthrie noticed that "h" too. She thought Dylan borrowed it from Woody, whose "voice was slurred by Huntington's chorea" when Dylan met him (Sounes: 83), but that breath is a common feature of Upper and Western Midwestern speech.

And hwen I really listen closely, I hear that inversion in Dylan — some of the time, not all of the time — more often early than late, and especially in songs of the first disc in the Bootleg Series. It's "how many seas must a *hwite* dove sail?" It's "Who killed Davey Moore, *hwy* and *hwat's* the reason for?" "It ain't no use to sit and wonder *hwy*, babe." The *hwaves* will pound when the ship comes in. In "Talkin' John Birch Paranoid Blues," them gol-darned Reds were "*everyhwere*" but they "got *ahway!*"

Speaking of an intrusive letter "h", the "overhauls" for "overalls" pun Michael Gray finds in *Lyrics, 1962–1985* and attributes to blues singers including Howlin' Wolf (*Song and Dance Man*: 321) is just another Upper Midwest mis-pronunciation, heard daily in cafés and bars. It can also be found in lines like Woody Guthrie's "My uniform's my dirty overalls," in the song "Dirty Overalls," a title which is actually printed "Dirty Overhalls" on the jacket of Vanguard's *The Greatest Songs of Woody Guthrie*. Guthrie writes "overhauls" in *Bound for Glory* (19); Dylan writes "overhauls" on the jacket of *Planet Waves*.

Many Minnesotans also have a problem with the word "hundred," which may come out "hundurd" or "hunurd" or even "hunurt." Dylan very clearly sings "hundurd" in "a hundred miles an hour" ("Motorpsycho Nightmare"), but (correcting his performance voice?) he clearly sings "hundred" in "The Lonesome Death of Hattie Carroll" and "It's Alright, Ma." He says something about halfway between the two in "A Hard Rain's A-Gonna Fall."

Unaccented first syllables can easily be lost: "be" in "beneath" and "because," "un" in "until," "a" at the beginning of "about." Again, these are not unique usages, but as Harold Allen points out, these syllables are lost more often in northern Midwest dialect than below the Minnesota line (*Atlas* 3: 16).

Sometimes Minnesotans talk right. They are, for example, pretty careful about an internal "b" following an "m" ("scramble," "number"). Around the country, "number" tends to become "nummer," but not at Zimmy's Restaurant in Hibbing, where a teenaged girl orders "number 5" with the "b". Dylan sings "your days are numbered," with the "b", on both the album version of "When the Ship Comes In" and in the demo version of that song on the first disc of the Bootleg Series. He sings "number eleven" in "North Country Blues." Iron Rangers are also careful with "t" between "n" and long "e", as in the word "twenty," which in other parts of America often becomes "tweny." Dylan retains that second "t": "twenty years of schoolin'" ("Subterranean Homesick Blues"), "at twenty-four years" (Lonesome Death of Hattie Carroll"), and "on her twenty-second birthday" ("Desolation Row").

Minnesotans are more careful with their final and internal "r" than, say, New Yorkers. "R" is sounded (with a slight palatal resonance) in words like "ear," "runner," "burglar," "weird," "poor," "marshal," "bar," "four."[17] However, listening to people interviewed for a television documentary titled *The Iron Range: A People's History*, one hears a slight loss of "r" in words like "father" and "dollar." It's slight: not nearly as obvious as the lost "r" of East Coast and British accents. The first of two r's can disappear in words like "mirror," "error," "nearer," and "terror," reducing those words almost to a single syllable. John Herdman takes the rhyme of "mirror" and "near" in "Visions of Johanna" for intentional half-rhyme (126), but admits it probably "sounds much less strange to American ears than to British ones." Probably it's just Minnesota dialect: in "Mama, You Been on My Mind," Dylan rhymes "mirror" with "clear." "Dylan seems to have a fascination with mirrors (despite not being able to pronounce the word properly)," observes Nick Hawthorne wryly (27). This pronunciation can be heard in "the palace of mirrors" ("Changing of the Guards") and "glance through the mirror" ("No Time to Think").

While spelling may not technically be a feature of dialect, some minor features of *Tarantula* are interesting. One is Dylan's regular spelling of *a lot* as *alot*, which also crops up on the back cover of *Another Side of Bob Dylan*: "an i dream alot." (This was corrected in *Lyrics, 1962–1985*, but note "It Takes Alot To Laugh" in the list of Dylan and The Band numbers performed on the 1974 tour on page 137 of the *Rolling Stone* anthology *Knockin' on Dylan's Door: On the Road in '74.*) Given his other spelling eccentricities and experiments in *Tarantula* (lowercase letters on proper names, but not on God, Allah, Jesus Christ, Suzy Q, or Des Moines, Iowa); "&" for "and"; omitted apostrophes in "dont," "youre," "doesnt," "theyve"; "nite" for "night"; "tho" for "though"), *alot* may be an intentional attempt to be hip and po-mo . . . but it's a misspelling I see in alot of my freshman comp. themes . . . almost as much as "and" for "to" in things like "try & touch my kid" (*Tarantula*: 14).

Another interesting spelling is "does she wanna nother one" (*Tarantula*: 90). In the expression "a whole nother thing," which is common in the Midwest, the "n" has detached itself from the end of *an* and reattached itself to the beginning of *other*, with the word *whole* intruding between the two. Thus *nother* becomes a variant of *other* . . . which may be what Dylan is hearing in his brain.[18]

Also relevant to an understanding of the Midwest base of Dylan's language are the larger traits of Minnesota speech. In *How to Talk Minnesotan*, Howard Mohr points out that Upper Midwest speech is even flatter than most Midwest speech, and Minnesota phrases and sentences have a level accentual pattern and a flat or falling sequence of pitches which mirrors the landscape. A rising pitch, Mohr warns, might indicate enthusiasm, excitement, or overstatement, which would be "a big mistake" (3). "If you have to overdo it in Minnesota," he warns, "overdo it on the downside, not the upside" (6). David Alan Stern, training actors in *Speaking without an Accent*, emphasizes this flatness: "Perhaps the most important difference between the 'Southern' and the 'Mid-West' dialects is the presence of an inner-vowel lilt or pitch change in 'Southern' speech which *does not* exist in most farm belt speech," he writes (8). This is what Michael Gray describes as "ease of tone and vocabulary [and] careful straightforwardness of what is being said" (*Song*: 77), and "language of extreme simplicity" (*Song*: 161). Greil Marcus, in *Invisible Republic*, describes this voice as "a barbed Plains States drawl" (12); "the voice it makes you might call Yankee Midwestern . . . the sound of bluesman Frank Hutchison, . . . the sound of drugstore speech in Hibbing" (51, 52). In the *New York Times* review which launched Dylan's career, Robert Shelton wrote, "Mr. Dylan seems to be performing in a slow-motion film" (McGregor: 17); later he described the "flat Midwestern tones" as "gratingly mesmeric" (Cott: 94).

This is the sound Dylan heard at twilight, on the street, way back home when he was growing up. Minnesota flat may explain why Dylan sometimes levels accent or stress across a string of syllables, words, or phrases, from the early "admit that the waters" to the late "I get up in the dawn and I go down and lay in the shade." It is in this low-key, wary, masked tone, even more than specific verbal references, that Marcus locates the "Americanness" he finds permeating *The Basement Tapes*.

This speech is powerful and suggestive, but in addition to being musically flat, it's filled with pauses and suspensions, especially in rural Minnesota (you don't find the same tone in Twin Cities natives like Prince or The Replacements). "The heartbeat of conversation in Minnesota is the pause," says Mohr (204), the kind of pauses which fill Dylan's introduction to "Baby, Let Me Follow You Down" at one end of his career, and his interviews in *No Direction Home* at the other. Garrison Keillor writes in *Lake Wobegon Days*,

> I grew up among slow talkers, men in particular, who dropped words a few at a time like beans in a hill, and when I got to Minneapolis, where people took a Lake Wobegon comma to mean the end of the story, I couldn't speak a whole sentence in company and was considered not too bright. (6)

"Ain't talkin', just walkin'," sang Dylan in a song which may depict one of these rural Midwest types.

Sometimes this speech talks around the real subject in non sequiturs and repetitions, saying words but saying nothing. With tongue just partially in cheek, Mohr presses his analysis a step further:

> Most Minnesota conversations do not, however, need a common theme. The only rule is to pause briefly between what seem to be unconnected statements. . . . This peculiarity of the Minnesota language was picked up some years ago by Samuel Beckett (he spent a week near Worthington, Minnesota, when his car broke down). He wrote the first draft of his most famous play in a motel room that looked out on a bare field. He called it *Waiting for the Mechanic*. . . . What happens is, one guy says something in a monotone — "I don't know, it could be the alternator" — and the other guy waits until the drum is struck and then he says in a monotone, "The fruit is balanced on the vestibule." It went on like that for almost three hours. I was fascinated. (145)

Growing up in an environment with this kind of conversational disconnect may explain Dylan's fascination with ballads and folk songs in which so much remains mysterious and unsaid, where motivations remain so submerged as to be inexplicable, where key parts of the story are not reported, where nine-tenths of the iceberg remains submerged, where obfuscation, not clarity, seems the principle of composition. It may also explain, better than Faulkner and Joyce,[19] his modernist habit of composing line to line, by association. As

Mohr suggests, there's a lot of absurdist surrealism in day-to-day Minnesota life and conversation.

These Midwest conversations are often so guarded that they never reach any real conclusion. In *Invisible Republic*, Greil Marcus records this conversation overheard in McPherson, Kansas, by artist Bruce Conner: "'Hi, Joe.' 'Hi, Nick.' 'How're you doing.' 'I'm doing fine.' 'Great day, isn't it.' 'Sure is.' 'Think we might get some rain?' 'Could be.' 'How's the wife?' 'Real good.' 'Well, gotta go now.' 'Well, see you.' 'See you.'" (138). The novel *Being Youngest*, by Iowa author Jim Heynen, contains the following dialogue:

> "Not so far," said Henry. "And this here is our new neighbor, just moved over here from North Dakota."
>
> "So," the old man said, and rocked his head and shoulders. "North Dakota."
>
> "Yep," said Gretchen. "North Dakota."
>
> "So," the old man said again. "North Dakota. That's quite a ways."
>
> "Yep," said Gretchen. "That's quite a ways."
>
> "That's an awful long ways for a little girl like you to be going. You come over here in a car then?"
>
> "Yep," said Gretchen. "We come over in a car."
>
> "You musta got tired," said the old man.
>
> "Sure did," said Gretchen. "Ridin in a car makes you tired."
>
> "You mustn't get too tired," said the old man.
>
> "Nope," said Gretchen. "That ain't good." (65–6)

Sometimes these conventions mark a false cheerfulness, a fear of offending anyone which characterized Minnesotans long before the day of speech codes, and a general unwillingness to confront problems evident in quintessentially Minnesota lines like "It's All Good" and "times are hard everywhere / We'll just have to see how it goes" ("Floater [Too Much to Ask]"). This evasiveness is often called "Minnesota Nice" (as in "wouldn't say 'shit' if he had a mouthful"). In fact, far from being inoffensive or reassuring, Minnesota Nice makes a person wonder just what's really going on beneath the bland façade. Marcus goes on to quote Sarah Vowell:

> the congenial Midwest makes me tremble. I know for a fact that steam rises from the gates of hell in downtown Fargo and the Antichrist, laying low, shovels snow off the streets of Dubuque for extra cash. Forget the Big Bad Wolf, the fear of God, the hands of time — they can't stand up to Minnesota Nice. (138)

Apparently, this was the habit of Abe Zimmerman, whom Dylan recalls as "plain speaking and straight talking" (*Chronicles*: 107), and whose speech Robert Shelton reports as "slow and deliberate" and peppered with double negatives (*Home*: 33). "We never did too much talkin' anyway," Dylan sang in "Don't Think Twice," and Suze Rotolo, Joan Baez, Echo Helstrom, and Carole Childs have all remarked on how little talkin' Dylan does, even with his women.

This flat delivery is useful in the Woody Guthrie-style "talking blues" at which Dylan is so adept — "long, long monologues, with no point, and no punch line" (Nissenson quoted in Heylin, *Shades*: 55). He uses this voice most notably in mundane shaggy-dog sagas that start nowhere and go nowhere, like "Talkin' World War III Blues" ("I lit a cigarette on the parking meter and walked on down the road") and "Clothes Line Saga." "Clothes Line" began as a parody of "Ode to Billy Joe" (see Marcus, *Invisible Republic*: 143), and Andrew Muir discusses the song in the context of existential absurdity (*Troubadour*: 155), but most of all it sounds like a parody by Jim Heynen or a typical Mark Twain tall tale: "The humorous story is told gravely," Twain explained in "How to Tell a Story"; "the teller does his best to conceal the fact that he even dimly suspects that there is anything funny about it." Twain, Heynen, and Dylan all speak in the same going-nowhere-in-a-hurry Midwestern voice:

> I reached up, touched my shirt
> And the neighbor said, "Are those clothes yours?"
> I said, "Some of 'em, not all of 'em"
> He said, "Ya always help out around here with the chores?"
> I said, "Sometime, not all the time"
> Then my neighbor, he blew his nose
> Just as Papa yelled outside,
> "Mama wants you t' come back in the house and bring them clothes"
>
> ("Clothes Line Saga")

"Saga" is, of course, an ironic reference to the great heroic epics of Northern Europe, whence originated the ancestors of so many North Country citizens, whose present-day speech is so guarded, so very unheroic, an "exercise in phatic communion," as Muir calls it (*Troubadour*: 156), in which things are said merely to fulfill some kind of social convention or simply as a sign of sociability. Muir finds this Joycean. Aidan Day interprets this kind of chatter in "Isis" — "Where ya been?" "No place special" — as "a reflection of language's failure to hold the ideal" (46). To me this talk sounds just typically Minnesotan, like the restaurant monologue and the rest of "Highlands," full of Midwest tall-tale non sequiturs, redundancies, and shifting verb tenses that would have made Mark Twain envious:

> I'm crossing the street to get away from a mangy dog
> Talking to myself in a monologue
> I think what I need might be a full-length leather coat
> Somebody just asked me
> If I registered to vote

THE ARC OF DYLAN'S LANGUAGE

In most of this discussion, I have treated Dylan's performance language as a constant, drawing examples from early songs and late songs to support points about vocabulary, idiom, and pronunciation. Insofar as the object of discussion was to describe a layer of linguistic bedrock, that approach makes a certain sense, but the heaves and shouldering of life shift that bedrock, and our language, like our personality, changes from decade to decade. In a subsequent chapter I will talk about Dylan's physical and intellectual journeys away from and back to his home place, and forward and backward in time. Those journeys are partially linguistic. Dylan's language has its going out and coming back. A look at highlight albums and some of the more arcane repositories of Dylan shows just where Dylan was at certain points along this journey. Call it linguistic archeology, and if you're already bored, skip to the next chapter.

Bootlegged Beginnings

In *Rain Unravelled Tales*, Clinton Heylin lists several early "Folk Circle Tapes," extant or rumored (1–7). One of the earliest is the tape made by Bonnie Beecher in September of 1960, when Dylan had returned to Minnesota after nine months in New York City. The tape records Dylan already in performance voice. Foreign influences are very evident: Dylan sounds Dust Bowl Oakie on the talking blues (including Guthrie's "Jesus Christ"), and he's two-thirds of the way to being Irish on "Johnny I Hardly Knew Ye." "My" is in the process of becoming "mah," "I" is turning into "ah," and the letter "r" is disappearing, but those developments are still in process. In the tape's first song, Dylan actually seems intent on deleting the "r" from "waterbucket," but that "r" sneaks back in when he's not paying attention. However, the Iron Range dialect prevails: "hundred" is Upper Midwest "hunerd," "get" is "git," and the long "o" is everywhere apparent. "I'll do *a couple* verses of it," Dylan says by way of introduction to Guthrie's "Jesus Christ." In an improvised song about his roommate, "Lazy Hugh Brown," Dylan drifts into one of those Midwestern conversations that go nowhere: "I says 'oh?' He says, 'yeah.' I says, 'oh?' Hugh Brown never closed the window. . . ."

In the talk between songs and in the songs like "Red Rosey Bush" which do not require a particular accent, Dylan's voice is even closer to his natural dialect. He sounds very flat, level, understated, and very Midwestern . . . with "I," "my," "every" pronounced without borrowed accent or dialect. "Cynthia, don't be that mean to me." "Oh hell, I can't do it." "Can't do a talkin' blues in a tape recorder." "Oh, I got one here."[20] That is the same voice we hear when Dylan reads "Last Thoughts on Woody Guthrie" after his Town Hall concert in April, 1963. He reads the poem quickly, a little nervous perhaps and unsure of his stature as a poet, or intent on emphasizing the tetrameter lines. His speaking voice is Minnesota flat and understated, a sharp contrast to his performance voice. He's doing Guthrie "ah" for "I," but the Minnesota long "o" is everywhere, and r's are present and accounted for in "heard" and "supper club" and "cardboard."[21] Dylan throws a little breath into "wheel" to convert it to "hweel." "Hundred" comes out Minnesota "hunert," and "figured" is "figgerd." "Window" stays "window" (not Guthrie's "winder"), and Dylan says "furgit it," "furever," "git" and "gittin'," "yer" for "your."

Early Sixties

The voice Dylan used on his early records is more difficult to pin down. His first album was mostly songs by persons other than Bob Dylan, sung in performance voice by a Bob Dylan who was perhaps too intent on being a southern bluesman or an Oklahoma hillbilly. However, the songs of his second album, *The Freewheelin' Bob Dylan*, offer a legitimate barometer. They are all Dylan compositions performed by a singer using fewer borrowed voices, the three exceptions being "Down the Highway" (Dylan singing the blues), "Talkin' World War III Blues," and "Bob Dylan's Blues" (Dylan being Woody Guthrie).

Overall, we notice plenty of Iron Range vocabulary: "dawn" in "Don't Think Twice," "casket" in "Masters of War," "string bean" in "I Shall Be Free" (although the text printed in *Lyrics: 1962–2001* reads "jumped a bean stalk"). The songs contain lots of working-class vernacular: plenty of "ain't" and plenty of double negatives, sometimes in the same line: "It ain't no use to sit and wonder why." The songs are full of nonstandard verb forms common in the Midwest: "I seen a man," "I seen a Cadillac," "our hats was hung, our words was told, our songs was sung" (two of these three verbs are changed to "were" in *Lyrics: 1962–2001*), "life don't mean a thing," "I give her my heart." In "Don't Think Twice, It's All Right," Dylan goes both ways in the same song: "never *did* too much talkin'," and "like you never *done* before." And while in "Oxford Town" he sings "don't even know why we *come*," in "Talkin' World War III Blues" he goes with "a crazy dream *came* to me."

Listening closely to Dylan's vowels, one senses an Iron Range performer whose background keeps slipping in when he is trying hard to sound like somebody else. The long Minnesota "o" is everywhere on this album — especially the "nose" and "grow" and "Bridget Bardot." That long "o" even intrudes into the bluesy "Down the Highway" on the word "ocean," a word which gets a hearty Minnesota articulation elsewhere in "a dozen dead oceans." The long, pure "e" can be heard in "Anita Ekberg," "steeple," "people," "seen," "Mr. Clean" of "I Shall Be Free." "Been" is Midwestern "bin" in "Where have you been, my blue-eyed son?" "Window" becomes Midwest "winduh" in "look out your window" ("Don't Think Twice"). "I" is clearly [aI] in "I wish there was somethin' I could do or say," "I've often prayed," and virtually all of the lines of "A Hard Rain's A-Gonna Fall," and Dylan sings "my" — not "mah" — in "darkness of my night" and in "I'll know my song well." Elsewhere — "hope that you *die*," "while *rid*ing on a train" — the vowel "i" is a nice, clean, Midwestern [aI] without glide after or before.

"For" is "fur" in "runnin' *fur* office on the ballot note," but it's "for" in "sit *for*ever in fun." "Get" is often Midwest "git" ("to *git* along with you," "death count *gits* higher," and "just" is often "jist": "Honey, *Jist* Allow Me One More Chance." A slight glide slips into Midwestern "for" and "fire" before the "r" in "for others to fire." We hear plenty of "coulda done better," "kinda wasted my precious time," "outa their bodies," "talk outa turn," "musta told em." And in "Masters of War" one wonderful "Lemme ask you one question."

We can also hear a little of that "h" breath that precedes the letter "w" in "wild wolves" ("Hard Rain"), "white dove sail" ("Blowin' in the Wind"), "why we come" ("Oxford Town"), and "wonder why, babe" ("Don't Think Twice"). And sometimes we hear the unvoiced "s" plural where we should have a voiced "z" sound, as in "build all the guns" and "build all the bombs."

When he's not singing blues, Dylan retains his r's in many places where he will later lose them, in places where good Midwesterners retain their r's: "bird that whistles" ("Corrina, Corrina"), "before they're forever banned" ("Blowin' in the Wind"), most "r" words in "A Hard Rain's A-Gonna Fall," and every "r" word of the second stanza of "Bob Dylan's Dream."

In contrast to the energized, kinetic sound of the middle sixties electric albums, this album seems slow, deliberate, almost flat. "Blowin' in the Wind," "Masters of War," "A Hard Rain's A-Gonna Fall" all address big-picture issues which in the late 1950s and 1960s elicited street riots, shouted obscenities, tear-gassing if you were lucky and police batons/bullets if you were not. Dylan is steely and resolved, but Midwest matter of fact: "I just want you to know"; "I'm a-goin' back out 'fore the rain starts a-fallin.'" Neither the words nor the tune of "Blowin' in the Wind" is angry or militant — merely Midwest resigned. There is nothing you can do about the injustice in Oxford Town except go back where you came from and hope somebody investigates soon, which is Dylan's offhand suggestion, made in the flat Midwest voice which masks so many emotions. The dark side of Minnesota Nice sounds in "I'll stand o'er your grave / 'Til I'm sure that you're dead," and Dylan hopes that the masters of war die soon, but he will not kill them, nor, when we look at the song closely, will he celebrate their death. He'll make sure they are dead, and move on to the next matter (which on this album happens to be his girlfriend's departure for Italy). The song's simple, repetitive, hypnotic melody enhances its understatement.

Middle Sixties

In contrast to *The Freewheelin' Bob Dylan*, which celebrates freedom in the voice of the Midwest, *Highway 61 Revisited*, despite the geographical reference to home, is *not* particularly Midwestern in either its tone or conception. "Revolutionary and stunning," Michael Gray calls the album in *Song and Dance Man III*; "The whole rock culture, the whole post-Beatle pop-rock world — in an important sense the 1960s started here" (5). The New York influence is evident in both the subjects and images of the songs (not our interest here) and in Dylan's language (which is our interest here). But old habits of speech and vocabulary die hard, and beneath the hip sound of the sixties one hears atavistic vestiges of the North Country.

Dylan's performance voice has lost most of its Guthrie borrowings, and he has synthesized blues with rock enough that only in rare cases like "It Takes a Lot to Laugh" (with its borrowings of phrasing and pronunciation from Leroy Carr's "Alabama Woman Blues" and Elvis Presley's version of "Milkcow Blues Boogie") does Dylan sound like a blues singer. The "d" is Midwest absent in "used to it" and "used to be" in "Like a Rolling Stone." An occasional breathy "h" can be heard in lines like "hwat's mine?" ("Ballad of a Thin Man"). The "g" at the end of "ing" words is more present, but not always present: "something is happening here" ("Ballad of a Thin Man"), but "puttin,'" "comin,'" "killin,'" and "rovin'" in "Highway 61 Revisited." We hear more "get" ("get used to it," "could not get across"), but plenty of "git" remains: "*git* sick in," "math book to *git* thrown," "*git* your kicks for you," "*git*ting ready for the show." We hear more "just" ("I've just been made" in "Tombstone Blues"), but plenty of "jist" remains: "*jist* like I said," "*jist* stand around and boast," "*jist* arrived here," "lookin' *jist* like a ghost." "For" is more often "for" ("kicks for you," "roadmaps for the soul"), but an occasional "fur" remains. Where Dylan would once have sung "do you wanna make a deal?" he now sings "Do you want to make a deal?" but he still sings "you're gonna have to get use to it." In "Like a Rolling Stone" he sings "didn't you" where he might once have sung "didnchu," but in the next stanza it's "taucha" for "taught you." Elsewhere it's "got to run" in "Highway 61 Revisited" but "wonchu" in "Queen Jane Approximately." Howard in "Highway 61 Revisited" must be from the north end of that highway because he's "ol' Howard." "Heave their plastic" ("Queen Jane Approximately") is an Upper Midlands vocabulary preference, as is "pants" in "Desolation Row," and while Dylan does not sing it on record, the particle verb "pick up" appears in the text of stanza four of "Just Like Tom Thumb's Blues." Double negatives are still everywhere — in fact Dylan sings one into "Like a Rolling Stone" that is not (surprise, surprise) in the *Lyrics: 1962–2001* text: "when you ain't got nothin', you got nothin' to lose."

Dylan's vowels are more controlled, especially the long "o" sounds in "Like a Rolling Stone," but lend an ear to "don't talk so loud" in the first stanza, and watch that long "o" sneak right back into "home" and "unknown" in later choruses. Listen closely to "nose," "clothes," "go," and "know" in "Highway 61 Revisited," and the various rhymes with the title line of "Desolation Row" (especially "joke" in the final stanza). And while "steal," "deal," and "conceal" in that song have glides stronger than anyone hears in Hibbing, "feel" is Minnesota pure, as are the i's in things like "eyes" and "alibis."

The letter "r", though fading fast (gone from "barbell" and Jack the Ripper, gone from "graveyard" and "four" in "From a Buick 6," gone from "sergeant at arms" in "Just Like Tom Thumb's Blues") is hanging in there in "ain't it hard," "your useless and pointless knowledge," "wear earphones," and — perhaps most significantly, "I'm goin' back to New York City."

D. A. Pennybaker's classic documentary *dont look back* dates to this time, following Bob Dylan on his 1965 tour of Great Britain. Whatever Dylan thinks of the film, it does record Dylan's out-of-studio speech of this period, as well as the speech of a host of Brits sounding like Brits of various classes and geographies, and Albert Grossman sounding like a Chicago mobster: "you're one of the dumbest assholes and most stupid person I ever talked to in my life. If we were someplace else, I'd punch you in your goddam nose."

And there is Dylan, trying to give "bloke" and "rubbish" their proper U.K. pronunciation, injecting a little Southern twang into "Only a Pawn in Their Game" (this footage was shot in Greenwood, Mississippi, not in the U.K.), and pumping the twang and diphthongs into "Lost Highway" as he and Baez duet on that classic. Mostly, Dylan sounds like just plain Midwest Bob Dylan:

wonderful Midwest "shuure," "ya know," "tomorrow" with the full "o" sound, and "bone" and "stone" in "The Times They Are A-Changin'." Plenty of "r" in "here," "number," "other," "car," "world," "person," "very," and "for." Plenty of r's in the version of "It's All Over Now, Baby Blue" that he sings to Donovan in a hotel room. "Wanna," "kinda," "gonna," "gotta," "donchu." "Whatdaya like about it?" Both "or" and "er," both "just" and "jist." "Misquotin'" and "callin'" without the "g." A little "h" intruding before the "w" in "twirled" and "away from your face" in some refrains of "Lonesome Death of Hattie Carroll." A couple of big, fat "furs" in "for a piano player" and "for her." Double negatives: "I don't wanna hear nobody." A wonderful Midwestern explosion in the hotel: "gonna git the fuck outta here." (And a wonderful Prophet Bob Dylan attack on *Time* magazine: "I don't take it seriously. If I want to find out anything, I'm not gonna read *Time* magazine! They'd go off the stands in a day if they really printed the truth.")

Early Seventies
What followed Electric Bob, we recall, was Country Bob. While we might expect a retreat to rural Minnesota dialect during this period, that's not quite what we get, because Dylan's voice always seems to lag slightly behind his mind. *Nashville Skyline* (1969) represents Dylan well into his country stage. Artistically, it cannot measure up to the other albums in this sequence, but it's an honest indicator of Dylan's performance voice at this stage of his career. The Johnny Cash–Bob Dylan duet which opens the album offers an instructive contrast between Dylan's soft, almost New York, lost r's and Cash's relatively harder Arkansas r's, especially on words like "north," "for," "there," "remember," "fair," and "hair." In the balance of the album, "r" is half present at best ("ticket out the door," "here with you"), gone most of the time. It's mostly "mah" for "my," and "ah" is back as "I," although in a few cases Dylan retains the pure [aI]. Plenty of "ain't," plenty of "oughta," "whatcha," "and "by golly." Dylan sings "I wish the night was here" even where he writes "I wish the night were here." He appears to be going for a country sound by singing "on" as "awn" ("One More Night") and "want" as "waunt" ("Tell Me That It Isn't True"), but what he should have done was add a "t" to "across" on "lay across my big brass bed" and converted "window" to "winder" in the first line of "Tonight I'll Be Staying Here with You." Below the surface, Country Bob sounds less rural than Bob Dylan, Folksinger or even Electric Bob.

Middle Seventies
Coming off of the slack albums of the late country music period, *Blood on the Tracks* (1975) was a reassuring festival of imagery, subtle sounds, and voices: an

album of genius to stand with *Highway 61 Revisited* and *John Wesley Harding*. Dylan was reborn yet one more time, and once again reflecting the peculiar stage of life (self-reassessment) which hits people in their middle thirties . . . just about the time members of his own generation were entering that stage. There is a certain melancholy in reaching that point when your life is turning out as well as it's probably going to turn out, but also less frenzy and more transcendence and acceptance. This is a time of catching breath, of enjoying health and success, of being honest with self and world, of enjoying time. Less pose, less angst. "More on target," as Dylan puts it. And Dylan's performance voice reflects the singer's long, rich, and varied musical and personal history. It is worth remembering that in 1975, his many musical explorations aside, Dylan had been away from the Iron Range nearly as long as he had lived there, so it is not surprising to find the voice on this album pretty distant from drugstore talk in Hibbing. Yet in some respects this voice seems closer to the Midwest standard than *Nashville Skyline*. Dylan was spending a lot of time on a farm west of Minneapolis, and in the album's songs he mentions snow, hail, mourning doves, the great north woods of the Iron Range and Wabasha in Minneapolis.

In *Blood on the Tracks*, Dylan has his r's mostly on half-articulation. Medial and terminal r's are appropriately turned off in the bluesy "Meet Me in the Morning," but the songs of this album have more hard r's than we've heard in a long time, including some words where we might expect to find the "r" missing: "weather," "horses," "heart," "boxcar door," "apart," "anymore." Some of these are hard r's in a snarling song — "Idiot Wind" — but some are in soft, appreciative ballads like "Shelter from the Storm," where Dylan almost caresses the letter "r". There are several rich Minnesota o's, especially in the word "know": "you can make me cry if you don't know," "I know where I can find you," "you still know how to breathe" (this last, in "Idiot Wind," is nasal and long and very Minnesotan). Appropriately, there's a little "h" breath in "workin' for a *hwile* on a fishin' boat" ("Tangled Up in Blue"): the boat is outside of New Orleans,[22] but the singer is just in from the great north woods, and the songs are filled with lots of "gonna" and hafta" and "a lotta people." "Made you" becomes "madja" ("Idiot Wind") "yellow moon" becomes "yelluh moon" ("If You See Her, Say Hello"), and a "d" gets lost in "used to it" ("If You See Her, Say Hello"). Dylan sings "gimme a lethal dose" ("Shelter from the Storm"), sings "I seen" and "them words" ("Tangled Up in Blue"). The first "girl" in "You're a Big Girl Now" is pure, but the second time through it picks up a slight Midwest glide between the "r" and "l". Even though the voice is not really the voice of Hibbing, Dylan's rich tapestry of sound — especially in "Tangled Up in Blue" and "Idiot Wind" — sounds like the old voice of the North Country, "heavy on the vowels."

"Lily, Rosemary and the Jack of Hearts" is Dylan at his most Midwestern, full of "up" particle verbs ("filling up," "drew up," "kept up," "covered up"), "jist" for "just," "git" for "get," "who" where we'd want "whom," and a lovely double negative: "couldn't go no further." "Across" comes without the "t" it picks up below the Iowa line. And plenty of Minnesota o's, including the last "o" on "window."

Eighties

The 1980s were rough on Bob Dylan — and on anyone else living in America — and almost nobody has anything good to say about Dylan's work during this decade. Part of the heat he takes is undoubtedly due to the uncompromising, dogmatic Christianity of some of his songs, although that kind of strong assertion of principles was — we see in retrospect — the correct response to the flaccid, PC sociology and the leveling reader-response school of cultural studies which enervated intellectual thought during those times. "Disease of Conceit" sounds like a Southern Baptist sermon complete with Hammond organ, although it was probably exactly what the times needed and deserved. The dominant linguistic influences of Dylan's eighties life were far from the Midwest, although he was by this time such a master of voices that in performance he could do, and did do, about anything he chose.

Oh Mercy (1989) is not only Dylan's strongest album of the decade, it constitutes a convenient milestone in the history of his voice. There's plenty of familiar verb slang here — "crime don't have a face," "She ain't even in my mind," "when you give me that kiss," "[I] seen a shooting star tonight." The many particle verbs in these songs strike a listener as Midwestern: "cover up," "pick up," "hold up," "match up." "Comes up" in "Where Teardrops Fall" and "going down" in "Ring Them Bells" might reflect Upper Midwest exceptions to the Lower Midwestern prejudice against "come up" and "go down" for rising and setting of the sun. The songs also contain a rich lode of Midwestern idiom and cliché: "sticks in the throat," "both feet on the ground," "deal with the situation," "right down to the bone," "head is on straight," "comes right down the highway," "down for the count," "too good to die," "miss the mark," "tomorrow will be another day." There is some characteristically Midwest ungrammaticality in "Ring Them Bells."

Among the songs' Midwestern pronunciations are "mirror" in "Political World" with its missing internal "r", "I *jist* might have to come see you" in "Where Teardrops Fall," "*willuh*" for "willow" in "Ring Them Bells" and "*winda*" for "window" in "Man in the Long Black Coat," "kinda wondered" in "Shooting Star," and a "been" that rhymes with "within" in "What Good Am I?" Dylan sings "when you gimme that kiss" and "*git* it back" in "What Was *Itchu* Wanted?" (later in the song, however, it's "am I * get*ting it wrong?"). Long Minnesota o's appear ("broken bones") and disappear ("broken phones"), sometimes, intriguingly, in the same word repeated in the refrain of a song that appears to be Minnesota based: the "coat" of "Man in the Long Black Coat." "Of" is "a," and final g's have gone missing, including the "g" on "croaking" to rhyme it with "broken" ("Everything is Broken"). A little "h" breath sneaks into "wheel" on "the wheel and the plow" ("Ring Them Bells"), and into the whole final stanza of "Ring Them Bells."

"Man in the Long Black Coat" contains a lovely piece of Minnesota ambivalence: "It is true sometimes you can see it that way"; "Most of the Time," that lovely piece of self-deluded rationalization, is a song full of Minnesota ambivalence and lowered expectation: "Most of the time / I can keep both feet on the ground . . . Most of the time / I'm halfway content. . . ." Dylan was by the close of the 1980s such a subtle manipulator of voice, it is hard to say exactly what he sounds like — except Dylan.

Nineties

Consensus winner of the award for Dylan's greatest album of new material in the 1990s is *Time Out of Mind* (1997). It's the only album in the category, other nineties albums being officially released bootlegs, greatest hits, and collections of Dylan singing other people's songs. *Time Out of Mind* is an album of great emotional loss and enervation, and its songs are flatter even than *Blood on the Tracks*: none of the anger of Dylan's protest period, none of the exciting explorations of his twenties, none of mellow Country Bob's pleasures in family and nature, none of the religious intensity of Reverend Bob Dylan. Love in this album is not the joy of pursuit or sex, but the devastation of unrequited desire and affection which would rather run away and hide than strike another match and start anew. "Yesterday everything was going too fast," Dylan sings in "Standing in the Doorway"; "Today, it's moving too slow." The songs express tremendous indecisiveness. It's like a long winter afternoon snowed in on the Range, when you can't go anywhere and there is nothing to do but look out the window and watch time seep away. All Dylan can say is "There's a way to get there and I'll figure it out somehow" ("Highlands"). Talk about Midwest lowered expectations!

In contrast to the brilliant surrealism of the middle sixties albums and the lush pastoralism of other material, the images in these songs are foggy, and the landscape is muddy, snowy, stormy, dead. With its flat, indecisive, level-to-the-point-of-being-soporific intonations, Midwest English is perfect for this album. Dylan's halting, level delivery of lines like "I can't even remember what it was I came here to get away from" sounds like something out of Garrison Keillor.

The disconnected thought processes of "Highlands" sound like a conversation out of Howard Mohr. And on *Time Out of Mind*, Dylan seems to backburner all linguistic riches in favor of the sound of drugstore speech in Hibbing. If absence of ornament is the largest identifying feature of Midwest English, this album is it. When Dylan sings "I was born here and I'll die here against my will / I know it looks like I'm moving, but I'm standing still," and "I'm twenty miles out of town, in cold irons bound" he is talking about his intonation as well as his life. After all the rich tapestries, imagistic and vocal, of other albums, he's now stuck in the North Country.

It is this general flatness that sounds most Midwestern, although other markers of Iron Range speech are present: infinite lost g's, "furgit" in "Love Sick," mixed "just and "jist," "get" and "git" ("It's not dark yet, but it's *gittin'* there"), plenty of "gonna" and "bin," "tomorrow" reduced to "tomorruh" ("Til I Fell in Love with You"), a little "h" in "whiskey" ("Cold Irons Bound"), "then" for "than" in "Not Dark Yet" and in "Highlands" (the text in *Lyrics: 1962–2001* even prints "then" — a common mistake among my Minnesota students), a crisp Midwestern second "t" in "twenty." We hear some familiar idioms as well: "gone down the drain," "torn me to shreds," "on your case," "what in the devil," "seal up" and "put me up" and "smashing up." And some double negatives: "ain't looking for nothin'," "won't be back no more," "ain't seen nothin' like me yet."

Dylan's long a, e and o vowels are pure and simple in these songs, most noticeably the "o" of "window," "meadow," and "shadow" and "road" in "Love Sick." He usually uses a flat "i", although "fire" in "Til I Fell in Love with You" gets a long, hard and very noticeable, and very Upper Midwestern, glide. But what we hear most in Dylan's voice on this album is the bleak amplitudes of a long winter afternoon on the Iron Range.

2000s

With the new millennium, Bob Dylan seemed to recover from the loss of love and self that colors *Time Out of Mind* . . . and survived the early conviction that he would die young. He has become, in fact, a legend of longevity — the performer who keeps on performing, the composer who keeps on composing, the DJ who keeps on talking. *Modern Times*, which appeared in 2006 to thunderous applause, represents the best of new Dylan, and it is a good measure of Dylan's present performance voice — or voices.

When you think about it, as early as *Nashville Skyline* Dylan was giving us the kind of music we loved him in the sixties for being an alternative to. That's what he does on *Modern Times* — which as all Dylan fans know is a kind of joke, because the musical styles are not modern at all and the lyrics allude to or borrow from material that dates to long before Dylan was born. The most interesting thing about the album, though, is that Dylan's dominant voice is more old-time Midwest than anything he had done in a long time. The overall sound is perhaps not as flat and foggy as *Time Out of Mind*, but the language is rural Midwest: "ruckus," "twister," "for the love of God," "dawn of day," "sweating blood," "feel like laying down," "[I] seen the rising sun return," "a whoppin' good time" (do you believe that one?), "get up in the dawn," "when the deal goes down," "I'm gonna wring your neck," "the edge of the creek," "break your horns," "outta whack," "yella dog." "Gonna make a lotta money, gonna go up north" *sounds* like somebody who has been up North. The r's are back on this album, harder than ever before, especially in the first stanza of "When the Deal Goes Down." Sometimes Dylan revels in the vowel, as if embracing a long-lost friend. There's more [aɪ] for "i" and less "ah" than we've heard from Dylan in a long while. The long vowels of "Rollin' and Tumblin'" are north woods full: "I git up in the *dawn* and I *go* down and *lay* in the *shade*."

Listening to Dylan's personal voice on the *No Direction Home* interviews, taped in 2005, one is struck more than anything by how much Dylan's voice sounds like your father talking — your older, reflective, thoughtful Midwestern father. Perhaps this is Abe Zimmerman's voice — certainly, it is the voice of the hardware salesman in Hibbing True-Value. The vowels are long and sonorous: "playin' 'Mule Train' and 'Ghost Riders in the Sky,'" "be," "me." R's are all present and accounted for: "there," "furniture," "father," "for" (which occasionally slips out as "fur"), "Gorgeous George," "hard-core," "star," "hair," "heard." Dylan mixes "eye" and "ah" pronunciations of the pronoun "I." Like all of us he uses "outta" and "lotta," and "kinda," "er" for "or" and "a" for "of." He says "just" and he says "jist." He uses plenty of that reliable old Minnesota filler expression, "ya know." There's a little bit of "h" in "overwhelmed" and a couple other words. At one point, speaking in the past tense, he says, "that *come* across on the pop stations." He uses expressions familiar in this neck of the woods, like "what the gripe was all about" and "came outta Canada."

Most of all, one is struck by the Upper Midwest pitch and rhythm of his speech: low, sonorous, relatively even, often halting and suspended in mid-thought, and if not clipped, then terse. He does not overstate, and his vowels are not fluttery or ornamented with diphthongs. When the voice trails off, then picks up again, one cannot help remembering Howard Mohr's observation that the heartbeat of Minnesota conversation is the pause, and the Garrison Keillor remark quoted earlier: "people took a Lake Wobegon comma to mean the end of the story" (6).

Dylan is verbally adroit, but most commonly he uses a plain speech which reflects his plain thought. And for all the influences of pop culture, new age theory, Christian theology, and French surrealism, that thought is Midwest pragmatism based on a variety of simple down-home ideas. Similarly, a long journey of linguistic exploration brought Dylan finally to a speech not much different in its larger features and finer details than the voice he grew up with.

Chapter 3

Bob Dylan and the Pastoral Tradition

"I can see God in a daisy. I can see God at night in the wind and rain. I see creation just about everywhere. The highest form of song is prayer. King David's, Solomon's, the wailing of a coyote, the rumble of the Earth. It must be wonderful to be God. There's so much going on out there that you can't get to it all."

— *TV Guide*, September 11, 1976

AMERICAN PASTORALISM

"The pastoral ideal has been used to define the meaning of America ever since the age of discovery, and it has not yet lost its hold upon the native imagination," wrote Leo Marx in 1964, opening his classic analysis of the subject, *The Machine in the Garden: Technology and the Pastoral Ideal in America*.[1] Even if it becomes sometimes inchoate, isolationist, sentimental, nostalgic, essentially contradictory, and to all appearances irrelevant in the modern world, the ideal has persisted even as the percentage of the American labor force represented by farmers dropped from 60 percent in 1860 to 30.5 percent in 1910 to 2.3 percent in 1990 (Conlogue: 3). It underlies the high sixties' retreat from cities to Woodstock, to communes, and to country music; the seventies' exodus to the suburbs; the nineties' dream of "homesteading on a few acres"; and the present campaign for small-scale, sustainable agriculture, and a green earth.

Actually, the belief that life is better in the country — safer, healthier, simpler, lovelier, less stressful, more ethical and honest — antedates the discovery of America. Both Marx and Conlogue begin their studies of American pastoralism

105

with the Latin poet Virgil, a nod to the Judaic-Christian legend of a lost Eden, and describe a European and British tradition in which sophisticated but vaguely discontent city folks "retreat into a 'green world' to escape the pressures of complex urban life" (Conlogue: 6). Eighteenth century British poets like James Thomson and Alexander Pope firmly established that tradition in literature with their rich descriptions of the rural environment. Later poets Oliver Goldsmith ("The Deserted Village") and Thomas Gray ("Elegy in a Country Churchyard") added the trope of loss, setting the stage for William Wordsworth ("Lines Written a Few Miles Above Tintern Abbey"), William Blake (*Songs of Innocence*), and John Keats (who looms so large in Christopher Ricks's study of Dylan). Wordsworth especially was notorious for sentimentalizing honest country farmers and ruined abbeys, and for localizing British hopes for the future in the Lake District, far from London. With literary pastoralism came a visual pastoralism which produced the spectacular British and American landscapes displayed today in any major art museum, including Hudson River School painters like Thomas Cole and Albert Bierstadt. "In the record of Western culture there is nothing to compare with the vogue for landscape that arose in this period," Marx writes (88). Travelers on both sides of the Atlantic journeyed great distances just to gaze at inspiring vistas.

Monastic ruins were hard to come by in the colonies, but North America was loaded with sublime landscape. "Wilderness was the basic ingredient of American culture," writes Roderick Nash; "From the raw materials of the physical wilderness, Americans built a civilization" (xi). American pastoralists developed the social-political system of Jeffersonian agrarian democracy,[2] creating the strong, independent, self-sufficient American farmer celebrated by expat Jean de Crèvecoeur in his influential *Letters from an American Farmer*. Then, in the early nineteenth century emerged the first truly American literature, written by Romantics like Lowell, Whittier, Bryant, and Longfellow, and American Transcendentalists like Emerson and Thoreau — the poems and stories and essays which Dylan, like every American who attended school in the 1950s, read and discussed and memorized, until their words echoed and re-echoed in our minds, and their ideas became an ingrained mental frame of reference.

The American view of nature and human nature is partly literary, partly biblical, and partly philosophical. The components are intertwined. In the Judeo-Christian mind, the Garden of Eden linked godliness with nature, Noah showed that a man of God was also a friend to animals, and the Exodus story established the idea of finding spiritual renewal in the wilderness. Christianity associated virtue with a lost Edenic state, which it sought to recapture. When Protestant Christianity added a work component, life in the New Eden was no longer just party hearty in Cloud Cuckoo Land. Then Luther elevated secular work to a status equal to that of spiritual work when he gave following one's calling — "a task set by God" — status it had lacked in Catholic theology (Weber: 79), and suggested that "the fulfillment of worldly duties is under all circumstances the only way to live acceptable to God" (Weber: 81). Luther could not be a true capitalist, since he believed that the pursuit of material gain beyond personal needs suggested an absence of grace, but he did incorporate the idea of a work ethic into religious thought. Calvin pushed it further in this direction by equating election with serving one's calling — working hard for the sake of working hard, not so much to purchase salvation (which Calvin saw as impossible), as to allay fears of damnation (Weber: 115). Good works would not get you into heaven, but good works — and the rewards they brought — were an indication of election. "The connection," suggests Rev. Stephen Pichaske, "is probably Matthew 6: 33: 'But seek ye first the kingdom of God, and his righteousness; and all these things shall be added until you.'"[3] The work may be for the Kingdom, but it brings plenty of earthly rewards. One thing we notice about American pastoralism at least is that when work goes out of country living, pastoralism itself goes slack, and the Protestant Midwest is justifiably famous for its work ethic. In its cover story on "The Good Life in Minnesota," *Time* magazine (August 13, 1973) proclaimed that Minnesota was "a state that works." All of this is relevant to Bob Dylan. "One thing about that child I loved," said Sidsel Gleason, who hosted the Woody Guthrie gatherings Dylan attended upon arriving in New York City, "if there was snow to be shoveled, he shoveled; if there were dishes to wash, he washed dishes. Bobby didn't bum" (Scaduto: 64). "This one phrase was going through my head," Dylan told Jon Pareles of the *New York Times* regarding the songs of *Time Out of Mind*; "'Work while the day lasts, because the night of death cometh when no man can work'" (Cott: 394). "I've never stopped working," he told Mikal Gilmore proudly in 1986 (Cott: 341).

Moreover, as Leo Marx notes, the conversion experience, or calling, typically happens in the countryside — starting with John the Baptist, the Christian Moses, and Elijah, who preferred the wilderness to Jerusalem for his own ministry. American preacher Jonathan Edwards describes grace coming to him "as he walked alone in his father's pasture." More recently, Anglo Kevin Kline and Afro Danny Glover achieved a state of racial harmony at the end of Lawrence Kasdan's 1991 film *Grand Canyon*, breaking down the social barriers of L.A. in the very place Bob Dylan recommended in "Last Thoughts on Woody Guthrie" — the Grand Canyon at sundown.

The philosophical component of American pastoralism came mostly second-hand from French philosopher Jean-Jacques Rousseau. Rousseau differed from

Christian doctrine on how Eden was lost: for the writer of the book of Genesis, and subsequent Christian theologians, Adam and Eve lost Eden due to an inherent character deficiency called sin. There's nothing you can do about sin, but God (as Dylan came to believe) will forgive and forget and repair, and when that happens, we'll be back in a state of grace. To Rousseau, however, human nature is not inherently flawed. People in their natural state are inherently good. Nature and people are contaminated by the complexities of human history and elements of human society, including many things customarily considered beneficial: science, material comforts, the arts, and learning in general.[4] Get things back to their natural state, Rousseau suggests, and all will be well again. Rousseau, his followers, and pastoral writers including Dylan suspected cities, where social institutions overbalanced nature . . . where country boys, cut off from nature's support, turn to theft and alcohol, and country girls turn to prostitution. Rousseau is thus the opposite of Thomas Hobbes, who believed that the natural selfishness of people could be contained only by social interactions . . . and even Rousseau, as much as he idealized the freedom and spontaneity of life lived close to nature, in the last analysis advocated not a severing of all ties, but a movement away from society and in the general direction of nature.

The New World, which was short on social institutions and long on nature — and sought an excuse, as D. H. Lawrence argued in *Studies in Classic American Literature* (1923), a good excuse to cut its ties to the old parenthood of Europe — borrowed enthusiastically from Rousseau even while reading its Bible and listening to Calvinist preachers. The proto-evolutionist Comte du Buffon thought that people removed from the level of climate and food to which evolution had brought them would degenerate quickly: deprived of the civilization they knew in Europe, colonists would degenerate to rodents in a matter of one or two generations. No, no, Americans could argue, citing Rousseau: come to America, the "new Eden unspoiled by Old World history" (Carpenter: 4). Be a new Adam, reconnected to nature and to your inherent goodness; you will grow big and strong in our American landscape. Give your tired, your poor, your huddled masses a farm in Pennsylvania or 160 acres in South Dakota, and they will prosper. "Where is that station which can confer a more substantial system of felicity than that of an American farmer possessing freedom of action, freedom of thoughts, ruled by a mode of government which requires but little from us?" asked Jean de Crèvecoeur rhetorically (52). "If ever man was permitted to receive and enjoy some blessings that might alleviate the many sorrows to which he is exposed, it is certainly in the country, when he attentively considers those ravishing scenes with which he is everywhere surrounded" (62). Closing "Letter II from an American Farmer," he enthused,

I bless God for all the good he has given me; I envy no man's prosperity, and with no other portion of happiness than that I may live to teach the same philosophy to my children and give each of them a farm, show them how to cultivate it, and be like their father, good, substantial, independent American farmers — an appellation which will be the most fortunate one a man of my class can possess so long as our civil government continues to shed blessings on our husbandry. (65)[5]

Crèvecoeur, who combined a good Protestant work ethic and material gain with his appreciation and management of nature, provided an ideal model for later Americans, and in his classic essay on "The Frontier in American History," Frederick Jackson Turner was still attributing to the yeoman farmer all the American virtues:

coarseness and strength combined with acuteness and inquisitiveness; that practical, inventive turn of mind, quick to find expedients; that masterful grasp of material things, lacking in the artistic but powerful to effect great ends; that restless, nervous energy; that dominant individualism, working for good and evil, and withal that buoyancy and exuberance which comes with freedom. (37)

In the early nineteenth century, even as the nation's intellectuals moved off the plantation and into town, out of settlement mode and into arts-and-philosophy mode, the idea of nature retained its privileged status. For transcendentalists Emerson and Thoreau, nature was a more important source of inspiration than books, the countryside a richer experience than civilization. While life in town provided resources for training the mind, reason was inferior to the vision and inspiration offered by nature. "Standing on bare ground," Emerson wrote in his essay "Nature," his head "bathed by the blithe air, and uplifted into infinite space," he was poised for a post-Unitarian conversion experience: "all mean egotism vanishes. I become a transparent eye-ball; I am nothing; I see all; the currents of the Universal Being circulate through me; I am part or particle of God" (16). "Is it not likely," Sherwood Anderson mused in a letter to Waldo Frank, "that when the country was new and men were often alone in the fields and the forests, they got a sense of bigness outside themselves that has now in some way been lost?" (Crèvecoeur, Letters: 23).

While scholars who track American pastoralism debate finer points and broad interpretations, they agree that in the American consciousness, unspoiled nature was relocated gradually westward. New England and the South failed the pastoral vision early, since the soil was rocky in New England and thin in the South, and both quickly developed a materialistic society, art, and culture (including slavery in the South). Already in 1835 Alexis de Tocqueville was looking to the western side of the Appalachian Mountains: "The valley of the Mississippi is, on the whole, the most magnificent dwelling-place prepared by God for man's abode," he wrote in the first chapter of *Democracy in America* . . . and so it was, until a series of locks and dams designed to facilitate barge traffic slowed the water, clogged the shallows, and necessitated the constant dredging which still does not prevent flooding every five or ten years. So the West became paradise regained (did not Dylan trade the Huck Finn cap of his younger years for the cowboy hat of his later years?), until America ran out of frontier and thus of unspoiled nature, and — in the immortal words of Frederick Jackson Turner, thus "closed the first period of American history" (38). Wallace Stegner notes that "the distinct downturn in our literature from hope to bitterness took place almost at the precise time when the frontier officially came to an end, in 1890, and when the American way of life had begun to turn strongly urban and industrial" ("Wilderness Letter": 150).

In one sense the American frontier — and with it unexplored American wilderness — backwashed in the late nineteenth century, from the California coast to the still sparsely populated Upper Midwest . . . Bob Dylan's back yard. A Conoco roadmap as recent as 1953 (the time of Dylan's youth in Minnesota) shows not one continuously paved north–south highway traversing North or South Dakota, and only U.S. 2 in North Dakota and U.S. 14 in South Dakota paved all the way east–west. In Dylan's neck of the woods, the U.S. highway 53 miles north of Virginia was still gravel, although it was paved Virginia to Duluth. Even today, when the U.S. highways are paved and interstates transverse the Dakotas north–south and east–west, one mile off the interstate the emptiness is emptier than ever. So the Upper Midwest inherited by default the virtues of the American West. James Shortridge argues that not until the West failed as a home to American pastoralism did the Midwest emerge as a conceptual unit, at which point "the two concepts — pastoralism and the Middle West — which initially were similar in several respects, rapidly intertwined and soon became virtually synonymous" (28).[6]

Pastoralism fills American literature, most of it familiar to American students of Dylan's generation. Henry Thoreau was a role model for millions in his retreat (with a few books and occasional visitors) to Walden Pond, there to live simply and confront only "the basics of life" so that he would not, when it came time to die, discover that he had not lived. *The Adventures of Huckleberry Finn*, which Hemingway claimed was the wellspring of all modern American literature, recounts Huck and Jim's escape from civilization, renewal on the Mississippi, and return to the village, ending with Huck seeking further renewal in what was then the frontier: "I rekon I got to light out for the Territory ahead of the rest, because Aunt Sally she's going to adopt me and sivilize me and I can't stand it. I been there before" (229). In Chapter 2 of Henry James's *The American* (the title is significant), Christopher Newman (the name is significant), recalls a moment of lighting out from New York City in a hack that was "greasy . . . as if it had been used for a great many Irish funerals" (the simile is significant):

> We pulled up in front of the place I was going to in Wall Street, but I sat still in the carriage, and at last the driver scrambled down off his seat to see whether his carriage had not turned into a hearse. I couldn't have got out, any more than if I had been a corpse. What was the matter with me? Momentary idiocy, you'll say. What I wanted to get out of was Wall Street. I told the man to drive down to the Brooklyn ferry and to cross over. When we were over, I told him to drive me out into the country. As I had told him originally to drive for dear life down town, I suppose he thought me insane. Perhaps I was, but in that case I am insane still. I spent the morning looking at the first green leaves on Long Island. I was sick of business; I wanted to throw it all up and break off short; I had money enough, or if I hadn't I ought to have. I seemed to feel a new man inside my old skin, and I longed for a new world.[7]

In Chapter 22 of Upton Sinclair's novel of urban injustice, *The Jungle* (1906), Lithuanian immigrant Jurgis, an American Everyman nearly destroyed by long hours in the Chicago stockyards, abandons his wife and the city for an all-too-brief rebirth in nature. Work on a farm (20 cents and supper, sleep in the barn) and "the perfume of fresh fields, of honeysuckle and clover" restore his health and

> all his lost youthful vigor, his joy and power that he had mourned and forgotten. . . . What with plenty to eat and fresh air and exercise that was taken as it pleased him, he would waken from his sleep and start off not knowing what to do with his energy. (215)

Too bad Jurgis later returns to the city, and to calamity after calamity! Willa Cather's signature novels *O Pioneers!* (1913) and *My Ántonia* (1918) both contrast strong women who stayed close to nature to be healthy with weaker males who went for the big bucks in the big city, only to return to the farm for restoration. In *O Pioneers!* Carl sums up life in the city this way:

> When one of us dies, they scarcely know where to bury him. Our landlady and the delicatessen man are our mourners [Gatsby's experience exactly], and we leave

nothing behind us but a frock-coat and a fiddle, or an easel, or a typewriter, or whatever tool we got our lives by. . . . We have no house, no place, no people of our own. We live in the streets, in the parks, in the theatres. We sit in restaurants and concert halls and look about at the hundreds of our own kind and shudder. (123)

Contrast that with the vision of perpetual renewal in nature which closes the novel: "Fortunate country, that is one day to receive hearts like Alexandra's into its bosom, to give them out again in the yellow wheat, in the rustling corn, in the shining eyes of youth!" (309).

Restoration in wilderness remains the dream of East Coast characters in East Coast stories of the mid-twentieth century, like Holden Caulfield in J. D. Salinger's *The Catcher in the Rye* (set in New York City), who dreams of escaping urban phoniness by hitchhiking out West; and Biff Loman in Arthur Miller's *Death of a Salesman* (also set in New York City); and Sal Paradise in Jack Kerouac's *On the Road* (which uses New York City as a point of departure). Restoration in nature (plus a little sex, cards, and sports) is the main point of Ken Kesey's West Coast *One Flew Over the Cuckoo's Nest*, and Michigan novelist Jim Harrison (*Legends of the Fall*) has repeatedly found his renewal in nature, especially in water and rivers: "If you're willing to say try it sometime, sit down on a stone or a cushion or just on the bank of a river for two solid hours. And you find, if you're willing to give up everything, or open up a bit, the river does absorb rather nonchalantly your poisons" (DeMott: 180). Pastoralism can be postmodern.

The pastoral theme sounds clearly in the music beloved by the Woodstock generation, beginning with the folk revival of the late fifties–early sixties, when even the Greenwich Village leftists used old folk songs, as Greil Marcus says, to pitch "a scale of values that placed, say, the country over the city, labor over capital, sincerity over education, the unspoiled nobility of the common man and woman over the businessman and the politician, or the natural expressiveness of the folk over the self-interest of the artist" and also "a yearning for peace and home in the midst of noise and upheaval" (*Invisible Republic*: 21). Marcus quotes Robert Shelton to the effect that

What the folk revivalists were saying, in effect, was: "There's another way out of the dilemma of modern urban society that will teach us all about who we are. There are beautiful, simple, relatively uncomplicated people living in the country close to the soil, who have their own identities, their own backgrounds. They know who they are, and they know what their culture is because they make it themselves." (*Invisible Republic*: 20).[8]

That pastoral tradition continued in popular music long after the civil rights component disappeared, from Joni Mitchell's "Woodstock" ("We got to get ourselves back to the garden") to Canned Heat's version of the old blues song "Goin' Up the Country" to the songs of John Denver (who, incidentally, married a girl from St. Peter, Minnesota): "Take Me Home, Country Roads," "Rocky Mountain High," "Thank God I'm a Country Boy," and "Wild Montana Skies": "Give him a fire in his heart, give him a light in his eyes, give him the wild wind for a brother and the wild Montana skies." It is curious but true that pastoralism should appeal to a generation of people who had not, like Bob Dylan, had the inestimable benefit of a youth "spent wildly among the snowy hills and sky blue lakes, willow fields and abandoned open pit mines" (Dylan in a letter to the Emergency Civil Liberties Committee, responding to their reaction to his speech in 1963 [Engel: 95]). The attraction of the countryside became even stronger at the far end of the sixties, after the Grant Park Riots, the shootings at Kent State, and the violent Rolling Stones concert at Altamont. As America began to unravel, people tuned out to politics and tuned in to Garrison Keillor's *A Prairie Home Companion* . . . and the rebirth of country music that Dylan's *John Wesley Harding* helped spawn.[9]

DYLAN ON NATURE

American pastoralism begins, as we have seen, with the plentitude of landscape — with the fact of the land itself. Landscape is especially prominent in the Midwest and on the Great Plains, where the view is not confined by mountains. The Midwest landscape may not be mountain majesty, but it is damned near overwhelming. "The great fact was the land itself," writes Willa Cather (*O Pioneers!*: 15), and again, "There was nothing but land: not a country at all, but the material out of which countries are made" (*My Ántonia*: 8). Here is Jean Ervin introducing an anthology of Minnesota writers:

> In their writing Minnesotans seem to be more aware of the land and climate than writers from the East. . . . One does not have to look far to find geography and weather woven into a short story or novel either metaphorically or explicitly. The violence of winter blizzards and summer thunderstorms, the vastness of the prairies, the importance of the lakes and rivers and of the ever-present wilderness in the north — all inform the literature of Minnesota. (9)

Although her anthology does not even include Bob Dylan, she could not more accurately have described his work.

In fact, the most striking feature of nearly half a century of Dylan's songs is simply the many references to nature, especially to weather. In Chapter 3 of *Invisible Republic*, Greil Marcus makes a big deal out of Dylan's focus on weather in *The Basement Tapes*, with all its various metaphysical expansions, but it's not just *The Basement Tapes*: early, middle, and late, in songs and poems and writings like *Chronicles*, there is plenty of wind, rain, snow, river, creek, mountain, meadow, day, night . . . all the components of an overwhelming Midwestern American landscape. Not without cause was Dylan's first Theme Time Radio Hour show devoted to the subject of weather (opening with a song about wind, of course).

Familiar Dylan lines echo and re-echo in our ears: "I'm a-goin' back out 'fore the rain starts a-fallin'"; "you'll be drenched to the bone"; "You don't need a weatherman / To know which way the wind blows"; "I couldn't see when it started snowin'"; "Two riders were approaching, the wind began to howl"; "I pity the poor immigrant / Who tramples through the mud"; "I long to see you in the morning light"; "under that apple suckling tree, oh yeah!"; "May you have a strong foundation / When the winds of changes shift"; "'Come in,' she said, / 'I'll give you shelter from the storm'"; "Idiot wind, blowing through the flowers on your tomb"; "she was there in the meadow where the creek used to rise"; "There's a wicked wind still blowin' on that upper deck"; "I can see the Master's hand / In every leaf that trembles, in every grain of sand"; "When the storm clouds gather 'round you / And heavy rains descend"; "There's smoke on the water, it's been there since June / Tree trunks uprooted, there's blood on the moon"; "Well my heart's in the Highlands with the horses and hounds"; "The fog is so thick you can't spy the land"; "Thunder on the Mountain," "Spirit on the Water" . . . "if it keep on rainin' the levee's gonna break."

The marvels of modern technology — namely the lyrics available online at bobdylan.com and an electronic version of *Chronicles* — let us run hard-nosed, almost scientific searches to substantiate general impressions. How many hits on "rain" do we come up with in "Search the Lyrics"? 102 . . . but many of those are "brain" and "train." The count for "rain," as in non-frozen precipitation, is 49. The word "thunder" appears in 14 songs. The word for frozen precipitation — "snow" — appears in 15 songs, with "ice" (including ice water, but not, of course, the "ice" in "nice" or "twice") showing up four times; "frost" three times; "hail" six times; "freeze" six times; and "sleet" twice. "Wind" (including "whirlwind" but not "window") appears in 58 Dylan songs. In one song Dylan uses the word "cyclone," and in another "twister." Dylan uses "winter" in 13 songs, "spring" in 12, "autumn" and "fall" in a total of six, and "summer" in 17. The word "water" appears in 55 Dylan songs, "waterfall" in two, "river" in 43, "creek" in four, "stream" in 13, "brook" in two, and "lake" in nine. The word "tree" appears in 31 Dylan songs, and "leaf/leaves" in 12. The word "flower" appears in 25 songs (including "wallflower" and "wildflower"). Variations of "hill" (including "hilltop" and "hillside") show up in 31 Dylan lyrics, "mountain" in 24, "island" in three, "wood(s)" in nine ("forest" in two, "grove" in one), "meadow" in six, "grass" in ten, "sky" in 37, "earth" in 21, "pond" in three, "flood" in eight, "desert" in five, "garden" in six, and "cloud" in 25 songs. "Sand" is mentioned in 17 songs and "beach" in four. The word "mud/muddy" shows up in 16 Dylan lyrics; "dirt" appears in eight (with plenty of "dirty" elsewhere), and "dust" in 18. "Storms," from tropical to snowstorms, rage in 17 Dylan lyrics. "I like storms," Dylan told Jon Pareles of the *New York Times* in 1997; "I like to stay up during a storm. I get very meditative" (Cott: 394). Shelton says that Dylan's favorite metaphor is the tempest (*Home*: 220).

Dylan's songs to date are home to 30 dogs, 28 horses (and six ponies), 25 birds, 13 cats, 11 cows, six fish, six rabbits, six snakes, four frogs, four wolves, three ducks, three hogs, three trout, two bulls, two wildcats, two orchids, one wild rose, one briar, one robin, one bluebird, one locust, one groundhog, one donkey, one skunk, one weasel, one reindeer, one coyote, one turkey, one drake, one meadowlark, a herd of moose, a hound dog howling, a bullfrog croaking, and all together in one splendid song, a bear, a cow, a bull, a pig, a sheep, and a snake.

In *Chronicles*, a mature Dylan looks back over his career, recounting episodes and visions from his early years. Its 88,000 words contain a wealth of Midwestern idioms and vocabulary preferences, as well as plenty of weather, from the snowstorm that greets Dylan upon his arrival in New York City to the "shit storm" that undoes the pastoral idyll of the Village's folk revival in the book's closing paragraph. In that book Dylan mentions "snow" 27 times (not counting Hank Snow and Snow White); "rain" 12 times (not counting Ma Rainy or "Singin' in the Rain"); "storm" ten times (including "lightning storm," "thunderstorm," and the aforementioned "shit storm," but discounting the song "Stormy Weather"); and "wind" 26 times. He uses the word "cloud" ten times, "leaf/leaves" ten times, and "tree" 26 times (including oak trees, elms, and banana trees). He uses the word "earth" 14 times, "mountain" 11 times, "river" 13 times (not including "Joan Rivers"), "wood(s)" nine times (not including Woody Guthrie or Woody Allen, but counting "my neck of the woods" and "woodpecker"). Other word scores: "bird," four; "mud," six (excluding "Muddy Waters"); "frost," six (excluding "Robert Frost"); "creek," one; "stream," two; "lake" nine; "water," 11 (excluding Barry Goldwater); "grass," five; "mountain," 11; "island," six; "sky," eight; "beach," four; "fish," 20 (including catfish, sucker fish, and "the ultimate fish story"); "sleet," two; "freeze," three; "winter," 12; "spring," 15; "summer," 17; "autumn," three. He mentions "thunder" four times and "lightning" (including "heat lightning") seven times. Dylan's river, mountain, island, and lake references are sometimes specific, as in Mississippi River, Sierra Madre Mountains, Coney Island, and Lake Superior, and he mentions specifically volcanoes, tidal waves, earthquakes, dogs of several varieties (including underdogs and hot dogs), jackrabbits, mountain laurel, marshlands, water lilies, and wetlands.

And these are not just passing word usages. Dylan's similes and metaphors are often drawn from nature: "like a great tree had fallen" (96), "didn't come gently to the shore" (34), "like a sea of frost" (35), "roared in like a storm" (44), "my haystacks weren't tied down and I feared the wind" (149), "left on the floor like shot rabbits" (182). Then there is that line that echoes and re-echoes through Dylan's songs and now his prose: "a thousand miles from [my] home," empty, unspecific miles but rich with a sense of the vast, overwhelming American amplitudes. And *Chronicles* is full of extended passages describing the weather:

> Outside the wind was blowing, straggling cloud wisps, snow whirling in the red lanterned streets, city types scuffling around, bundled up — salesmen in rabbit fur earmuffs hawking gimmicks, chestnut vendors, steam rising out of manholes. (4)

> It was noontime and I was shuffling around in my old-fashion garden. Cutting across the vacant lot to a bank of field flowers where my dogs and horses were, the strangled cry of a gull came whipping through the wind. Walking back to the main house, I caught a glimpse of the sea through the leafy boughs of the pines. I wasn't near it, but could feel the power beneath its colors. (162)

> Wind whipped in the open doorway and another kicking storm was rumbling earthward. There was a hurricane a hundred miles away. The light had gone out of the day. In the trees, a solitary bird warbling. (217)

The simplest explanation for all the nature and weather is that Dylan came from the North Country, where snowflakes fall, the winds hit heavy on the borderline, and changes in the weather are known to be extreme. Minnesotans pay attention to weather because they're so much out in it. What Bob Dylan did in his Tom Sawyer youth, he recalls in *Chronicles*, was "march in parades, have bike races, play ice hockey, . . . swimming holes and fishing ponds, sledding and something called bumper riding, where you grab hold of a tail bumper on a car and ride through the snow" (232). When Dylan sings, "I can feel it in the wind" ("Something's Burning, Baby"), he acknowledges his roots in the North Country, where you can indeed anticipate a change in weather by a change in the wind, by the smell and the tempo and the direction, and the sound. Grow up in the Midwest and learn about different kinds of wind. And weather. Minnesotans recognize "a blizzard sky"; naturalist Paul Gruchow talks of guestimating the winter temperature by the sound of snow beneath a boot heel (*Journal*: 4). As Howard Mohr says in *How to Talk Minnesotan*, "If you can't carry on a conversation about the weather in Minnesota, you might as well pack your bags and head back to where you came from" (25). Not everyone appreciates wind and rain the way Dylan does. Bob Spitz quotes Dave Van Ronk's reaction to "Blowin' in the Wind" as "Jesus, Bobby — what an incredibly dumb song! I mean, what the hell is 'blowing in the wind?'" (193). Well, whatever. Van Ronk was from Brooklyn. He was not North Dakota-Minnesota-Midwest; he didn't speak or think that way. Dylan did when he wrote "Blowin' in the Wind," and he still did when he wrote "Thunder on the Mountain." Tor Egil Førland writes, "the picture that fastened in [Dylan's] brain, developed by rural propaganda, was the agrarian myth" (348), but it's a Midwestern version of the agrarian myth.

Nature carries value in Dylan's thought, as it does in the thinking of most Midwesterners, and that value varies. It's "what a glorious day" one morning, and "fuck this snow, we're moving to Arizona" the next. Usually, Dylan finds nature, whether sunny or stormy, to be a source of sanity, restoration, escape, grace . . . and the right kind of girl, what Andy Gill calls "the unpretentious, undemanding earth-mother type" (86). Nature is an antidote to insanity, decay, confinement, corruption, and the wrong kind of girl. "Time and again in *Love and Theft*," writes Andy Muir, "it seems that 'majesty and heroism', if it is to be found anywhere, is to be found in or of country roots. . . . The agrarian world is depicted as the authentic alternative to all that has 'gone wrong'" (*Troubadour*: 277, 278). But not always: nature can be indifferent bordering on cruel, a cause of decay and death, something you escape from rather than to. Dylan is both a romantic and a realist. He's a little like the weather: you never really know quite what you're going to get.

The relatively simple trope of nature as redemption crops up in several Dylan songs, especially those written early in his career. In "Lay Down Your Weary Tune," the morning breeze blowing like a bugle, the wild ocean playing like an organ, the waves crashing like cymbals, the skies and clouds unbound by laws, the rain like a trumpet, the tree branches playing like a banjo, the river running like a hymn and humming like a harp all signal Dylan's departure from the confines of the folk revival and into the freedom of just being himself. It's a better music and a better deal, Dylan says, this natural song that no human voice could match, and it absorbs all your hassles. Dylan sounds a bit like Jim Harrison here, with the water absorbing his weariness and troubles. "Lay Down Your Weary Tune" also recalls a point made by Page Smith about Midwest small-town literature: "In every recollection of the town we find the symbol of water. In its classic form it is the old swimming hole or the broad Mississippi of Tom Sawyer or Huck Finn. It is the symbol for freedom and also for mystery and perhaps for something deeper" (219). Stephen Scobie argues that, in this song, Dylan's lines unite images of natural phenomena with cultural artifacts (usually musical) to create "a grand vision of transcendence in both man and nature" (*Alias*: 129). Possibly this is a vision of nature absorbed *into* music, but Scobie also reminds us that Dylan's invitation in this song is to "lay down your weary tune": forget the song and the abstracted, interiorized landscape, and go with the natural world.

As early as November 1964, Dylan had told a reporter for the *Kenyon Collegian*, "Man, if I went here [to Kenyon College] I'd be out in the woods all day gettin' drunk. Get me a chick . . . settle down, raise some kids" (Cott: 30). That early date suggests that in part of his brain Dylan held this pastoral vision, even as he was in the process of escaping the Upper Midwest for New York City. While it is Dylan's songs of the post-1967 country music period which best celebrate the pleasures of life close to benevolent nature, the cover of *John Wesley Harding* suggests America of the frontier/settlement period, and the songs themselves reflect Dylan's personal experience in Woodstock, New York, which began long before 1967, in the days "when Woodstock was a refuge, not yet a zoo or a 'nation'" (Shelton, *Home*: 262). "Bob was never more at peace with himself than that first summer in Woodstock," Peter Yarrow told Robert Shelton; "When Bobby and Suze went back to the Village, they were down. When they returned to Woodstock, their spirits inevitably rose" (163). Some reports suggest that Dylan at Woodstock in the 1966–69 years was so laid-back he was almost boring to be around. Tim Riley calls *The Basement Tapes*, recorded later in this period, "a classic statement of rural virtues" (157), with Dylan getting all kinds of practical, honest advice from all kinds of practical, honest, direct, quirky western types in songs like "Open the Door, Homer," "Tears of Rage," and "Too Much of Nothing." The songs of Dylan's country period sound a bit simple (and therefore uninteresting, if not unconvincing), but the message is clear: the big fat moon is gonna shine like a spoon, and we're gonna let it, you won't regret it. "Can't you feel that sun a-shinin'?" Dylan sings to open "New Morning"; the ground hog is running by the country stream, the sky is blue, and this is the day all dreams come true. "Sign on the Window" celebrates expectations and pleasures as simple as its language:

Build me a cabin in Utah
Marry me a wife, catch rainbow trout
Have a bunch of kids who call me "Pa"
That must be what it's all about

After a period of uncertainty and reassessment in the eighties and the nineties regarding both Christianity and pastoralism, Dylan appears to have recovered in later songs the sense of salvation in nature that he formerly felt, as well as a preference for what Mikal Gilmore calls the "country-gentleman finery he has tended to favor in recent years" (Cott: 411). In "When the Deal Goes Down," wisdom grows up in strife with the world as it is, and Dylan's bewildered brain toils in vain as it always has. Amid the deafening noise, disappointment, and pain, however, he feels occasional joy which is again expressed in images from nature: moonlight, flowers (including a rose), a winding stream. In a mostly unsuccessful search for "Dignity" in a song of that title, Dylan suggests, with a possible reference to Walt Whitman or Carl Sandburg,[10] that a wise man might consider "lookin' in a blade of grass." "Beyond the Horizon" also looks long-range, beyond death, past countries and kingdoms and temples of stone, to the end of the game and the soft light of morning beneath crimson skies, to what can only be described as salvation. At the end of the rainbow, Dylan tells us, life has only begun, and beyond the horizon the sky is so blue that it affords more than a lifetime of life loving the right kind of country girl.

The idea of nature as renewal reappears in other late songs like "Where Teardrops Fall," in which, "far away from the stormy night" and "rivers of blindness," Dylan discovers a place "where soft winds blow" and the shadows of moonlight offer "a new place to start" . . . and a new love to go along with it. In the first two songs of *Modern Times*, "Spirit on the Water" answers and redeems "Thunder on the Mountain" (with its angry twister bearing down on all of us). "Thunder on the Mountain" closes with Dylan headed up north to plant and harvest what the earth brings forth — a pastoral idyll which recalls his *New Morning* days. Other examples of redemptive nature are easy to find in *Modern Times*, including the dawn of day in "Spirit on the Water," and the greenwood glen of "Rollin' and Tumblin'." "In nature there's a remedy for everything," Dylan writes in *Chronicles*, "and that's where I'd usually go hunting for it. I'd find myself on a houseboat, a floating mobile home, hoping to hear a voice — crawling at slow speed — nosed up on a protective beach at night in the wilderness — moose, bear, deer around — the elusive timber wolf not so far off" (147).

Nature may also be an escape from a bad relationship, which is definitely a form of salvation. In "Don't Think Twice, It's All Right," the rooster crowing at dawn signals Dylan departed from a relationship that was just a waste of time (in that respect, this song anticipates "It's All Over Now, Baby Blue"). Nature as escape appears early in "Don't Think Twice" and in later songs like "Summer Days," where Dylan promises to leave in the morning, as soon as the clouds lift. His departure here is less gracious than his morning departure in "Don't Think Twice": in this song he's going to "break the roof in — set fire to the place as a parting gift." But he's gonna get out anyway.

Receiving an honorary doctorate from Princeton University is not exactly a bad relationship, or even an uncomfortable situation, for someone to whom schools have always represented 20 years of ideology before a lifetime working the day shift, the whole deal is uncomfortable. The Black Hills of South Dakota form the perfect polar opposite to modern American academia: spiritual and organic as opposed to intellectual and theoretical. (Like fellow Minnesotan F. Scott Fitzgerald in *This Side of Paradise* and *The Great Gatsby*, Dylan is not kind to the Ivy League.) Dylan had skipped the black-tie dinner the night before commencement and looked "noticeably ill at ease" according to Princeton President Robert Goheen, slightly weeded up according to David Crosby (Sounes: 259). The Black Hills, one of the most unpretentious vacation spots in the nation and a weekend get-away for many Upper Midwesterners even today, are a studied choice in this song. Nature acts as an escape in Dylan's description of the event (June 9, 1970), in a song with a title borrowed from Nathanael West's 1939 catalog of shallow American stereotypes, *The Day of the Locust*:

I put down my robe, picked up my diploma
Took hold of my sweetheart and away we did drive
Straight for the hills, the black hills of Dakota
Sure was glad to get out of there alive[11]

So nature is an escape, and nature is renewal. In many songs, Dylan attaches a specifically religious significance to the renewal he finds in nature, which is well within the American pastoral tradition. Even before his conversion to Christianity, Dylan tended to see nature within a biblical context. As early as "11 Outlined Epitaphs," Dylan had suggested that what is natural reflects the Master's hand, and what disturbs the balance of nature also disturbs a moral and ethical equilibrium:[12]

"I am raginly against absolutely
everything that wants t force nature
t be unnatural (be it human or otherwise)

an I am violently for absolutely
everything that will fight those
forces (be them human or otherwise)"

In this poem, Dylan moves from nature to the Boston Tea Party to the Ku Klux Klan to the "brainwashed dream" he was sold at Hibbing High School, but his argument is a religious version of Rousseau: God made the world the way He wants it to be, and what corrupts nature corrupts God. We need to stop corrupting, recover what we can, restore the rest. Dylan reasserts the proposition in "Father of Night," linking God the Father to (scanning the song's lines) day, dark, bird, rainbow, rain, night, mountain, cloud, rivers, streams, grain, wheat, cold, heat, air, and trees . . . not, be it noted, to skyscrapers, bars, supper clubs, condos, taxicabs, subways, power plants, telephone lines, tractors, trains, or paved roads.

There's more religion in other Dylan nature. Stephen Scobie suggests that the lowlands of "Sad-Eyed Lady of the Lowlands" owe something to Jeremiah 51.42-3: "The sea is come up upon Babylon . . . Her cities are a desolation, a dry land, and a wilderness, a land wherein no man dwelleth" (145).

As Dylan moves into his Christian period, of course the biblical context increasingly colors his view of nature, and the identification of nature with God the Creator and with Salvation becomes even stronger. In "Every Grain of Sand," every leaf that trembles, every grain of sand, every sparrow falling (this reference at least is New Testament — Matthew 10.29), even the sun that beats down all serve to remind us of the Judgment to come, and thus of our need for confession and repentance for "the flowers of indulgence and the weeds of yesteryear." Dylan plays with metaphors of light and dark (= illumination and ignorance = Christian faith and all else) in a manner that recalls the us/them, good guys/bad guys dichotomies of "When the Ship Comes In." Theology (and larger implications) aside, the sun in "Precious Angel" is the wisdom of Christian faith, as the rock of "Solid Rock" is the wisdom of Christian doctrine: "I'm hangin' on to a solid rock / Made before the foundation of the world." "Covenant Woman" shines like a morning star; the garden of "In the Garden" is the Garden of Gethsemane. In "Death Is Not the End," the storm clouds and heavy rains are the perils and temptations which afflict Pilgrim Christian in the Slough of Despond, and the cities on fire with the burning flesh of men are Vanity Fair, and the tree is the Tree of Life, and the bright light is the bright light of salvation. In a later song like "Something's Burning, Baby," Dylan is less dogmatic — this is another one of his love-gone-wrong songs — but the religious overtones are still there: the edge of the road "where the pasture begins" is identified, by rhyme and proximity, as the place "where charity is supposed to cover up a multitude of sins."

Like Bunyan in *Pilgrim's Progress*, Dylan likes to contrast the countryside with the city. There is a biblical context here of course — come the apocalypse, Dylan reminds us in "Death Is Not the End," we'll see burning cities as well as the Tree of Life — but Dylan operates within a typically Midwestern pattern in which "in story after story, the hero or heroine despises the town and loves the land" (Sanders: 32). This is not to say that the countryside is always sunny skies over woods and meadows, but where nature has plusses and minuses, the city is always a modern Babylon: a City of Destruction right out of *Pilgrim's Progress*. "Modern Gomorrah," Dylan called it in *Chronicles* (9). Following Rousseau, American pastoralism has always been fundamentally antiurban: "Though urban life is obviously superior in wealth and formalized knowledge, the country has its own special values. Pastoral plays the two against each other," writes John Lynan (10). "I don't like the city," Dylan sang recently in "Can't Escape from You"; "not like some folks do." Like most Midwesterners, Dylan usually ignores Big Windy and the Motor City, locating his evil cities mostly east or south, and his country mostly midwest or west. In Dylan's earliest songs, "western skies" act as a counter-symbol to New York City, and even the dust of the Oklahoma Plains and the dirt of the Rocky Mountain mines are "all much cleaner than the New York kind." In "Talkin' New York," Dylan is making a little joke when the western skies turn out to be East Orange, New Jersey, but he's not joking about the trope: the West = nature = good. Similarly, in "Let Me Die in My Footsteps," he is serious in contrasting "mountain streams," "the smell of wildflowers," and "meadows with green grassy leaves" with the subterranean fallout shelter in which the song opens. This fallout shelter is not the New York City subterranean homesick hideaway in Ralph Ellison's *Invisible Man*, but the song's final stanza implies that the shelter is an eastern city, to be contrasted with the western country: "Go out in your country where the land meets the sun / See the craters and the canyons where the waterfalls run." If you're going to die anyway, go down free and in your footsteps, in Nevada, New Mexico, Arizona, and Idaho — not in some city out East.

That New York–countryside contrast reappears, reversed, in "Last Thoughts on Woody Guthrie," where Dylan recognizes lightning, thunder, and "hours of storm," but finds hope and restoration finally in nature — not on "Macy's window sill" or "cardboard-box house," but in nature.[13]

In later songs like "Mississippi," Dylan describes the city as "just a jungle, more games to play," adding, significantly, "I was raised in the country, I been workin' in the town / I been in trouble ever since I set my suitcase down." Other songs on *Love and Theft*, like "Po' Boy" and "Honest with Me," also play the trope of a country boy lost in the city, coming full circle to his early compositions where it was hard times for the country boy living in New York town.

Dylan's antiurban bias is especially strong in songs of his middle sixties rock period: songs like "Subterranean Homesick Blues" (with the man in the trench coat, his badge out, looking for a pay-off), "Desolation Row" ("a purgatory that seems to have no escape," and "a direct reference to *The Wasteland*" — Carpenter: 31), and "Stuck Inside of Mobile with the Memphis Blues Again." Mobile is peopled with whacked-out characters literary and imaginary: Shakespeare in the alley hitting on a French girl, Mona warning Dylan against railroad trains, Grandpa building a fire on Main Street and blasting away with his revolver, some undoubtedly corrupt senator promoting his son's wedding, Ruthie the stripper hitting on Dylan ("your debutante just knows what you need / But I know what you want"), and various "neon madmen" swarming all over Grand Street. It's an insane world made more depressing, despite the up-tempo melody, by the remembered musical legacy of Memphis, Tennessee: "can this really be the end?" *Blonde on Blonde*, Andy Gill writes, evokes a "dark urban netherworld that reflected the New York demi-monde of Warhol Factory 'stars', dodgy drugs and late-night clubs into which Dylan had recently been sucked" (Blake: 102).

"Dirge" paints another portrait of the American urban landscape, this time New York in the mid-seventies. For Dylan, the city in this song is a bad relationship born of a moment of weakness: a bad situation (the song hints at a one-night stand) on Lower Broadway with some city girl all pepped up about progress and the Doom Machine. In "No Time to Think," the Federal City is one decoy after another: notoriety, high society, memory, mortality, reality, alcohol, duality, mortality, and all the –isms: socialism, hypnotism, patriotism, materialism. In the Federal City, Dylan tells us, you're attracted to the Empress called "Suckcess," but you're distracted by oppression and you just end up feeling violent and strange. Even the virtues — equality, liberty, humility, simplicity, loyalty, unity — become fuzzed by distraction when, in the middle of the chaos of The City of Man, there's no time to think. Such, he suggests, is the plight of most people in the late twentieth century: like the busy passersby down on the concrete of Tenth Avenue in "Three Angels," they are locked in their own little worlds, and miss the angels and the message they bring.

"The Groom's Still Waiting at the Altar" is yet another Bosch-like urban horror show: the massacre of the innocent, cities on fire, phones out of order, nuns and soldiers dying, fighting at the border. Goodness is persecuted, or misrepresented as evil. "Someone's Got a Hold of My Heart" mentions "a city of flaming red skies" which it later identifies as Babylon. While these songs offer hope of some curtain rising on a new age, that new age will not be found in any city. Nor can Dylan's assessment of the city be dismissed as an older man looking back on the wild excesses of a hip young kid, because these were things Dylan had said about the city when he was a hip sixties kid.

Dylan's pastoralism causes him to associate good women with benevolent nature, and bad women with the city. "Dylan attempts to seek shelter from the storm of shallow city life through women who have stayed outside of the culture he so clearly abhors," write Kevin Krein and Abigail Levin (54);

> Just as a certain kind of woman seems to exemplify Dylan's discontent at a larger social pattern of consumption, so also a certain kind of woman harkens toward a possible resolution of this angst and transcendence of that system. The kind of woman Dylan praises . . . suggests a resolution to the crisis of vacuous consumer culture in images of a pre-industrial, pastoral archetype. (58)

This association of good girl with country life is not unusual in American thought, and may have religious origins. In his study of the American pastoral, Mark Peter Buechsel notes, "The conflation of the Virgin, Woman, Midwestern nature, and sacramentalism in opposition to an ideological cluster centered around the Dynamo (mechanical culture), abstraction, industrialism, literalism, and the New England tradition can be traced in any number of Midwestern works" (21). Dylan is in this regard a typical Midwestern pastoralist.

Examples of good girls connected to nature come from all points of Dylan's career. These good girls include — but as the lawyers like to say "are not limited to" — the Girl of the North Country, with her Minnesota winds and snowflakes; the unnamed girl, also probably of the North Country, in "Tomorrow Is a Long Time," with her beauty beyond the beauty of silver, singing rivers and the sunrise in the sky; the girl from the "Red River Shore," who offered him the sound advice to "go home and lead a quiet life," was the only one to really see Dylan, and is probably also the Girl of the North Country if Dylan means the Red River of the North; the proletarian Ramona, with her watery eyes and cracked country lips (a contrast to the deathlike flowers of the city); Suze Rotollo in "Ballad in Plain D," whom Dylan, in the summer of their love, likened to an innocent lamb and a gentle fawn; the girlfriend who's been troubling Dylan's thoughts in "Mama, You Been on My Mind," memories of whom are triggered by the color of the sun or the weather or something like that; the magical, mysterious, always-giving woman of "Love Minus Zero/No Limit," who laughs like the flowers and cannot be bought, who is true like ice and fire; the equally attractive

"Sad-Eyed Lady of the Lowlands," with her eyes like smoke, voice like chimes (those bells again!), magical silhouette when the sunlight dims, and mysterious eyes where the moonlight swims; the lovely mermaids who live by the sea where fishermen hold flowers and nobody has to think about "Desolation Row"; John Wesley Harding's lady, helping straighten out the situation in Chaynee County; the little bundle of country joy in "Down Along the Cove" and the unnamed country babe of "I'll Be Your Baby Tonight," with the mockingbird and big, fat moon; the Heaven lost by Dylan when "I Threw It All Away," who was, metaphorically, mountains in his hand, rivers that ran every day; Peggy by golly Day; Winterlude that little daisy, that little apple, that corn in the field and snowflake on the sand ("an ice skater's waltz, right off one those old Victor records," writes Scaduto [271], right out of Dylan's North Country youth, where that kind of music was quite popular); that other mysterious girl of the North Country (named Ruth?) in "Something There Is About You," who personified all the wonder of rainy days on the Great Lakes and walking the hills of old Duluth (is·she the same girl keeping company with Dylan on a snowy night in "On a Night Like This" while the winds blow and the snow falls around the old cabin?); the lovely girl (Ellen Bernstein?) of "You're Gonna Make Me Lonesome When You Go," with her purple clover and Queen Anne's lace; Sara the Great, sweet love of Dylan's life, moonlight on the snow, asleep in the woods by a fire in the night, playing with the kids on the beach; the siren of "One More Cup of Coffee (Valley Below)," with a voice like a meadowlark, a heart like an ocean, and loyalty to the stars above; the fisherman's daughter-siren of "Golden Loom," who appears and then disappears under the eucalyptus trees one smoky autumn night; the controversial lady of "Is Your Love in Vain?," who can cook, sew, and raise flowers; the mysterious woman of "I'll Remember You," who understood and came through in the clutch, and will remain in Dylan's memory when "the wind blows through the piney wood" and he's forgotten all the rest. The gal who looks so fine coming after Dylan in "It Takes a Lot to Laugh, It Takes a Train to Cry" is linked to the moon shining through the trees and the sun going down over the sea. The gal who offers Dylan a new place to start in "Where Teardrops Fall" is located in a place of rivers, soft winds, and moonlight. "Spirit on the Water" is associated in the first verse of that song with a girl who, later in that song, is "a blossom on a stem." The girl Dylan remembers when their romance was "Born in Time" comes with snow, rain, fog, and hills.

The girl in "Marchin' to the City" could have been one of those girls, but she blew it: "I was hoping we could drink from life's clear streams / I was hoping we could dream life's pleasant dreams. / Once I had a pretty girl but she done me wrong."

Not surprisingly, Dylan's good women who are close to nature are sometimes associated with religion. This is especially so in the later songs, but as early as his interview with Robert Shelton in 1966, Dylan was describing Sara as "holy" and "Madonna-like" (Cott: 87). The beautiful stranger of "I and I" must, in another lifetime, surely have been wed to a righteous king who wrote psalms beside moonlit streams. The woman in "Caribbean Wind" is the Rose of Sharon. The woman of "In the Summertime" visited in the summer, in a place where trees hung low by a soft and shining sea, and she seems to have brought, or be associated with, Dylan's Christian experience, with "the flood / That set everybody free." The gift this woman brought was not good sex or even good love, but salvation, which will remain with Dylan "unto the grave and then unto eternity."

As he associates the right kind of woman with nature, Dylan associates bad women with the city. Five- and ten-cent women with nothing in their heads, he calls them in "Bob Dylan's Blues." The woman in "Dirge" is just "a painted face on a trip down Suicide Road," an urban misadventure in an old hotel which has left him hating himself for loving her and the weakness it shows. "Can't recall a useful thing you ever did for me," he says looking back on the relationship. Among the unpleasant features of the city in "The Groom's Still Waiting at the Altar" is Claudette, who for all the singer knows might, by this time, be respectably married or running a whorehouse in Buenos Aires; fifty-fifty odds either way. In "Abandoned Love," a Spanish moon rising on the hill calls to Dylan, but he returns from the flaming moon to town and to the woman whom he needs, even though he knows she's a ball and chain. In the much later "Honest with Me," Dylan finds himself stranded in the city with a bunch of city girls who just give him the creeps. In "Love Sick," Dylan walks through streets that are dead, with his head buried in a girl he wishes he'd never met. Dead streets, dead girl. Next song on the album, same deal: in "Standing in the Doorway" the girl's gone and Dylan's bummed (once again the antipastoral midnight train intrudes mysteriously out of nowhere). "If I saw you, I don't know if I'd kiss you or kill you," says a boy in serious need of rebirth in the countryside.

The girl in the "Mississippi" city is not particularly evil — she is just a sell and a disappointment or distraction from which Dylan is now free, walking through the autumn leaves. Dylan's reaction is no regrets — "you're sorry; I'm sorry too" — and, as the song closes, an invitation to this city girl to escape with him onto the road. In "Rollin' and Tumblin'," Dylan actually invites the young lazy slut who charms away his brains every night in to renewal in nature. This woman is so crazy she's driving him to tears, and there's nothing so depressing as trying to satisfy her, but instead of taking off (or staying away — in this song he himself appears to be already in touch with warm weather, rising sun, a glowing landscape), he suggests they go together down to the greenwood glen and (echoes of Neal Cassady in Jack Kerouac's *On the Road*) "forgive each other darlin', . . . / Let's put old matters to an end." Can this girl can be saved? Perhaps out in the countryside.

THE MACHINE IN THE GARDEN

But there is much more in Dylan's gardens than good times and good girls. Leo Marx and William Conlogue are not the only critics to track the pastoral tradition from classical times to *The Grapes of Wrath*, but they are particularly useful in framing a discussion of Bob Dylan because of their insistence, almost from the get-go, on ambivalence within that tradition.

Smack-dab in the middle of the American garden, both Marx and Conlogue point out, is usually The Machine: the watermill, the steamboat, the railroad train, the textile factory, the power plant, the whaling ship, the dynamo, the scoop shovel, the automobile (or motorcycle), the tractor and combine, the television, the computer, and now the cell phone and iPod. (And, in fall, in Minnesota corn fields and the great north woods, those machines Marx does not mention: the shotgun and the deer rifle.) Some thinkers, Marx notes, went so far as to suggest machines could improve the garden, as the shotgun "harvests" surplus deer and pheasants. For all their pastoral proclivities, nineteenth century Americans made the machine a hip pop icon: the locomotive was nineteenth-century-totally-awesome, then the telephone and the Victorola. Inventors were the heroes of the age, and the Mississippi River steamboat and the Pullman car were the equivalents of our '57 Chevy or '65 Mustang convertible. In the early twentieth century, Midwestern farmers (if not their wives) fell in love with the tractor, a romance commemorated today in institutions like Minnesota's (Farm) Machinery Museum in Hanley Falls, Minnesota, and the "Old Time Threshing Show" celebrations popular in the Upper Midwest in August, where a Case steam-powered tractor is belted to an old Harvester threshing machine, and young farmers in 1940s straw hats toss bundles of oats onto the conveyor belt at one end (for a bindle stiff astride the thresher to pitch into the beaters), while a shower of grain pours into a horse-drawn wagon parked on one side of the machine, and a rain of straw spews forth on the other. Conlogue's focus in *Working the Garden* is *industrial* farming in American literature, and Barillas, in *The Midwestern Pastoral*, examines at some length the "version of pastoral ideology" of Henry Ford, raised on a Michigan farm, who saw the car as a means of transporting families to hours of pleasure in God's great open spaces (42–3) — which remains today one important function of the car, or truck, or motorcycle, or snowmobile, or four-wheeler in rural Minnesota today.

Clearly, some versions of the American pastoral tradition reached an accommodation with what some might call the dark or technological side of civilization. They settled for some middle way, usually in the spoken or unspoken hope that plus would outweigh minus, that the enormous American landscape would absorb factory impurities, that the busy railroad would counterbalance what Thoreau called the "quiet desperation" of men's lives. Leo Marx identifies an "industrialized version" of the American pastoral in Whitman and Emerson, especially in Emerson's 1844 lecture titled "The Young American," where he hails the locomotive and the steamboat which, "like enormous shuttles, shoot every day across the thousand various threads of national descent and employment" (344), conveying immigrants to "amelioration in nature" (352), facilitating trade (!!!), and forging a national pastoral consciousness which agrees well with Transcendentalism.

Not all Americans agreed — or agree — with these developments, of course. Marx points out that even Emerson's optimism waned in the late 1840s; that Emerson's contemporaries Hawthorne and Melville felt "a widening gap between the facts and ideals of American life"; that Twain in *Huckleberry Finn* found "everything all busted up and ruined" with the only solution to "light out for the Territory ahead of the rest"; that for Henry Adams, writing at the dawn of the twentieth century, the dynamo had crushed the virgin — and Adams too. Beuchsel argues that Midwestern pastoralists of the early twentieth century resented New Englanders precisely because they had betrayed the American pastoral ideal by conflating industrialism (Henry Adams's dynamo) with nature (Adams's sacramental Virgin-woman) on the very land which held most promise of a pastoral idyll (21), and consciously sought to "locate an existential, spiritual anchor amidst what seemed like the final disintegration of the already long-battered American dream" (33).

There is much support for Buechsel's position among Minnesota writers. In a story titled "Harvest," in *Ripening*, Meridel Le Sueur tells the story of a marriage gone sour when immigrant farmer Winji uses his young wife's dowry money to buy a new threshing machine against her wishes. Herbert Krause's Minnesota farm novel *The Thresher* (1946) is about Johnny Black's ugly obsession with making a bundle of money with his threshing machine which — like Winji's in Le Sueur's story — animates itself into an ugly character in the novel. And while her husband's automobile drives Carol Kennicott to countryside and to a "dignity and greatness which had failed her on Main Street" (Lewis: 61), the entrepreneurs of Gopher Prairie — including Percy Bresnahan, president of the Velvet Motor Company returned to Gopher Prairie for a hometown visit — drive Carol Kennicott right out of town. In the Midwest literary tradition, machines devour the land and destroy human relationships. Then the machines themselves turn to junk, litter the groves, or pile mountains of scrap iron beside the railroad tracks. Especially in Hibbing. "Junk defines the Range," observes Aaron Brown (87).

Perhaps because Dylan had seen the destructive effects of technology on the landscape early on in Hibbing and Duluth, the "industrialized version" of American pastoralism is not much present in Dylan after the mid-sixties albums. The machine itself is undeniably there, including the motorcycle T-shirt Dylan wears on the cover of *Highway 61 Revisited*, which a San Francisco student asks him to deconstruct at the beginning of the 1965 KQED press conference (*No Direction Home*). But these are bad machines. Dylan himself used to tear ass around the back roads and trails of Hibbing and Woodstock on the Harley-Davidson 74 his parents bought him in 1956 (which is what he's apparently doing at the beginning of "Motorpsycho Nightmare"), but all he did was get in accidents. Motorcycles appear in two other Dylan songs, in both cases with negative connotations: the motorcycle black Madonna two-wheeled gypsy queen of "Gates of Eden," and the disaster waiting to happen in his cover of Hank Snow's "Ninety Miles an Hour (Down a Dead End Street)," a woman "as bad as a motorcycle with the devil in the seat."

In "Masters of War," what poisons Dylan's world (not specifically described as a garden) are the machines of war: guns, death planes, bombs. The pastoral idyll of "Last Thoughts on Woody Guthrie" turns into a nightmare Dylan describes as "a pinball machine." As we saw in Chapter 1, trains are one of the most frequently used memories of Dylan's youth, but the train is separate from, and opposed to, nature: train and grass are opposite, unassimilated images. Agrarian charity in "Something's Burning, Baby" is contrasted with the midnight train-machine. In "Walk Out in the Rain," Dylan maintains a pastoral nature-versus-machine contrast: walk out with me, your own true love, your own true dreams, in the rain tonight . . . or catch the next train out of here.

Dylan opens the reminiscence written for *Joan Baez in Concert, Part 2* with himself as a child, kneeling in the grass by his aunt's house in Duluth and hearing the iron ore cars rolling down the train tracks: a classic machine-in-the-garden scenario. Distracted by the train, he would bite his lip and tear the grass out by its roots:

But when the echo faded in the day
An I understood the train was gone

It's then that my eyes'd turn
Back t my hands with stains a green
That lined my palms like blood that tells
I'd taken an not given in return
But glancin back t the empty patch
Where the ground was turned upside down
An the roots lay dead beside the tree
I'd say "how can this bother me"
Or "I'm sure the grass don' give a damn
Anyway it'll grow back again an
What's a patch a grass anyhow' [sic]

At the poem's conclusion, an older (all of 23 years) Zimmerman, with the help of Joan Baez, understands just how wrong young Zimmerman was. Trains are bad machines in the garden — nothing but trouble, trouble, trouble.

The guitar, on the other hand, is a kind of counter-machine, a means of attacking ugliness, or an escape vehicle from ugliness along the lines of Henry Ford's automobile. Woody Guthrie had written on his guitar, "this machine kills fascists,"[14] and poems like "Last Thoughts on Woody Guthrie" and songs like "Mr. Tambourine Man" suggest that a music machine might function in alliance with nature to restore the damage done to the garden by other bad machines. Folk revivalists and topical protest crusaders (overlapping but not identical groups) who believed that songs could effect political change certainly viewed the acoustic guitar — if not the electric guitar — as a machine which might cleanse a corrupt garden. For Dylan, however, the electric guitar of "Mr. Tambourine Man" is a magic swirling ship that offers an escape from the city's ancient, empty, sense-numbing and very dead streets. These streets are similar to the world outside of Eden in the *Bringing It All Back Home* companion song "Gates of Eden," and to the world of "It's Alright, Ma (I'm Only Bleeding)": eclipsed sun, poisoned waterfalls, and a twisted society full of flesh-colored Christs that glow in the dark, lying advertising signs, old lady judges pushing fake morals, and flowers that are nothing more than investments. Whereas the rat race of "It's Alright, Ma" is inescapable and the Gates of Eden remain closed and inaccessible, the tambourine-music machine-ship transports Dylan into a rebirth in music and art. Interestingly, Dylan links the tambourine machine with elements of nature, early in the song, with the implicit rebirth of night turning into "the jingle jangle morning," but especially at the end of the song: leaves, trees, beach, sky, sands, waves. He suggests in that last stanza that damaged nature (the leaves are frozen, the trees are twisted) is restored through the agency of the artist and his music machine into some kind of cultivated, or at least reasonable facsimile of, Eden of "diamond sky," "circus sands," and all-forgiving waves.

Something rather similar happens at the close of "Percy's Song," a little-known ballad about a friend of Dylan's sentenced to a rather excessive 99 years in jail for involuntary manslaughter on a vehicular homicide charge. The ballad's refrain — "turn, turn to the rain and the wind" — makes the traditional association between bad weather and bad news, but in the song's final stanza, Dylan uses his guitar not exactly to free his friend, or to right what he considers to be an injustice, but, as he plays "Oh the Cruel Rain and the Wind" over and over to himself, to get him through the night. The guitar-machine thus buffers the weather, and insofar as day resolves night, acts as an avenue of escape from bad nature to good nature.

An actual escape into nature via instrument-as-machine occurs at the end of "Visions of Johanna." The song opens with the singer as a "little boy lost," dead-ass devastated by visions of some distant Johanna-Madonna in a room where heat pipes cough and a country music station plays soft. Escape comes with the aid of some tough talk from Louise, a mule laden with jewels and binoculars (suggesting the reward won by vision and sight) . . . and a mysterious fiddler and Dylan's own harmonicas. In the song's final stanza, the cage that imprisoned Dylan's old self corrodes as his harmonicas play "the skeleton keys and the rain." Either "and the rain" adds a second subject to "the harmonicas play," and both the music machines and the rain effect his release, or "and the rain" adds a second object to the sentence, and the harmonicas act as both the key to escape and as the rain which is forgiveness and renewal. Either way, in this song the harmonicas and nature work together to the prisoner's benefit.

Music machines aside, however, Dylan does not integrate technology with pastoralism in the manner described by Leo Marx.

THE DARK SIDE

However, the general ambivalence Marx finds in colonial depictions of nature is very much part of the nature that we find in Dylan, for like Robert Frost he knows that the woods, although lovely, are dark and deep.[15] American colonists, who actually lived in or close to the countryside or wilderness, were aware not only of "all those happy Advantages which Nature hath given them" (the words are those of Robert Beverley in closing *The History and Present State of Virginia* [83]), but also of some very unhappy Disadvantages which Nature hath also given them. "Anticipations of a second Eden quickly shattered against the reality of North America," writes Roderick Nash (25), and even the grand landscapes of Hudson River School painters like Thomas Cole sometimes depict an Eden ominous with clouds, fires, storms, blighted trees, ruined buildings, and dark foreboding. Dylan himself writes in *Chronicles* that he was raised not in Walden Pond, "where everything was hunky-dory," but in "the dark demonic woods, same forest, just a different way of looking at things" (14), and when push comes to shove, the land around Hibbing was too stony for farming, too swampy for timber, and frozen half the year. In *The Machine in the Garden*, Marx argues that what finally allows us to take the idea of a therapeutic return to nature seriously is its temporariness (69); it is a journey into and then out of. The experience in nature is, to borrow another phrase from Robert Frost, only "a momentary stay against confusion," as per Thoreau's *Walden*: after two years, two months, and two days at Walden, Thoreau cleared out, went home, took what he had gathered from coincidence, struck another match, and started anew. What he gathered at Walden (including an afternoon spent observing under a magnifying glass a war between red ants and black ants: one warrior chewing another to pieces bite by bite) shaped the odd combination of reformer and hermit that was Henry David Thoreau, and the lecture on "Civil Disobedience" he would deliver a year after leaving Walden. "If the city is corrupt, it is men who have made the journey of self-discovery who must be relied upon to restore justice, the political counterpart of psychic balance," Marx argues (71), but the journey is only a camping trip. Such seems to be the case not only with Henry Thoreau, but also with Bob Dylan, who, let us be honest, spends most of his time far from North Country pastoral retreats and who knows that, in Minnesota, there are more days in the year when the temperature drops below freezing than days when it remains above 32°F.

As I suggested regarding the North Country origins of Dylan's death fixation, Midwestern writers have understood nature's dark side since settlement times. Scott Russell Sanders writes, "The dark side of fecundity is wholesale death. Beneath the Midwestern writer's affirmation of the country there is often a shudder, as there must be for anyone who looks wilderness in the teeth" (40). Mark Peter Buechsel writes, "Already before the ascent of Midwestern modernism, the region's naturalists, such as Joseph Kirkland, Edgar Watson Howe, and Hamlin Garland, sought to thwart pastoral idealism, portraying the harsh facts of rural life" (70). Later — citing Cather's Jim Burden and Neil Herbert, Fitzgerald's Amory Blaine and Jay Gatsby, Floyd Dell's Felix Fay, Glenway Wescott's Jim Towers, Josephine W. Johnson's Kerrin Haldemarne, and Sinclair Lewis's George F. Babbitt — Buechsel notes that in "virtually every case," escapist, romantic pastoralism is a negative symptom in a character of some unwillingness or inability to engage with objective spiritual and physical realities (155).

In Rölvaag's *Giants in the Earth*, Per Hansa's wife, Beret, goes temporarily insane in large part because of her daily confrontation with vast expanses of hostile nature. "You haven't heard how terribly the wolves howl at night," she tells her husband; "I shall die to-night. . . . Leave here as soon as spring comes! Human beings cannot exist here! . . . They grow into beasts" (228). (Why are you thinking of the Comte du Buffon right now?) Rölvaag opens the final section of the novel with a set piece on the adversities of homesteading:

> But more to be dreaded than this tribulation [Indians] was the strange spell of sadness which the unbroken solitude cast upon the minds of some. Many took their own lives; asylum after asylum was filled with disordered beings who had once been human. It is hard for the eye to wander from sky line to sky line, year in and year out, without finding a resting place! (413)

Willa Cather writes in the first chapter of *O Pioneers!*, "It was from facing this vast hardness that the boy's mouth had become so bitter; because he felt that men were too weak to make any mark here" (15). In his own memoir of pioneering, *A Son of the Middle Border*, Hamlin Garland echoes Cather: "No man knows what winter means until he has lived through one in a pine-board shanty on a Dakota plain with only buffalo bones for fuel" (309).

In the thirties, of course, nature reasserted itself with a vengeance: hard winters but brutal, dry summers, drought, dust. The evidence collected by Roy Stryker's Farm Security Administration photographers has become iconic. In an essay published in *American Mercury*, September 1934, Meridel Le Sueur described western Minnesota:

> On Decoration Day the wind started again, blowing hot as a blast from hell and the young corn withered as if under machine gun fire, the trees in two hours looked as if they had been beaten. The day after Decoration Day it was so hot you couldn't sit around looking at the panting cattle and counting their ribs and listening to that low cry that is an awful asking. We got in the car and drove slowly through the sizzling countryside. Not a soul was in sight. It was like a funeral. (*Ripening*: 168)

That experience, and the whang-leather toughness it bred in those who survived, remained with Midwesterners long after World War II ended. "If you go a few minutes from here in Hibbing into the desolate bush," high school teacher Bonn Rolfsen told Robert Shelton, "you'll know why we are so independent here" (*Home*: 43).

Or nature can just wreck things bit by bit. Gradually, slowly, inch by inch and block by block, she reclaims human incursions. Bridges ultimately collapse, levees inevitably fail. Just below North Hibbing, on the east side of Third Avenue opposite the Greyhound Bus Museum, is the old cemetery — perhaps the unconscious "graveyard of my mind" in "Can't Wait," where Dylan remembers playing as a child in "Nobody 'Cept You" and in "11 Outlined Epitaphs":

> dogs howled over the graveyard
> where even the markin stones were dead
> an there was no sound except for the wind
> blowin thru the high grass
> an the bricks that fell back
> t the dirt from a slight stab
> of the breeze . . . it was as tho
> the rains of wartime had
> left the land bombed-out an shattered

And it is not just death that haunts Dylan and the Upper Midwest — it is the oblivion after death wrought by nature. Hibbing is not unique in this respect. Driving around the back roads of Minnesota and the Dakotas, it is common to happen on a lost graveyard of four or six markers in a settlement long abandoned . . . or even on a single gravestone off in the nowhere, its inscription, perhaps in a language nobody speaks any more, weathered nearly to illegibility. In a collection appropriately titled *The Color of Mesabi Bones*, Mesabi native John Caddy opens a poem on "Mine Towns" with these words: "Much abandoned now, forced out or grown over, gone, thrown into memory's hole" (17). Customs too are lost, Caddy notes, and causes, countries, recipes, languages: "Serb, French, Italian, stubborn Finn, merchants who could speak them." And whole towns gone, the houses knocked down, the open cellars choked with raspberries, rhubarb and mint and lilies struggling with long grass, which seeks to reclaim everything.[16]

Nature often shows her dark side in Dylan's work. In "Ballad of Hollis Brown," natural disasters are both a reflection of the South Dakota farmer's mental state and an objective reality: coyotes, rats, drought. In other songs, floods roll through New Orleans, Vicksburg, and towns along the Red River, the Mississippi River, the Minnesota River. Several of the country comfortable songs of *Nashville Skyline* are actually songs of lost, discarded, or threatened love figured by gray skies or "dark and rolling sky." In a later song "Under Your Spell," the countryside into which Dylan escapes a bad relationship does almost as much damage as the woman: "the desert is hot, the mountain is cursed." Nature does not work its healing magic in *Time Out of Mind*, Stephen Scobie suggests, finding a conscious strategy on this album of "sneaking up very dark and ominous images under a cover of apparent innocuousness" (*Alias*: 307) — something along the lines of what Dylan does in the 2001 song "Moonlight": melodious songbirds, moonlight, orchids, black-eyed Susans, petals pink and white, purple blossoms creating a mystic glow . . . and then sharp hills rising behind twisted oaks. What's that all about? In the earlier "Romance in Durango," Dylan even reverses the escape-from-city-to-nature paradigm. To his girlfriend/companion, an outlaw-on-the-lam paints a picture of the good life after an escape from barking dogs and a posse pursuing them through the blistering sun of the desert. They will disappear into the anonymity of Durango, sitting in the shade, reciting wedding prayers in a little church this side of town, enjoying the fiesta and dancing the fandango. Michael Gray actually finds a conscious contrast between love and the harsh natural landscape in songs like "Can't Wait" (*Song*: 796).

Dylan sometimes uses wind, rain, flood, hurricane, snow, and hail metaphorically, to signal isolation, lost love, personal hardship, prison, death, or judgment. These are, for the most part, conventional metaphorical usages, noteworthy more for frequency of appearance rather than for any striking use Dylan makes of them. A cold reception is symbolized by cold weather, so young Bob Dylan, just blowed into New York City from the wild open spaces out West, is met with the coldest winter in 17 years. What could be simpler? His friend Percy gets 99 years for involuntary manslaughter? It's raining. If a guy's life is a disaster, they maybe call him "Hurricane" (not Dylan's invention, but it certainly fits Rubin Carter). A washed-out road and weather unfit for man or beast reflect a warped social order in "Lonesome Day Blues." Your own life is a mess? It is like an idiot wind, blowing from the Grand Coulee Dam to the Capitol. You have "Buckets of Rain" coming out of your ears; you're under the gun and clouds are blocking the sun ("You Changed My Life"). Maybe your messed-up life is like a storm, until you meet the right girl who takes your mind off the mess, and she is like "Shelter from the Storm." Maybe you can't find the right girl and "It's been raining in the trenches all day long" ("Need a Woman"). "If Not for You," you tell the girl you love, the sky would fall and rain would gather. (Or perhaps *her* life is a mess — rain blowing in her face — and you offer her a warm embrace to "Make You Feel My Love.") The girl leaves, and you're back in the rain with a pain that stops and starts, like a corkscrew to your heart ("You're a Big Girl Now"). Or maybe your faith in God causes a "driving rain / I know I will sustain / 'Cause I believe in you." (Did Dylan ever sustain a hard rain of criticism for his Christian witness?)

In "Cold Irons Bound," Dylan uses parched fields to reflect his personal situation: he's all used up, there's nobody around, and whatever friends he had have proven false. Rölvaag echoes in our heads: "I shall die to-night. . . . Leave here as soon as spring comes! Human beings cannot exist here!"[17]

Disorder in nature may reflect matters cultural. Dylan portrayed the cultural disorders of the 1960s as a flood in "The Times They Are A-Changin'": "the waters / Around you have grown / . . . You better start swimmin' or you'll sink like a stone." A decade later, during the soporific seventies, he reissued the warning in "Down in the Flood": "Water's gonna overflow, / Swamp's gonna rise, / No boat's gonna row." Thirty years after that he re-reissued the warning using the same metaphor: "If it keep on rainin' the levee's gonna break" (George Bush's rain machine ran at full tilt, and sure as shootin', in 2008, the levee broke big-time).

For Dylan, rejuvenation (literal rejuvenation in a song like "My Back Pages," with its refrain "I was so much older then / I'm younger than that now") often comes with a certain amount of trauma and pain, which he may deliver in a metaphor or simile involving rain, snow, wind, or storm. In these cases, bad weather becomes purgative and thus long-term beneficial. In "You Changed My Life," the right woman comes "in like the wind" to straighten out Dylan's troubles. Conversely, in an even later song, "Seeing the Real You at Last," rain and storm bring a clearness of vision that lets him break off a bad relationship.

In "Chimes of Freedom," bolts of lightning, blowing rain, electrical storm, "the mad mystic hammering of the wild ripping hail" all signal release for the outcast and the abandoned and "[f]or the countless confused, accused, misused, strung-out ones an' worse" — and for hung-up people everywhere in the universe. This idea will make sense to country people who understand that heavy winds and rains clear trees of dead limbs, that forest fires purge deadfall and prepare for new growth (sometimes we even do "controlled burns"), that the raging rivers use periodic floods to flush out silt and cleanse their channels — that storms clean out old shit. Dylan's Iron Range experience is certainly as germane to a song like "Chimes of Freedom" as his reading poetry — you don't need Rimbaud when you have a Minnesota winter or a good Midwestern thunderstorm. The experience is terrifying but exhilarating.

Yet another purgative apocalypse is found in "When the Ship Comes In." Here Dylan associates nature with the young, righteous, correct, winning side in a generally mean-spirited song which envisions a hurricane blowing away the old, corrupt, incorrect, losers and carrying the ship of good guys finally to journey's end and the safety of shore. The seas split as the wind and waters pound, and the bad guys end up "drownded in the tide" (more like Pharaoh's horsemen than Goliath).

The howling wind of "All Along the Watchtower" promises an imminent apocalypse which may be cleansing. At 12 lines as printed in *Lyrics*, this is the shortest song Dylan had written to that date, but the song radiates meanings. "The Watchtower" suggests the Jehovah's Witness Watchtower Society and the monthly illustrated magazine, *Watchtower*, printed by the Watch Tower Bible and Tract Society of Pennsylvania, which Witness missionaries passed out when they descended upon your town for door-to-door ministry. I think all of us who lived in the sixties were handed a *Watchtower* at least once in our lives. The name of the magazine is in turn an allusion to Isaiah 62.6: "Upon your walls, O Jerusalem, I have set watchmen." So the song has biblical overtones even before the joker starts talking about wine. Given the apocalyptic overtones of the song, "the thief" suggests one of the thieves crucified with Christ, which might make "the joker", talking about his communion wine and his earth, Christ himself. Their discussion, then, concerns the approaching end of all things ("the hour is getting late"). The growling wildcat recalls the leopard (representing lust or incontinence) which, along with a lion (pride) and a she-wolf (avarice), greets Dante in the opening canto of *The Divine Comedy*. The approaching riders recall the horsemen of the apocalypse, and the howling wind recalls the dislocations which accompanied the Crucifixion and will mark the Final Judgment. The wind, of course, echoes the hard rain which Dylan has already prophesied in other songs, and that is the point of "All Along the Watchtower": the disturbances of nature which accompany judgment are usually a result of human misbehavior (individual and social), which precipitates the judgment. That admonition, cast in the metaphor of predatory wildcats and howling winds, is a message I think Dylan likes to leave with his audiences.

A similar suggestion infuses "The Wicked Messenger," also on *John Wesley Harding*, and the wicked, apocalyptic wind "blowing on the upper deck" will be purgative in the much later song "Señor (Tales of Yankee Power)."

Examined closely, "Death Is Not the End" is another dark prediction couched in terms of dark nature. Dylan sees the Tree of Life better than he does in "All Along the Watchtower," but the landscape immediately around him at his (presumably country) crossroads is strictly storm clouds and heavy rains. The song promises that — to reference Walt Whitman's lines on grass — to die is different from what anyone supposed, and luckier, but in the incomprehensible here and now Dylan gives us only cities afire, sadness, injustice, and isolation. In "Tryin' to Get to Heaven," Dylan looks yet again toward eternal salvation, again seeing the afterlife from mucked-up nature, in this case "high muddy water" through which he's been wading, hoping against hope to make Heaven before they close the door. That feeling of doubt, of futility, of failure, carries into *Time Out of Mind*'s next song, "Not Dark Yet," where Dylan has lost his sense of humanity, his burden seems more than he can bear, and — more significantly — he doesn't "even hear a murmur of a prayer." Again he locates himself in dark nature — shadows and a sea he reached by following a river after escaping London and gay Paree. He specifically mentions scars that the sun hasn't healed, denying the restoration he has so often found in nature. "I can't even remember what it was I came here to get away from," he admits. And he begins his final stanza with the extremely suggestive line, "I was born here and I'll die here against my will." Is this perhaps a reference to his own biography, a life of growing up in Minnesota, attempting to escape, willing himself to be something he could not become, and falling back into rural place which — in this song — offers nothing at all?

So is nature your ally or your enemy? Perhaps the best way of looking at nature is as a contest in what does not kill you makes you stronger. Nature-as-a-test is a common enough motif in American literature, including the stories of Ernest Hemingway, whom Dylan specifically mentions reading and appreciating in a 1964 interview with Nat Hentoff (Cott: 25), and Tim O'Brien's first book, *Northern Lights*, in which two brothers get lost and nearly killed in the Boundary Waters region of Minnesota, north of Duluth. Nature-as-a-test often comes combined with the journey archetype which we will examine shortly: if we survive the test of nature, even though we fail to recover the treasures sought in "Isis" (or the grail sought in *Indiana Jones and the Last Crusade*), we return home with the true wealth of self-knowledge which makes adult life possible. If we fail the test, we become the fruits of Darwinism. If we decline the challenge, we remain forever adolescent. In Arthur Miller's quintessentially American allegory *Death of a Salesman*, protagonist Willy Loman declines the adventure in Alaska offered by his older brother Ben, partly at the insistence of his wife Linda, and partly because he thinks he is doing okay right where he is. He thinks he's prospering where he is, but in fact he is deluded . . . and dying. One son, Happy, likewise deluded, also declines the challenge; the other son, Biff, goes out into the West, is beaten, but comes back to New York with the wisdom of experience: "I know who I am, kid" (132). Uncle Ben, who accepted the challenge and won, reminds Willy, "The jungle is dark but full of diamonds, Willy. . . . One must go in to fetch the diamonds out" (127). Willy Loman never entered the jungle, and remains always the low man, always "the Shrimp." Al Capone, Dylan says in *Chronicles*, "seems like a man who never got out alone in nature for a minute in his life. . . . He's not even worthy enough to have a name" (39).

Dylan sees nature as a challenge/test in at least some songs. In "Farewell," an early departure song, Dylan bids goodbye to his own true love as he heads off for the Bay of Mexico or the coast of California or perhaps the Mexican plains. He knows he will encounter hardships — "the weather is against me and the wind blows hard" — but he might strike it lucky, and if he does he'll be back. On the results of this quest, we receive no report. Dylan is a little more optimistic in "Paths of Victory," another early song: the singer again confronts dusty trails of troubles, rough roads of battles, bumpy gravel roads, a one-way wind blowing — again a mysterious evening train in this rural landscape — before walking paths of victory. He is less optimistic in "Born in Time": "the ways of nature will test every nerve," warns Dylan, and "you won't get anything you don't deserve."

The key to "Isis" is most probably the goddess' role as fertility goddess and the various vegetation and death–rebirth myths associated with her, and the song reflects some new age fascination with old-age myths.[18] The song is fuzzy in several respects: Dylan heads to the cold of the North but rides back in from the East; he's excavating a pyramid but traveling through snow and chopping through ice; he leaves the benign country not for a city but for a hostile country which is not, as John Herdman notes, the simple countryside of pastoral myth, "where, according to American myth, issues are clear-cut and uncomplicated, and man's only struggles are with Nature" (74); this countryside is a test. But Isis herself is associated with nature, the meadow, and the creek, in contrast to "the center of town" where the quest for big bucks begins, dreams of turquoise, gold, diamonds right out of *Death of a Salesman*. These dreams morph into the fantasy of a mummy buried in a pyramid embedded in ice which, if brought out successfully, will bring a good price. As the wind howls and the snow blows, the narrator chops through the night only to find . . . no jewels, no nothing. His mission unaccomplished, he returns to Isis. He is different but "not quite" different: he tried but he failed. In this song, however, failure is irrelevant. What is important is that he took up the challenge of nature. At the beginning of the song, he could not hold on to Isis very long; by the end of the song, she's asking him to stay.

All of these songs contain an ambiguity found in one of Dylan's best known songs, "Blowin' in the Wind." Thanks in part to the melodious recording of Peter, Paul and Mary, "Blowin' in the Wind" became the battle hymn of the sixties protest movement, supplanting the historically richer "We Shall Overcome." This song was everywhere in the early 1960s, on everyone's lips, bringing every civil rights rally to a spiritual and satisfying conclusion. The song asked all the right questions: how many roads must a man walk down before he is called a man? How long can we ignore injustice and death? How deaf, blind, insensitive can people be? How long does it take to solve a problem? The problem is mostly civil rights, but Dylan also suggests the other great sixties crusade against the war in Vietnam (to his everlasting credit as a seer, he wrote the song before

Vietnam even cranked up). And Dylan uses metaphors from nature to ask the questions: peace is a white dove sailing wide seas in search of rest on the beach; victims of injustice are men looking up but unable to see the sky; racism is a mountain yet to be eroded. So social problems are depicted as elements of nature against which we struggle: sea, sky, mountains. Simple enough. The problem with this song is the answers. Unlike "We Shall Overcome" and "Paths of Victory," this song does not promise victory in the near future or even the distant "some day." This song asks questions, but the answers are "blowing in the wind." Dave Van Ronk had a point: what the hell is "blowin' in the wind?" This is a non-answer, and the song may even be defeatist. Certainly, Dylan makes no promises. Dylan closed his election-eve 2008 performance in Minneapolis with "Blowin' in the Wind," prefaced by the statement "It looks like things are going to change now"; in reviewing that performance, Jon Bream of the Minneapolis *Star Tribune* wrote, "Dylan, who usually closes with the rocking 'All Along the Watchtower,' ended this evening with a warm, gracious answer to America's problems" (C2). But the song is no such thing. The wind is a test, and Dylan gives us no indication of the test's outcome.

Nor does Dylan make any real promises in "A Hard Rain's A-Gonna Fall," except the promise to keep fighting. Again, elements of nature are used symbolically to give the song the vaguely allegorical flavor of "Blowin' in the Wind." Dead ponies, black branches, roaring waves, wild wolves, misty mountains, sad forests, dead oceans become the test against which humans prove or fail to prove themselves. While the hard rain should be long-term beneficial, Dylan again leaves us hanging: in the final stanza he promises to head out into the deepest black forest (danger) in the face of rain (hardship), and to testify atop the mountain or ocean so that all souls can see it . . . but he also suggests that he will sooner or later start sinking. In this song there are no paths of victory; the ship does not come in. The important thing is to have accepted the challenge and sustained commitment.

Several songs, mostly from the middle to later stages of Dylan's career, might be categorized as "ambiguous" or "problematic" when it comes to Dylan's view of nature, either because he can't get to the good nature he seeks, or because he can't make up his mind about nature, pro or con. One such gated paradise is Eden in "Gates of Eden" — incommunicative, an imagined shelter from the nightmare urban world of the song. This paradise is something like Kafka's *Castle*: a presence there but not there, except that Eden, unlike the Castle, sends no messages or messengers. It's an inaccessible retreat. In "Highlands," Dylan imagines another inaccessible rural paradise "gentle and fair." As Gray points out, this is "a dream future in time and space, and not an idealised past" (*Song and Dance Man*

816), but paradise past or paradise future, the point is that Dylan's not there. He's stuck in the urban rat race with a wrecked soul, surrounded by reminders of his own age, and tangled up in a dead-end conversation with some ding-dong feminist waitress. The song is filled with allusions religious ("chariots that swing down low") and literary (Scobie sees Donne in this song as well as Burns, and Smart suggests an allusion to the Yeats poem "Lake Isle of Innisfree"), and all manner of benevolent nature, but the passage from here to there is blocked or hidden. "I'll figure it out somehow," Dylan concludes at the end of the song, but for the moment it's all in the mind, and that will have to do for now. Scobie notes that the image of the highlands remains as split and equivocal as any of the other possible images of redemption on *Time Out of Mind* (*Alias*: 303).

"Where Are You Tonight? (Journey Through Dark Heat)" opens with a train rolling through the rain — again the machine in the American garden. We're in New York City with neon lights blazing along Elizabeth Street, and a couple of city girls: one a mother in a rage, and the other a golden-haired stripper. (Bells are also present but ignored; they ring in a valley of stone.) Dylan cleared out before the trouble started — or he cleared out at some time in the past — and there's another girl who at one point agreed with and supported Dylan's decision to leave, but hung back herself with some other guy. She is in some respects city-corrupt (her beauty is faded), and the singer feels corrupted by their "horseplay"; she's associated with flowers on the one hand, diamonds on the other. The song suggests that she's a forbidden fruit, and Dylan knows she's forbidden, but he's still interested. Or was interested. Or knows he should avoid her, but misses her, which makes him still interested. In terms of Dylan's use of nature, the song is problematic because the singer is — or says he is — in some kind of Paradise, but it is a Paradise Lost, a "landscape being raped." Clearly, it's not what he wants. The final verse predicts a restorative new day at dawn and grace after the rain, but nothing is guaranteed: Dylan sings "*if* [italics mine] I'm there [where? Back in the city with the woman? In Paradise?] in the morning, baby, you'll know I've survived." But he'll survive only with scars, and the song closes on a note of unrepentant regret for lost city and girl — "without you it just doesn't seem right" — foreshadowing the resignation in exile of "Red River Shore."

In "Jokerman" Dylan presents another one of those autobiographical males who preaches redemption while looking around with interest and desire. Nick de Somogyi connects Jokerman with the joker in "All Along the Watchtower," and both of them with the holy fool, the trickster, and The Fool of the Tarot, where he appears on the Waite deck with a small dog which also shows up in this song. Perhaps "Jokerman" also owes something to the Beatles' "Fool on the Hill." Michael Gray devotes nearly 30 pages of *Song & Dance Man III* to the song: a complex web of biblical allusions and personal confessions, emphasizing the book of Ecclesiastes and the biblical significance of the song's natural components, especially water and sun. The song is a favorite of other Dylan exegetes as well, all of whom are fascinated with its ambiguities, contradictions, multiplicities . . . and moral neutrality. Gray concludes, finally, that Dylan not only accepts but exults in unresolvablity and ambiguity. Certainly, nature is ambiguous here: snakes and hurricanes, nightingales (and other birds), and "a small dog licking your face." "The law of the jungle and the sea." Rural seems jumbled up with urban: "Nightsticks and water canons, tear gas, padlocks / Molotov cocktails and rocks behind every curtain." The world is shadowy, Dylan suggests; the skies are "slippery gray" and Jokerman shows no response at all. Dylan has not quite reached the enervation of *Time Out of Mind*, but he's headed in that direction, and his loss of direction is reflected in his depiction of nature. Dylan, as usual, said it best: "That's a song that got away from me. Lots of songs on that album [*Infidels*] got away from me. They just did. . . . That could have been a good song. It could've been" (Cott: 378).

"Floater (Too Much to Ask)" is also troubling, but Dylan is more upbeat about things . . . or pretends to be. Or assumes the persona of a rural redneck who pretends to be. On the surface, life is peachy in this pastoral idyll: over the window comes the dawn of another beautiful day, honeybees buzzing, summer breeze blowing. Sit in the boat fishing, meditate on the attractions of your second cousin, ignore the boss and his pain-in-the-ass hangers-on. Times are tough, but it doesn't bother me. Dylan mentions a squall moving in, but suggests the obvious solution: just stay out of the wind and the cold rain. If you don't like it, then just shove off. It's all good. Neither grandpa nor grandma had any real dreams or hopes, although I had hopes once, but that was long ago; "I left all my dreams and hopes / Buried under tobacco leaves." There's nothing left to do with life except smell the wood stove burning, hear the school bell ring . . . and if you ever cross my path, I just might blow you away. In another chapter we will consider what Dylan expects us to make of this redneck, but the song presents a rural lifestyle in which, taken on its own terms, the livin' is easy . . . but dangerous.

The recent "'Cross the Green Mountain" contains perhaps the most ambiguous nature of all: out of the sea comes the Civil War monster which sweeps through the land of the rich and free, and the ground is frozen hard as frost, but the singer-soldier takes pride in having walked "in fair nature's light" and having remained loyal to truth and light. Nature in this song seems as inscrutable as nature in Stephen Crane's famous Civil War novel *The Red Badge of Courage*, one of the most naturalist works in American literature, which I am sure Dylan

— like the rest of us — read in high school.

Given a subject as rich as nature, and a career as productive as Dylan's, it is not surprising to find contradictions and multiple perspectives. The bottom line, however, is that even in his moments of reassessment, Dylan reflects the attitudes of his birthplace: anyone who lives in proximity to nature, and especially those who live in the Upper Midwest, is reminded almost daily of the extreme dualities of what Hemingway called "the Big Two-Hearted River": mesmerizing countryside and threatening desolation. A dark side is part and parcel of Midwestern pastoralism. And as long as nature remains natural, and as long as nature remains part of our lives, that's the way it's gonna be.

Chapter 4

Going Out/Coming Back

"Probably sometimes I'd like to go back for a while. Everybody goes back to where they came from, I guess."

— *Chicago Daily News*, November 27, 1965

THE ARCHETYPAL JOURNEY

It was Carl Jung himself who once pointed out that although most people do not know *why* the body needs salt, they crave it nevertheless. Other aspects of our lives are like that — we do things instinctively, unconsciously, out of need or habit. So if archetypal patterns are indeed archetypal patterns, we do not need Jungian psychologists and archetypal critics to tell us where we're going. We'll get where they tell us we're headed without their direction, as a matter of course. Each generation will continue to make its own mistakes, the same old mistakes. And, all things considered, it might be better not to have someone telling us we're "just going through a stage." While "terrible twos" is a thought to comfort distraught parents, "midlife crisis" reduces major life decisions, and the people confronting them, almost to insignificance. This kind of psychological analysis is more dismissive than helpful. When power structures educational and governmental dismissed sixties civil rights and anti-Vietnam War protests as "adolescent rebellion," we naturally suspected their agenda was designed more to trivialize our critique than to comfort our parents. (And we were right.)

Archetypal analysis may not even be particularly useful when applied to art. While it explains the tremendous impact a new work of art has on us, and the enduring power of art that has lost its immediate cultural context, its analysis is after the fact (like, we already knew this was high-octane material) or vaguely coercive ("you should have enjoyed this play, because, as you will understand when I explain it, the hero is acting out a pattern still relevant to your world"). And when a writer or filmmaker, even if he's George Lucas or she's J. K. Rowling, consciously manipulates Joseph Campbell myth into story, the result is rarely great art. It makes a ton of money, but like theory-driven art of all sorts, it weaves a magic that is too deliberate, too mechanical. Or it gets lost in new age mumbo-jumbo . . . like the films featuring or about Bob Dylan: *Renaldo and Clara, Masked and Anonymous,* and *I'm Not There.*

Still, I own the books and even read them. Sir James G. Frazer's *The Golden Bough* is, as the dust jacket of the 1951 abridged version claims, "one of the great books of all time": the sacred marriage, perils of the soul, killing the divine king, the myth of Adonis, the story of Osiris and Isis, eating the god . . . you can't invent great stuff like that, and the psychological-mythological background they provide expands our understanding of life. Carl Jung explains more writers than James Joyce, T. S. Eliot, and Herman Hesse (who were very popular in the sixties); *The Hero with a Thousand Faces,* by Joseph Campbell (who edited *The Portable Jung* for Viking Library), is useful for so much more than *Star Wars* and *Harry Potter.* We use archetypes not as a template for assessing the correctness of a story ("whereas the hero typically returns with some gift, in this case . . .") or for measuring its value ("this film contains six of eight essential components of the myth; I score it 8.4 out of a possible 10"), but as ideas in their own right, and as a context for talking about life and art — although, as I suggested earlier, we could develop that context on our own just by doing what Jung and Frazer and Campbell did: examining relevant examples.

In Dylan's case especially, an understanding of the journey as an archetypal pattern, and of the hero as an archetypal figure, sheds light on Dylan's own life journey and the journeys in many of his songs. "The usual hero adventure begins with someone from whom something has been taken, or who feels there's something lacking in the normal experiences available or permitted to the members of his society," writes Joseph Campbell; "This person then takes off on a series of adventures beyond the ordinary, either to recover what has been lost or to discover some life-giving elixir. It's usually a cycle, a going and a returning" (123). Campbell's version of Arnold Van Gennep's *The Rites of Passage* (1909) actually divides the hero's journey into *three* stages, which are very applicable to Bob Dylan: the "preliminary" stage, or departure; the "*liminaire*" stage, or separation from home on a road fraught with dangerous adventures in marvelous environments; and the "*postliminaire*" stage, or return. The second stage produces the most exciting material — Beowulf's contest with Grendel, Gawain's adventures with the Green Knight and his hot wife — while the third stage produces most of the understanding, but also a sense of confusion: Gawain back in Arthur's court, trying to explain to pals who weren't there just what he learned in Wales, and just what his really cool and totally awesome green belt actually symbolizes.

American literature is rich in on-the-road epics, from Lewis and Clark's *Diaries*, through Cooper's *The Pathfinder* and *The Prairie*, to Melville's *Moby Dick*, Twain's *Life on the Mississippi* and *The Adventures of Huckleberry Finn*, Lindsay's *Adventures While Preaching the Gospel of Beauty*, Steinbeck's *Travels with Charlie* and *The Grapes of Wrath*, Miller's *The Air-Conditioned Nightmare*, Kerouac's *On the Road*, Wolfe's *The Electric Kool-Aid Acid Test*, Pirsig's *Zen and the Art of Motorcycle Maintenance*, William Least Heat-Moon's *Blue Highways*, not to mention a whole string of on-the-road flicks from *The Wizard of Oz* to the great *Thelma and Louise*.[1] Behind them all stands Walt Whitman who, Mark Ford notes, "first embodied in poetry the ideal of the archetypal American self journeying down the open road into a future where anything might happen" (129). And behind Whitman and all those American road trips and trippers lie the on-the-road adventures of Aeneas, Odysseus, Christ, Dante, Chaucer's Canterbury pilgrims, the Christian hero of *Pilgrim's Progress*, and the not-so-Christian hero of Fielding's *Tom Jones*. I doubt that Dylan read *Tom Jones* or *Pilgrim's Progress* in Bonn Rolfsen's Hibbing High School English class, but Dylan's reference to Aunt Sally in "Sugar Baby" is just one of many reflections of his familiarity with *The Adventures of Huckleberry Finn*, including the signature Huck Finn cap he wore on the cover of his first album.

Most Americans, and young people in general, are not much interested in the first and third stages of that three-part process, and tend to skew their tales. Americans prefer adventure over wisdom eight days a week. Condense part I, cut part III, expand part II. Or give us a short Phase III, followed by Phase II redux. *The Adventures of Huckleberry Finn*, it will be remembered, ends not with Huck settling down to respectable village life with Aunt Sally, but with Huck striking another match and starting anew, as if Twain were setting up a sequel he never got around to writing. The Joads do not return to Oklahoma, and the real high point of Steinbeck's *The Grapes of Wrath* is Tom's famous forward-looking farewell to his mother:

> "Then I'll be all aroun' in the dark. I'll be ever'where — wherever you look. Wherever they's a fight so hungry people can eat, I'll be there. Wherever they's a cop beatin' up a guy, I'll be there. If Casy knowed, why, I'll be in the way guys yell when they're mad an' — I'll be in the way kids laugh when they're hungry an' they know supper's ready. . ." (572)

John Ford's 1940 film closes with an even more forward-looking scene not in the novel: Ma Joad at the wheel of the family jalopy headed somewhere, forward, further, preaching about the people's will to carry on:

> "Scared, ha! I ain't never gonna be scared no more. I was though, for a while it looked as though we was beat, good and beat. Looked like we didn't have nobody in the whole wide world but enemies. Like nobody was friendly no more. Made me feel kind of bad, and scared too. Like we was lost and nobody cared. . . . Rich fellas come up an' they die an' their kids ain't no good, an' they die out. But we keep a-comin'. We're the people that live. They can't wipe us out. They can't lick us. And we'll go on forever, Pa . . . 'cause . . . we're the people."

"The road is life," observes Jack Kerouac in *On the Road*, and he closes the novel with a panoramic look across America reminiscent of *The Great Gatsby*, ending with a dark meditation on aging worthy of late Bob Dylan:

> So in America when the sun goes down and I sit on the old broken-down river pier watching the long, long skies over New Jersey and sense all that raw land that rolls in one unbelievable huge bulge over to the West Coast, all that road going, all the people dreaming in the immensity of it, . . . and nobody, nobody knows what's going to happen to anybody besides the forlorn rags of growing old, I think of Dean Moriarty, I even think of Old Dean Moriarty the father we never found, I think of Dean Moriarty. (310)

Growing too old to be on the road in America is a sad song indeed. "He who's not busy bein' born is busy dyin'," sang Bob Dylan in a line that is poster material. May we all stay forever young.

Even authors who make good literary currency writing about the home place often opt to stay away, especially if they are from the Midwest. In his meditation on Midwest writers titled *Writing from the Center*, Scott Russell Sanders notes that while Thoreau, Frost, Hawthorne, Faulkner, O'Connor, Welty, and others were "stay-at-home" American writers of place who lived in the places central to their art, Midwestern authors have often left their native place and remained on the road, in permanent exile, or great remove with infrequent (and short) visits:

> Eggleston recollected Indiana life from New York as Samuel Clemens recollected life on the Mississippi from his mansion in Connecticut. Hemingway recalled Michigan from the clarifying distance of Paris. Willa Cather and Wright Morris wrote about Nebraska from opposite coasts, Cather on the Atlantic, Morris on the

Pacific. William Stafford kept making poems about Kansas while living in Oregon. The pattern continues today, for Toni Morrison writes about Ohio from New Jersey, Louise Erdrich writes about North Dakota from New Hampshire, and W. P. Kinsella writes about Iowa from various spots in Canada. (24–5)

These authors may have come home in voice and subject matter, but not in person.[2] Even the art of writers I discussed in *Rooted: Seven Midwest Writers of Place* (2006) remains bipolar, an odd fusion of Midwest realism with distant influences: postmodernist fiction, magical realism, surrealism, symbolist poetry, jazz or classical music, philosophy or history.

America's bedrock Protestantism, stronger in the Heartland than in the East or West, may also be a reason its citizens avoid stage three of the tripartite journey paradigm, as Christianity is based upon a linear history that keeps its hand on the plow and looks always ahead and out. Psychological and mythological paradigms aside, there is no return from New Jerusalem, as Chaucer's pilgrims discovered way back in 1400. Also, America likes to think of itself as a young country still in stage two of its mission: tame the wilderness, drill for oil on the North Slope, grow the economy, push the technology, see what's out there. "Mission accomplished" was George Bush bullshit to cover plans for expanding the war in Iraq: America must keep going, keep growing, do more and then more. Down with the old; your job is to make it new, even if — like Pound and Eliot, and Joyce as well — you make the new from fragments of the old. "There'll be time enough for countin' when the dealin's done," sings Kenny Rogers.

Some thinkers have suggested a vestigial Victorianism in America's obsession with an eternal stage two — with Progress — and Tennyson's great Victorian poem "Ulysses," about an aging king setting out again in search of adventure, was a particular favorite in high school classrooms in the fifties, much discussed and oft recited at graduations and declamation contests.[3] Looking back on his Minneapolis youth in an essay titled "The Victorian City in the Midwest," Harrison E. Salisbury recalls a life where open religion played little role, but submerged Protestantism in the form of Progress was omnipresent:

> All of this was in the great Victorian tradition — go out into the world and make a fortune. Build a mill, erect a city, plow the prairie, dig the riches from the bowels of the earth. This was, as I understood it, man's right. No, man's duty. He was not placed on earth simply to contemplate nature and its beauties. (56)

That was gospel in America in the 1950s, and it was gospel in the Zimmerman household in Hibbing: Abe reportedly once explained to his son that Micka

Electric had to repossess appliances because the people who had bought them mismanaged their time and money and needed to maybe work a little harder. In regard to the journey archetype, the gospel of business and the gospel of Beat are similar: whether you work or whether you play, you stay on the road to your dying day. The road was life for traveling salesman Willy Loman as for Jack Kerouac, and news that Willy will no longer be representing his firm as a traveling salesman precipitates his suicide . . . at the exact moment when Willy has planted his garden, the mortgage has been paid off, and "home" is free and clear at last. Victoria trumps Jefferson. "There ain't no goin' back," sings Bob Dylan, the man who never quit working.

In its obsession with doing always more, the American journey sometimes loses direction, becomes neither Progress nor vacation, neither a going out nor a coming back. Just going. "Sal, we gotta go and never stop going till we get there," enthuses Dean Moriarty in *On the Road*. "Where we goin', man?" Sal Paradise wants to know. "I don't know" is the answer; "but we gotta go" (238). It doesn't matter whether the car is headed for the city or the country, or pointed north, east, west, or south. It doesn't matter whether you're headed toward a good woman and a promising situation, or away from a bad woman and a bad situation, as long as you're in a car, or on a train, or even hiking — moving somewhere.[4] Americans are notorious for their restlessness, even when incessant relocation works them into economic hardship (discarding perfectly serviceable Old just to buy New And Improved, which is usually not in any way improved), psychological pain (how much mental stress do we impose upon ourselves in constantly adjusting to New, with change accelerating just ahead of our capacity to absorb it?), and cultural loss (Dylan told Bono that he admired the Irish for their capacity to hold on to the Old, which Americans so willingly give up [Blake: 8]). American restlessness made car songs an American rock-'n'-roll genre in the fifties and sixties, and before that our songs were full of ships, covered wagons, Erie Canal barges, and railroad trains. We all knew the songs; Carl Sandburg includes groups of "Railroad and Work Gang" songs, "Sailorman" songs, and "Road to Heaven" songs in *The American Songbag*, published in 1927.

For rural Minnesotans, the American journey contains a few wrinkles. The first is directional: because in America the archetypal journey is often overlaid on a pastoral vision, for most Americans the road of departure, when it does take direction, usually leads toward some unsettled paradise "out West." "A sweet little nest somewhere in the West" has been the American dream from settlement times, from the days when Boston and Philadelphia were west of England, Ireland, Germany, and Italy. "The world began in Eden, but it ended in Los Angeles," sang Bob Dylan's buddy Phil Ochs in his own song of westward movement, ending with an ironic "so this is where the Renaissance has led us!" We move west and then further west, from corruption to hope, pursued always by disillusionment and decline.[5] But Minnesota is already west — in the 1950s, most of us would have included Hibbing in our maps of the American West. So when they think of going out, many young Minnesotans look east.

And they often look to the city. Here is wrinkle number two: if you're already living in Eden, where can you go except out to Los Angeles or back to New York? Kids have been leaving the farm and the small town for the city for many, many decades. Page Smith titles successive chapters of *As a City upon a Hill* "Small-Town Boy" and "Makes Good." Smith mentions that a study of Marshall, Oklahoma's first high school graduating class shows "only two remained in Marshall. The rest scattered, going for the most part to the cities. Sims's observations in Aton were similar. Of 299 high school graduates in the years from 1877 to 1910, ninety percent left the community" (231). "The town exported its most able and energetic youth, who found places in the higher occupational ranks of the cities and in many instances carved out distinguished careers on the national scene," he writes (235), citing one Illinois study of "outstanding scientists" which shows that the smaller the city/town of birth, the higher the incidence of outstanding scientists: one in 23,000 persons for Chicago, one in 1,800 for Centralia and Dixon, one per 800 for Henry, and one per 120 for Granville (250). Both Henry Ford and Frank Lloyd Wright, industrial and architectural geniuses of the early twentieth century, grew up on Midwest farms, but lit out at the first opportunity "to the nearest major city to apprentice in technical fields" (Barillas: 46). To rural teenagers of the later twentieth century, looking for a good career and made conscious by books, radio, television, and movies of the great world Out There, the case for departure is even stronger. And today they leave with parental and community approval: "We raise our most capable rural children from the beginning to expect that as soon as possible they will leave and that if they are at all successful, they will never return," writes Paul Gruchow, who grew up on a farm just north of Montevideo, Minnesota (*Grass Roots*: 99).

An artist especially must clear out to become successful. Hibbing High may be a palace, and the countryside around Hibbing (the part which has not been mined) may be Edenic, but Hibbing itself is just a mining town literally on the disappearing edge of nowhere, and no place for an aspiring artist. In *Tarantula*, Dylan wrote, "i will be an old man — & i am only 15 — the only job around here is mining — but jesus, who wants to be a miner . . . i refuse to be part of such a shallow death" (109). Much later in his career, looking over a packet of poems handed him by a kid in Lincoln, Nebraska, Bob Dylan told Robert Shelton, "I know how that boy feels. I know what it's like being a boy in a small town, somewhere, trying to become a writer" (*Home*: 361).

Departure is a cliché of Midwest small-town literature. Jay Gatz came from some place in North Dakota, met Dan Cody one summer day on the shore of Lake Superior, and that was it for Jay Gatz. He left the Midwest, went East — to Louisville, to England, to Long Island — and reinvented himself into *The Great Gatsby* ("helluva book / just a helluva one. that cat sure / tells it like it is," writes Dylan of *Gatsby* in *Tarantula* [46]). George Willard, Sherwood Anderson's main character in *Winesburg, Ohio*, is from a town so small, Anderson could draw a map for his book: a total of four streets, two labeled "alley way." George, like Bobby Zimmerman, is privileged: his father owns the town's hotel. Unlike Bobby Zimmerman, George moves easily among all strata of the town's society and writes for the local newspaper; he is on his way to becoming a small-town success, a writer even. But George — like Bobby Zimmerman — must leave the small town for the city to discover himself. "I'm going to get out of here," he tells his mother early; "I don't know where I shall go or what I shall do but I am going away" (47). In a final chapter of *Winesburg, Ohio*, titled "Departure," Anderson takes George out of town on a train, and "when [George] aroused himself and again looked out of the car window the town of Winesburg had disappeared and his life there had become but a background on which to paint the dreams of his manhood" (247). That in a nutshell is the preliminary stage of the Midwest archetypal journey.

Winesburg, Ohio made Sherwood Anderson famous for the same reason that *Main Street* made Sinclair Lewis famous: millions of Midwesterners found the stories of George Willard and Carol Kennicott true to their own lives. Carol Kennicott, whom Sinclair Lewis himself admitted was modeled on himself, finds *Main Street* smug, and stultifying. A good wife and mother, if a bit flighty, Carol ultimately leaves Gopher Prairie to find a new self in Washington, D.C., working for the Bureau of War Risk Insurance. She discovers a world "which did not cleave to Main Street," and is for a time fulfilled. The ones who stayed in Gopher Prairie, who never get out, are not fulfilled; they remain blindered or "baked in a pie" as Dylan put it in "Under the Red Sky." Anthony Channell Hilfer describes these books (along with Edgar Lee Masters's *Spoon River Anthology*) as "the Revolt from the Village," a movement toward a less idealized depiction of the small town than had been depicted in popular literature and song, with an emphasis on departure.[6]

"In 'getting away,'" writes Nicholas Roe in an essay titled "Playing Time," "Dylan resembles a poet with whom, so far as I know, he hasn't yet been linked:

John Betjeman" (87) — but to explain the departure–return trope in Dylan's songs and life, we do not need John Betjeman when we have Anderson and Lewis, Fitzgerald and Hemingway . . . and more recent writers like Bill Holm and Garrison Keillor.

But there is a wrinkle in the wrinkle: if you grow up in a rural Midwest Eden, even if it seems not so Edenic, your escape is necessarily a journey into the non-Edenic city, and you might not like what you see there. In fact, rural people are at one level suspicious of the city even as they depart for the city. Country folk have seen boys like Ned Curry, in Sherwood Anderson's story "Adventure," move to the city and drop off the radar entirely. Maybe they've heard Carl Linstrum in Willa Cather's *O Pioneers!* describe city life: "there are thousands of rolling stones like me. We are all alike; we have no ties, we know nobody, we own nothing" (123). Maybe they have read Dreiser's *Sister Carrie*, in which the author describes Carrie's move from rural village to urban Chicago this way:

> When a girl leaves her home at eighteen, she does one of two things. Either she falls into saving hands and becomes better, or she rapidly assumes the cosmopolitan standard of virtue and becomes worse. The city has its cunning wiles, no less than the infinitely smaller and more human tempter. (1)

Perhaps they have read — or even memorized — a poem by Carl Sandburg, which Dylan references in *Tarantula*, about the city Chicago:

> They tell me you are wicked and I believe them, for I have seen your painted women under the gas lamps luring the farm boys.
> And they tell me you are crooked and I answer: Yes, it is true I have seen the gunmen kill and go free to kill again.
> And they tell me you are brutal and my reply is: On the faces of women and children I have seen the marks of wanton hunger.
>
> (*Harvest Poems*: 35)

These days they might even know Dave Etter's 1985 parody of Sandburg in a "Chicago" of his own:

> the hustlers still come to the big city by the lake. They come with their neon shirts, their glass pants, their plastic eyes. Yes, and they come with their loaded dice, their two-headed coins, their marked cards. And the rigged games go on twenty-four hours a day, with no letup on Sunday, no time out for Thanksgiving or Christmas.

"Business," they tell you. "Business is America and America is business. You got that straight, buddy?" (*Selected Poems*: 145).

Or maybe they haven't read these books, but this is what they think. "The madly complicated modern world was something I took little interest in," Dylan writes in *Chronicles* (20); "It had no relevancy, no weight." What Dylan found attractive about Minneapolis and New York were the bohemian enclaves of Dinkytown and Greenwich Village, shelters *from* modern urban chaos (as well as connections to other alternative enclaves from Boston to Madison to San Francisco), places where Protestant-Victorian-materialistic America did not exist (*Chronicles*: 55). The University of Minnesota and Manhattan north of Fourteenth Street neither impressed nor interested Dylan. They confirmed, in fact, his darkest suspicions. Izzy Young's explanation for the low attendance at Dylan's Carnegie Chapter Hall concert on November 4, 1961 (only 53 people attended), was that Village people wouldn't go uptown (Hajdu: 103).

So there is a certain ambivalence to the departure archetype as it plays out in the rural Midwest. Folks living close to nature see both its benevolent and destructive sides; they see that the American countryside amounts to a colony exploited by banks, manufacturers, and agribusinesses like U.S. Steel and Archer Daniels Midland; they face cultural deprivation, limited opportunity, and a slow pace of life bordering on boredom. They also sense that both nature and the Midwestern village itself have been corrupted into a marked-down version of urban industrialism, full of "tradespeople and shopkeepers, interested only in making money and swindling one another and the rest of the country," as Ohioan Louis Bromfield puts it in his 1933 novel *The Farm* (8). So why settle for the knock-off when you can get the real thing?

On the other hand, the city remains, in Upton Sinclair's words, *The Jungle*. What to do? Where to go?

Usually, they go out, have their worst suspicions confirmed, and then come back, to see their old place with new eyes and some degree of befuddlement. At least in their stories Midwest writers come back; there is more return in the Midwest journey archetype than in other American versions of on-the-road. In *O Pioneers!*, Alexandra Bergson has the last word in her debate with Carl Lindstrum. She tells him about

> Carrie Jensen, the sister of one of my hired men. She had never been out of the cornfields, and a few years ago she got despondent and said life was just the same thing over and over and she didn't see the use of it. After she had tried to kill herself once or twice, her folks got worried and sent her over to Iowa to visit some relations.

Ever since she's come back she's been perfectly cheerful, and she says she's contented to live and work in a world that's so big and interesting. She said that anything as big as the bridges over the Platte and the Missouri reconciled her. And it's what goes on in the world that reconciles me. (Cather: 124)

You go out, and then you come back. That's what Carl will do. That's what Carol Kennicott will do at the end of *Main Street*, when her active hatred of Gopher Prairie has run out and Washington seems a little hectic: return to the town and her husband, mostly accepting both for what they are, with the faint hope that in a matter of, oh, a hundred thousand years or so, things might improve. Hamlin Garland's story "God's Ravens" tells of one Robert Bloom, who left his country village as a youth to work in the city as an editor for the *Star*. Overworked in the city and stirred by spring winds whispering "sweet reminiscences of farm life," Robert gives up Chicago, where "the struggle is too hard," leaving "the great grimy terrible city" to return with his wife and sons to his native town in northwestern Wisconsin. Of course home is not what he remembers, and he is initially disconcerted by small-town gossip and the Wisconsin version of "Minnesota Nice," but after suffering a stroke, he comes to appreciate how these country people minister to him and his wife like "God's Ravens."

Minnesota writer Bill Holm, born two years after Bob Dylan, recalls his journey out of Minneota, Minnesota, in a 1985 essay titled "The Music of Failure":

At fifteen, I could define failure fast: to die in Minneota, Minnesota. . . . To be an American meant to move, rise out of a mean life, make yourself new. Hadn't my grandfathers transcended Iceland, learned at least some English, and died with a quarter section free and clear? No, I would die a famous author, a distinguished and respected professor at an old university, surrounded by beautiful women, witty talk, fine whiskey, Mozart. . . (56)

Holm's one great desire as a teenager was to see Minneota disappearing, for the last time, in the rearview mirror of his car. He went off to college, studied music and literature, found a job on the East Coast, traveled to Iceland . . . and then "settled almost contentedly back into the same rural town which [he] had struggled so fiercely to escape" (57). Back in Minneota, Holm formed a close friendship with poet Robert Bly, who himself had escaped Minnesota for Harvard and New York, before returning to what he once called his "crumby little place" on the old family farm near Madison. Concluding his tale of going out and coming back, Holm writes, "Whatever failure is, Minneota is not it.

Nothing can be done about living there. Nor should it be. The heart can be filled up anywhere on earth" (87).

Both Holm and Bly, of course, know Garrison Keillor, host of radio show *A Prairie Home Companion* and author of *Lake Wobegon Days* and *Leaving Home*. Keillor himself left Minnesota in 1966, for New York, hoping to land a job with the *New Yorker*. Then he came back to Minnesota. Keillor's persona in Chapter 1 of *Lake Wobegon Days* leaves his home to enroll, like Bob Dylan, at the University of Minnesota. At the university, again like Bob Dylan, he busies himself in creating a new identity:

> I tried out a Continental accent on strange girls at Bridgeman's lunch counter. "Gud morning. Mind eff I seat next to you? Ahh! Ze greel shees! I zink I hef that and ze shicken soup. Ah, par*don* — my name ees Ramon. Ramon Day-Bwah." This puzzled most of the girls I talked to, who wondered where I was from. "Fransh? *Non.* My muthaire she vas Fransh but my fathaire come from Eetaly, so? How do you say? I am *internationale.*" I explained that my fathaire wass a deeplo*mat* and we traffled efferyvhere, which didn't satisfy them either, but then my purpose was to satisfy myself and that was easy. I was *foreign.* I didn't care where I was from so long as it was someplace else. (19)

Relatives from Lake Wobegon visit, and he does not acknowledge them. His composition teacher tells him to write from his own personal experience, but says it with a smirk that suggests his experience is limited and irrelevant, so the narrator writes "the sort of dreary, clever essays I imagined I'd appreciate if I were him." Keillor's narrator erases his youth in Lake Wobegon as completely as Dylan, in *No Direction Home*, says that he sealed the Iron Range from his mind while at the University of Minnesota. Palming one's self off as *internationale* is the supreme moment of searching for a double, looking for complete evaporation, the instant of Rimbaud's "Je est un autre," which so attracted young Dylan. Before long, however, Keillor's narrator tires of the university (and the city) and returns home . . . where he lives the tales of *Lake Wobegon Days*, which became a national best seller.[7]

When it comes to going out and coming back, however, *The Wizard of Oz* is the quintessential Midwestern journey story. Dorothy leaves home, humbly accepts her mission, embarks on her journey down the Yellow Brick Road collecting confidence and friends as she passes from one adventure to the next, gains entrance to the Emerald City, wins her battle and reaps her reward, realizes the shallowness of these city folk (most of whom speak with high-class British accents) . . . and then returns home to Kansas.[8] And, even today, every American kid knows the last line of that film.

And here emerges a twist in the wrinkle in the wrinkle: you can't go home. Nat Hentoff once wrote of Dylan, "You can only go home for a visit, unless you've stopped growing" (117), but that's not it, really. You can't go home again because the person returning home is not the person who left home, and home is not the way you remember it. Actually, in the Midwest these days, home is probably falling apart. Dave Etter's collection *Alliance, Illinois*, loosely based on Edgar Lee Master's *Spoon River Anthology*, opens with a serviceman returning from Korea to his hometown, thinking with a combination of relief and resignation, "nothing has, nothing could have / really changed since I went away" (2); as the collection's 222 poems unwind, however, we learn that what he finds is mostly creeping decrepitude, including, in the last poem, the abandoned train depot "of many fierce goodbyes." *Alliance, Illinois* is full of nostalgia, and decline everywhere apparent. Of course change is a constant, and the American penchant for New means that Old is always being discarded, but American demographics of the second half of the twentieth century — population shifting rural to urban and suburban, Midwest to East Coast, West Coast, Florida, and Arizona — play an important role here. In most of America, decaying Old must be demolished or rehabbed into the New demanded by growing populations of ambitious young people, but in most of the Midwest, Old is merely abandoned. It becomes more visible than it might be elsewhere, and it haunts people perhaps more than it would elsewhere in the country.[9]

Thus develops the sense of bewildered nostalgia which colors so much of the departure–return literature of the Midwest, including the late songs of Bob Dylan. You remember why you left, you know that what you found away from home was in many respects no better than what you had at home, you know that home is even deader now than it was when you left, you know you no longer fit in at home, so you might as well be away. "I'm a stranger here in a strange land," Dylan sings in the tremendously important "Red River Shore" (1997), adding with resignation "but I know this is where I belong."[10] Nothing looks familiar, the dream died a long time ago . . . and yet he dreams the dream, tries somehow to resurrect the past by going back in time. Midwest literature of the twentieth century — even from Revolt from the Village writers — is so filled with nostalgia that it becomes an important component of the departure–return archetype. Nostalgia becomes the understanding one gains in stage two of the journey.

BOB DYLAN, HOME AND AWAY

Keillor's *Lake Wobegon Days*, Dave Etter's *Alliance, Illinois*, and Holm's *The Music of Failure* had not been published, or even written, when Dylan was a lad in Hibbing, so they of course had no influence on him. These books merely record the experiences of others growing up in the same neighborhood at the same time. Even Kerouac's *On the Road* was not published until Dylan's junior year, and Dylan probably did not read it until his year at the University of Minnesota, which was when he first read Guthrie's *Bound for Glory*. Both *On the Road* and *Bound for Glory* fuse two things important in the life of young Dylan (and, coincidentally, in the lives of young Keillor, Bly, and Holm): travel and music. And in a way travel and music represent the same thing in both books: escape from place. In *On the Road* the place escaped is New York — gloomy, crazy, "brown and holy." From page one, Kerouac uses the West as a contrast to New York, an escape, a lifelong dream of seeing America in its great immensity and variety.[11] *On the Road* presents a simple self-contained myth: the road is episodes and visions, and "somewhere along the line the pearl would be handed to me" (11).[12] "In three hundred pages these fellows cross America eight times," wrote Paul Goodman in opening his review of *On the Road*; "and they have kicks." Goodman, the author of *Growing Up Absurd*, was certainly one sympathetic to the alienation which drove the Beats, but for him the book, and the Beats, represented "a lot of sugar for animal energy, but not much solid food to grow on" (283). Young Dylan — like many others of the sixties generation — was less critical, although he later came to share Goodman's opinion:

> Within the first few months that I was in New York I'd lost my interest in the "hungry for kicks" hipster vision that Kerouac illustrates so well in his book *On the Road*. That book had been like a bible for me. Not anymore, though. I still loved the breathless, dynamic bop poetry phrases that flowed from Jack's pen, but now, that character Moriarty seemed out of place, purposeless — seemed like a character who inspired idiocy. He goes through life bumping and grinding with a bull on top of him. (*Chronicles*: 57, 58)

Dylan mentions Kerouac only twice in *Chronicles*.

In contrast, Dylan writes incessantly of Guthrie, his reason for going east in the first place. Legend has it that Dylan first read *Bound for Glory* in a copy loaned to him by Harry Weber, a student friend in Minneapolis, and Dylan "sat in the [Ten O'Clock] Scholar, cutting the pages, until he had finished the book"

(Sounes: 64). Dylan says he borrowed the book from Dave Whittaker, but confirms that he "went through it from cover to cover like a hurricane" (*Chronicles*: 245). Guthrie's book had the right kind of music (folk, not jazz); moreover, *Bound for Glory* reinforced the vision of the journey found in Steinbeck's *The Grapes of Wrath*, and the sense of alternative societies that Dylan had found in music. In the film *No Direction Home*, Dylan makes the point that the folk scene delivered the world as he had always understood it, the world he had discovered outside of Main Street, Hibbing, on late-night radio and records. Folk music jibed better with Dylan's North Country rural roots, his political proclivities at the time, and his notion of the singer as a kind of prophet-bard. Guthrie not only sounded real, he had something to say, something more than "kicks." "Even a lost cause, I thought, would be better than no cause," writes Dylan in *Chronicles*; "To the Beats, the devil was bourgeois conventionality, social artificiality and the man in the gray flannel suit" (247); to Guthrie, the devil had a political dimension, was more akin to the devils prowling the Iron Range. Guthrie's road trip was a better deal than Kerouac's.

The first chapter of *Bound for Glory*, with the alluring title "Soldiers in the Dust," opens with a scene that is *The Grapes of Wrath* on a railroad train — a train which, coincidence of coincidences, had departed from the city of Dylan's birth, Duluth, Minnesota:

> I could see men of all colors bouncing along in the boxcar. We stood up. We laid down. We piled around on each other. We used each other for pillows. I could smell the sour and bitter sweat soaking through my own khaki shirt and britches, and the work clothes, overhauls and saggy, dirty suits of other guys. My mouth was full of some kind of gray mineral dust that was about an inch deep all over the floor. We looked like a gang of lost corpses heading back to the boneyard. Hot in the September heat, tired, mean and mad, cussing and sweating, raving and preaching. (19)

Then, right up front, Guthrie brings the mission: ten or 15 guys are singing, "This train don't carry no gamblers, this train is bound for glory." Then Guthrie brings the politics: "I pulled my guitar up on my lap and told him, 'Gonna take somethin' more'n a dam bunch of silly wisecracks ta ever win this war! Gonna take work!'" (19, 20). "The songs of Woody Guthrie ruled my universe," Dylan remembers in *Chronicles* (49), and later,

> I listened all afternoon to Guthrie as if in a trance and I felt like I had discovered some essence of self-command, that I was in the internal pocket of the system feeling more like myself than ever before. A voice in my head said, "So this is the game." (244)

For a time Dylan spent every waking hour trying to become Woody Guthrie, even though Jon Pankake told him he could not be Woody Guthrie because Jack Elliott already was. In the *Playboy* interview of 1978, Dylan claims to have learned close to 200 Woody Guthrie songs (Cott: 205). On a subconscious level, Guthrie was more important to Bob Dylan than Kerouac and the other urban Beats because of his pastoral vision and his commitment to the working class. Guthrie's ramblings through the West were a journey into blue-collar labor, into the land of leftists (Jeffrey Johnson's book on the Pacific Northwest is titled *"They Are All Red Out Here": Socialist Politics in the Pacific Northwest, 1895–1925*), and into the natural landscape.

Well. Adolescent Bob Dylan really left Hibbing, Minnesota, not on a political mission, but for the reason kids from the farms and villages all over the Midwest have been leaving for decades: for the adventure of leaving. His departure, in the mode of Keillor and Holm, was fuzzy: not so much a grail quest as an escape, a restless looking around for "something more." "I'm not going to fake it and say I went out to see the world or I went out to conquer the world," Dylan told the *L.A. Free Press* in 1965; "I had to get out . . . and not come back. Just from my senses I knew there was something more than Walt Disney movies" (Engel: 104). In 1966 he told Nat Hentoff that Hibbing was not the right place for him to stay and live:

> There really was nothing there. The only thing you could do there was be a miner, and even that kind of thing was getting less and less. . . . *Everybody* about my age left. It was no great romantic thing. It didn't take any great amount of thinking or individual genius, and there certainly wasn't any pride in it. (Cott: 109)

Hard census statistics show no significant decline in the population of either Hibbing or St. Louis County until the 1980s,[13] but the operative phrase in Dylan's explanation is "my age." The young depart, and even if Dylan exaggerated the idea of Hibbing dying in the 1950s, as events transpired his vision was prophetic and his departure perspicacious. "When I left home the sky split open wide," Dylan recalls in "Honest with Me."

The conventional understanding is that Dylan left Hibbing for New York, with a one-year pit stop in Minneapolis. In fact, Dylan's first goings out — beyond high school excursions to relatives in Duluth, to Camp Herzl in Wisconsin, to Matt Helstrom's cabin in the woods south of town, to disc jockey Jim Dandy in Virginia, Minnesota, and down to Minneapolis on weekends of his senior year — were trips west. The summer after his graduation in 1959, Dylan worked as a busboy at Red Apple Café in Fargo, North Dakota. According to David Kemp and Lynn Aspaas — both respected historians associated with the Center for Western Studies at Augustana University — Dylan spent a month or two in Sioux Falls during the winter of 1959–60 (even when he was enrolled at the University of Minnesota), living on Summit Avenue, chasing a local girl (their candidate for the Girl from the North Country), and practicing an acoustic guitar. This may be true: Clinton Heylin reports Dylan AWOL from Sigma Alpha Mu fraternity around Christmas, 1959, and starting to perform at the Purple Onion Pizza Parlor in St. Paul in January, 1960, but he also reports that "according to Terri Wallace this did not occur until Spring 1960" (*Stolen Moments*: 8). One thing is for sure: the summer of 1960 found Dylan in Central City, Colorado, playing piano at a strip joint called The Gilded Garter while living with one of the strippers, before making off with some of Walt Conley's and Dave Hamil's folk records (Heylin, *Stolen Moments*: 9). Not until December of 1960 did Dylan head east: Chicago, Madison, and finally New York.

In many early poems and songs Dylan celebrates his departure from Hibbing, with some of the "stretchers" we noted earlier. The poem "My Life in a Stolen Moment," which was printed on the program of the Town Hall Concert of April 1963, is especially rich in invented tales. Although fictional, these tales do document Dylan's nonfictional desire to see Hibbing disappearing, for the last time, in the rearview mirror of his car.[14] Dylan's stories of life at the University of Minnesota are also apparently part bullshit ("I was enrolled, but I never went to class," Dylan tells us in the film *No Direction Home*), but they too honestly reflect his desire to live life straight up. "My Life in a Stolen Moment" ends with Dylan, after weathering the New York winter (true), pulling out in the spring for Florida (not true), ending up in Sioux Falls, South Dakota (he had been there, apparently, once) . . . you get the idea. The point of this mini *On the Road* tale is simply getting out: you arrive one place and you leave for another; you arrive there and leave again. Travel opens your eyes and ears, even if you can't name all your many influences and tell why it is you do what you do. The road is life, as Kerouac says and Dylan would prove again, after a fashion, in the Rolling Thunder Review concerts.

Elsewhere, Dylan was more honest, more focused, and more thoughtful about leaving Hibbing. "11 Outlined Epitaphs" (1964) is a look back at the road already traveled. He first surveys Duluth with its rocky cliffs and rainy mists, and calls it "a dyin town." He then surveys North Hibbing where "even the markin stones were dead," and South Hibbing where "the winds of the / north came followin and grew fiercer." "I was young / [and] so I ran," Dylan remembers, "an kept runnin." He talks about his arrival in New York City, which he depicts as a graveyard akin to the North Hibbing cemetery: "where

are those forces of yesteryear? / why didn't they meet me here / an greet me
· here?" Parodying Idris Davies's poem "The Bells of Rhymney" (which Pete
Seeger set to music and recorded on a disc produced by Dylan's producer, John
Hammond[15]), he continues: "the underground's out a work / sing the bells of
New York . . . the underground's gone / cry the bells of San Juan." He flashes
back to education (at Hibbing High School? at the University of Minnesota?),
but education is nothing more than rote memorization: study this and get
an A. The immediate solution is the road — in this case a road away from dead
Duluth, dead Hibbing, dead New York, dead school, a dead culture with dead
justice and ridiculous expectations, and into . . . the night, into nature, into the
proletariat, (into Suze Rotolo), into poetry (Villon, Brecht, Behan, Ginsberg,
Blake, and Yevtushenko among others), and into song (Miles Davis, Johnny
Cash, Pete Seeger among others), "t make new sounds out of old sounds / an
new words out of old words" (prophetic, eh?). The journey of "11 Outlined
Epitaphs" is a journey from death to rebirth in not a place, really, but in art and
music. "[M]y road is blessed / with many flowers," Dylan concludes, because
it's endless and it's all songs; flowers and the mirrors of flowers (nature and
nature in art?) answer his isolation; outside the chimes rung, and they are still
ringing.

In his liner notes to *Joan Baez in Concert, Part 2*, which take another close
and closely focused look at his experience in leaving home, Dylan presents a
similar vision. Dylan begins his poem on the Iron Range with the contrasting
images of grass (organic, rooted) and train (a mechanical device for transporting displaced earth). He then moves to self-analysis:

> In later years altho still young
> My head swung heavy with windin curves
> An a mixed-up path revolved an strung
> Within the boundaries a my youth

A place-bound Dylan retreats into a world of symbols and imaginary foes in
which ugly (especially the railroad) is perceived as beauty and rebellion is the
best option. Dylan tracks himself to New York, where he finds more ugly in
the dust and grime, in the cracks and curbs, in the "crackin' shakin' breakin'
sounds." Then, in rural Woodstock, on the edge of the Catskill Mountains State
Park, the drums and gongs and cathedral bells in Joan Baez's voice break down
his defensive pride, open his senses, and straighten out his mind . . . taking him
back, at the poem's conclusion, to a revised vision of grass and train: the grass
is not to be uprooted, and the train becomes less a vehicle for escape than an

excuse to talk to the engineer. Dylan opts finally not for neither, but for a road somewhere between the grass and the train, for he has learned "not t' hurt / Not t' push / Not t' ache / An' God knows . . . not t' try." The journey in this poem, like that in "11 Outlined Epitaphs," has been a psychological journey in the best Jungean-Campbellean tradition, outward to self-knowledge, and then home again with recovered wisdom. Score the poem 9.2 out of 10.

Dylan's songs of this period are generally less thoughtful than these poems, although they frequently tell of journeys west, like the songs he had performed in the summer of 1961: "California Brown Eyed Baby," "Colorado Blues," "Over the Road," and "I'll Get Where I'm Going Someday." These songs do not appear on Dylan's records or in printed anthologies of his lyrics, but "Rambling, Gambling Willie" does. Willie has seen the country from the White House to Cripple Creek and clear down to New Orleans — he's fathered 27 children, yet has never had a wife. "Ride, Willie, ride / Roll, Willie, roll." The justly obscure song "Farewell" is simply (and only; that is the song's weakness) an adolescent male heading out into the world to seek his fortune in the Bay of Mexico, the coast of California, the old Mexican plains, the highway goin' west. The song's tune and tempo reduce the singer's nod to a girl left behind to mere lip service: "I will write you a letter from time to time / As I'm ramblin' you can travel with me too." This is Dean Moriarty placating one of his women before rushing off to adventures with his buddies. "Dusty Old Fairgrounds" is a catalog of all the great times Dylan did (not) have on the carnival circuit: leave Florida for Michigan, Wisconsin, Minnesota, South Dakota, Montana . . . dancing girls, red wine, harmonicas in the lonesome nighttime. This is the adventure contemplated by Kerouac's Sal Paradise in Shelton, Nebraska: "I had visions of a dark and dusty night on the plains, and the faces of Nebraska families wandering by, with their rosy children looking at everything with awe, and I know I would have felt like the devil himself rooking them with all those cheap carnival tricks" (23). Dylan takes an entirely imaginary song from the novel he read in Minneapolis, the novel which helped send him East, not West.

In these songs, Dylan celebrates the simple, naive joy of getting out, of finding himself on a road other men have gone down, in Guthrie's world of paupers, peasants, princes, and kings. Dylan loves the idea of being "a thousand miles from my home"; you can hear the excitement and the wonder in his adolescent voice: here we go, man![16] He has escaped a shallow death in Hibbing, and could not be happier:

my road it might be rocky,
The stones might cut my face.

But as some folks ain't got no road at all,
They gotta stand in the same old place.
Hey, hey, so I guess I'm doin' fine.

("Guess I'm Doin' Fine")

In "Let Me Die in My Footsteps," Dylan promotes travel to Nevada, New Mexico, Arizona, Idaho. "Paths of Victory" takes Dylan on a trip along the river of life, across the fields to adolescent dreams of easy and glorious victories over utterly outclassed Goliaths, promising roads of battles and paths of victory.

The whole point of *The Freewheelin' Bob Dylan* is the independence of life "Down the Highway." Travel is escape, and Dylan is pleased to be going. "I Shall Be Free," he announces. That's the message of *Freewheelin'*, and that's the overall message of Dylan's kick-ass sixties rock albums. That was the attraction of England early on, and the Dylan-Baez duet on Hank Williams's "Lonesome Highway" is one of the more positive moments of Pennebaker's documentary film of that tour, *dont look back*. The sixties were a period of exploration for an entire generation which had not spent four years away from home fighting in Europe or the Pacific, and — far from being content to settle down in the hometown, buy a house, marry the high school sweetheart, and fill her and it up with kids — was understandably antsy to go somewhere. Dylan spoke to these people, fans and critics alike. In a 1965 *Jazz Monthly* piece on Dylan, Maurice Capel made the case succinctly: "To arrive, to succeed, to rest, are synonymous with personal destruction, the triumph of an anonymous and freedom-hating society. Authentic liberation can only be found in movement, in a determined wrench from the 'Leviathan's' encroachments" (113). In *Chronicles*, Dylan describes his early songs: "'I'm a rambler — I'm a gambler. I'm a long way from home.' That pretty much summed it up" (55).

There is something else in some of Dylan's early departure songs. Robert Bly, whose poems and prose books (especially his best seller, *Iron John: A Book About Men* and his later *The Maiden King*) delve deep into archetypes and myth, spoke early in his career of the need of a certain type of boy-god male and his need to leave a girlfriend:

He wants to be tied down to no one, especially not to a woman, and so he is always with "his hand on his lips, bidding farewell." The boy-god typically explains the reason for his departure (which for him is the most exciting part of the love) as caused by vast, whirling forces so cosmic that to obey is to be "pure," and so complicated in their working, that they could, of course, only be understood by "special people" like himself. ("Being": 210)

The boy-god's fare-thee-well is a tender goodbye, but it's a goodbye nevertheless, and one cannot help seeing the girlfriend as embodying the home place, and the young male's excitement over leaving her as excitement over leaving what she represents, as much as who she is. In the pastoral tradition, the land has always been feminine; Page Smith sees the Midwestern small town as being feminine as well after 1920 or so.[17] (In later songs like "Born in Time" and "Red River Shore," the girl also represents a lost home place, or dream, which an older Dylan seeks to reclaim after having mistakenly abandoned it in his youth.)

Several of Dylan's early journey songs, including "Farewell," reflect the need of this "special" male to be gone, to not be tied down, to follow his calling: "One Too Many Mornings," "Don't Think Twice, It's All Right," "Farewell Angelina," "Restless Farewell." This last song begins with a truth about boy–girl relationships lost on many people these days: "ev'ry girl that ever I hurt / I did not do it knowin'ly." Likewise the foes we fight, the arguments we get into, the money we steal "right or wrongfully," the petty bullshit we get entangled in. Most men do not intend the harm they cause to women or anyone else, and most men — especially Upper Midwest men — are more inclined to retreat into themselves than to sit down and talk matters out. Dylan's solution in this song (written perhaps with an eye to the November 1963 *Newsweek* article) smacks of Bly's departing boy-god: "the dirt of gossip blows into my face / And the dust of rumor covers me. . . . [but] I'll bid farewell and not give a damn." Of course most women do not intend the harm they cause either, and the fact that Joan Baez recorded this song suggests that departure might work for a strong woman as well as for a Minnesota boy-god.

On the other hand, some songs, even early material including songs on *The Freewheelin' Bob Dylan* album, temper their celebration of independence with a note of caution, remorse, and even a look — if not a movement — backwards. John Herdman makes the interesting observation that most of Dylan's love songs are "what might be called after-love songs" (18), and in "Don't Think Twice, It's All Right" we hear a hint of regret mixed with accusation in "You're the reason I'm trav'lin' on." As Andrew Muir points out in his detailed analysis of this song (*Troubadour*: 20–9) there is more self-examination, regret, ambivalence in Dylan's lyric than in Johnny Cash's companion song with much the same borrowed melody, "Understand Your Man." At least three girl-left-behind songs are so full of sincere regret that they almost break your little heart. In "Tomorrow Is a Long Time" lost love makes all the beauty of life on the road irrelevant: the beauty in the silver river and the bright sunrise is no match for the beauty in the eye of the right kind of girl . . . if she were still around. Which she is not, for if she were, the singer would return immediately to his own bed back home. In this song the loss of love (Suze Rotolo, we all think) not only outweighs the joys of life on the road, it apparently destroys Dylan's identity and his ability to understand himself: "I can't see my reflection in the waters . . . I can't remember the sound of my own name." Dylan will not be knocked this much for a loop until "Love Sick." Memories of the "Girl of the North Country" are not quite so devastating, but she's obviously been on his mind, and memories of the past are a more immediate concern than any pleasures of life on the road, for Dylan mentions none. No silver river, no beautiful sunrise, just fuzzy memories and doubts: "I'm wonderin' if she remembers me at all." In "One Too Many Mornings," blame and guilt become blurred. "You're right from your side / I'm right from mine," sings Dylan as he looks down the street ahead of him, with a deep breath and a shrug of the shoulder.

"Boots of Spanish Leather" is a little harder. The song recounts the now-famous departure of Suze Rotolo for Italy when her mother and sister decided that a scruffy folksinger was not quite right for their 18-year-old daughter/sister and hauled her off for an extended stay in Perugia, Italy. The male sings the song: the girl is leaving in the morning and offers to send him something to remember her by; he begs her to stay . . . or at least return to him unspoiled; she's equivocal. The strained relationship unravels in a letter that announces, "return date uncertain." And, with some ironic advice to "take heed of the western wind" (a reference to the medieval lyric "Westron Wind"; the lines Dylan is really pointing to are "Christ, that my love were in my arms, / And I in my bed again"), he cuts himself loose: "yes, there's something you can send back to me / Spanish boots of Spanish leather" (a possible allusion to "Black Jack David"). She took her trip; he'll take his. But not without obvious regrets.

Beyond the ambiguities of boy–girl relationships and blame, in some of his sixties travel songs Dylan suggests that the journey itself is a dubious adventure. "The Death of Emmett Till" and "Only a Pawn in Their Game" are not celebratory civil rights songs: they are cautions that any journey south of the Iowa line is dangerous. South is where you go to wear the ball and chain and live your life in sin and misery in the House of the Rising Sun. In the land of the "ghost-robed Ku Klux Klan" you too might get shot; someone might be hiding in the dark behind a bush with a bullet bearing your name. "Oxford Town" is Dylan's 1963 song on the riots and demonstrations that attended the registration of James Meredith at the University of Mississippi in 1962.[18] Dylan was not there, with or without his girlfriend; he was not met with teargas; two people were not killed at the university, as the song implies. But things like this might happen, Dylan suggests, which is reason enough to reconsider such a journey and stay the hell where you come from. In "Blowin' in the Wind," a song of journeys by land and sea, Dylan asks rhetorically "How many trips do you have to take?" He gives no answer. If the journey is a walk or a sail to nowhere, what exactly is the point of the journey?

Bringing It All Back Home and *Highway 61 Revisited* are suggestive titles for rock-'n'-roll albums: rock is not usually so retrospective. Usually, the references are interpreted in a musical context — Dylan returning to the rock-'n'-roll and the electric guitar he had played in high school — or in a social context: cut through the insanities of modern Amerikkka to fundamentals like a good woman and good music. Oddly, while Dylan's new electric sound presses him (and American pop music) forward from folk-protest to rock, the many allusions and references in the songs themselves look backward into cultural history. They are a return to the cultural roots. So while Dylan appears to suggest the familiar solution of lighting out for the Territory — "On the Road Again," "Can You Please Crawl Out Your Window?" "Outlaw Blues" — and while it appears that the "home" to which we are bringing it all back is the home dream of life on the road, such is not really the case. As many critics have observed, "How does it feel / To be on your own / With no direction home / Like a complete unknown / Like a rolling stone?" implies as much angst as relief: the road is not necessarily life — for Princess on the Steeple, for the folk music crowd, for the sixties generation, for Dylan himself.

The opening lines of "It's All Over Now, Baby Blue" suggest similar reservations about the journey: "You *must* leave now, take what you *need*." The journey liberates us from the dead we leave behind, but it's an act more of desperation than of exploration or inspiration, and Dylan's emphasis is as much on finding fragments of the past that he can hold on to as it is anticipation of starting anew. Seasick sailors, orphans, and vagabonds do not promise paths of glory; they are roadsick refugees tired of the journey and looking for a place to hole up. The acoustic version of this song recorded at Manchester on May 17, 1966, and released on *Biograph*, has an especially haunted feel to it, with Dylan's tentative start, the soft guitar and the softer harmonica drifting into and out of silence, the elastic vowels — Dylan shrugging his shoulders in musical resignation. Bob Dylan is not a happy traveler here, and this song and performance are definitely Dylan on Dylan. Talking with John Cohen and Happy Traum in 1968, Dylan made the point himself: "I'll tell you another discovery that I've made. When the songs are done by anybody on a record, on a strange level the songs are done for somebody, about somebody and to somebody. Usually, that person is the somebody who is singing the song" (Cott: 122). Talking to Paul Zolo in 1991, he repeated himself: "My songs were written with me in mind" (Cott: 381).

"Farewell Angelina," while something of a boy-god departure song, also suggests a journey which is compelled, not chosen: "The sky is on fire / And I must go." The song's final lines suggest an escape out of urban chaos into some country place "where it's quiet," but the road in this song is not life — it's only a necessary, and hopefully temporary, laying low while you nurse your fears and anxieties. This angst about being rootless (in Dylan's case, at having lost his Minnesota moorings) is absent in both Robert Shelton's *No Direction Home* and Martin Scorsese's *No Direction Home*, which celebrate as only postmodern urbanites could do the adrenalin rush of losing one's place.

Dylan's electric albums are no celebration of the city scene, with its hectic life of drugs, sex, and rock-and-roll, but mostly depictions of an urban landscape full of painted women and hired gunmen, with implicit or explicit desire for escape from the nightmare. Often that escape is impossible, as in "Gates of Eden," where those gates are locked and impenetrable. When escape does come, it's escape into music ("Visions of Johanna," "Mr. Tambourine Man"). A few lines in a few songs suggest that Dylan misses something or some place, but at this point he's not thinking of any Midwest pastoral idylls — in fact, a throwaway line in "One of Us Must Know (Sooner or Later)" suggests that he's way too hip for that kind of stuff: "you were just kiddin' me, you weren't really from the farm." In terms of his dress, performance persona, girlfriends, and style, Dylan — like the Beatles — had traveled a long way in a short time: adventure after adventure in his Kerouacian road trip into the American dream.

This is the point at which many Dylan biographies (printed and cinematic) end, partly because it makes a good ending, especially backed with a rousing chorus of "Like a Rolling Stone": youthful energy, the thrill of success, the excitement of the unfolding sixties, drugs, and momentum.

We now know that the journey took a terrible toll. "I was on the road for almost five years," Dylan told Jann Wenner in 1969; "It wore me down. I was on drugs, a lot of things. . . . And I don't want to live that way anymore" (Cott: 140). As David Boucher suggests, "Paradise in New York or Los Angeles ironically became more of an illusion than the great American dream itself. . . . The rediscovery of the dream would come, not by severing oneself from the culture one despised, but by rediscovering tradition through a new communion with nature." Looking beyond the electric rock albums, Boucher adds what we noted in the previous chapter: "the countryside became the promised land and the city the site of a new biblical Exodus from Egyptian enslavement" (*Dylan & Cohen*: 66). Biographically, this process had already begun even as Dylan was recording the electric albums; the motorcycle accident in Woodstock merely provided a road-weary Dylan with the excuse he finally needed to quit the road, stop touring, and come back to an approximation of home.[19]

So just when did Dylan first contemplate the return phase of the going out-coming back paradigm? A remark made by one of his Dinkytown friends to Anthony Scaduto suggests that even in Minneapolis, when Dylan tells us in the film *No Direction Home*, "I'd forgotten all about the Iron Range, where I grew up. It didn't even enter my mind," Dylan was playing a rural role which suggests an unspoken memory of, and fondness for, one aspect of the North Country: "I used to ask him, 'How's the man of the soil today?' And that's what he was. Full of the Jesse Fuller thing, being down to earth, being a man of the soil" (44). That was Dylan's role in Minneapolis and New York: "the American primitive role," Scaduto calls it, quoting Van Ronk: "Being a hayseed, that was part of his image" (82). Dylan's early songs reflect a fondness for the rural West over urban New York, and one very early unrecorded, unpublished lyric written during Dylan's first month in New York is about "a lonesome man who feels 'so bad' stuck in Texas City, which 'ain't no friend of mine,' and who is pining away for old East Colorado" (Scaduto: 80). As early as 1962, Dylan spoke of Minnesota as quiet and pleasant (Shelton, *Home*: 148). By 1964, in "11 Outlined Epitaphs," Dylan seems to have made some peace with Hibbing:

an I know I shall meet the snowy North
again — but with changed eyes nex time round
t walk lazily down it's [sic] streets
an linger by the edge of town
find old friends if they're still around
talk t the old people
an the young people
running yes . . .
but stoppin for a while
embracing what I left
an lovin it — for I learned by now
never t expect
what it cannot give me

And even while explaining his reasons for leaving Hibbing to Nat Hentoff in 1966, Dylan equivocated: "As I think about it now, though, it wouldn't be such a bad place to go back to and die in. There's no place I feel closer to now, or get the feeling that I'm a part of" (Cott: 109).

Doubts, reservations, and memories are not exactly going back, but we know that Dylan returned to Minnesota, as early as May, August, and December of 1961. He returned to Hibbing for his brother's graduation in 1964, for his father's funeral in 1968, for his tenth-year class reunion. And he was pretty pepped up about that reunion:

> "When I was fifteen, I said to myself, 'They treat me pretty low-down here now, but I'll be back one day and then they'll all run up and shake my hand.' And it actually came true, in the summer of 1969. I sat there in Hibbing and signed autographs for an hour, more than an hour." (Shelton, *Home*: 16)

Shelton also reports that Dylan's brother David found him at this point a very mellow, mature person, "amazingly like his father. . . . Could he have become what he had so long opposed?" (*Home*: 61).

These were only visits, and Dylan did not move back to Hibbing and take a job at Micka Electric. He did, however, retreat to a series of rural hideouts. As early as 1962 Dylan holed up for a time with friend Paul Clayton in a log cabin in Charlottesville, Virginia, that resembled Echo Helstrom's dad's place: "The place had no electricity or plumbing or anything: kerosene lamps lit the place at night with reflective mirrors" (*Chronicles*: 73). Then he started hiding out in Woodstock, New York, 75 miles north of Manhattan, at places owned by Peter Yarrow's dad and Albert Grossman, first with Suze Rotolo, then with Joan Baez, and later with Sara. In 1965 he bought his own home in Woodstock, where he had his famous motorcycle accident on July 29, 1966, and jammed with The Band (then the Hawks) at Big Pink the year following. "Truth was I wanted to get out of the rat race," Dylan writes in *Chronicles* (114). When the retreat from chaos to Woodstock boomeranged as the rat race followed Dylan to Woodstock, he returned briefly to New York City in 1969 ("It was even worse," writes Dylan in *Chronicles*: 118), then started spending a lot of time on Fire Island, off of Long Island.[20] At various points in the 1970s, Dylan bought a ranch north of Phoenix, Arizona, and then a home on the Point Dume peninsula north of Malibu Beach, and then an 80-acre farm tract just west of Minneapolis near the Crow River, where he remodeled the barn into a house and hid out during the summer, playing with his kids, writing songs, romancing his current woman. Ellen Bernstein (for whom we think "You're Gonna Make Me Lonesome When You Go" was written) recalls Dylan on the Crow River farm: "He was at his best there, at his most comfortable, with his brother's house down the road. He had a painting studio out in the field, and the house was far from fancy, out in the middle of nowhere" (Gill and Odegard: 40). "Rural domestic bliss," Gill and Odegard call Dylan's life in Minnesota (41). Clinton Heylin pointed out, in the introduction to the 1988 edition of *Stolen Moments*, that Dylan constantly veers between bouts of frenetic activity in New York, Los Angeles, or around the world, and relaxation on his Minnesota farm or some equivalent thereof (xix); in *Revolution in the Air* he reports the revealing bit of information that the working title of "My Back Pages" was "Ancient Memories" (206)!

So we can say that, in his own life, Bob Dylan had escaped Hibbing for Minneapolis, then escaped Minnesota for the East Coast. New York City itself he found hostile and cold, but within the city he found an enclave which, in distancing itself from the materialism of modern urban America, critiqued the commercial life which one side of Hibbing mirrored, while valuing the kind of rural existence he had found on the other side of Hibbing. In going into folk music, Dylan departed from Iron Range polka and Top 40-schlock songs, rode the folk revival for a time, then departed from it by going electric, transforming himself into the epitome of postmodern urban hip and temporarily transforming the nature of Top 40 as he birthed modern rock-'n'-roll. But even as he appeared to be forging ahead musically, Dylan was retreating personally, to a landscape which resembled more Minnesota than Manhattan. As the sixties unfolded, Dylan continued to venture forth literally all around the globe, and he continued to retreat to pastoral hideaways. The music went in one direction while Dylan's life went in two directions, until, with *John Wesley Harding*, Dylan's music caught up with his life.

In *John Wesley Harding*, Dylan returns not exactly to folk songs, but to something approximating rural music. This album came as a shock in 1969, but with the clarity of hindsight we can see hints of Dylan's disillusionment in the songs of those three great electric albums (conversely, many of the "country" songs on this album are full of the surreal images, condensed narratives, and startling jumpcuts that characterize Dylan's electric songs). In *John Wesley Harding*, Dylan seeks to repair a journey gone too far by moving out of the (eastern) city into the (western) countryside. The album is generally claustrophobic, especially on its first side, but ultimately Dylan celebrates escape from corruption into the right kind of rural place. In "I Pity the Poor Immigrant," Dylan even suggests that if all immigrants (including himself) had just stayed home, they would not need to passionately hate their lives while also fearing their death.[21] Dylan predicts that in the final end, all visions must shatter like glass (an echo of the glass of "St. Augustine"?), but the shattering of visions will be a release, a moment of grace, and a return home. The album closes with an anti-trip: close the door, open a bottle, and "I'll be your baby tonight." The album which began in an outlaw raid on the System — very much in the Campbell mode — closes with hunkering down at home. It thus touches two of the three Van Gennep-Campbell stages, and receives an 8.7 on the archetypal critics' scorecard.

Certainly after *John Wesley Harding*, Dylan too went home and, as he puts it in the last song of *Nashville Skyline* (1969), threw his ticket out the window. So as Dylan moved from New York City to a series of rural retreats — returning in many respects to his home place — he moved the sound of the city to the sound of the country.

Not only does the music sound rural, the songs of Dylan's country period contain several references, or possible references, to Dylan's Minnesota past, including an encore of "Girl of the North Country." Stephen Scobie suggests that the "Frank" in Dylan's liner notes to *John Wesley Harding* is really Frank Hibbing, the German prospector who founded the town where Dylan grew up: "the key is Frank," Dylan writes — not faith or froth (19). Michael Gray suggests that the whole *Planet Waves* album "devotes itself to revisiting, as the adult with the mid-1960s surreal achievement behind him, the Minnesota landscapes and feelings from which he had emerged in the first place" (*Song*: 179); Robert Shelton remarks, "*The Basement Tapes* could have been titled *Roots*" (*Home*: 385), and notes that Dylan singled out "Something There Is About You" during the Tour '74 as a favorite, an echo of times with Echo and "an evocation of times past in Duluth" (435). In that particular song, Dylan admits that he thought he'd shaken "the wonder and the phantoms" of his youth, but the woman addressed in the song has brought him out of the whirlwind to "some better place" which is very much like back home. It is interesting that "Went to See the Gypsy," from the *New Morning* album, ends with the sun rising "in that little Minnesota town." Extrapolating from a remark Dylan made in recording this song, both Michael Gray and Howard Sounes say the song is about Dylan meeting Elvis, but when and where they met is "unclear" (Sounes: 259). Just what Minnesota might have to do with the jester and the king is equally unclear.[22] Perhaps the song is better interpreted as Dylan going into a big hotel in an urban area to meet a force he hopes will cure his anxiety ("Drive you from your fear"), but finding no answer and escaping, finally, into the natural world outside the hotel window: river, dawn, rising sun. In Minnesota.

"On a Night Like This" sounds like the North Country, with the four winds blowing around the old cabin door and folks inside reminiscing over hot coffee. And although Gray finds *New Morning* artificial and forced, at least part of Dylan seems to enjoy himself again during this period and dropping out of the serious journey-become-rat-race has made Dylan a mellow, if boring, man, disinterested in complex philosophical matters. As Dylan asks less and receives more, *The Basement Tapes* is full of post-Guthrie Guthrie characters, vacations, and runs to the bar, like "Goin' to Acapulco," "Lo and Behold!" and "Tiny Montgomery." They're also full of pleasant non-journeys, like "You Ain't

Goin' Nowhere" and "This Wheel's on Fire," in which Dylan decides to unpack his things and just be.

"For the public eye, I went into the bucolic and mundane as far as possible," Dylan recalls (*Chronicles*: 123). He told Robert Shelton that the songs of this period "reflect more of the inner me than the songs of the past. They're more to my base" (*Home*: 399). Dylan was living a kind of North Country pastoral on record royalties and taking his kids camping, boating, rafting, canoeing, fishing. Did he not wish for them — and us — a strong foundation to anchor us from the winds of change?

Well, you can't retire in your twenties, no matter how the winds of changes are blowing. Going home to lead a quiet life is not Bob Dylan, or the proper role for any kid with a Midwestern work ethic. "He wasn't born for this," writes John Hinchey in an essay titled "*New Morning* and Beyond: Biding Time, Biting His Tongue" (4). "If Bob had indeed been content as a country squire, it didn't last long," writes Anthony Scaduto (263). Hints of a growing boredom can be heard in a song like "Time Passes Slowly," where Dylan sits lost in a dream, fishing, with no inclination to go to town, to the fair, anywhere. "Time passes slowly," he concludes, "and fades away." "Wish I was back in the city / Instead of this old bank of sand," sings Dylan in "Watching the River Flow." Ultimately, the stasis got to him; he returned briefly to New York City, decided (again) that the "apartment block feeling" was an environment "no longer at the centre of his consciousness" (Gray, *Song*: 429), and hit the road for "Tour '74," to be followed by Rolling Thunder tours of 1975 and 1976, the very un-laid-back-rural insanities of which have been recorded in the film *Renaldo and Clara* and Sam Shepard's *Rolling Thunder Logbook*. "Dylan finally admitted that although 'being settled' may result in personal happiness, the romantic agony of loss and search are goads to greater art," writes Robert Shelton (*Home*: 441).

These tours replicated the frenetic tours of the middle sixties. At the start, Dylan was optimistic and enthusiastic about returning to life on the road. He began the opening performance of "Tour '74" with a rewritten version of "Hero Blues," a song he'd written in the early sixties: "almost yelling that he had 'one foot on the highway, and one foot in the grave'" (Sounes: 275). The music on the Rolling Thunder tour was terrific — even if the film lacked shape and sense. "I been playin' it straight," Dylan sings in a 1973 lyric "Going, Going, Gone"; "Now, I've just got to cut loose / before it gets late." Sounding like a sports broadcaster calling a home run, he announces his departure: "I'm going / I'm going / I'm gone."

But it wasn't long before Dylan — going out for the second (or third? or tenth?) time in his career — felt the old ambivalence. "Going, Going, Gone" is a subtle road song: just how will the baseball feel when, after the exhilarating ride up and away, it disappears right out of the park? How will Dylan feel when the book is closed on pages and text? The song does not look back, but it moves forward only with effort and the old misgivings of "How does it feel to be out on your own?" In the song's original lyrics, Dylan receives advice and reassurance from his grandmother: "Boy, go and follow your heart / And you'll be fine at the end of the line . . . / Don't you and your one true love ever part." As Dylan gradually rewrote the song, "true love" became "long, long dream," the old dream of going out. The true love, which might imply place or stasis or roots — anything that would stake a claim on the singer — disappears from that dream. Hit the road, Grandma seems to be saying. But the very fact that Dylan needs this encouragement suggests that reservations remain, and it is not without some effort of will that Dylan concludes, "I've just got to cut loose." As in the later "Red River Shore," Dylan knows he's estranged from whatever gave meaning to his life, but the road is, regrettably, where he belongs and is what gives him his song.

In other words, the journey has become a necessary effort, not a release, and one which will cost as much as it yields. It did. The Rolling Thunder tours became increasingly incoherent, and left Dylan again weary of the road, psychologically adrift, and in hock to the film *Renaldo and Clara*, which bombed in all but the artiest of circles. "He doesn't know what he's doing half the time," singer Mick Ronson claimed (Blake: 161). Sam Shepard wrote, "You begin wishing you could just go back into the kitchen with the waiter and wash a few dishes or even go back home with him and watch color TV with his grandmother. Anything just to get the taste back of 'normal everyday life'" (82).

Joseph Campbell warns that the return phase of the hero's adventure is difficult:

> All these different mythologies give us the same essential quest. You leave the world that you're in and go into a depth or into a distance or up to a height. There you come to what has been missing in your consciousness in the world you formerly inhabited. Then comes the problem either of staying with that, and letting the world drop off, or returning with that boon and trying to hold on to it as you move back into your social world again. That's not an easy thing to do. (129)

Return seems especially disappointing in the rural Midwest, where adolescents found such compelling reasons for getting out, and left with such high expectations. It involves that compromise with dreams that comes upon us in our thirties and forties and never becomes quite acceptable. Besides, when we return to reclaim it, the old world is disappointing and, as I have mentioned, full of decay. Minnesota author Bill Holm did return to his hometown to retire a distinguished professor, but from a not particularly distinguished state school with little whiskey or Mozart, a history of 40 brief years, incessant committee meetings with zero witty talk, a shrinking library . . . and, okay, a couple of beautiful women. Meanwhile, the Minneota Holm had left as a teenager was collapsing in the streets, a mere memory in the local consciousness. Holm wrote a book titled *Landscape of Ghosts*, introducing it as "a book full of pictures of stuff nobody wants to look at and of essays on subjects no one wants to read about" (7). So you go out and you come back again, and, yet again, comfortable with neither the road nor the home. After 1975, but especially in the 1980s and 1990s, Dylan found himself strung out on the idea of journey for the rest of his career, a man constantly searching for but never able to find the home place. A man "unraveling" on foreign shores, as he put it in "Emotionally Yours," pleading for somebody, something to take him back to where he once began, where he belongs emotionally.

SIX TYPES OF DYLAN JOURNEYS

Reviewing Dylan's career of journeys and journey songs, we notice several *kinds* of journey, all tangled to some degree in myth or theology, all except the first more subtle than jumping on a boxcar or hitching a ride out of town. Journeys of all types can be found in early and late Dylan material, although certain journeys tend to concentrate in the songs of certain periods. Some journeys we have already discussed in following Dylan's career from 1960 to the mid-1970s; others show up later. Although many of these journeys fail, all, I would argue, are compatible with and may reflect Dylan's rural Midwest origins.

The Journey into Freedom
The simplest of these is the attempted journey into absolute freedom through renunciation of present loves, successes, comforts, and ambitions in return for the rewards of the road. As we've seen, these journeys are especially common in the early songs, and the songs of the years of touring: Rolling Thunder, the world tour of 1978, the "Never-Ending Tour" which began in 1988. "Running for the sake of running," Dylan called this in a mid-sixties interview with Nat Hentoff (Cott: 25), and Nick Smart opens his discussion of "Bob Dylan from Place to Place" with this quip "Place . . . is where you should leave from" (179). The idea is to keep on keeping on, a phrase which Dylan uses in "Tangled Up in Blue." Andy Gill points out that songs of departure on Dylan's 1970s albums

rarely arrive anywhere, but at that time Dylan didn't seem to care (112). "I'm not getting caught by all this rot," he had written in the jacket notes to *Another Side of Bob Dylan*; "as I vanish down the road with a starving actress on each arm."

This journey-for-the-sake-of-journey accords well with "He who's not busy bein' born is busy dyin'," and with what Dylan had to say to Robert Shelton in the middle eighties: "The important thing is to keep moving. . . . I guess that's about the best thing anyone can do" (*Home*: 14). There is an American Protestantism to this journey, the old relentless Midwestern Neo-Victorianism, but also an existentialist quality, as Rick Furtak points out in an essay subtitled "Passion and the Absurd in Dylan's Later Work":

> Dylan shows us something about the possibility of finding hope in a blighted world, and he even considers how one might continue to live without hope if necessary. In doing so, he makes a valuable contribution to the literature of the existential tradition, which is represented by such philosophers as Søren Kierkegaard (1813–1855) and Albert Camus (1913–1960). (16)

Dylan's line "standing next to me in this lonely crowd" ("I Shall Be Released") is probably a conscious or unconscious reference to David Riesman's 1950 book *The Lonely Crowd*, which stood — along with William H. Whyte's *The Organization Man* — as the standard analysis of the fifties American existential predicament. Irwin Silber also sees Dylan as a proto-existentialist: "Life is an absurd conglomeration of meaningless events capsuled into the unnatural vacuum created by birth and completed by death" (103). Shelton's 1986 biography *No Direction Home* caught this dimension in Dylan's thought, ending in an allusive hymn to the road as Dylan's answer to existential absurdity:

> There may be blood on those tracks and nothing is revealed, but he'd told us there must be some way out of here. There may be no direction home for him or a lot of us, but with one foot on the highway and the other in the grave, we try to get outside the empty cage that holds us. Desperation and hope fight in the captain's tower, a pairing of twins. Although it's all over now, we renew ourselves by leaving the dead behind. We're younger than that now. Death and rebirth. For every seven people dyin' there's seven new ones being born. (497)

In "Visions of Johanna," a complex and beautiful song, Dylan escapes what appears to be a sequence of selves to achieve freedom in music and the road. "Ain't it just like the night to play tricks when you're trying to be so quiet?" he asks to open the song. Everyone is stranded, although everyone is denying he's stranded. Louise and her lover (perhaps Dylan himself), flickering lights, coughing heat pipes (those who should know claim this was a description of the Hotel in New York, where Dylan lived with Sara), a radio which nobody bothers to turn off, and visions of Johanna that conquer the poet's mind: in these images Dylan depicts his own exhausted enervation. Craig Scobie (259) sees "Johanna" as a pun on Gehenna, the burning garbage dump in the Valley of Hinnon, near Jerusalem, a place set for the destruction of the wicked and of all things evil. If that is even part of Dylan's intention, his situation is desperate indeed. The song proceeds through a series of perspectives on himself to escape into music, or into something with the assistance of music. From the arid room of the first stanza, Dylan's song opens to the empty lots where the night watchman asks that crucial question, "Just who's nuts around here?" From there the scene shifts to a hallway where new Dylan leaves the old Dylan (little boy lost) paralyzed by self-pity. "All we have to get hung up on is hang-ups themselves," he suggests as he prepares to energize himself by the simple act of leaving, a symbolic act he has used so often before. The pros and cons of fame are weighed, and the cons win: you can be the greatest ever, you can be Mona Lisa, but you're still going to have those old highway blues. In a favorite guise of a peddler (cf. "Like a Rolling Stone") Dylan confronts the countess alter ego (fame?), who's pretending to care for him, denies that self, and breaks free in an explosion of psychological debris, leaving the visions of Johanna — whatever they represented — as all that remain. "We're even, and I'm gone," Dylan sings, rejecting the world, the country, and himself for the freedom of the open road. This song is Dylan's most unequivocal affirmation of the road, stronger even than "Like a Rolling Stone."

Whatever the successes or failures of Rolling Thunder and the Never-Ending Tour, Dylan's escape songs almost always fail. Moreover, the failure worsens as Dylan's career unfolds. The journey fails because Dylan loses his sense of direction, because he can't escape pursuit, because he can't break old habits, or because he's strung out on the past. The 1986 memory song "Brownsville Girl" is a return to *On the Road* outlaw adventures, but direction is lost and the journey is pointless, as Paul Williams observes (263): "the song doesn't have much to say" and "the love story contained within the frame is unconvincing." Or, Dylan suggests, our journey becomes less exploration than escape from some unseen Pat Garrett, or some posse up in the hills outside of Durango, or rival mobsters outside a New York clam bar, or New Jersey cops. This journey is no fun, because, try as we might, we cannot escape what pursues us.

The most fully realized mature song of this journey-for-the-sake-of-journey — "Where Are You Tonight? (Journey Through Dark Heat)" — is far from the celebratory "Visions of Johanna." Michael Gray (*Song*: 228–30) reads the song as tracking Dylan's path from Sara (the woman he longs to touch) to Christian salvation (the new day at dawn) through the years in New York City (Elizabeth Street, and more generally "that valley of stone"). In a more general sense, the song recalls/recounts a journey into distraction: a good woman, now "drifting like a satellite," has been lost when the singer left town at dawn, producing the disasters of a million dreams gone, a landscape being raped. Sacrifice, "the code of the road," produced only estrangement, loss, and scars; Christopher Ricks sees this song as Dylan's *Paradise Lost* (342). The beginning of the song finds Dylan writing a tearful letter from a long-distance train that rolls through the rain; the end of the song finds Dylan hoping to make it to morning, congratulating himself on surviving so far, and calling out to the woman he abandoned, without whom things just don't seem right. Dylan might be free — he might even be on the road to salvation — but he certainly does not sound happy. A choice between life in the valley of stone and a journey of this nature is not much of a choice, but a fellow might just as well see what's out there.

The Journey toward Salvation

In many songs, Dylan explores a more purposeful journey: the Christian journey into redemption and righteousness, vaguely overlaid with the American mission into the wilderness, and sometimes identifying Dylan as, or with, Christ. The journey in these songs is usually allegorical: the miracle of metaphor transforms a walk down the highway, a train ride or even the quest for an idealized Sara into a journey toward salvation. Read allegorically, "Paths of Victory" (1964) becomes one such journey from struggle to grace, from this world to the heavenly city. "The Times They Are A-Changin'," filled with biblical allusions, offers the old road of corruption and the new road of reform and "please get out of the new one if you can't lend your hand." Songs of the Christian period especially make this journey: there's a slow train coming, and you better be ready to ride it; the road is rough in "What Can I do for You?" but Dylan is ready to shake the dust off his feet, not look back, and press ahead ("Pressing On"). As Gray points out, Dylan's "Dignity" parallels Christian's quest for the Celestial City in *Pilgrim's Progress* (*Song*: 625), and "Covenant Woman" uses the familiar image of "strangers in a land we're passing through." The fact that Dylan reintroduced Christian songs — including hymns he had not written himself — into his twenty-first century performances suggests not only his acknowledgment of their importance in the history of American music and culture, but a continued commitment to this allegorical journey.

Despite bushwhackers in the City of Destruction, temptations in the Slough of Despond, and discouragements in the Valley of Humiliation, prospects in

Christian journey songs are generally brighter than the prospects in most journey-for-the-sake-of-journey songs, at least until the twenty-first century. "Nothing can hold you down," Dylan tells us in "Pressing On," as he presses relentlessly on to the higher calling of his Lord. "Just remember that death is not the end," Dylan sings in the hypnotic song of that title, and "the bright light of salvation shines / In dark and empty skies." "There's only one road and it leads to Calvary," Dylan tells us in "Saving Grace," but he promises that beyond Calvary is life everlasting. "Ye Shall Be Changed," Dylan promises in his brightest song of the Christian journey. The song, an outtake from the sessions which produced *Slow Train Coming* (an album more of jeremiads than journeys), was finally released in the Bootleg Series. As its title suggests, it celebrates that moment after resentment and emptiness, after working "from early in the morning 'til way past dark," after drinking bitter water and eating the bread of sorrow, when Christ comes in glory, the last trumpet blows, the dead arise, and justice prevails. "The path you've endured has been rough," Dylan admits, but at the end of life's journey is eternal salvation for the faithful.

While the idea of life as a journey to heaven or hell lends meaning to our lives, it also raises questions which cloud the path. Not all of these questions are present in the songs themselves, but they have troubled some listeners. The Christian journey is, in one sense, escapist in a manner reminiscent of the Puritan founders: it would rather run away from evil than confront it, analyze it, or try to change it. We just might become complacent. If the first will be last and the last will be first, as Jesus promises us in Matthew 19.30 and Dylan promises us in "The Times They Are A-Changin'," one might as well stay last. But even if this kind of self-effacement and low expectations sound Midwestern, one would never, in the Protestant Midwest, give one's self over to a life of sloth.

Or we might become smug: "You've chosen me to be among the few" ("What Can I Do for You?") is a bit much, especially for a Midwestern boy.

Or we might become neurotic: the same theology which promises heaven also teaches us that salvation is a gift we can never earn, that we will never on our own carry ourselves to that golden strand just beyond the river, that this is a world, as Paul Nelson put it, "where things aren't often pretty, where there isn't often hope, where man isn't often noble" as the folkniks and Marxists imagined (McGregor: 75). So despite our best intentions and efforts on behalf of the world and our own selves, all we will get is relapses, setbacks, failures, and the angst they bring. This truth Greil Marcus grasped in his 1979 review of *Slow Train Coming*: "What Dylan does not understand . . . is that, by accepting Christ, one does not achieve grace, but instead accepts a terrible, life-long struggle to be worthy of grace, a struggle to live in a way that contradicts one's natural impulses, one's innately depraved soul" ("Amazing": 239).[23] "The war won't cease / Until He returns," Dylan sings in "When He Returns." As for self-examination, you might go nearly insane coming to terms with what you find inside yourself: "Hope I don't find out anything . . . hmm, great God!" Dylan had sung light-years before in "Talkin' John Birch Paranoid Blues."

The Americanized version of the Christian journey is the foundation of "No Time to Think," where Dylan reads the full indictment of a system which leads Average Pilgrim from nature into the city, there to strip him of all virtue, leaving him to crawl through dirt and feel plenty guilty about his journey. The man who struggles through life with child, wife, job, house ("the full catastrophe," Zorba the Greek called it) never thinks his way clear, never finds an exit, never prepares for the future, never manages to move an inch. This journey is not very successful; neither is the Christian-American journey of "Señor (Tales of Yankee Power)": whether it's headed down Lincoln County Road or toward Armageddon, America is hopelessly corrupt, and the judgment upon it will be severe. In "I Believe in You," Dylan expresses a kind of blind faith in salvation for the individual, but the individual is lost and bereft of friends in a hostile town a thousand miles from his home. This is not a particularly pleasant prospect.

The Journey into Memory
In the notes to *Planet Waves*, an album which contained "Going, Going, Gone" and "Forever Young" and "Never Say Goodbye," Dylan makes the interesting observation that the old days are gone, and the present will soon be gone too . . . that everything melts into a collage of time-places on a vaguely biblical time line. The notes to this planetary album are themselves a sentimental journey, a Ginsburgesque retrospective about a mad trip out of a New York bar and back to old Hibbing, with its pinball machines and polka bands, its headwinds and snowstorms — all the things that Dylan left in his late teens. Looking over his shoulder, Dylan recalls his hometown, Hibbing's carnival characters, and the teenaged ethos of love at first sight. He recalls lighting out for parts unknown (some of them the invented escapes he claimed when first he arrived in New York) and buying into the past of Woody Guthrie and American myth as he shaped himself into a folksinger. These notes are a curious mixture of styles and Dylans, and anticipate two developments in Dylan's future career: his increasing sense of loss, and his use of the journey as a trip back into his own and a communal remembered past.

This is Dylan's third journey option: a journey into the past through memory, along the lines of his mental trips back to Minnesota in 1963, in the songs "Girl of the North Country" and "Bob Dylan's Dream" (1963). Many of Dylan's sixties

songs express impatience with permanence and a desire for change ("Blowin'
in the Wind," for example, and "When the Ship Comes In"), and others suggest
a contempt for the past, especially old girlfriends Dylan has outgrown or who
just don't get it ("Just Like a Woman" or "To Ramona"). "There is no yesterday,
so what's left is today," he had told Anthony Scaduto (178). But that was 1966.
Dylan's position regarding the past changed, and changed quickly. Toward the
end of his 1971 biography, Anthony Scaduto has Dylan working on his autobiography: "I never thought of the past," Dylan told Scaduto. "Now I'm doing
it. Now I realize that you should look back sometimes. Back then I didn't look
at the past because today was important. But now the past seems meaningful
and I'm getting a kick at looking back" (273). "I have more memories for the
past than for the future," he said, speaking of *John Wesley Harding* in *Sing Out!*
(Cott: 123), indicating that despite his own admonition "don't look back," he had
reached the moment when one does indeed look back. Terri Van Ronk recalls
Dylan visiting her toward the end of 1969: "He was looking for a piece of his
past," she says. "When he came, he looked at his old corduroy cap which I still
have. He said he wanted to see it. I held it and he looked at it and he said, 'Wow,
what a great cap.' . . . He asked, 'You got any other old stuff has anything to do
with me?' (Scaduto: 265). In 1974's "Shelter from the Storm," Dylan was musing
aloud, "If I could only turn back the clock. . . ." Howard Sounes concludes his
version of Dylan's 1985 visit to his boyhood home in Hibbing with the observation, "His nostalgia for his home, and the town where he had grown up, was
obviously very strong" (368).

Two decades later, Bono was explaining to *New Musical Express* that Dylan
"feels he's trapped in his past, and in a way, he is" (Heylin, *Shades*: 398). Dylan
became increasingly interested in sometimes embarrassingly sentimental journeys into old times. In "Precious Memories," arranged by Dylan and released
on the 1986 *Knocked Out Loaded* album, the return home via memory is quite
explicit:

> As I travel down life's pathway,
> Know not what the years may hold.
> As I ponder, hopes grow fonder,
> Precious memories flood my soul.
>
> Precious father, loving mother,
> Glide across the lonely years.
> And old home scenes of my childhood
> In fond memory appears.

Precious memories, how they linger
How they ever flood my soul.
In the stillness of the midnight
Precious sacred scenes unfold.

What could be clearer? A journey out, with return home via memory. "Though the line is cut / It ain't quite the end," Dylan had written in "Restless Farewell." I'll remember you when I've forgotten everybody else, Dylan had promised some unidentified girl in the 1985 song titled "I'll Remember You" (perhaps she's the old Girl of the North Country, since it's wind blowing through the piney wood which triggers this memory).

In the 2008 Bootleg Series, *Tell Tale Signs*, Dylan released a 1992 recording of Jimmie Rodgers's "Miss the Mississippi" that is interesting in regard to Dylan journeying back to his roots. "I've grown tired of these big city nights, / Tired of the glamour and tired of the sights" the song goes; "I miss the Mississippi and you." The Mississippi River figures prominently in Dylan's songs and thought, especially on *Tell Tale Signs*, and one wonders if this 1992 recording was perhaps a source of, influence on, or reflection of some of Dylan's post-1992 "longing for the homeland" songs.

Usually, these remembered trips leave Dylan only funkful and blue. A character in Dylan's "Open the Door, Homer" advises, "Take care of all your memories . . . For you cannot relive them." "Forget the dead you've left, they will not follow you," Dylan sang in "It's All Over Now, Baby Blue." In "Wedding Song" Dylan sang (perhaps to Sara), "What's lost is lost, we can't regain what went down in the flood." "Time is a jet plane, it moves too fast" Dylan sings in "You're a Big Girl Now." "Time is an enemy," he sings in "Up to Me." "Situations have ended sad," Dylan announces on the first cut of *Blood on the Tracks*, "You're Gonna Make Me Lonesome When You Go." Even though this particular relationship — probably with Ellen Bernstein — is a going affair, Dylan is bummed out by past losses, so convinced of and obsessed with the inevitable failure of this relationship, that the girl's departure is pretty much a self-fulfilling prophecy. It's like the present is already past even when it's present. "You're gonna have to leave me now," Dylan sings, promising to look for her in Honolulu, San Francisco, and Ashtabula (Ohio). And if he thinks he'll have to settle for seeing her in the sky and tall grass, however, it's pretty clear he doesn't expect to reconnect. "You're a Big Girl Now," he sings, admitting that the memory of lost nights together serves only to drive him out of his mind with a "pain that stops and starts" at the thought that this big girl is now in a room with somebody else. Here's a memory-journey no male ever wants to take, and it is the futility of these journeys into the past that causes Dylan to abandon journeys altogether.

"Tangled Up in Blue" is perhaps the quintessential memory-journey song. It reflects Dylan's studies with Norman Raeben, who "brought Dylan to a more fruitful understanding of time, enabling him to view narrative not in such strictly linear terms, but to telescope past, present, and future together to attain a more powerful, unified focus" (Gill and Odegard: 39). The lovers' first meeting, the break-up, the narrator's experiences before and after the event, even other women are all remembered, but jumbled, "tangled up," as Dylan puts it. The biography is also jumbled. Dylan's point of departure smacks of rural Hibbing, with the great north woods and an escape to the East Coast; however, the song also incorporates New Orleans and Greenwich Village. No matter: all of the past is simply a lost illusion to which Dylan, "still on the road" in the song's final stanza, seeks to return. "I got to get to her somehow" he sings, but he sounds more desperate than hopeful, and the odds on reconnecting seem slim to none. Most probably, Dylan will remain trapped in the blue of memory.

"Highlands," that epic imagined journey of *Time Out of Mind*, suggests return in mind or heart to Midwest pastoralism. Metaphorically "highlands" is probably heaven, but there is also a remembered physical highlands, the exact location of which has been the subject of some discussion. The point of this song, however, is that Dylan's *heart* is in those highlands gentle and fair; they are a memory which has become a dream. Dylan himself is in a restaurant in Boston "where nobody's going anywhere," entangled in conversation with some ding-dong eighties feminist waitress. He's in the rat race, insanity smashing up against his soul, drifting abstractedly from scene to scene. Memory is little comfort when the party's over and there's less and less to say. Dylan is simply not one of those young men with their good-looking women, full of plans and adventures, and the fact that he is no longer a player seems to send him off to the countryside where a guy doesn't have to be a player. Whether Dylan will get where he's going — or hopes to go — is debatable at best, probably unlikely. The heartfelt return fails, regardless of where Dylan's heart is.

So part of Bob Dylan is Nick Carroway, and part of Bob Dylan is Jay Gatsby in the famous exchange Dylan himself will quote in "Summer Days":

"I wouldn't ask too much of her," I ventured. "You can't repeat the past."

"Can't repeat the past?" he cried incredulously. "Why of course you can!" (Fitzgerald, *Gatsby*: 73)

The larger part of Dylan, however, is Nick: "You can always come back," he sang in "Mississippi", "but you can't come back all the way." "You can't come back," he sang in "Sugar Baby," the last song in *Lyrics: 1962–2001*; all you can do is remember. And some of those memories you learn to live with, and some you don't.

The Journey of Abandonment

Dylan seemed to abandon the memory-journeys, just as he gave up the religious journeys in the 1990s, melding the Christian journey and the journey into personal freedom into what Michael Gray calls pointless "compulsive walking" (*Song*: 822), or abandoning the idea of journey entirely. This is Dylan's fourth journey option: a half-hearted review of life's journeys past, expressing some degree of regret and perhaps attempting some (usually failed) recovery of the old vision, then dragging his aging bones onto the streets that are dead for a night of joyless wandering, or giving up the journey entirely. "We try and we try and we try to be who we were," Dylan told *Newsweek* in 1997; "Sooner or later you come to the realization that we're *not* who we were. So then what do we do?" (Gates: 68). He titles one of his most recent songs, "Beyond Here Lies Nothin'."

Although it becomes more pronounced in the 1990s, the aimless or abandoned quest is not a new idea with Dylan, and Steven Heine tracks a long history of what he suggests is Zen-like disengagement, or at least zigzagging, all across Dylan's career. Several songs on the three great middle sixties albums suggest disengagement. "Bob Dylan's 115th Dream" opts out of the great American Journey with a polite "Good luck" to Columbus as he arrives in the New World. Heroic enterprises and expeditions — this one at least — are not for him. The title "Subterranean Homesick Blues" definitely suggests a retreat from engagement. Dylan's final solution in this song ("jump down a manhole") is a marked contrast to "Let Me Die in My Footsteps": hunker down, be invisible, forget the engines of social and economic development, because they don't work anyway, the vandals took the handles. The liner notes to *Bringing It All Back Home* begin, "i'm standing there watching the parade. . . ." Watching — not in it, not a part of it, neither coming nor going. Dylan is just staying put — no desire for paths of victory, or for journeys anywhere.

Increasingly as Dylan's career unfolded, the past seemed to entangle him so much that he was too wounded to run. The title and songs of *Blood on the Tracks* (1975) are a case in point. The album is one song after another of going nowhere. Dylan seems to just quit. "If You See Her, Say Hello," he requests of some messenger to lost love in a song of enervation and pointless walking. He might bump into her himself, or he might not. Although he is still moving from town to town, Dylan's message — "tell her she can look me up" — suggests a disinclination to pursue his own the girl and all she represents (unlikely given his fond memories), a feeling that she — like the Girl of the North Country — is no longer interested in him, or an admission that both his journey and hers are so random as to make the odds on reunion nil.[24] Really, he's given up on the attempt.

"Abandoned Love" (1975) is really an abandoned journey song. The man who would follow where his patron saint leads, who marches in the parade of liberty, who knows it's time to make a change, just can't break old habits and affections (girl, power, wealth itself), and is thus not free and never gonna be free. The talk goes one direction ("before I turn you loose," "I've got to leave," "before I abandon it"), but the action goes the other, and one more time is going to lead to one more more time, to yet one more more more time, and the journey will never happen.

In "Don't Fall Apart on Me Tonight" (1983), Dylan seems strung out and enervated: "Yesterday's just a memory," he sings, "Tomorrow is never what it's supposed to be." "The dream dried up a long time ago," Dylan sings in "Red River Shore" (1997); "Don't know where it is anymore." Living in the shadows of a fading past, he remembers a trip "back to see about it once," a trip (perhaps his visit to Hibbing in 1984) which came to nothing: nobody back home could remember what he was talking about. Offhandedly, he mentions a man who lived a long time ago (Jesus Christ) who could bring the dead back to life, but the words have been lost, and "they" don't do that kind of thing anymore. There's nothing for it but to live life, every day being another day away from the girl — and the dream — of the Red River Shore. "Red River Shore" dates to *Time Out of Mind*, an album filled with aimless wandering, missing-my-baby songs, and abandoned lovers lost in time. "I'm walking through streets that are dead / Walking with you in my head," sings Dylan in "Love Sick." Nothing but ticking clocks and silences, images of lovers in the meadow and silhouettes on the window. "It doesn't matter where I go anymore, I just go," he sings in "Can't Wait" (1997). "I feel like I'm being plowed under," Dylan admits; "I just don't know what to do." "I got no place left to turn, / I got nothing left to burn" is the couplet in "Standing in the Doorway." The ghost of old love haunts him still, and even though the weather is pleasant and warm, he's lost and enervated "in the dark land of the sun." The ringing church bells suggest death more than wedding, and Dylan's allusion to the John Donne's line he will quote almost verbatim in "Moonlight" (also borrowed by Ernest Hemingway to title a novel), "never send to know for whom the bell tolls," suggests the completion of that line: "it tolls for thee." Romantic options exist in this song — new journeys as it were — but he's paralyzed in the doorway, suffering like a fool.

In "Tryin' to Get to Heaven" (also 1997), Dylan plods toward heaven without memory (which every day grows dimmer), eschewing further explorations of "the lonesome valley" in "the middle of nowhere," and renouncing visions of a future (a train runs through this song, but it's other people — not Dylan — waiting on the platform) to sleep down in the parlor and relive dreams of life in Sugar Town and past travels "all around the world." Everything is hollow — or *seems* hollow — and even the vaguely religious overtones of this song (the river of life, the road of life, the thunder of apocalypse, the lonesome valley of life, the promise of heaven itself) seem flat. "If the Bible is right, the world will explode," Dylan tells us in "Things Have Changed," but he personally is out of range.

In "Not Dark Yet," Dylan is stalled again — "I know it looks like I'm moving, but I'm standing still" — frozen in a state of complete physical and spiritual enervation. Buried somewhere inside of him is apparently a will to be elsewhere, but the nerves which might translate impulse into action are shot. He's lost his sense of humanity, and his very soul has hardened into steel. And time is running away. "I used to care, but things have changed," Dylan sings. Talking with *Newsweek* reporter David Gates in 1997, Dylan said, "I don't feel in tune with anything" (65).

What a far cry these lyrics are from early boy-god "I am leaving, I am leaving" songs like "Don't Think Twice, It's All Right" and "Visions of Johanna," or from Dylan's request for walking boots of Spanish leather!

With the new millennium, Dylan seemed less depressed about his enervation — and as *Modern Times* followed *Love and Theft* — less enervated. Still, a journey anywhere lacked appeal, and even the idea of escape seemed unlikely. "We struggle and we scrape," Dylan sings in "Mississippi," but "We're all boxed in, nowhere to escape." "Mississippi," in fact, is a suggestive song. Dylan himself has strong personal connections to the Great Father of Waters,[25] and in his essentially pastoral mental landscape, water often represents some form of healing. Water does not necessarily have to be the water of baptism; sometimes a hard, apocalyptic rain or flood can be good for us in the long haul. In many songs Dylan seems to think this way. But "Mississippi" is a song about loss, not restoration: leaves are falling from the trees; Dylan feels like a stranger with no future or past; the emptiness is endless. His problem is that he was "raised in the country," came to the city which is "a jungle," and in so doing lost his future and his past beyond reclamation. Dylan is not bitter in this song, but he is stranded, going nowhere.

"High Water (For Charley Patton)" hints at empathy with suffering fellow travelers, but again Dylan is inactive. "I told her I didn't really care," he sings here; in "Honest with Me" he repeats himself: "I don't care." We all eventually reach the point where praise and blame are difficult to differentiate, and there is a strong temptation to not care. "But in that case" balances "what if" at life's remembered crossroads. Martin Luther's "Here I stand; I can do no other" becomes less a ringing declaration than a shrug-of-the-shoulder resignation. Or we say, "I don't much care, because I don't have to care. I ain't goin' nowhere anyway."

Or perhaps we rationalize: you can't turn back even if you know you've gone too far, half the time when you try to help someone you end up hurting her, happiness comes and goes willy-nilly, so "Sugar baby, get on down the road / you ain't got no brains no how."

The Journey through Cultures Past, Present, and Future

Dylan's fifth conscious journey option, and his most satisfying, is a mental-musical journey through time-place, using cultural artifacts to collapse time past and time present, recovering the moment when all options were open, and "when anything was possible" (Dylan in Marcus, *Invisible Republic*: 69). These songs resemble simple memory songs, but they are more successful because Dylan seems to realize that time is a dimension, and life itself is what he once called "A Series of Dreams," among which those past are no less alive than those present or future. "The past is ubiquitous on *Planet Waves*," notes John Hinchey, "but there are many pasts," including "a past that, although grounded in historically real personal experience, exists outside time altogether, a time out of mind, if you will, that beckons us always from the future" (*Planet Waves*: 15). Dylan suggests in "Bye and Bye," that even "the future for me is already a thing of the past."

Here is a weighty philosophical matter as well as an aesthetic proposition. At the beginning of "Burnt Norton," the first poem in "Four Quartets," T. S. Eliot wrote, "Time present and time past / Are both, perhaps, present in time future, / And time future contained in time past." Opening the second of the quartets, "East Coker," he reiterated the idea: "In my beginning is my end." In the third quartet, "The Dry Salvages," Eliot used the metaphor of the river, which some critics believe to be the Mississippi of his youth, bridged and tamed as civilization expands, "almost forgotten / By dwellers in cities," but implacable, lurking, "reminder / Of what men choose to forget." The "Four Quartets" were written by Eliot mid-career, looking ahead and looking back. As he matured, Dylan also began to think of transcending linear time: "Went on the Rolling Thunder tour, made *Renaldo and Clara* — in which I also used that quality of no-time. And I believe that that concept of creation is more real and true than that which does have time," he told Jonathan Cott (261). "Time is running backwards," Dylan sings in "Ring Them Bells" (1989). In many songs Dylan uses water as a metaphor for time in a manner very reminiscent of Eliot: "I followed the river and I got to the sea"; "like a river that is flowing" ("Coming from the Heart [The Road Is Long]"); "Time is an ocean but it ends at the shore" ("Oh, Sister"). Increasingly, the river of time annihilates place by fusing everything into one time-place. Analyzing the songs of *Planet Waves*, John Hinchey observes,

> There is, in other words, the history we carry around with us — and that will drag us down if we don't carry it forward as a refreshed present ["Never Say Goodbye" and "Something There Is About You"] — and there is the history ["Dirge"] we walk away from — and that will destroy us if we don't. But there is also a past that, although grounded in historically real personal experience, exists outside time altogether, a time out of mind, if you will, that beckons us always from the future. (15)

This journey, as Ben Child points out, reflects modernism's interests in the flexibility of concepts like time and place (202). It is also the habit of many of us in our older years of jumping quickly from time-place to time-place, usually with the aid of photographs, letters, tapes, and books. Is this the beginning of wisdom as we recognize the interconnectedness of things, or the beginning of Alzheimer's? I do not know. Regardless, this journey through time-place lets Dylan recapture the moment when things were just getting started ("Born in Time"), or exciting, enjoyable, relaxed, whatever. More importantly, the journey through time-place affords Dylan the same legitimate excuse it gave T. S. Eliot for raiding the treasury of cultural history to construct complex collages out of Herman Hesse's *The Glass Bead Game*, a novel very popular in the hip sixties. Dylan has been raiding the treasury of cultural history since his first song. "I am a thief of thoughts," Dylan admitted in his 8th Outlined Epitaph; "I have built an' rebuilt / upon what is waitin'." The individual talent operates within tradition, and, by incorporating elements of old into new, keeps tradition alive in an eternal present. Dylan has always worked this way. Andrew Muir sees the seven years between *Under the Red Sky* and *Time Out of Mind* as "re-immersion in the musical roots that nourished him and led to his early creative breakthroughs" (*Troubadour*: 189); at a time when Dylan was "goin' nowhere" artistically, he "strapped himself to the tree with roots" (191). Michael Gray even interprets the nursery rhyme songs of *Under the Red Sky* as a journey into the past appropriate to Dylan's age and situation at the time:

> It is unsurprising that in middle age, and with his own children grown, Bob Dylan should revisit the arena of the nursery rhyme and the fairy tale. Like me, he is the sort of age at which re-examinations of the central self, impelled by what is not called "mid-life crisis" for nothing, become unavoidable and important. (*Song*: 666)

The bewildering eclecticism of the list of songs Dylan sang in concerts and recorded in studio during the last two decades of the last millennium constitutes a monumental excavation of the musical past, and provides a context for the kind of Dylan journey which was to come, a journey which, Richard Brown says, amounts to "redeeming space through time" (214).

Perhaps Bono says it best in his introduction to Mark Blake's *Dylan: Visions, Portraits & Back Pages*:

> Dylan was at one point in time the very epitome of what was modern, and yet his was always a unique critique of modernity. Because in fact Dylan comes from an ancient place, almost medieval. . . . The anachronism, really, is the '60s. For the rest of his life he's been howling from some sort of past that we seem to have forgotten but must not. That's it for me. Bob Dylan keeps undermining our urge to look into the future. (8)

While time is often an enemy in Dylan songs, undermining the singer and his world and threatening more than it promises, reducing time to a dimension like any other marker of place makes it as permanent as any other marker of place. And "permanence, not change, is what is craved," writes Pádraig Hanratty in an essay titled "Time Is an Enemy" (51).

The idea of a journey through time-place ties nicely to the Christian journey where "what's to come has already been" ("Pressing On"), and to pastoralism. American pastoralism especially was always an attempt to revoke the ravages of industrialism and materialism by stepping outside of (or reaching back before) the line of time which stretches from the Fall to the Present, to timeless Eden. Dylan "sought safety in a retreat to the countryside that was also a retreat in time, or more precisely, a search for timelessness" writes Marqusee of *The Basement Tapes* (211), and what he says is true of other Dylan songs. In looking back to look ahead, pastoralism denies linear time: in a book titled *The Uses of Nostalgia: Studies in Pastoral Poetry*, Laurence Lerner observes,

> Both Eden and the New Jerusalem — the myth of the Golden Age and the myth of the millennium — are ways of refusing history. If the ideal version of man's life is placed outside ordinary time, then we have a way of protecting ourselves against the incessant suffering that human history offers. (72)

Although Dylan was not particularly optimistic about *reclaiming* lost time-place through memory during most of his career, recovering elements of culture is comparatively easy, especially if the culture is a performed culture. In a 1993 interview, Dylan had talked about blues singers and songs this way:

[P]eople like Son House, Reverend Gary Davis or Sleepy John Estes. Just to sit there and be up close and watch them play, you could study what they were doing, plus a bit of their lives rubbed off on you. Those vibes will carry into you forever, really, so it's like those people, they're still here to me. They're not ghosts of the past or anything, they're continually here. (Gray, *Song*: 292)

Recreating the past in the present is especially easy in an age of electronic media — everything from TV shows to tape recorders to computers — which reproduce voices and images from the past as faithfully as if the actor were there before us. (This is especially true if our initial experience of the song or the show or the game was electronic — then, save for our own hearing loss, the experience is duplicated exactly.) Dylan heard the old singers on record and radio — except for the static and the scratches on the record, they sang as if standing beside him. Now we hear Dylan on record and on radio — that's where Dylan exists for most of us — and Dylan on record or radio is eternally present for us. Driving to the grave of Jack Kerouac on the Rolling Thunder tour, Dylan and Ginsberg annihilated time by listening to a tape of Kerouac supplied by driver Tony Sampas, Kerouac's brother-in-law. Sam Shepard writes, "and suddenly there's the voice of Jack. Speaking like a ghost over time" (91). Dylan was there and Ginsberg was there and Kerouac was there. As Greil Marcus notes in *Invisible Republic*, the very basement tapes in which Dylan advised us that we cannot relive our memories are an annihilation of time in music:

[T]he basement tapes could carry the date 1932 and it would be as convincing, as one listens, as 1967, if not more so — as would, say, the dates 1881, or 1954, or 1992, 1993. In those last two years, Bob Dylan, then in his early fifties, suddenly recast what had come to seem an inexorably decaying public life with two albums of old blues and folk songs, *Good as I Been to You* and *World Gone Wrong*. . . . in Bob Dylan's repertoire they preceded the material on his first album, issued thirty years before. Unlike other songs he had sung in nearly a quarter century, they removed him from the prison of his own career and returned him — or his voice, as a sort of mythical fact — to the world at large. (xiv–xv)

Although later albums like *Love and Theft* stand out as especially dense conflations of times and places, Dylan has jump-cut across times and cultures throughout his career. He used U.S. 61 to unite not just America north and south, but to connect past, present, and future, and to join biblical history with American history and human history. In like manner, the songs of *Blood on the Tracks*, while they could not reclaim remembered love, did manage to reconstruct the past in song. The album's key theme, Paul Williams argued, is the "evocation of the past as a universal, omnipresent now" (23). "She still lives inside of me, we've never been apart" Dylan sings in the *Lyrics, 1962–1985* version of "If You See Her Say Hello." And it's not just old flames who live on in this album: *New Republic* noted in its review of the album,

> Nearly every cut refers to earlier songs by Dylan himself or others. "Idiot wind" recalls "Blowin' in the wind," "You're a big girl now" reappraises "Just like a woman" and "She belongs to me"; "If you see her, say hello" evokes "Girl from the north country"; "Buckets of rain" reminds us of "A hard rain's a-gonna fall"; and so on down the line. (Thomson and Gutman: 196)

Robert Craig Snow suggests that Dylan plays the same game in the songs of his Christian period: "Saving Grace" echoes "Song to Woody," "Slow Train" echoes "Train A-Travelin'," "When You Gonna Wake Up?" echoes "I'd Hate to Be You on that Dreadful Day," "Jokerman" echoes "A Hard Rain's A-Gonna Fall," "Precious Angel" echoes "Oh, Sister," "I Believe in You" echoes "I Don't Believe You, "Shot of Love" echoes "Rainy Day Women No. 12 & 35" (290, 91). In *Song & Dance Man III*, Michael Gray spends whole chapters tracking Dylan's quotations from blues songs, rock-'n'-roll songs, films, nursery rhymes, his own works, and from literature.[26] When all is said and done, Dylan's greatest talent is for bringing home the past, wrote Greil Marcus in "Dylan as Historian," "giving it flesh — and proving, as the ethnologist H. L. Goodall, Jr., puts it, that 'in addition to the lives we lead we also live lives we don't lead'" (*Dustbin*: 83). "Dylan seems almost on a crusade to turn the new generation's attention back to the past," Andrew Muir noted (*Troubadour*: 203) three years before Dylan's Theme Time Radio Hour program. It's all a matter of archeology . . . and receptivity.

In the song "Born in Time" Dylan is lost (as he always was in 1990) in a lonely night, stranded in the hills of mystery and the foggy web of destiny, but in his isolation he dreams a vision of his youth, returning him to a woman and a time of black-and-white photos "when we were made of dreams." Dylan apparently found the woman — and the experience — exhausting and ultimately destructive, but his desire to reclaim her (the past and the forward vision she embodies) is strong enough that he offers her what's left of him if he can transverse time and find her. In the *Tell Tale Signs* version of this song he sings, "Just when I thought you were gone, you came back . . . when I was ready to receive you." Receptivity involves first rethinking his own situation, and then finding a road out, forward, back, or all three directions at once.

The rethinking of the 1990s apparently worked a change in Dylan's situation: on the first song of *Modern Times*, Dylan sings, "Feel like my soul is beginning to expand." In light of Dylan's earlier withdrawal from the world into self-imposed isolation, this statement is important. A soul which had congealed to steel is beginning to thaw. The song itself ("Thunder on the Mountain") also puts Dylan back on the road back to Minnesota ("gonna go up north"), and to some kind of salvation beyond linear time: "some sweet day I'll stand beside my king." There is a certain two-sided pastoralism to the songs of this album, as I have argued earlier, but I'd suggest that the road Dylan walks is a cultural road, the road of music and literature, which takes him backwards and laterally through time-place into every form of music imaginable ("where the music's coming from"), and every English idiom from Minnesota folk talk ("a whoppin' good time") to the language of Ovid's *The Art of Love*. Hot stuff here, everywhere you go! Stephen Scobie calls this "Dylan's archaeology of traditional lyrics" (100) which "produces a loose, nonlinear structure which serves Dylan's avowed aim of 'stopping time'" (101). It's as if Dylan has awakened from a long sleep, and is back in the game, including the game of love . . . or at least desire.

For this journey he doesn't need any guide — he knows the way, because he's already been there. Some songs even explicitly suggest the annihilation of time by music: "I've been conjuring up all these long dead souls from their crumbling tombs" ("Rollin' and Tumblin'"). In "Workingman's Blues #2" a reawakened Dylan promises a new crusade nearly in folk protest mode ("I'm sailin' on back, ready for the long haul"). "The words fans have been waiting thirty years to hear Dylan say," someone said of this song — back to the sixties thinking and music. "Beyond the Horizon" is anything but a sixties protest song, but Dylan's new road leads to swing as well as folk protest . . . and to all of the musical styles and forms Dylan alludes to and imitates in the other songs of this album, and in the songs of *Tell Tale Signs* and *Together Through Life*: waltzes, blues, rhythm-'n'-blues, gospel, country. And to all the culture that these songs carry, high and low, corny or sophisticated, deep or mindless.

The journey through literature, nursery rhymes, films and music, in the form of albums, concerts, radio programs, films — what Eliot called tradition, and Yeats called the artifice of eternity — seems to be the best journey after all.

Traveling through Systems of Belief

I have identified five types of conscious Dylan journey: the journey as escape, the allegorical Christian journey from sin to redemption, the journey into memory, the journey which abandons goals and hope and even journey itself, and the journey through culture in a universal time present. These are "conscious journeys" — Dylan knows what he's doing when he does it. In addition to these journeys, however, Dylan has made at least two trips, probably unconscious, into slippery, postmodern relativism and then back to the relatively coherent, conservative (some would say narrow) value systems of his Midwestern youth. These may be his most significant journeys.

In addition to Hibbing's limited opportunity, its failure to appreciate his genius, and Hibbing High's strict codes of dress and behavior, what alienated young Dylan was Main Street, Hibbing's aggressive small-town boosterism, its orthodox and narrow-minded way of looking at life. To Studs Terkel in 1963, Dylan described the people he knew there, especially his schoolmates, as "little small-town people. . . . They still have a feeling that's tied up, where it's tied up in the town, in their parents, in the newspapers that they read which go out to maybe five thousand people. They don't have to go out of town, their world's very small" (Cott: 9). There is no need to rehearse that story again, except to point out that Dylan did know another side of Main Street which the power structure did its best to suppress. I want merely to point out the obvious fact that the dominant culture Dylan left on his journey out of Hibbing was conservative socially, intellectually, and artistically.

What college students find at schools like the University of Minnesota is an alternative to this Main Street thought: a wide range of beliefs and behaviors which can threaten or exhilarate them, depending on their strength of character. (Today the pall of political correctness limits exploration and expression on some campuses as much as religious orthodoxies limit them on other campuses.) At first glance, this appears to be what Dylan found in Minneapolis — not at the fraternity house or in classes, but in Dinkytown. He rejoiced in this world, thrived on its art and ideas. In Greenwich Village he found a larger version of Dinkytown values and art, and he thrived on them until, to his ever-expanding mind, they too seemed orthodox and blindered. Preaching is preaching, Dylan decided, whether it's from the right or the left. This is the crux of the debate between Dylan and the "traditional" folkies who wrote open letters to him in *Sing Out!* and booed and hissed and hollered "Judas!" and "sing protest songs" when he came on stage with an electric guitar and a backup band: he was exploring new territory and they remained "in a box," "baked in a pie." By the middle sixties, Dylan was traveling very far and very fast, on momentum from the cultural opportunities opened by Suze Rotollo (see *Chronicles*: 268–88), Greenwich Village friends, and musicians from across the Atlantic, opening his mind to music, art, and ideas of the most current, international, highbrow sort. In so doing, Dylan was in synch with his generation, found very marketable material, and quickly achieved not only a global audience among members of that generation, but a reputation for being "the hippest person on earth ... my Existential hero, the gangling Rimbaud of rock" (Marianne Faithfull, quoted in Boucher, *Dylan & Cohen*: 84), a man one step ahead of everyone else.[27]

A journey into that kind of artistic and philosophical environment, although productive, can produce uncertainty, confusion, and even insanity. In the 1990s, perhaps even earlier, we began to realize that modernism and its descendant postmodernism proceeded perhaps too easily from a rejection of received truth as preached by church, school, and the Rotary Club to a blanket rejection of religious doctrine, rational truth, and even the intuited truth of Romanticism. modernism had at least continued the search while lamenting the loss of certainty; postmodernism abandoned the search and settled for a not very satisfying celebration of the all-too-transient moment.[28] In a book titled *The Culture of Interpretation*, Roger Lundin puts it this way: "If modernism represented a desperate effort to have art and culture fill the void created by the decline of religion in the West, then postmodernism stands as the affirmation of the void, as a declaration of the impossibility of ever filling it" (3). Jean-François Lyotard in fact defined postmodernism as "incredulity toward [all] metanarratives" (xiv). Postmodernism is less interested in discovering reality than in inventing reality, and all invented reality is equal. "Good an evil are but words / invented by those / that are trapped in scenes," Dylan writes on "Some other kinds of songs; "i know no answers an no truth . . . there are no morals." Nothing means anything, and everything means anything . . . which makes everything mean nothing at all.

Not only does truth collapse upon itself, art collapses on itself: high culture and low culture are equally commodified, all part of the world of pop, where Michael Jackson, not Bob Dylan, is king, every bit as important (someone actually said this, in the days after he died) as Mozart. Postmodernism is pop, and pop is postmodernism. In this world of five-minute, media-generated fame, quality and insight are discounted as meaningless notions. Andy Warhol's silk screens are neither more insightful nor more irrelevant than a song like "How Much Is that Doggie in the Window?" — the inane stuff Dylan disliked on Top 40 radio when he was a teenager.[29] Inevitably, the postmodernist celebration of artistic-license-become-chaos collapses upon itself, as Arthur Rimbaud found when he dropped over the edge and quit writing at a relatively young age. Why write when culture becomes so hip as to lose its ability to communicate? Why write when text, dissociated from its author and even itself to become "reconstructed" in the mind of each reader, has been reduced to gibberish?

On this point Andrew Muir quotes Henry Miller:

it is gibberish if, out of two billion people who make up the world, only a few thousand pretend to understand what the individual poet is saying. The cult of art reaches its end when it exists only for a precious handful of men and women. Then it is no longer art but the cipher language of a secret society for the propagation of meaningless individuality. (*Troubadour*: 106)

Later Muir writes, "On the poetic corpse of Rimbaud we have begun erecting a tower of Babel" (112). This Dylan understood relatively early on. Talking about Dylan visiting her place in Carmel Valley in the film *No Direction Home*, Joan Baez remembers,

Bob liked to write there. . . . He would always say, 'What do you think of this?' And I didn't understand the thing at all. But I loved it. So, well, okay, I'm gonna figure this one out. So I read through it and I gave back my interpretation of what I thought. And he said, 'Uh, that's pretty fuckin' good.' And he said, 'A bunch of years from now, all these people, these assholes, are gonna be writing about all this shit I write. I don't know what the fuck it's about. And they're gonna write about what it's about.'

Looking back in 1997, he told David Gates that in the late 1980s he was beginning to think his songs were "like what all these people say, just a bunch of surrealistic nonsense" (66).

Where does surrealistic nonsense leave the artist? In *Tarantula*, Muir notes, "the 'eye' and 'I' are fragmented beyond repair, and the 'I' writes his own epitaph: 'here lies Bob Dylan'" (*Troubadour*: 111). Dylan's electric songs, most of us believe, are not a Tower of Babel, although some of us have reservations about Dylan's prose pieces and poems, including *Tarantula*, of which Clinton Heylin writes, "Perhaps only *Finnegans Wake* among works of modern literature is as sustainedly unreadable as the prose sections of *Tarantula*" (*Shades*: 129). Even Dylan admitted that when reading galleys he was embarrassed at the nonsense he'd written (Heylin, *Shades*: 179).[30] During the 1960s, many people in the media misperceived postmodernist protest for postmodernist hip, and asked a lot of very stupid postmodernist questions, to which Dylan gave very hip postmodernist answers. Was he playing them (and us)? Who can say? Is Richard Hishmeh even a little bit correct in suggesting that Dylan's very much publicized relationship with poet Allen Ginsberg — Dylan's move in the direction of postmodernist "poetry" and musical cut-ups, Ginsberg's "experiments" in music, plans for a joint *Holy Roll Jellyroll* album (Shelton, *Home*: 424) — was just a marketing strategy in the postmodernist tradition of advertiser-turned-artist Andy Warhol, intended to turn both poet and folksinger into acceptable sixties rebels, and promoted everywhere from opening scene of *dont look back* to the liner notes of *Bringing It All Back Home* to (later) the Rolling Thunder visit to Kerouac's grave? In the film *No Direction Home*, Dylan suggests that the French did not understand his albums because they are French postmodernists, but Pennebaker's *Eat the Document* documentary shows that Dylan could be as postmodernist as the French.

Postmodernism is a fun game, but exhausting. Robert Shelton titles his chapters on this period of Dylan's life "Several Seasons in Hell" and "Inside the Coliseum." *Post hoc* and perhaps *propter hoc*, a strung-out Dylan returned to the relatively stable philosophical roots he had once rejected, in the country songs which so disturbed his sixties fans in the early seventies. "Truth was the last thing on my mind, and even if there was such a thing, I didn't want it in my house," he writes in *Chronicles* (125). This retreat did not sit well with Dylan fans at the time, because Dylan sounded . . . well, not like Dylan at all. And the music — *New Morning* is Dylan's first ever #1 album in the U.K.? You're kidding. "Lay, Lady, Lay" is Dylan's message for America, with half the country rushing out to buy brass beds? Nashville cracker music from Bob Dylan?! Nashville cracker thought from Bob Dylan? You call this poetry? Yet there can be no denial: Dylan's country songs represent a return not only to acoustic guitar and folk song structures, but to a very non-hip language and, as Michael Gray points out, an "acceptance, after all those years, of an outside, handed-down moral code" which Dylan as proponent of American individualism elsewhere finds offensive (*Song*: 207). Dylan had, in short, embraced a system of received truth, sometimes different in content but not much different in nature from the received belief he had heard in Hibbing. He himself had become one of those who tell you everything is all right, when everything is not all right. Here endeth voyage one of going out and coming back.

As we saw, Dylan lit out again, in his life and in his art and thought. When Dylan took to the road in the mid-1970s, he sent his brain on tour as well, with artists like Norman Raeben, new age spiritualist wives, nannies and girlfriends, long-time accomplices like Jack Kerouac Naropa School of Disembodied Poetics poet Allen Ginsberg, and pop psychologist-collaborators like Jacques Levy. He even bought a house in California. The results? Coked-up, po-mo "I and I" events like Rolling Thunder, European "auteur" style films like *Renaldo and Clara* (and the whacked-out explications that accompanied it[31]), and goofy songs like "Jokerman" coming out of "very mystical" Caribbean spirits called *jumbis* (Cott: 303).

And then? A strung-out Dylan collapsed again into an even more narrowly defined system of beliefs with his baptism into Evangelical Christianity, and songs (not to mention sermons) which are distressingly, starkly, black and white in a manner reminiscent of fifties Hibbing orthodoxies. Once again, Dylan had gone out intellectually only to come back to a mental framework similar to the one he knew as a youth.

These are broad generalizations indeed, and even broader speculations, but I think they will hold water. Coincidentally, Dylan's explorations are similar to those of other Midwest writers from Hamlin Garland (whose last book, *The Mystery of the Buried Crosses*, was a defense of psychic phenomena he'd absorbed in California), through F. Scott Fitzgerald (who departed Minnesota physically and mentally for Princeton, New York, Paris and the French Riviera, and then Hollywood) and Ernest Hemingway (Paris, Africa, Key West, Bimini), to Garrison Keillor (whose "Guy Noir, Private Eye" and "The Lives of Cowboys" intrude upon the News from Lake Wobegon). Perhaps great writers need new material to keep from going stale; perhaps smart people explore multiple possibilities; perhaps great artists become easily bored and — as Cather said of her mentor S. S. McClure, go in for everything and get tired of everything. Perhaps, as Fitzgerald once wrote in *The Crack-Up*, the test of a first-rate intelligence is the ability to hold two opposed ideas in the mind at the same time, and still retain the ability to function. Or perhaps smart Midwestern kids never tire of going out physically and mentally . . . and then coming home again.

Chapter 5

Bob Dylan's Prairie Populism

"Do I consider myself a politician? Oh, I guess so. I have my own party, though."
— Press Conference, KQED TV, 1965

I n his 1920 best seller *Main Street*, Sinclair Lewis presents two views of the Midwestern village in which most of the novel takes place. Gopher Prairie is a thinly disguised version of Lewis's own hometown, Sauk Centre, Minnesota, about 150 miles southwest of Hibbing, but Lewis sees it as Everywhere, U.S.A. "This is America," he writes in his preface; "its Main Street is the continuation of Main Streets everywhere. The story would be the same in Ohio or Montana, in Kansas or Kentucky or Illinois, and not very differently would it be told Up York State or in the Carolina hills." The town's name — Gopher Prairie — tells you all you need to know: its rodent inhabitants live in an underground city in the middle of nowhere, sticking their noses above ground only occasionally to sniff the fresh air and view the scenic vistas before darting back into their dark, narrow, protective dens. Gopher Prairie lies close to Lac-qui-Meurt, "The Lake which Dies," another name which says it all (this name is a reference to "Lac qui Parle" — "the Lake which Talks" — a river, a nature preserve, and a county in southwestern Minnesota). Fifty years from its founding, Gopher Prairie has grown to 3,000 people, with bankers and doctors, grain elevator, barber shop, pool room, feed store, Christian Science Library, lumberyard, school . . . and two ladies' social organizations: the Jolly Seventeen and a book study group named Thanatopsis ("meditation on death," a reference to William Cullen Bryant's famous poem of the same title). But Gopher Prairie is still a small place:

the newly arrived bride of Dr. Will Kennicott covers the entire town on foot in exactly 32 minutes, north to south, east to west.

The town's vision is also narrow; the Protestant, cognitive, male, commercial agenda that so many Midwest writers saw as destroying the old, pagan, intuitive, female, pastoral heartland. Carol Kennicott, young and idealistic, socializes uneasily with her husband's friends among the town's Republican upper class, listening to speeches like the one given by lumberyard owner Jack Elder in Chapter 4 of the novel:

> It's a lot of these cranky, wage-hogging, half-baked skilled mechanics that start trouble — reading a lot of this anarchist literature and union papers and all. . . . I stand for freedom and constitutional rights. If any man don't like my shop, he can get up and git. Same way, if I don't like him, he gits. And that's all there is to it. . . . All this profit-sharing and welfare work and insurance and old-age pensions is simply poppycock. Enfeebles a workingman's independence — and wastes a lot of honest profit. . . . And it's my bounded duty as a producer to resist every attack on the integrity of American industry to the last ditch. Yes — SIR!" (53)

The town is smug, suspicious, cheap, cliquish, insecure, and filled with double, even triple standards. "It is negation canonized as the one positive virtue," Carol decides in Chapter 22; "It is slavery self-sought and self-defended. It is dullness made God" (257).

In short, Gopher Prairie is the merchant class's vision of what an American small town should be, and what most people today picture when they imagine the Midwestern town: a little Peoria, Illinois, with its Caterpillar Tractor Company, Bradley Polytechnic Institute, and Ronald Reagan Republicanism. A town full of the vaguely lobotomized characters Philip Roth created in *American Pastoral* (1997), Swede Levov types, who never confront the larger questions, write off dissent as youthful craziness, and vote Republican every election against their own best interests. It's the kind of place Norman Mailer had in mind when he wrote in *The Armies of the Night*, "the true war party of America was in all the small towns" (174).

Gopher Prairie is the middle-class Hibbing depicted early in *No Direction Home*, with its Fourth of July parades and boosters and insanely cheerful Johnny Mercer advice to "accentuate the positive, eliminate the negative," in a song which Shelton reports four-year-old Bobby Zimmerman singing to his Grandmother Anna at a Mother's Day celebration in 1946 (*Home*: 30). It's Hibbing chanting banalities like the refrain/title of Dylan's most recent song: "It's all good, all good, it's all good." Hibbing, whose small-town Philistinism had supplied motive, energy, ferocious drive, and will to an escaping Bob Dylan. Hibbing, the Rotary-Kiwanis Club town that published a 75-year anniversary of the *Hibbing Daily Tribune* in August, 1968, without a single mention of Bob Dylan (Shelton, *Home*: 58). It's the kind of town in which farmers and the businessmen plot against the "Sad-Eyed Lady of the Lowlands."

THE OTHER SIDE OF MAIN STREET

In *Main Street*, however, Carol encounters other residents of Gopher Prairie, including the cranks who question the honesty of Jack Elder's profit. These people, whom Philip Roth seems to have missed, take a different view of the town and of life: lawyer Guy Pollak, domestic Bea Sorenson, the town's handyman Miles "The Red Swede" Bjornstam, and two farmers Carol overhears conversing below her husband's law office:

> Sure. Course I was beaten. The shipper and the grocers here wouldn't pay us a decent price for our potatoes, even though folks in the cities were howling for 'em. So we says, well, we'll get a truck and ship 'em right down to Minneapolis. But the commission merchants there were in cahoots with the local shipper here: they said they wouldn't pay us a cent more than he would, not even if they was nearer to the market. Well, we found we could get higher prices in Chicago, but when we tried to get freight cars to ship there, the railroads wouldn't let us have 'em — even though they had cars standing empty right here in the yards. There you got it — good market, and these towns keeping us from it. Gus, that's the way these towns work all the time. They pay what they want for our wheat, but we pay what they want us to for their clothes. Stowbody and Dawson foreclose every mortgage they can, and put in tenant farmers. The *Dauntless* lies to us about the Nonpartisan League, the lawyers sting us, the machinery-dealers hate to carry us over bad years, and then their daughters put on swell dresses and look at us as if we were a bunch of hoboes. Man, I'd like to burn this town! (223)

Lewis's novel gives you most of what you need to know about Minnesota politics in the twenties, and the fifties, and even the late twentieth century, when the president of our local Farm Machinery Museum board, no recent immigrant or socialist but a prominent farmer and the son of a prominent farmer, told me after President Reagan died, "I didn't much care for the son-of-a-bitch when he was alive, and I don't much care for him now. Leave the flag up; if people ask, tell 'em we forgot to lower it."

In most Upper Midwest small towns there are literally two sides to the tracks.

Prairie towns further east were typically built around a central square — with a band shell, a Civil War memorial, and perhaps a county courthouse — surrounded by the town's merchant establishments, two-story buildings with businesses below and residences above. Ronald Reagan grew up in just such a building in Tampico, Illinois. But in the Upper Midwest one finds mostly railroad towns, planted every seven or eight miles along the track to collect grain from pioneer farmers still using horse-drawn grain wagons. Across the main highway, which runs parallel to the tracks, sat the Farmers and Merchants Bank and the hotel, backed by churches, businesses and the residences of their owners. On the other side of the highway, literally "the wrong side of the tracks," sat the grain elevator, the lumberyard, and the humble abodes of the town's Miles Bjornstams. Folks on the right side of the tracks read the local newspapers, attended the English Lutheran Church, and joined the Elks or Moose Lodge. People on the wrong side of the tracks read *The Theory of the Leisure Class* (written by Wisconsin native Thorstein Veblen), voted for William Jennings Bryan, attended the Swedish Lutheran Church (if they attended church at all), and socialized at meetings of the Nonpartisan League. They were leftist from the git-go. Whatever Republican apologists for the System tell you today, progressive-to-radical politics are as much a Midwest heritage as the Lutheran Church, the Rotary Club, and the Carnegie Library: Grangers, Progressives, Knights of Labor, Farmers' Alliance, People's Party, Socialist Party, Communist Party, Nonpartisan League, Industrial Workers of the World, Farm Holiday Movement, Co-Op Movement, Farmer-Labor Party, National Farm Organization, Students for a Democratic Society, and trade union organizations in general. These groups constitute a populist tradition, still strong in the Upper Midwest and on the Iron Range, which helped shape Bob Dylan's own politics.

Earliest among these groups was the Patrons of Husbandry, popularly known as the Grange, which was powerful enough in the early 1870s to establish state control over railroads, thereby asserting the interests of the Midwest against those of the power elites "back East." Oliver H. Kelley, founder of the Grange, was from Minnesota, and the organization was powerful in the state. After the Panic of 1873, the Grange was supplanted by the Farmers' Alliance, with Ignatius Donnelly, who had moved to Minnesota in 1857, as its most powerful spokesman on the Chautauqua Circuit. Mary Elizabeth Lease, of Kansas, provided its most memorable slogan: "raise less corn and more hell." A. L. "Doc" Bixby provided a song:

I cannot sing the old songs,
My heart is full of woe;

But I can howl calamity
From Hell to Broken Bow.

(Blegen: 387)

The Alliance was strong in Minnesota, and the election of 1890 "marked the emergence of third-party protest on a large scale in the traditionally conservative state" (Blegen: 388). Gradually, the Farmers' Alliance yielded ascendancy to the broader-based Noble Order of the Knights of Labor, which founded a Seaman's Benevolent Union and organized a longshoremen's strike in Duluth in 1883 (C. Miller: 212). Then came the People's Party, or Populist Party — successor to the Knights of Labor — which was strong enough to run a slate of its own in the 1892 election. With Democrat William Jennings Bryan — Vachel Lindsay's "prairie avenger, mountain lion" — as its endorsed candidate, the Populist Party won 22 electoral votes in the 1892 election (including some from North Dakota). It did even better in 1896, when Bryan lost to McKinley by a mere 600,000 votes nationally.

The Nonpartisan League mentioned by Lewis's *Main Street* farmer was formed in 1915 by former Socialist Party organizer Arthur C. Townley, a North Dakota wheat-flax farmer originally from Minnesota. Convinced that the unfair trade practices of the grain-railroad-banking combine cost North Dakota farmers 55 million dollars a year in usurious loan interest (at least 10 percent, as high as 40 percent per year), dockage fees for "impurities," commissions on resales from one subsidiary company to another, bogus shipping charges, bogus switching charges, jiggered grading, and storage fees,[1] the League called for state ownership of terminal elevators, flour mills, packing house and cold-storage plants; state inspection of grain and grain dockage; tax exemptions for farm "improvements"[2]; state crop insurance; and rural credit banks operated at cost (Morlan: 26). Its program attracted wide support all across the Upper Midwest, including Minnesota, where membership reached 50,000. In light of the fact that the target of many of its reforms was the grain processing and shipment operations headquartered in Minneapolis and Duluth, its success merely highlights the split political vision of the Upper Midwest populace.

The League was less a political party than an agenda which advanced the interests of producers and small merchants against the powerful influences of monopolies, trusts, and corporations which used government regulations and license to steal the fruits of their labor. Historian Theodore Blegen calls it "an experiment in state socialism" (468). The league endorsed a Republican candidate for governor in 1918, one Charles Augustus Lindbergh, a former U.S. Congressman who had opposed American entry into World War I. That election marked the beginning of Minnesota's farmer-laborer alliance, and Lindbergh became "the farmer-labor candidate," losing the election to pro-war incumbent governor J. A. Burnquist.

More radical than the Populists, and therefore more to be feared, were the Industrial Workers of the World, or the I.W.W., the "Wobblies." This group went after the lumberjacks first, then the miners, organizing strikes on the Iron Range in 1916. "Duluth was said to have been the nerve center for the I.W.W. lumber strike, and another immediately following it against the old Oliver Iron Mining Co., predecessor of U.S. Steel's Minnesota Ore Operations," writes Curtis Miller (217). A photo in Dave Engel's book *Just Like Bob Zimmerman's Blues* (22), taken "in the early 1900s," shows Industrial Workers of the World parading in North Hibbing. Iron Range miners struck in 1907, led largely by Finnish workers, and again in 1916 with the help of the Industrial Workers of the World (Landis: 110). At a time when five iron ore workers in a thousand were dying annually (Gilman: 6), their demands were reasonable enough — an eight-hour day, no work on Saturdays, pay twice a month instead of once a month, extra pay for miners in "wet" areas — but the results were disastrous. In 1907 the Finns were replaced with workers from the Balkans and Italy; in 1916 the union leaders were arrested and striking miners were blacklisted. The I.W.W. retreated from the Iron Range, the mining companies developed a network of spies, and — although Iron Rangers availed themselves of consumer co-operatives like the Mesabi Range Co-operative Foundation and the Range Foundation for Oil Products (founded in 1928) — miners finally unionized only after the National Labor Relations Act of 1935 offered them the protection of federally supervised labor elections.

Despite limited success with strikes and at the Minnesota polls, the Nonpartisan League and the I.W.W. pressured both Republican and Democrats to move toward reform and ushered in a broad program of progressive legislation, which increasingly incorporated labor concerns like taxation which directed money out of the pockets of large corporations and into the pockets of local municipalities. These included a tonnage tax on iron ore (based on the argument that an irreplaceable natural heritage was not to be removed from the state without appropriate compensation), which benefited Iron Range towns like Hibbing. From the turn of the century until World War I, Carl Chrislock notes, "a consensus based on progressivism dominated state politics, at least on the rhetorical level" (182).

There was an antiwar component to this populism. Unlike reformers in other parts of America, Midwest progressives opposed World War I, even during the period of American neutrality, partly because they had always been isolationists, partly because they saw it as an unnecessary diversion from the real job at hand, and partly because of their own ethnic heritage. Suspicion of East Coast owners and management also played a role: in 1916, Harold Knutson, U.S. Congressman from Minnesota, suggested nationalizing the manufacture of all war materials (Førland: 344). But patriotism usually trumps reform, at least in the short run: Burnquist, from the "right" side of the tracks, was a key member of the near-dictatorial Minnesota Commission of Public Safety, which regulated alcohol traffic, mandated the registration of all "aliens," suppressed Minnesota's growing labor movement, and intervened to break a transit strike vital to unions of the American Federation of Labor on the grounds that the world war was "everybody's business" and not to be disrupted by men trying to make a living wage (John Earl Haynes: 10). At one point Burnquist recommended that Wisconsin's Populist Senator "Fighting Bob" La Follette be expelled from the United States. He told the Minnesota manager of the Nonpartisan League, Arthur Le Sueur, that the unpatriotic utterances of Senator La Follette "put a stamp of disloyalty on [the League] that can never be erased" (Chrislock: 164), and he never tired of pointing out to media that Le Sueur himself had provided legal counsel to I.W.W. organizer William D. "Big Bill" Haywood.[3] When Iron Range miners struck in June of 1916, Burnquist — worried that law enforcement officials in Hibbing might be too soft on their fellow citizens — telegraphed John Maining, sheriff of Duluth, instructing him to

> arrest forthwith and take before magistrate, preferably in Duluth, all persons who have participated and are participating in riots in your county, and make complaints against them. Prevent further breaches of the peace, riots, and unlawful assemblies. Use all your powers, including the summoning of posse, for the preservation of life and property. The violations of laws in Saint Louis County must be stopped at once. (Lillie: 37)[4]

Given the mindset of World War I America, that was pretty much it for the League. Several important members, including Townley, were arrested, and general membership declined. The high prices for agricultural commodities brought by the war also undermined the League's argument that farmers were being exploited, although most of the profits went not to farmers but to grain exporters.

Even though radical leaders had been jailed and radical reform was on hold throughout the decade, rural Minnesota remained a stronghold of populism in the 1920s. A Farmer-Labor Party did elect moderate Henrick Shipstead to the U.S. Senate in 1922 and keep him there until 1946. Within the state, in 1921, Minnesota legislators passed a bill — authored in part by Andrew Volstead of

Granite Falls, the very man who penned the prohibition amendment — which declared commodity exchanges "open markets" obliged to admit co-operative selling agencies as members, thereby enabling the Farmers Co-Op Elevators which dot the Minnesota landscape to this day.

Then came the Great Depression, which had actually begun in the Upper Midwest in the 1920s, as grain prices fell from their wartime highs and the wartime demand for steel ended. Depression-era discontent helped elect Farmer-Labor Party Governor Floyd Olson in 1930. Although he seemed leftist, Olson was in many respects a moderate compromise. More radical Minnesotans were looking at the Community Party (Haynes: 12, 13), and at newly reinvigorated unions, like the meat packers who struck at the Hormel packing house in Austin in 1933 (when the National Guard was not called in), and the teamsters who struck in Minneapolis in 1934 (when Governor Olson did call out the troops — to support the strikers). The more radical side of Minnesota's agrarian reform movement resurrected itself in the National Farmers' Holiday Association, formed in Des Moines, Iowa, in 1932. Under the leadership of Milo Reno in Iowa and John Bosch in Minnesota, farmers acted to protect themselves with a variety of actions: withholding commodities from markets, disrupting delivery of produce shipped by non-strikers, and "penny sales" at which friends of a foreclosed farmer bid a penny or a nickel for whatever the sheriff put up for sale, then stopping further bidding by "all means necessary." If an outsider bid ten dollars, he was "corrected": "I'm sure you meant ten cents." Sometimes a crowd of two or three thousand farmers simply detained the sheriff until an hour after the announced sale time, at which point the auction became void. John Bosch remembers one sale:

> A U.S. marshal was there, and I bet I had about 10,000 farmers there. Well, I never tried to conceal who I was, and I had never met this fellow before so I came in and introduced myself. And we had developed tactics, techniques, and so on. I told him that I felt that if he would let me talk to him, that I could convince him that he should not proceed with the sale. "Well," he said, "it doesn't make any difference how much I agree with you, I must proceed with the sale." Well, out in the hall where you couldn't identify somebody, somebody would holler, "Let the son of a bitch out here and we'll cut a hole in the ice and push him down twice and pull him up once." Somebody else would say, "Let's tie him up with one hind leg behind the car and haul him back to St. Paul," and this type of thing and he was white as a sheet. (Nass: 192)

As these tactics became known and the Holiday demonstrated in St. Paul, the mere threat of a Holiday presence was enough to stop a sale. Minnesota

Governor Floyd Olson, and then President Franklin Roosevelt, adopted the idea of a holiday on mortgage payments, and radical protest was subsumed into a more temperate reform.

Although the Farm Holiday was more active in southwestern and western Minnesota than on the Iron Range, it is inaccurate to suggest, as does David Boucher, that Dylan had come from a small country town in Minnesota, and to a large extent learned of the injustices in society through music (*Dylan & Cohen*: 124). It is true that, by the 1920s, militant activity in the mines had declined from its earlier level, but earlier activity had left its mark. Carl Chrislock reports a change in Hibbing heart one strike to the next: "In 1907 middle-class opinion in the numerous small towns that dotted the range had stood with management. In 1916 for a number of reasons it identified to a considerable extent with the strikers" (117). And there they stayed. "Iron birthed red," Mesabi native John Caddy writes in a poem titled "The Color of Mesabi Bones," including dust, rust, "SCAB" slashed in paint across a store front, and "Wobblies, union bombings, socialist Finns" (125). "The last Republican elected in the heart of the Iron Range won during the Eisenhower 1950s," Aaron Brown notes; "There are Republicans around. They vote and run for office, but they always lose" (184).

Iron Range Finns especially tended to be left-wing and active even in the twenties and thirties. Many had left their homeland to avoid long hitches in the Russian army as the tsar tried to Russify Finland; they joined the Finnish socialist clubs popular in the early twentieth century, and read "workers" newspapers (communist, socialist, and I.W.W.) published in Duluth, Minnesota and Superior, Wisconsin. "Finnish socialists and Wobblies in Northern Minnesota had developed an elaborate system of cultural institutions by the end of 1916," notes David Carter Lisa. "The Work People's College, the *Tyomies* and *Socialisti/Industrialisti* newspapers, the Finn halls and cooperatives acted to keep radical values alive. They also gave activist Finns alternatives to the churches and the mining companies for meeting material and psychological needs" (66). Barbara Wiener's KTCA documentary titled "The Iron Range: A People's History" reports a Socialist Hall opened in 1913, a Young Communist League active in 1927, and Mesabi Park built by Finns as a communist headquarters. Curtis S. Miller's history of organized labor in Duluth reproduces a photo of a Communist labor rally at the Duluth Civic Center in 1931, and John Earl Haynes discusses at some length the complex relationship between the Popular Front faction of the Farmer-Labor Party and the Communist Party in the 1930s. A blacklisted miner — John Bernard — was elected to Congress on the Farmer-Labor Party in 1936, although he lost his bid for re-election in 1938 when his opponent labeled him a communist. Even popular music could be a political statement, like the "CIO Polka" mentioned by Robert Shelton (*Home*: 22).

Midwestern isolationism also reasserted itself in the Depression years. In 1931, U.S. Congressman William Pittenger, from the Iron Range, told colleagues in the House that they should "look at world affairs from the standpoint of what is good or what is bad for America and not from the standpoint of the international financiers" (Førland: 347). In 1934, Senator Gerald P. Nye, a Progressive Republican Senator from North Dakota (1925–45), launched a Senate investigation into the profits and political machinations of the U.S. munitions industry. World War II — not to mention the Cold War and the Bush wars in the Middle East — continued to distract national attention from matters closer to the Midwestern home.

The Iron Range leftist tradition continued through World War II and after. As Dylan himself notes, the ethnic composition of the Iron Range undermined the appeal of anti-Soviet Cold War propaganda, so war continued to be unpopular there. Miners struck again 1949, more successfully, demanding pensions and insurance; they struck again in 1951 for 55 days in support of a national shutdown, and yet again in July of 1958. In school, Bob Dylan absorbed at least some populist history: whereas early in the century the school system, sensitive to the mining companies, had offered "Americanization" classes designed to wean immigrants from their radical ethnic heritages, in the fifties Social Studies 12 at Hibbing High was taught by Union president and Democratic-Farm-Labor Party captain Charlie Miller (Engel: 205). Bob Dylan was there. *Hibbing Daily Tribune* editor George Fisher noted in 1951 that Minnesota ranked ninth on the FBI list as a haven for reds, and that Gus Hall, chairman of the Communist Party USA and the party's presidential candidate (who spent eight years in Leavenworth during the McCarthy era for violating the Smith Act), had been born near Hibbing (Engel: 77). Walter Eliot of the *Duluth News-Tribune*, a man from the "right" side of Main Street," later cited Hall and Dylan as evidence that "a lot of strange characters have come off the Iron Range" (Shelton, *Home*: 84).[5] *Hibbing Daily Tribune* columnist Aaron Brown, a member of the younger generation from the "other" side of Main Street, was the last reporter to have interviewed Hall, shortly before his death in 2000. In the fifties, progressive-populists refused to support Joe McCarthy and his communist witch hunts, questioning McCarthy's targets even while supporting his populist attack on centralized government. "It was a popular thing to be a radical," says a woman from Eveleth interviewed for the *Iron Range* documentary, and as Aaron Brown points out in his own book on the Iron Range, "the most exciting human events of the region all happened within the lifetimes of people who still wander around downtown" (12).

Dylan heard this history; he even lived some of it. In *Chronicles*, he recalls his youth and the Iron Range's radical political tradition: "The upper Midwest was an extremely volatile, politically active area — with the Farmer–Labor Party, Social Democrats, socialists, communists. They were hard crowds to please and not too much for Republicanism" (231). The fact that Abe Zimmerman made his life on the right side of the tracks may account for some of the father-son tensions in the Abe Zimmerman-Bob Dylan relationship. Dave Engel reports that early in his Duluth years, Abe had been elected leader of "a company union" formed by his employer, Standard Oil, to keep workers away from the Congress of Industrial Organizations (CIO); "Loyalty to management may account for his rise through a 75-employee office to junior supervisor, and in 1941, to supervisor," Engel speculates (34). His son lined up on the other side of the picket line: on his February, 1964, trip across America, Dylan stopped in Colorado at the site of the Ludlow Massacre of 1914, in which 30 miners striking against the Rockefeller Mines were shot by National Guardsmen (Woody Guthrie had sung a song on the massacre). Mr. Rockefeller, who shows up in Dylan's early "Hard Times in New York Town," had helped the U.S. Steel Company buy the Iron Range.

RADICAL WRITERS

Writers being what they are, the reformist tradition is much stronger in Midwest literary tradition than what we can call the Main Street tradition.[6] Hannibal, Missouri's Mark Twain began the movement in this direction when he followed the idyllic *The Adventures of Tom Sawyer* (1876) with the revisionist *The Adventures of Huckleberry Finn* (1884) — one insane scheme after another all along the Mississippi River shore — and followed that with "The Man That Corrupted Hadleyburg" (1899), but Wisconsin's Hamlin Garland best formulated the aesthetics of realism in the stories of *Main-Travelled Roads* (1891) and in a passage in his autobiography *A Son of the Middle Border*: "Obscurely forming in my mind were two great literary concepts — that truth was a higher quality than beauty, and that to spread the reign of justice should everywhere be the design and intent of the artist" (374). Garland, who had earlier joined the Anti-Poverty Society, weathered a storm of Main Street criticism leveled at his "totally inaccurate depictions of Midwest farm life," and traveled around the Midwest speaking at Populist picnics and reading stories to audiences who grasped the truth of what he said.[7]

Sinclair Lewis was another one of those commie pinko authors. Like his novel's heroine, Lewis moved comfortably through all strata of Sauk Centre society. Although a bit of a nerd, Lewis knew what he knew, which was what

Bobby Zimmerman knew: both sides of his Midwestern small-town heritage. Like Dylan, Lewis headed east as a teenager (Oberlin College, then Yale); like Dylan he met serious leftists, especially during his brief stay at the "Home Colony" which Upton Sinclair had founded in Englewood, New Jersey, in 1906 with royalties from *The Jungle*. The Sauk Centre *Avalanche* described Home Colony as a "Communist colony," but according to Mark Schorer "membership implied no central political commitments but represented all varieties of radical opinion and shaded over into lunacy: there were socialists, anarchists, syndicalists, single-taxers, New Thoughtists, spiritualists" (113). Most were writers, and Lewis fit right in . . . for a month. Soon, like Dylan in Greenwich Village, he broke with the ideologues, but not before writing a fictional account of life on Sinclair's Farm, which the *New York Sun* published on December 16, 1906, under the headline "Two Yale Men in Utopia" with the subhead, "Sinclair Lewis and Allan Updegraff Tell How They Performed Manual Labor and Cultivated the Intellect at Upton Sinclair's Colony Up on the Palisades" (Schorer: 114). Lewis actually joined the Socialist Party (for a little over a year — number 12157, Branch One, New York Local), read Marx, and even met Jack Reed and "Red Emma" Goldman at the 1910 Anarchists' Ball. Yet Sinclair Lewis never wrote for the *Masses* or for the *New Masses*. In the opinion of his biographer, Mark Schorer, "what most concerned the young Lewis was material for fiction, and the social rather than the concretely political occasion" (180). The New York and New Jersey crowd gave intellectual credibility to less theoretical leftists Lewis had heard back home, and his own assessment was, finally, positive: "Taking it by and large, where else than at Helicon Hall could I have learned so many new things every minute, . . . [have] seen so many novel yet vital things and have met in intimacy and equality so many thoroughly worthwhile people?" (Schorer: 115). This was Dylan's experience almost exactly. "I've got nothin' but affection for all those who've sailed with me," he sang in 1977, looking back at his own weird crew of socialists, anarchists, syndicalists, single-taxers, New Thoughtists, spiritualists.

One scarcely thinks of Willa Cather as a Red Emma Goldman, but Cather did work for years as managing editor of *McClure's Magazine* with other muckrakers like Lincoln Steffens and Ida Tarbell. As a youth she — like Sinclair Lewis and Bobby Zimmerman — had moved freely among all strata of society, hanging out with hired girls in town and riding into the countryside for chats with immigrant farm women, and listening to political views from the other side of Main Street. For *O Pioneers!* she wrote this exchange between Lou Bergson and Carl Lindstrum, just returned to Nebraska from New York City:

Lou sat down on the step and began to whittle. "Well, what do folks in New York think of William Jennings Bryan?" Lou began to bluster, as he always did when he talked politics. "We gave Wall Street a scare in ninety-six, all right, and we're fixing another to hand them. Silver was n't the only issue," he nodded mysteriously. "There's a good many things got to be changed. The West is going to make itself heard."

Carl laughed. "But, surely, it did do that, if nothing else."

Lou's thin face reddened up to the roots of his bristly hair. "Oh, we've only begun. We're waking up to a sense of our responsibilities, out here, and we ain't afraid, neither. You fellows back there must be a tame lot. If you had any nerve you'd get together and march down to Wall Street and blow it up. Dynamite it, I mean," with a threatening nod. (112)

That line still has a certain ring to it in an age of 9–11 and Wall Street bailouts.

Vachel Lindsay was the son of a Springfield, Illinois, doctor who early in his career used his father's money to publish the *Village Magazine*, filled with his own reformist poems and visions of a transformed Springfield. In the 1920s, Lindsay toured the country reciting poems like "General William Booth Enters Heaven" in a manner that rejoined poetry with music, something between chanting and singing. Most large school libraries contained the Caedmon Records recording *Vachel Lindsay Reading The Congo, Chinese Nightingale, and Other Poems* (TC 1041), released in 1941 from a recording made in 1933. Lindsay's strong Christianity and dark portrayal of Africa have banished him from the anthologies since the 1970s, but Lindsay was quite popular in the 1950s, as much for his performance as for his poetry. Young members of the *Dead Poets Society* exit their subterranean headquarters chanting Lindsay's poem "The Congo." Lindsay's *Collected Poems*, not of course the Caedmon record recorded in New York in 1931, include gems like his 1909 "Why I Voted the Socialist Ticket" ("I am unjust, but I can strive for justice . . . Come let us vote against our human nature"), his 1910 "The Leaden-Eyed" ("Not that they die, but that they die like sheep"), his 1919 celebration of Populist candidate William Jennings Bryan ("Gigantic troubadour, speaking like a siege gun, / Smashing Plymouth Rock with his boulders from the West"), and his lament for the results of the 1896 election ("Where is McKinley, Mark Hanna's McKinley, / His slave, his echo, his suit of clothes?"). His *Collected Poems* includes celebrations of Abraham Lincoln and Illinois Governor John P. Altgeld, who pardoned the convicted Haymarket Rioters and lost re-election. And this screed under the title "To the United States Senate":

And must the Senator from Illinois
Be this squat thing, with blinking, half-closed eyes?
This brazen gutter idol, reared to power
Upon a leering pyramid of lies?

And must the Senator from Illinois
Be the world's proverb of successful shame,
Dazzling all State house flies that steal and steal,
Who, when the sad State spares them, count it fame?

If once or twice within his new won hall
His vote had counted for the broken men;
If in his early days he wrought some good —
We might a great soul's sins forgive him then.

(1: 134)

Carl Sandburg's popularity has also waned from what it was in the 1950s and 1960s, when poems like "Fog" and "Chicago" (which Dylan references in *Tarantula*, page 15: "chicago? the hogbutcher! meat-packer! whatever!") were familiar to anyone who got past the eighth grade.[8] His voice too could be heard on Caedmon records. Sandburg, the son of an immigrant Galesburg, Illinois, railroad worker, met his wife while working for the Wisconsin Social Democratic Party. He was corresponding secretary to Milwaukee Mayor Emil Seidal, the first socialist mayor of a major U.S. city (1910–12), and was active in the presidential campaign of 1912, when Seidal ran for vice president on the Socialist Party of America, with presidential candidate Eugene V. Debs. Later Sandburg returned to Illinois, writing for the *Chicago Daily News*, largely on labor issues. He wrote a magnificent multi-volume biography of Abraham Lincoln, an equally magnificent autobiography titled *Always the Young Strangers*, and poems like "The People Yes," which Dylan parodies on page 110 of *Tarantula* ("& said yes / to the people / yes the people") and at the end of "Talkin' World War III Blues." Sandburg could be Dylan when he writes,

The people is Everyman, everybody,
Everybody is you and me and all others.
What everybody says is what we all say. . . .
To work hard, to live hard, to die hard, and then to go to hell after all would be too damned hard.

You can fool all the people part of the time and part of the people all the time but you
can't fool all of the people all of the time. . . .
    The people will live on.
The learning and blundering people will live on.
   They will be tricked and sold and again sold
And go back to the nourishing earth for rootholds,
   The people so peculiar in renewal and comeback,
   You can't laugh off their capacity to take it.

(Harvest Poems: 91, 93, 103)

In *Invisible Republic,* Marcus reports that Kenneth Rexroth, "looking for a phrase to describe the country he thought lay behind Carl Sandburg's work" came up with the phrase "the old free America," a phrase which Marcus uses to describe the America of Dylan's basement tapes (89). Sandburg also edited a collection of American folk songs titled *The American Songbag* which is filled with outlaw and working-class songs like "The Poor Working Girl," "Been in the Pen So Long," "Poor Paddy Works on the Railway," "Jesse James," and "Shovelin' Iron Ore." As a collector of folk songs, Sandburg was an early Alan Lomax or John Hammond; as a poet-singer, he was an early Pete Seeger or Bob Dylan:

> Perhaps I should explain that for a number of years I have gone hither and yon over the United States meeting audiences to whom I talked about poetry an art, read my verses, and closed a program with a half- or quarter-hour of songs, giving verbal footnotes with each song. These itineraries have included now about two-thirds of the state universities of the country, audiences ranging from 3,000 people at the University of California to 30 at the Garret Club in Buffalo, New York, and organizations as diverse as the Poetry Society of South Carolina and the Knife and Fork Club of South Bend, Indiana. The songs I gave often reminded listeners of songs of a kindred character they knew entirely or in fragments; or they would refer me to persons who had similar ballads or ditties. (*The American Songbag*: ix)

Sandburg *was* the socialist ticket that Lindsay voted for.

In February, 1964, road-tripping across America with Pete Karman (who the year previous had visited Cuba), folksinger Paul Clayton, and Victor Maimudes, Dylan visited Carl Sandburg, who had retired in 1945 to Hendersonville, North Carolina. "Much as the young Sandburg had revered Whitman," Robert Shelton writes, "Dylan now revered Sandburg" (*Home*: 242). Sandburg and Dylan "had much in common," observes Jonathan Shimkin; "a mid-western background; an interest in folk song; an ardent espousal of the authenticity of the culture, language and regional accents that gave rise to folk songs; a streak of social activism" (61). The meeting was brief, perhaps 20 minutes, and Sandburg was obviously not as impressed with Dylan as Dylan was with Sandburg, but the older poet did tell the young folksinger that he regarded poetry and folk singing as kindred arts.

Had Dylan's high school teachers been more courageous or savvy, he might have made a road trip to visit socialist writers closer to home, like Meridel Le Sueur and Thomas McGrath. Meridel Le Sueur was the daughter of lawyer Arthur Le Sueur, whom Governor Burnquist attacked for his defense of Big Bill Haywood. Meridel was a gifted journalist, poet, and fiction writer who wrote stories about hungry labor organizers and newspaper "reportages" like "Cows and Horses Are Hungry," "I Was Marching," and "Women on the Breadlines." When, during World War II, Erskine Caldwell conceived the idea of a series of regional studies to be called American Folkways, written by authors "well acquainted with the localities in which they lived," he picked Meridel Le Sueur to write *North Star Country*. The book was published in 1945, with a dedication to her socialist parents and chapters like "Woe to My People!" and "Rise, O Days," and "Stride On, Democracy." Meridel sounds at times like a female Bob Dylan:

> Capitalism is a world of ruins really, junk piles of machines, men, women, bowls of dust, floods, erosions, masks to cover rapacity and in this sling and wound the people carry their young, in the shades of their grief, in the thin shadow of their hunger, hope and crops in their hands, in the dark of the machine, only they have the future in their hands. (*Ripening*: 239)

"The world is round, people," she would warn audiences at her readings, "and your shit will fall on your own head." She autographed her books and articles, "Salut, comrade!"

Le Sueur's friend Thomas McGrath, born in North Dakota, also autographed his books "Salut, comrade!" Like Le Sueur, McGrath found himself blacklisted after World War II. McGrath wrote poems like "Vision of Three Angels Viewing the Progress of Socialism" and "Proletarian in Abstract Light" and, in the long reminiscence "Letter to an Imaginary Friend," a remembrance of one of his father's workers, Cal:

> He read *The Industrial Worker*,
> Though I didn't know what the paper was at the time.
> The last of the real Wobs — that, too, I didn't know,
> Couldn't.

Played a harmonica; sat after supper
In the lantern smell and late bat-whickering dusk,
Playing mumbly-peg and talked of wages and hours
At the bunkhouse door. On Sunday cleaned his gun,
A Colt .38 that he let me shoot at a hawk —
It jumped in my hand and my whole arm tingled with shock.
A quiet man with the smell of the road on him,
The smell of far places. Romantic as all of the stiffs
Were romantic to me and my cousins,
Stick-in-the mud burgesses of boyhood's country

(17)

McGrath smoked cigarettes and told stories like Woody Guthrie and Bob Dylan. "I lived in L.A. and hated it all the time," McGrath told an audience in 1986; "New York — I didn't especially like either of these cities, though I loved New York at first, like we all do when we are young and juicy. . . . It seems to me I've never liked any city I've lived in."[9]

The next generation of Midwest writers carried the populist message to crusaders of the sixties generation. Dave Etter, from Elburn, Illinois, wrote, "It's not that I'm unhappy being a Democrat, it's just that I would be a whole lot happier being a Populist — a real bumping, jumping, thumping Populist" (*Selected Poems*: 149). In 1966, Robert Bly co-founded American Writers Against the Vietnam War, donated his prize money for an American Book Award to war resistance, and wrote political poems like "Asian Peace Offers Rejected without Publication." Bill Holm incorporated a story his father told him of the Farm Holiday Movement into a poem about a farmers' protest in Pope County:

They used to call it a sheriff's sale.
Had one over by Scandia in the middle of the Thirties.
My dad told me how
  the sheriff would ride out to the farm
to auction off the farmer's goods for the bank.
Neighbors came with pitchforks
to gather in the yard:
"What am I bid for this cow?"
Three cents. Four cents. No more bids.
If a stranger came in and bid a nickel,
a circle of pitchforks gathered around him,
And the bidding stopped. . . .

The sheriff's voice weakens
as he moves from hayrack to hayrack
holding up tools,
describing cattle and pigs
one at a time.
The space between those fork tines
is the air we all breathe.

(*Dead*: 28)

Garrison Keillor wrote newspaper column after column attacking George Bush and Company, and in 2008 Barton Sutter, poet laureate of Duluth, wrote a political play titled *Bushed*, which ran for six weeks in the city where Bob Dylan was born.

The young Bob Dylan knew only a few of these writers, like Sandburg and Lindsay, but he knew this great tradition well. While he would not have known most of the lines I have just quoted, the ideas would have been familiar. The one major weakness of Mike Marqusee's otherwise useful *Chimes of Freedom: The Politics of Bob Dylan's Art* is that Marqusee begins his study of Dylan's political awareness with New York City and not the Iron Range, and it is inaccurate, insular, and a bit self-congratulatory for Suze Rotolo to credit herself with forming Dylan's social conscience, writing in her memoir *A Freewheelin' Time*,

> Growing up in a politically conscious home during the Cold War and under McCarthyism, I had struggled through the issues of Communism, socialism, and the American way. I threw those interests out to Bob. I was exposed to a lot more than a kid from Hibbing, Minnesota, was, especially with my upbringing amid books and music and interesting, albeit difficult, people. And I was also from New York City. No contest there. (137)

The great Midwest reformist tradition made Dylan enthusiastic about Steinbeck's *The Grapes of Wrath* and Woody Guthrie's *Bound for Glory*. Steinbeck's *The Grapes of Wrath* won him a Pulitzer and then a Nobel Prize: the story of displaced Oakies migrating westward toward a Promised Land which turned out to be a valley of bitter ashes, of their struggles along the way against owners and merchants and cops, and of the change of thinking — as Steinbeck puts it early in the book — from "I" to "we." Two of the novel's three main characters — Tom Joad and Preacher Casy — are proto-socialists given to fine radical speeches, and the third — Ma Joad — leans increasingly to collective thinking as her biological family shrinks and she expands the sphere of her concern to outsiders. Steinbeck moves his narrative forward in alternate chapters; between those chapters he splices small vignettes or short discourses on topics as diverse as a dust storm, a turtle crossing the highway, crooked used car dealers, generous truckers eating lunch in a diner, and the excesses of a deregulated capitalism. "Socialist/communist propaganda" shouted Main Street apologists for the System, and certainly *The Grapes of Wrath* is a critique of the System as it existed in the 1930s and still exists today:

> Maybe he needs two hundred men, so he talks to five hundred, an' they tell other folks, an' when you get to the place, they's a thousan' men. This here fella says, "I'm payin' twenty cents an hour." An' maybe half a the men walk off. But they's still five hunerd that's so goddamn hungry they'll work for nothin' but biscuits. Well, this here fella's got a contract to pick them peaches or — chop that cotton. You see now? The more fellas he can get, an' the hungrier, less he's gonna pay. An' he'll get a fella with kids if he can, 'cause — hell, I says I wasn't gonna fret ya. . . . (259)

Bob Dylan read *The Grapes of Wrath* for an English class at Hibbing High School, and was instantly attracted to the book and to other works by John Steinbeck. His 22-page handwritten paper analyzing the character of Tom Joad was exhibited at the University of Minnesota in spring 2006 — the paper for which he got an A–, then "loaned" the following year to his friend John Bucklen.

In the long run, *The Grapes of Wrath* prepped Dylan for his career as a folksinger. In the short run, it prepped Dylan for another great American on-the-road saga, the story of another Dust Bowl refugee, Woody Guthrie's *Bound for Glory*. The book, and the songs, made Guthrie Dylan's most majorist of heroes (Guthrie was "just a little smarter, because he was from the country" Dylan told Robert Shelton [*Home*: 356]) and the excuse for his trip to New York in 1960. Guthrie himself had headed west to California, where he fell in with socialists and communists. Although he later claimed to have joined the Communist Party, he apparently never officially did; writing a column for the communist newspaper the *Daily Worker* was, however, more than enough to get him blacklisted in the 1950s. *Bound for Glory* is filled with Oakie adventures and passages not unlike those in *The Grapes of Wrath*, including familiar advice about the tactics employed by crooked owners:

> Anyway, you'll sign that credit slip tonight. You'll take it down in the morning to buy your stuff and go to work. You'll get a bill of goods and find out the crops have been held up a few days. So you'll buy a few more days. . . . You'll get about ten days or two weeks behind at the store. Might be a few scattered 'cots to pick, but not half

enough to feed and keep your bunch. Then the weather will warm up and force the boss to pick the 'cots. You'll go to work. Make enough to live on while you're working. . . . You'll just barely make enough to keep you going while you work. But you won't make enough to be able to pay the ten days' bill you owe. You'll just be ten days behind the world. Twenty dollars, twenty-five. Ten days! Behind the world. (284–5)

In his songs and in his book and in his life, Guthrie was no saint, but he stood for the honorable things in American life: the common working man seeking respect and dignity, the guitar-playing man, the traveling man, the hobo, the eccentric, the man outside of civilization and the law . . . everything that Dylan himself came ultimately to value and represent.

THE INDIVIDUAL AND THE ORGANIZATION

Looking at this tradition, especially as it is embodied in the writers, one notices a couple things. The first is that not all of the older ones were born into working-class families. Hamlin Garland, Robert Bly, and Bill Holm grew up on farms, and Sandburg's father worked on the railroad, but Sinclair Lewis's father — like Lindsay's — was a medical doctor; Cather's father was a respectable merchant like Abe Zimmerman. Steinbeck's father was Monterey County treasurer, and his mother had been a schoolteacher. These writers acquired their progressive-to-radical politics from experiences outside of their immediate families: friendships, reading, and adventures in nature and on the other side of Main Street.

One notices too that they are not particularly theoretical or programmatic. They respect hard work and enjoy the company of an honest person. They like to sit around a table listening to a good story. But they do not sit around the table distinguishing correct from incorrect steps in achieving the dictatorship of the proletariat. They have plenty of empathy for exploited workers, but little time for "the concrete political occasion." They're not even particularly good as depicting the moment of transition from "I" to "we." I like to think they are true workers, not bureaucrats, although someone else might say they are sunshine radicals who cannot be counted on for drudge work or ward politics. They spend very little time, in their lives or in their writing, with things like raising the minimum wage from $4.50 an hour to $4.75, passing an iron ore tax, or circulating petitions for the recall of Governor Blagojevich or President Bush.

They are not always reliable. They manufacture details, they ignore evidence, they misrepresent the specific situation in the interests of a wider point or a better story. Meridel Le Sueur in her *North Star Country* histories, Dave Etter in his poetic "reworking" of the Ruthton Banker murders, Bill Holm in his Farm Holiday poem (and in virtually all of his political statements) — they are true to the idea, but not always to the historical fact.

Nor are they theoretically coherent or ideologically consistent. Mark Buechsel notes that Red Oliver, in Sherwood Anderson's quasi-Marxist novel *Beyond Desire*, "does not positively identify with communism as such but rather just resents the callous dehumanizing of the striking workers" (228). He also notes,

> Anderson's somewhat facile lumping together of Puritanism, conventional Victorian respectability, abstraction in general, capitalism, industrialism, machine culture, the success myth, and jingoism as one large complex is . . . due to the fact that Anderson thought in large-scale associative mythic terms and was not prone to careful historical analysis and differentiation. (73)

This disorganization and inconsistency can be found in many of Minnesota's progressive political leaders, the state's blue-collar workers, and even in the voters themselves. Other states have elected military heroes, Hollywood stars, and professional athletes to high office, but Minnesotans elected a pro wrestler as governor and *Saturday Night Live* comic as U.S. Senator. However, mavericks like Jesse "The Body" Ventura (of the Reform/Independence Party) and Al Franken (of the Democratic-Farmer-Labor Party) are a Minnesota tradition. In his study of Minnesota Progressivism, Carl Chrislock portrays Governor Floyd B. Olson as

> more a rebel than a radical, a pragmatist who rejected the ideological approach to politics. Upon discovering the heavy political liabilities created by the 1934 platform — the content of which had been strongly influenced by a militant Olson speech to the convention that adopted it — the governor attempted the extraordinary feat of interpreting it as a reformist rather than a radical manifesto. (195)

Minnesota's Senator Eugene McCarthy, who took up the anti-Vietnam War cause and took on President Lyndon B. Johnson, was a man of tremendous integrity and powerful enough to knock Johnson out of re-election, but he could not assemble a machine to match those of Bobby Kennedy or Hubert Humphrey. (He wrote good poems, though.) Alpha Smaby introduces her study of that crusade in Minnesota with a lengthy history of "two decades of internecine strife" within McCarthy's own party, including Hubert Humphrey's purge of suspected communists in 1948, a campaign *against* Adlai Stevenson's nomination in 1956, and disarray on the taconite amendment in 1964. That kind of party dysfunction hurt McCarthy's campaign.

For all their leftist leanings and the state's strong populist tradition, Minnesota farmers, writers, and miners — even on the Iron Range — have proven notoriously difficult to organize. They are simply too individualistic, or too distracted, or too whatever. Discussing Iron Range labor history, Paul Landis points out that despite legitimate issues, "Labor organizations as such never have flourished on the Range" (108), something he attributes to the fact that miners were "poor material out of which to weld an organization that could in any way match strength and wits against the United States Steel and other great corporations whose subsidiaries mine the ores of the Mesabi" (109).[10] In his study of I.W.W. support for Finnish draft resisters on the Iron Range during World War I, David Carter Lisa notes that just as the Finnish Socialist Clubs had resisted assimilation into the Socialist Party of America in the early 1900s, and had broken with the I.W.W. in 1912, so "Finnish members of the I.W.W. in Northern Minnesota displayed a remarkable degree of autonomy in their efforts to offer support for their jailed comrades in the summer of 1917" (270). It's the old story: good at the extraordinary and dramatic, but not so good at the mundane that would avoid drama.

Dylan was not Finnish, but his girlfriend was, and in this respect Dylan might as well have been Finnish. Early on in New York, Dylan told Izzy Young, "I won't join a group. . . . When you fail in a group you can blame each other. When you fail alone, you yourself fail" (Scaduto: 99). After the Emergency Civil Liberties Committee Banquet he told Nat Hentoff, "I'm never going to have anything to do with any political organization again in my life. . . . I'm not going to be part of any organization. Those people at that dinner were the same as everybody else. They're doing their time. They're chained to what they're doing" (McGregor: 61).

The thinking of many Midwest reformers is sometimes almost antiliberal. Any collective ideology is suspect, right or left, and these "radicals" would agree with what Michael Gray said in regard to Dylan's "Desolation Row": "the liberal conscience marries an indiscriminate humanitarianism to an equally effete set of fashionable reforming aims but never achieves sufficient vision to begin to transform society and thus gets nowhere" (Song: 138). Or Midwest radicals look back more than they look ahead — they seem almost conservative even while trying to be progressive. Populist reformers are injunctive — but their blueprint for the future is a fuzzy picture of an idealized Jeffersonian democracy. If the country has indeed become a "dream gone bust," as Dylan puts it in "Clean-Cut Kid," the answer is probably not more Strategic Planning, whether it comes from corporate management or the U.S. Government or unions or the Communist Party. Karl Marx and Henry Kissinger share the same line of Dylan's "When You Gonna Wake Up?" Too much planning is what wrecked America in the first place: we need to get back to something older, less structured, and, often as not, American pastoral.[11] "You're headed in the wrong direction," they seem to say to the modern American; "And if it's recovery you want, don't recover what got you into the mess to begin with; go back before big and global, to little and local. Little, not big, is better. Like in the old days." Vachel Lindsay envisioned the Springfield of the future as "a little Athens," and Carol Kennicott wants to remake Gopher Prairie into one of those old New England villages. When that past is not recovered, writers tend to turn bitter and acerbic like Mark Twain or Bob Dylan ("When there's too much of nothing / It just makes a fella mean," he observes in "Too Much of Nothing"[12]), light out for the territories like Lindsay and Garland and Dylan, or shrug their shoulders and resign, like Bob Dylan and John Steinbeck when post-war America became a land not of simple yeoman farmers but of Levittown suburbs, shopping malls, and consumerism triumphant. In any case, the impulse to look back from the middle of a real mess to something that seems to have worked well is stronger than the desire to design blueprints for a brighter tomorrow.

These writer-reformers value *individual* freedom over the *collective* good. "The frontier is productive of individualism," Frederick Jackson Turner pointed out in 1893; "the tendency is anti-social. The tax-gatherer is viewed as a representative of oppression" (30); as a result, he went on to argue, "The ideals of equality, freedom of opportunity, faith in the common man are deep rooted in all the Middle West. The frontier stage, through which each portion passed, left abiding traces on the older, as well as on the newer, areas of the province" (155). Hard-core socialists like Meridel Le Sueur, Tom McGrath, and Woody Guthrie valued human dignity above collective well-being, and even John Steinbeck was suspicious of reform which lost the individual in the amorphous and often intolerant masses. In their hearts, Midwesterners are suspicious of anyone grown "too big for his britches," and the fact that the Industrial Workers of the World aspired to become the biggest pair of britches on the planet gave them cause for concern. "I am an I.W.W., but I don't carry a red card," Shelton quotes Sandburg as saying; "I am an anarchist, but not a member of the organization" (*Home*: 242). True protest is amorphous and individualistic. It responds to an overly intrusive System either by returning to some kind of low-level participatory village democracy, or by becoming an anarchist (Thoreau decided early on that no individual could, without considerable loss of integrity, be in any way associated with the American government, and looked forward to a government which "governs not at all"). At the very least it selects its role models from the ranks of cantankerous individuals, outlaws, characters, and curmudgeons . . . what Greil Marcus labeled the "old free America," America's "invisible republic." It was for this reason that in 1955 people disenchanted with what America was becoming preferred pre-World War II songs: "the older, pre-war songs which were the bread and butter of any folk performer's act came from a time before America had assumed imperial dominance over the world, and were considered unsullied by the plastic desires of the Fifties" (Gill: 9).

One wonders after a while whether these Midwest populists are political activists at all — perhaps they should more properly be called prophets . . . or just plain cranks. Steve Earle went so far as to say, "I don't think of Woody Guthrie as a political writer. He was a writer who lived in political times" (Corn: 21). Others thought of Guthrie as a prophet — like Dylan. A politician believes that a structured system is necessary to protect individual rights, so system is better than non-system. Politicians *inside* the system think that the machine works fine as is, and they connive to ensure its continued operations for their own benefit and perhaps for the benefit of others. Politicians *outside* of the system think the machine is flawed to one degree or another, and design new gears or a new machine, for the benefit of themselves and perhaps others. Politicians on both sides are programmatic and accept compromise. They tend to be calculating bean counters. Cranks, on the other hand, just throw monkey wrenches into the gears. They are, in their way, as active as politicians, especially in spurts, and they're more colorful. They are certainly not conventional, but are they inspired? Prophets are inspired and flamboyant, but not proactive. In a way they are the most passive of all, because even as they decry corruption in the system, they are convinced of a built-in judgment which makes politics irrelevant. Many Americans in the sixties believed that the country had its flaws, and most Americans today think the machine is broken. In *A Generation in Motion*, I identified at least four responses to America gone bad, three of them apolitical: prank the system, blow the system up, and walk away from the system. I quoted Ken Kesey to the effect that "There's only one thing that's gonna do any good at all . . . and that's everybody's just got to look at it, look at the war, and turn your backs and say 'Fuck it'" (73). The Old Left was political in seeking to retain a mended machine or, if they were Marxists, to replace it with a new machine. The New Left was programmatic and more populist in that it sought to demolish the machine, with dynamite or just by ignoring it.

DYLAN'S POLITICS

Bob Dylan turns out to be a typical prairie populist — more prophet than politician — whose songs like "Maggie's Farm" and "It's All Over Now, Baby Blue" are, as Clinton Heylin puts it, "individualistic expressions of rebellion, without any of the sense of community that was important to [Joan] Baez" (*Shades*: 115). Dylan would be pleased to learn, as he does at the end of the film *dont look back*, that the British press has dubbed him an anarchist. When Bobby Neuwirth observes, "In England it's cool to be a commie," Dylan responds, with a hint of pride, "I don't think it's cool to be an anarchist, though."

Friends in New York were not impressed with Dylan's political acumen. "Bobby was not a political person," Dave Van Ronk recalls in *No Direction Home*; "we thought he was hopelessly politically naïve. In retrospect, he was probably more sophisticated than we were." For his part in that film, Dylan — who has always tended to interpret political issues in personal terms, and to express politics in personal situations — points out that being on the side of people who are struggling for something is not the same thing as being political in the usual meaning of the term. In a way Dylan is political in the largest sense, in the act of distancing himself from politics in the smallest sense, especially in politically charged times, and especially if politics is just part of an illusion (Cott: 229). Marqusee reports that Guthrie's "indifference to hierarchy of any kind" caused his application for membership in the Communist Party to be rejected; he was considered unreliable (20). Dylan quickly proved similarly unreliable. "Although leftist organizations (such as the Students for a Democratic Society) may have adopted him in the Sixties, and Christian fundamentalists attempted to co-opt him in the eighties, Dylan offers no institutional agenda in his lyrics," argues Craig Robert Snow (16). Dylan testifies throughout his career on big-picture matters like education, justice, war, and human dignity, and he insists again and yet again on the equality of all common men (himself the most common among them), but his real agenda was radical individualism. To the extent that this agenda is political, Dylan is political.

However, in the early sixties, the general Greenwich Village milieu and specific friends like Dave Van Ronk, Terri Thal, and Suze Rotolo did move the prairie populist briefly in the direction of Old Left theory and collective engagement. Rotolo herself worked in 1961 for the New York City CORE office (Sounes has her demonstrating against nuclear arms with SANE as well) and in 1963 as assistant to the stage manager for a Sheridan Square Playhouse production of George Tabori's *Brecht on Brecht*. All of this, not to mention the politics of the *Broadside* crew, was not lost on Dylan, whose sense of social injustice allowed him to write civil rights songs like "Oxford Town" and antiwar songs like "Masters of War," and even to write an antiwar poem titled "Go 'Way Bomb" for an Izzy Young anthology. In 1962 he played at a benefit concert at City College in Manhattan for the Congress on Racial Equality. After the now infamous speech to the Emergency Civil Liberties Committee (ECLC), where he was accepting its 1963 Tom Paine Award,[13] Dylan offered to do a benefit concert for the ECLC and for Students for a Democratic Society. In July of 1963, he flew to Mississippi with Pete Seeger to sing at a SNCC-sponsored voter registration rally in Greenwood, a trip which got him ink in the *New York Times*, plus coverage on television. On the road trip of February 1964, he visited Harlan County, Kentucky, where coal miners were on strike, buying one miner a drink and bombarding him with Hibbing-Steinbeck-Guthrie questions: "Ever been in a cave-in? Gotta shop at a company store? Company cops ever beat you?" (Scaduto: 167). He offered a benefit concert to a Hamish Sinclair, secretary of the National Committee for Miners (Shelton, *Home*: 241); on the same trip he sang at Emory University in Atlanta and Tougaloo College at a SNCC demonstration organized by Tom Hayden among others. With Joan Baez and Pete Seeger and Phil Ochs, he performed "Blowin' in the Wind" like a member of some proletarian civil rights church choir, his hands joined to the hands of others, committed to the cause. We have photos of these great moments in early sixties history, and newspaper reports, and the film *No Direction Home*. "He is the voice of the oppressed in America and the champion of the little man," wrote the *Newport News* after the 1963 Newport Folk Festival (Shelton, *Home*: 182). Dylan's songs of this period reflect a commitment to politics strong enough to trouble Tony Glover and other old Minneapolis friends, who "stood resolutely for the old music, mostly blues, and were alarmed by Dylan's drift into political slogans and protest and topical writing" (Shelton, *Home*: 210).

But Glover had no cause to fret about Dylan drifting into politics: Dylan quickly withdrew from active participation in causes and movements, and in 2004, he would deny ever having been involved: "I never set out to write politics. I didn't want to be a political moralist. There were people who just did that. Phil Ochs focused on political things" (Cott: 435). (That may be one reason Dylan remains visible long after Ochs — who wrote some pretty good songs in his day — has disappeared from the American consciousness.) "I never signed their petitions," Dylan told Nat Hentoff with regard to the *Sing Out!* crowd (Cott: 91). And probably Dylan was right to hold back. The words "appropriation," "com-modification," and "paternalism" had begun to intrude on the rapidly evolving self-consciousness of leftists as early as the "I Have a Dream" speech of Martin Luther King, Jr. The notion that "being a spokesman for a cause" amounted to claiming the experience without having paid real dues gained currency: comfortable white college kids singing Negro spirituals and handsomely paid folk groups singing Depression-era labor songs, even with the best intentions, were pocketing the compensation due others, much as "Gucci Marxist" academics pocket the compensation due genuinely overworked and underpaid blue-collar, oppressed, and sometimes dead people from other times and geographies. Dylan's Gaslight tape performance of "No More Auction Block" is inspired, but Iron Range Bob Dylan pretending to be an escaped black slave is the ultimate in commodification, and Dylan wisely dropped the song from his repertoire. Dylan scored big points as a "platform guest" at the August 1963 civil rights march in D.C., listening to Martin Luther King, Jr. give his "I Have a Dream" speech beside Joan Baez and Mahalia Jackson, but, really, what was he doing there? The *Boston Herald* quoted Comedian Dick Gregory's reaction: "What was a white boy like Bob Dylan there for? Or — who else? Joan Baez? To support the cause? Wonderful — support the cause. March. Stand behind us — but not in front of us" (Marqusee: 13). Many black Americans would come to see this kind of "help" as a subtle hindrance: "Beware of the handshake . . . the pat on the back; it just might hold you back," sang The Temptations in "Smiling Faces" (1971). Many white members of the sixties generation came to believe that they could best help American blacks (other than George Jackson and Rubin Carter) by letting them solve their own problems.

So Dylan ducked the demonstrations. However, Dylan speaks on many larger issues, because, like Anderson, his political analysis comes in large-scale associative mythic terms while avoiding Old Left historical analysis and hairsplitting. What big-picture issues attracted Dylan's attention, and what does Dylan have to say about them?

War

On the Vietnam War specifically, Dylan has little to say. A conspicuous contrast to Phil Ochs, he mentions Vietnam only twice in all his published writing: in the 1986 "Band of the Hand (It's Hell Time Man!)," and in the jacket notes to *Bringing It All Back Home*, where a middle-aged druggist up for district attorney accuses Dylan of being "the one that's been causing all them riots over in Vietnam." Tor Egil Førland quotes an additional stanza Dylan added to "With God on Our Side" in 1988: "In the 1960s / Came the Vietnam War / Can somebody tell me / What we're fighting for / So many young men died / So many mothers cried / Now I ask the question / Was God on our side?" (340). In interviews like the one with Happy Traum in *Sing Out!* (Cott: 133, 136) and press conferences on the Australian tour (Marqusee: 244), where he was specifically asked about Vietnam, Dylan was evasive if not flip. Andy Gill suggests that "Tears of Rage" was the first American song to "register the pain of betrayal felt by many of America's Vietnam War Veterans" (117), and Andrew Gamble sees the line "sends them out to the jungle" as a reference to Vietnam (24). Jon Landau thought that *John Wesley Harding*, without mentioning Vietnam specifically, exhibited an awareness of the war's effect on America in "the mood of the album as a whole" (Marcus, *Invisible Republic*: 55). On Iraq, David Boucher points out, Dylan registered his objections/reservations on several occasions, including a concert in Madison Square Garden on Veterans Day, November 11, 2002, at which time President Bush had announced his intention to invade Iraq:

> Dylan stood at an electric piano for the opening numbers of the set, the first of which was "Tweedle Dee & Tweedle Dum" off *Love and Theft*. He and his band then reverted to acoustic guitars for the most pointed song of the night — "Masters of War." Its significance was not lost on the audience, who spontaneously cheered as Dylan rasped, "And I hope that you die, and that your death will come soon." (*Dylan & Cohen*: 176)

On the general subject of war, however, Dylan was not silent. Tor Egil Førland sees Bob Dylan's isolationist politics as "what so-called progressive isolationists from the Midwest would have advocated, had they been transferred into the United States of the 1960s or later." He views Dylan as "an anachronism, seeing the contemporary world through a set of cognitive lenses made in the Midwest before the Second World War — or to a large extent even before the First" (337).[14] And Dylan's take on both world wars in "With God on Our Side" does indeed reflect Iron Range reservations and resistance to two wars that had plenty of popular support elsewhere in the country: "the reason for fighting / I never got straight." This was Dylan's thinking on the Cold War as well, and he saw Vietnam and Iraq in the context of the Cold War. His isolationism is again shaped by Hibbing, with its strong Eastern European-Russian population that felt more threatened by American mine owners than Russian apparatchiks or even Fidel Castro down in Cuba. The Cold War is just another lie from those who corrupt the American Dream with one invented conflict after another to distract workers from their own real problems, to generate money for the Masters of War, and to wrap themselves in a misapplied reverence for the American Dream. Dylan speaks to the users and the used in songs like "Talkin' John Birch Paranoid Blues," "Let Me Die in My Footsteps," "John Brown," "Blowin' in the Wind," "Masters of War," "Talkin' World War III Blues," "Highway 61

Revisited," even later songs like "Legionnaire's Disease" and "License to Kill." "With God on Our Side" tracks the history of war through settlement, the Spanish-American War, World War I and World War II, to the Cold War (Dylan skips Korea), prefiguring the Kubrick movie *Dr. Strangelove* and paying special attention to the bogus ideologies used by each side to buttress their causes. Dylan concludes with the thought that perhaps Judas Iscariot believed he too had God on his side, but in war or peace, God is not on America's side . . . or anybody's side, Dylan tells us.[15] Dylan addresses the military industrial complex in "Masters of War"; "I see through your brain," he tells them, "Like I see through the water / That runs down my drain." He often mentions the killers they create and the death they bring. In "John Brown" Dylan describes a hometown hero returned from a foreign war in a manner which anticipates returning Iraq War veterans: his face is all shot up, his hand is missing, he wears a metal brace around his waist, and whispers in a voice as unfamiliar to his mother as his appearance. In the much later "'Cross the Green Mountain," Dylan gives us a latter-day John Brown who will never come home because he's not in a hospital bed recovering, as the letter to his mother says — he's already dead as a brick. In "Lonesome Day Blues," Dylan sings critically of a captain, well schooled and decorated, who cares not at all "How many of his pals have been killed."

The war industry accounts for at least one line/image cluster of "A Hard Rain's A-Gonna Fall," and a nuclear holocaust World War III is the springboard for "Bob Dylan's 115th Dream." Dylan also tosses a satirical barb at the Cold War/space race in "I Shall Be Free No. 10," observing that if the streets of heaven are lined with gold, it really wouldn't make much difference if the Russians get there first. In "Talkin' World War III Blues," Dylan imagines life in a post-nuclear world as a way of suggesting that we avoid the whole thing.

Class

"The Iron Range is a working place," observes Aaron Brown (45), and class is important to Dylan, whose high school friendships gave him a sharp sense of class distinctions as they shape relationships. Echo Helstrom suggested that Dylan's experience in repossessing furniture and appliances for Micka Electric store also gave him a firsthand experience with working-class blues:

> As soon as Bob was old enough, Abe would make him go out collecting hire-purchase payments in the poorer sections of town, even though he knew his customers wouldn't be able to pay. "I just wanted to show him another side of life," explained Abe. . . . "Bob hated it most of all when he had to repossess stuff from

people who couldn't pay," recalled his first girlfriend, Echo Helstrom. "I think that's where he started feeling sorry for poor people." (Gill: 46–7)

Dylan draws class distinctions in songs as early as "Hard Times in New York Town," a city which he — like other Iron Rangers — associated with mine *owners* who lived far from the *workers* in Hibbing: "the very wealthy people didn't live there, they were the ones that owned the mines and they lived thousands of miles away" (*Biograph*: 4). Class distinctions make New York City a town of kickers and kicked: Dylan links the kicked poor with the country — "It's hard times from the country" — while wealthy urbanites like "Mr. Rockefeller" and "Mr. Empire," sit silently on their comfortable perches. In his recording of this song, Dylan added a stanza missing in the printed lyrics which echoes Carl Lindstrum's description of city life in *O Pioneers!* and Jay Gatsby's lonely funeral at the end of *The Great Gatsby*:

> The weak and the strong and the rich and the poor
> Gathered there together, ain't room for no more
> Crowded up above and crowded down below
> When someone disappears, you never even know.

Class distinctions back home form the basis of both "Ballad of Hollis Brown" and "North Country Blues," where a distant and wealthy elite (the abstract "they") destroys a farm and a farm family, closes the mines, and wrecks a town, a marriage, and a life. "Maggie's Farm" is a "shorthand précis of the Marxist analysis of the alienating condition of capitalism upon the workers" according to Andy Gill (71). The brother pays in nickels and dimes for your custodial work, fines you big bucks every time you slam the door, and wants to know if you're happy. The father puts his cigar out in your face while protecting himself with the National Guard (he sounds like Iron Range mine executives). Everybody advises, "Sing while you slave."

Dylan will return to the subject of union issues in later songs like "Union Sundown," "Cry a While," "Workingman's Blues #2," and "Floater (Too Much to Ask)." The first song is an angry song targeting North American Free Trade Agreement and other formal and informal agreements that allow formerly American — now "multinational" — corporations to exploit both American and global workers by exporting production jobs here, there, everywhere, buying Taiwan one day, selling it the next to buy Malaysia, then moving out of Malaysia to set up in China. That job you used to have now belongs to someone down in El Salvador, Dylan warns. "They don't make nothin' here no more . . . it's sundown on the union." The union, of course, is both the labor union and the country; both good ideas until greed got in the way. Dylan suggests, as he did in "11 Outlined Epitaphs," that the union membership is complicit in its own demise, part and parcel of an America rushing headlong, greedily, into its own decline:

```
... they've changed
they've been remodeled
an those union halls
like the cio
an the nmu
come now! can you see em
needin me
for a song
or two
```

As Craig Robert Snow notes, "Dylan's condemnation of the modern workers' union may be viewed as an extension of Dylan's characteristic denunciation of institutionalized programs which by their very nature are antithetical to Dylan's vision of radical individualism" (275). Or as Tor Egil Førland suggests, Dylan's rejection of global capitalism may reflect his isolationist Midwest populism: "What happened — to the north country miners as well as to the factory work-ers of 'Union Sundown' — was that they came up against the economic logic of comparative advantages" (341). Dylan feels "a profound empathy with the pup-pets and a correspondingly profound lack of understanding of the mechanism by which the strings are pulled" (342). Where in the late nineteenth century individuals and smaller regions had been threatened by national mechanisms, in the late twentieth century those mechanisms became global — and Dylan is strongly antiglobal. In 1984 he told Kurt Loder,

> "Right now, it seems like in the States, and most other countries, too, there's a big push on to make a big *global* country — *one big country* — where you can get all the materials from one place and assemble them someplace else and sell 'em in another place, and the whole world is just all one, controlled by the same people, you know? ... actually, it's just colonization. But see, I saw that stuff firsthand, because where I come from, they *really* got that deal good, with the ore." (Cott: 293)

"Cry a While" is an angry song sung in union vernacular by just such a union puppet to the woman who has betrayed him, who might be America herself. Fed up with the bullshit, he warns her that it's her turn to cry awhile. "Floater (Too

Much to Ask)" is a lighter satire of the old farts and the young soon-to-be-old farts in Hibbing, fishing, gassing about cute second cousins, schoolteachers, grandfathers who trapped ducks, and grandmothers who sewed their own dresses . . . and about work. It suggests a similar approach to labor–management relations: if one of the boss's flunkeys tries to bully you, strong-arm you, you respond with counter-threats. "What good are you anyway, if you can't stand up to some old businessman?" Dylan will ask in "Summer Days," another of his twenty-first century larks that turns a swing tune into political commentary, much as the old Finns turned polka into political music.

"Workingman's Blues #2" fakes right, then runs left: the world has gone to shit, the singer's old place is only a memory, the worker is poorer than he once was, he's down on his luck and black and blue, but he says he's perfectly comfortable looking past the creek to the peaceful "sacred fields," sleeping off the rest of the day . . . and imagining the pleasure of dragging them all down to hell and selling them to their enemies. This is political solution number three: blow the system up.

Class distinctions frequently crop up in hard rock songs involving women. High-maintenance, upper-class women have been a problem since "It Ain't Me, Babe" and will continue to be a problem through "Leopard-Skin Pill-Box Hat," "Just Like a Woman," and "Absolutely Sweet Marie." In an essay titled "Just Like a Woman," Kevin Krein and Abigail Levin write,

> We want to suggest that we can view Dylan as an early seer of the corruption and eventual demise of the mass-utopian dreamworld of industrial production, and its corollary of a consumerist lifestyle. His songs critiquing women who have yet to see the catastrophic end to the dream that he sees are meant as stern warnings that this dreamworld is no longer utopian in its promise of a better future. (63–4).

"Like a Rolling Stone" is addressed to a fallen princess who spent too much of her life on a steeple thinking she had it made, amused by the bums and street people around her. Now, fallen and free, she knows better. "I Want You" contrasts a Queen of Spades — high-class, high-maintenance, highly desired — with a chambermaid who is good to the singer, even though she knows where he'd rather be. "You shouldn't let other people get your kicks for you" he warns the princess in "Like a Rolling Stone."

In these songs, Dylan warns of the dangers of materialism. The money which makes the upper class upper, according to Dylan, is not even worth considering. People with money obviously stole it with a gun or a fountain pen or by paying employees in nickels and dimes while asking solicitously if they're having a good time. "Money doesn't talk, it swears," Dylan sings in "It's Alright, Ma." The highway of diamonds has nobody on it. "For the love of a lousy buck, I've watched them die," sings Dylan in "When the Night Comes Falling from the Sky." "Will your money buy forgiveness?" Dylan asks the Masters of War. Last-minute redemption will cost more than you've got, he warns the wealthy kickers and takers on "I'd Hate to Be You On that Dreadful Day": "You're gonna look in your moneybags / And find you're one cent short." Sweet saint Aretha, of *Tarantula*, sings of the day of salvation, when "no one will have any money" (8).

"I don't want to make a lot of money," Dylan told Robert Shelton (*Home*: 147), and as Shelton points out, Dylan has turned down more money than most of us will see in a lifetime. What the hell — the pot of gold is only make-believe ("Abandoned Love").

The Judicial System

Dylan's take on American justice is that justice is for those who can pay for it and do pay for it. In the halls of justice, the justice is out in the hall. The worst thing you can do is become a lawyer or a judge. The line "To live outside the law, you must be honest" suggests what most Americans know instinctively and children of the sixties knew absolutely: you're much more likely to find justice outside of a courtroom than inside — a subject Dylan explores at length on the *John Wesley Harding* album. Even before Dylan's legal experiences in his divorces from manager Albert Grossman and wife Sara, his songs are full of slams like "I ain't a judge, you don't have to be nice to me" and "the hanging judge was drunk."

Even if you cut a deal with false judges, as Reilly's daughter does in "Seven Curses," they'll take your virginity and hang your father anyway. If you're black like George Jackson, maybe they'll just send you to prison and rub you out there. If you're young, you might get 99 years for vehicular homicide no matter what color you are ("Percy's Song"), and there's nothing you or your folksinger buddy can do about it. Especially in the South, Dylan suggests in his civil rights protest songs, cops and courts protect the real criminals. If you're from the North, stay the hell out of Oxford, Mississippi and New Orleans and even Baltimore, Maryland. Resistance to civil rights leaders — including Rev. Martin Luther King, Jr. — included police, governors, lawyers, and occasionally judges. The white jury will acquit white murderers of Emmett Till's every time, and even if some "old lady judge" does find a white William Zantzinger guilty of murdering black Hattie Carroll, he'll impose nothing more than a six-month suspended sentence. (The bitter irony of this song is sustained as far as the final stanza can possibly draw it out.) False-hearted judges are dying in their own webs in "Jokerman"; their only teachers are the books of Leviticus and Deuteronomy and the law of the jungle.

The odd thing is that many of Dylan's "victims" of the judicial system are admittedly guilty, including the early Donald White ("I killed a man / I did not try to hide") and the juveniles inside "The Walls of Red Wing." In singing their songs, Dylan is just looking for an excuse to attack the judge who walks on the stilts of false power ("Most Likely You Go Your Way"), the kings of Tyrus with their convict lists ("Sad-Eyed Lady of the Lowlands"). The observation "Sometimes I think this whole world / Is one big prison yard" ("George Jackson") and the song "I Shall Be Released" offer a key to Dylan's take on the American judiciary system: it is a metaphor for overregulated America. And you had best not complain too loudly. "They kill people here who stand up for their rights," Dylan sings in "Band of the Hand (It's Hell Time, Man!)." This is typical sixties thought, reflected in popular sixties novel-films *Cool Hand Luke* and *One Flew Over the Cuckoo's Nest*.

Investigations have shown that in his protest songs Dylan often distorted or ignored facts to make the American judicial system look worse than it really is. George Jackson had, on the morning of his death, called for tearing down the prison system from the inside, and apparently shot one of the guards with a smuggled pistol (Heylin, *Revolution*: 424). Hattie Carroll died not from William Zantzinger's blow, but from a rise in blood pressure in her enlarged heart, which, combined with hypertension, caused a massive brain hemorrhage. The prosecution's medical doctor contended that Zantzinger's verbal abuse and single blow placed Carroll in a position of "fear, frustration, or resentment," and "fear of a second blow," which triggered the event, but a doctor for the defense testified that "the blow had very little to do with the rise in blood pressure" (Coffino: 17). Clinton Heylin believes Dylan accepted without investigation a newspaper report of Hattie Carroll's death by one Roy H. Wood, who "got just about every important fact wrong" (*Revolution*: 163). The murder indictment was dismissed, and Zantzinger was convicted of manslaughter, and given the sentence Dylan records. In reporting the trial, the *Afro-American* newspaper actually praised the presiding judge for "the calm and impartial manner in which he conducted the trial."[16]

In "The Death of Emmett Till," written for a CORE benefit concert over half a decade after the murder, Dylan again "shows himself hopelessly confused about the facts of the case" (Heylin, *Revolution*: 73). Till's behavior had been "provocative" toward the wife of one of the murderers (although certainly it should not have provoked torture and death), so the murder was not "just for the fun of killing him"; the murderers had not, as Dylan tells us, confessed to the deed before the jury rendered its verdict; and a doctor, an embalmer, and a sheriff all testified that given its advanced state of deterioration, the body discovered in the river three days after Till's death was probably eight, perhaps 15 days dead before discovery. In concluding his discussion of the Till case, Michael A. Coffino writes, "Dylan's song mediates between historical facts and the demands genre imposes on him," supported by the postmodernist position that truth "is contingent on perception, which actively constructs the world at every moment" and acts to "deny the existence of an objective world that is independent of human observation" (15). For our purposes, the point is that Dylan's inherent suspicion of the judicial system — a legacy of both Midwest radicalism reinforced by sixties New Left thinking — led him to misrepresent those cases.

Accusations of similar distortion and questionable sympathies surrounded "Hurricane," Dylan's story of convicted boxer Rubin Carter, and "Joey," Dylan's topical song on Joey Gallo, a New York Mafia figure and pal of Jacques Levy, Dylan's co-writer for both "Hurricane" and "Joey." Robert Shelton called "Hurricane" Dylan's "*J'accuse* of the American judicial system" (*Home*: 460), but as Michael Gray notes in *The Bob Dylan Encyclopedia*, "Almost every line of Dylan's song ["Hurricane"] is inaccurate, from his description of events and who was where when through to its depiction of Carter" (123). Dylan played "Hurricane" at all 31 Rolling Thunder Review concerts, culminating in a penultimate Review concert in the prison which held Carter, and a final performance which was billed as a "Hurricane Benefit" in New York, attended by Muhammad Ali among other notables. The whole to-do helped win Carter (and co-defendant John Artis) a retrial in 1976, this time with a racially mixed jury. That trial ended in the same "guilty" verdict as the first trial, although the decision was overturned in 1985 by a district court in New Jersey and Carter was released. Joni Mitchell, alone among members of the Rolling Thunder tour in having spoken several times with Carter on the phone, decided "that he was 'faking it' to take advantage of 'a bunch of white, pasty-faced liberals'" (Blake: 166).

"Joey Gallo was a psychopath, as his biographer Donald Goddard confirms," writes Lester Bangs in "Bob Dylan's Dalliance with Mafia Chic" (Thomson and Gutman: 216). Dylan's portrait of Gallo is colored by his sympathies for outlaws: although many outspoken good guys run afoul of the system and end up in jail, not everybody in jail is necessarily a good guy. This lesson most children of the sixties had already learned by 1975. But Suze Rotolo had told Anthony Scaduto early on that Dylan "didn't read or clip the papers and refer to it later, as you would write a story, or as other songwriters might do it. With Dylan it was not that conscious journalistic approach" (116). Like so many leftist Midwest writers, Dylan tended to plug a specific person into a myth that was probably already in his head. Dylan, in other words, is a Jeremiah, not a reporter.

Education

Dylan's take on American education is that it is "ipso facto part of the Establishment" (Mellers: 111), a tool used by the power elite to anesthetize and distract, just "false instruction" which nobody should believe ("Tears of Rage"). Dylan's position reflects his experience at Hibbing High School and his class consciousness, since the upper-class people have more fancy degrees than the lower-class people ("high-degree thieves," Dylan calls them in "Gotta Serve Somebody"). And part of his position is simple American know-nothingism. "How can so intellectual a writer as Dylan be so anti-intellectual?" Robert Shelton wonders aloud (*Home*: 99). Neil Corcoran offers an answer: "This kind of anti-intellectualism, or at least anti-institutionalized intellectualism, in an intellectual goes deep in the American tradition" (8). In Dylan's neck of the woods it does. Midwestern pragmatism values experience — or at least practical knowledge — over theory. Besides, that's the pose which lets the rube con the city slicker, and it works 90 percent of the time.

Although by all accounts a thoughtful young man, Dylan was not impressed by Hibbing High School, where he was not among the favored few (mostly athletes, but also the student council types) whose names appear every other week in the school newspaper. Abe Zimmerman had played basketball, Dylan's grandfather had coached basketball, and Dylan claims to have played hockey at a young age; however, except for a year on the swimming team, being a member of the 1955–56 Teen-Age Bowling League championship team, and belonging to Latin Club(!), Bob was "notably *not* active in school activities" (Engel: 150).

Woody Guthrie's songs attracted Dylan because they were up front about "the contradictions between what they were teaching in school and what was really happening" (Cott: 430). During adolescence, "the geometry of innocent flesh on the bone" ("Tombstone Blues") has it all over abstract math problems, and teenagers know it. Kids can go to the finest schools all right (and Hibbing High School was the finest of schools, although schools of life can be anywhere, including schools of hard knocks), but they only get juiced in it. One suspects that it was the educational system, as much as anything, that made a killer out of a "Clean-Cut Kid," even though (or perhaps because) he was on the baseball team and the marching band. Dylan devotes the better part of two stanzas of "Subterranean Homesick Blues" to education: you hang around the inkwell, get sick, try hard but get barred, "Try to be a success" (clearly pronounced "suck-cess," and written "suck-cess" on the placard Dylan displays opening the film *dont look back*), follow all the rules, and after years of schooling end up with a blue-collar job working on the day shift. (Twenty years would mean a Ph.D., and more than a few people with Ph.D.s are driving taxicabs, waiting on tables, and studying to become electricians.) "They keep it all hid," Dylan sings, unconsciously echoing the words of Minnesota writer Meridel Le Sueur recalling her own school years: "Of course nobody told you the true history of anything" (*My People*).

As for classes — "The teachers in school taught me everything was fine," Dylan told *Life* magazine in 1964.

> That was the accepted thing to think. It was in all the books. But it ain't fine, man. There are so many lies that have been told, so many things that are kept back. Kids have a feeling like me, but they ain't hearing it no place. They're scared to step out. But I ain't scared to do it. (Welles: 114)

Schools had taught Dylan to hate Russians all through his whole life ("With God on Our Side"), and schools had taught Medgar Evers's assassin that the laws were with him, protecting his white skin, fueling his hate, and making sure that he never thinks straight about his own situation. *Tarantula* contains an extended chapter titled "Prelude to the Flatpick," in which Dylan critiques education in a series of short clips (21, 22), and "11 Outlined Epitaphs" contains a bitterly comic schoolroom exchange that seems to reflect Dylan's Hibbing experience:

> (here! take this kid an learn it well
> but why sir? my arms're so heavy
> I said take it. it'll do yuh good
> but I ain't learned last nite's lesson yet.
> am I gonna have t get mad with you?
> no no gimme gimme just stick it on top
> a the rest a the stuff
> here! If yuh learn it well yuh'll
> get an A . . . an don't do anything
> I wouldn't do)

High school is neither self-realization nor an introduction to useful knowledge, but an exercise in enforced conformity: teachers and classmates alike want you "to be just like them." Our high schools will not produce tomorrow's leaders because truth is essential to learning, and the loss of truth has broken that mechanism beyond repair.

Was the University of Minnesota any better in 1959? "I hung around college," Dylan told Robert Shelton, "but it's a cop-out from life, from experience" (*Home*: 354). Perhaps that's why, although registered, Dylan never went to class, finding his real teachers in Dinkytown. "Colleges are like old-age homes," he told Nat Hentoff (McGregor: 139); "except for the fact that more people die in college than in old-age homes, there's really no difference." Mr. Jones, the over-refined academic of "Ballad of a Thin Man," is very well read, but he is clueless when it comes to life. Into *Tarantula* Dylan introduces another academic, a character named "Scholar, his body held together by chiclets — raw beans & slaves of days gone by — he storms in from the road — his pipe nearly eaten . . . a moth flies out of his pocket" (72).

One suspects that Dylan accepted the honorary doctorate from Princeton University in June 1970 (he returned in 2000 to accept the Willard and Margaret Thorpe Medal for Excellence in American Arts and Letters) as something to wave in the faces of all his old teachers, fraternity brothers, and University of Minnesota acquaintances. The actual experience, as recounted in "Day of the Locusts," is filled with perspiration, tears, angst, paranoia, exploding egos, darkness, and the odor of a tomb. Dylan is as critical of Ivy League education as Fitzgerald in *The Great Gatsby* and Hemingway in *The Sun Also Rises*. "Sure was glad to get out of there alive," sings Dr. Dylan as he heads for the Black Hills of South Dakota.[17]

Politics

Just what is populist Dylan's position on traditional politics? We all know the answer to that question. "Politics is bullshit. It's all unreal," Dylan told Ochs (Scaduto: 176). "Politics is an instrument of the Devil," Dylan told Kurt Loder in 1984 (Cott: 291). The "Political World" is all a stacked deck, conspicuously hostile to love, wisdom, mercy, courage, and peace. Well, we all knew long before "Sweetheart Like You" that patriotism is the last refuge of rogues and scoundrels. Unidentified political figures and places dot Dylan's songs, always associated with corruption: the senators and congressmen who block up the hall in "The Times They Are A-Changin'," the drunken politician of "I Want You," the blood-sucking politician of "Summer Days," the low-down sinner pounding on the President's gate in "Quit Your Low Down Ways." The phony politician of "I Shall Be Free," telling voters how he loves all kinds of people, eatin' bagels, pizza, chitlins, anything for a vote, including bullshit. Wealthy politicians use the poor white man who shot Medgar Evers for their own gain as they rise to fame. The president of the United States stands naked in "It's Alright, Ma," and the Commander-in-Chief/King of the Philistines (President Lyndon Johnson), looking like Colonel Kurtz in the film *Apocalypse Now*, chases flies, taunts the sun for being chicken, and preaches "Death to all those who would whimper and cry." In "Clothes Line Saga," the vice president — Minnesota's own Hubert Humphrey, who had helped purge leftists from the party in 1948 and become an accessory to the fact of Lyndon Johnson's Vietnam War in the 1960s — goes mad, and people just yawn. An unnamed senator prowls the streets showing off his gun and his power in "Stuck Inside of Mobile," a city councilman is taking bribes on the side in "Gotta Serve Somebody," and Dylan opens his list of the many suspect characters who "Gotta Serve Somebody" with the government's hired apologists: "You may be an ambassador to England or France." Among the politicos, not one man righteous. With luck, "When the Ship Comes In" they'll all be drownded in the tide and conquered like Goliath.[18] Democracy does not rule the world; "This world is ruled by violence" ("Union Sundown"). "The political world is the alienated world which individuals must decide whether to seek to overthrow, to survive within or to escape from. There is not much room in [Dylan's] vision of politics for cautious, piecemeal reform of institutions and politics. Things are too far gone for that," writes Andrew Gamble (20). Dylan's favorite metaphors for political America are, Gamble says, the prison and the graveyard.

Dylan's position alienated Old Left "corpse evangelists" with their politics of ancient history ("My Back Pages"), but its urban confusions and rejection of organizations resonated with the New Left, especially as represented by the Students for a Democratic Society (SDS), which was in many respects just a sixties reincarnation of old Midwest populism. Mid-sixties recruits to the SDS, Marqusee notes, "hailed mainly from the Mid- and Southwest and came from working-class backgrounds. Jokingly, they referred to their own advent as 'prairie power. . . . They wore cowboy boots and smoked dope. They were Dylan's people" (134). "More than simple political activism," Anthony Scaduto writes, "the Movement abhors formal leadership. Dylan clearly was on the same wavelength" (183). Marqusee correctly reads in the ambiguities of "Blowin' in the Wind" a reflection of New Left politics as embodied in the Port Huron Statement of the Students for a Democratic Society. The statement

shares the song's mixture of idealism and subdued impatience, as well as its longing for a bigger answer to the growing questions posed by the events of the day. . . . Skeptical of both the liberal and Communist traditions, severed from organized labor by the cold war, and emboldened by their own experience of material comfort, they paraded their innocent openness. Year zero had been declared on the American left. It was a historical moment that was to shape Dylan's trajectory in the coming years as well as the evolution of many others. (58–9).

Religion

Finally, there is the matter of religion. Organized religion is as suspect as politics in Dylan's songs and thought, as it was in Woody Guthrie's mind, as it is in the minds of many Midwest writers, including Minnesota's Sinclair Lewis, who gave America *Elmer Gantry*, a very popular novel about a phony evangelist. Clinton Heylin reports an early song, which never reached even the demo stage, titled "The Preacher's Folly," a satire of a traveling preacher who is struck by lightning during a tent revival (*Revolution*: 46). Hermit monks sit sidesaddle on the Golden Calf in "Gates of Eden"; right beside the city councilmen taking bribes in "Gotta Serve Somebody" are the preachers full of "spiritual pride"; in "Man in the Long Black Coat" parishioner runs off with preacher, leaving not a word of goodbye, not even a note. Dylan is well aware of the false prophets, of the warmongers who think God is on their side, of the adulterers in churches ("When You Gonna Wake Up?"), of the false preachers with 20 pounds of head-lines stapled to their chest ("Stuck Inside of Mobile") who preach about man and God and law while peddling "flesh-colored Christs that glow in the dark" ("It's Alright, Ma"), of the men whose queens are in the church ("Abandoned Love"), of non-believers talkin' in the name of religion ("Slow Train"), and the churches which turn a "Clean-Cut Kid" into a killer. Andy Gill finds in Dylan a "deeply-rooted belief that God, in his role as publicity agent for the organized churches, was not on the side of the angels, but working for the system against the interests of the underdog. 'With God on Our Side' manages to articulate all these complex conflicts of interpretation" (44). One senses, however, that Dylan's critique of false ministry reflects a faith and respect, evident long before his Christian phase, for legitimate ministry. "If Jesus Christ, himself, came / down thru these streets, Christianity / would start all over again," Dylan writes in "Some other kinds of songs" on his *Another Side of Bob Dylan* album. Dylan never had that kind of faith in any kind of politicians, educators, judges, merchants, or soldiers.

ABOVE ALL ELSE, INDIVIDUAL FREEDOM
AND A QUIRKY EGALITARIANISM

Throughout his career, then, Dylan presented a harsh critique of the American Establishment, but his critique is neither systematized nor activist. It is consistent not with the Old Left agenda of his New York acquaintances,[19] but with the beliefs of people he had known in Minneapolis . . . whom Kevin McCosh, owner of the bookstore in Dinkytown, described as "Marxist-anarchists, sort of predecessors of the New Left. Maybe a fusion of all these things, along with a strong feeling of just hating the bastards. A feeling the system doesn't work so throw it out, or maybe a little feeling that it wasn't worth fighting it and you might just drop out" (Scaduto: 32). This is apolitical solution number four, the attitude expressed by Robert Bly, a Minnesotan who was not from Dinkytown, when he jokingly told Bill Moyers in a late seventies interview, "You can't effect the system — you can't even make it worse!"

Dylan, who did not play team sports and opted out of the politics of high school, was certainly no Joan Baez, who went from one demonstration to another and by the end of 1967 had served a total of 60 days in jail for antiwar protests (Shelton, *Home*: 188). Even his early attempts to organize a band were haphazard. Dylan is one, not group, and after a lifetime performing as Bob Dylan and His Various Bands, and sporadic collaborations with a handful of other writers and composers, Dylan looms largest as an individual talent. He is prophet, not politician.

At the root of Dylan's objection to the war machine, the political machine, the economic machine, big money, big justice, big System lies his commitment to individual freedom. We all have different talents — some, admittedly, more talent than others — and in a democracy, each person has his own integrity which is not to be imposed upon by systems economic, political, educational, or judicial. That is the crux of the famous *Port Huron Statement*, the SDS manifesto drafted by Tom Hayden of Michigan: the United States government frustrates democracy by confusing individual citizens and by consolidating the power of military and business interests; the true goal of individual people and collective society should be human independence. The Midwest has always prided itself on its egalitarianism; its petty cliques and social circles are nothing compared to the caste systems of the South and the East. Everyone is an Average Joe, no matter how much money he has, how fancy a car he drives, how many books he's published, or how many letters he has after his name. No Doctors, no Professors, no Colonels or Dukes. At least that's the pose. Poet John Knoepfle's Sangamon County Fair princess candidate announces, "I am in other respects / like everyone here" (95). Robert Bly speaks of "giving up all ambition" (*Selected Poems*: 46); "*Sumus quod sumus*" is the motto of Garrison Keillor's Lake Wobegon: "We are what we are." Your experience and your ideas are as good as anyone else's. That is the Minnesota gospel preached by writers like Bill Holm:

> Sacredness is unveiled through your own experience, and lives in you to the degree that you accept that experience as your teacher, mother, state, church, even, or perhaps particularly, if it comes into conflict with the abstract received wisdom that power always tries to convince you to live by. (*Music*: 12)

That's the Minnesota gospel preached by Bob Dylan in one statement after another: "You're better 'n no one / And no one is better 'n you," he tells Ramona. "Each of us has his own special gifts," Dylan tells "Dear Landlord." "We are all the same [on the Rolling Thunder caravan]. No one is on any higher level than anybody else" (Shelton, *Home*: 453).[20] "Jim, Jim [apparently James Forman, executive secretary to the Student Nonviolent Coordinating Committee], where is our party . . . where all members're held equal?" ("11 Outlined Epitaphs"). In 1997, Dylan told David Gates, "I don't like to think of myself as in the high-falutin' area" (68). In "I Shall Be Free No. 10" he sang,

> I'm just average, common too
> I'm just like him, the same as you
> I'm everybody's brother and son
> I ain't different from anyone
> It ain't no use a-talkin' to me
> It's just the same as talking to you.

When *Chronicles, Volume One* appeared in 2004, it took nearly 12 days for the *Hibbing Daily Tribune* to mention the fact.[21] People probably figured there was no sense reading Bob Dylan, it would be just like reading themselves. Or maybe they thought he was getting highfalutin'. Duluth poet laureate Barton Sutter titles one of his stories, "Don't Stick Your Elbow Out Too Far" (25). Keep it small, buddy: "There's no success like failure, / and failure's no success at all."

Whoever organized the Bob Dylan exhibit in the Hibbing Public Library, September 2008, sprinkled only three Dylan quotations among the exhibit's many record albums and photos. Those three included that first stanza of "I Shall Be Free No. 10" about being average, common too, and a remark from the 2001 *Rolling Stone* interview: "I don't consider myself a sophist or a cynic or a stoic or some kind of bourgeois industrialist, or whatever titles people put on people. Basically, I'm just a regular person" (Cott: 419). This is the way Hibbing likes to see Bob Dylan, this is the way Dylan likes to be seen, and this is the way Dylan likes others to be, especially women.

This self-effacement dovetails nicely with Christianity, and may in fact be born of Christianity: Christ himself was the humble servant, washing his disciples' feet. He also hung out with prostitutes, tax-collectors, fishermen and other low-life types. He was poor and he dressed like a bum. "Do unto others," He advised his followers; if you see your neighbor carrying something, help him with his load; take the lowest seat because the last shall be first; inasmuch as you have done it to the least of these my brethren, you have done it unto me; and endlessly on.

Christ was also a prophet-outlaw, who in setting himself against the authorities of his day earned himself death on a cross. The American founding fathers were outlaws as well as egalitarian visionaries . . . or perhaps *because* they were egalitarian visionaries. Both Christ and the Fathers were far more radical than many red-white-and-blue-blooded Americans like to admit. Henry Thoreau, that guru of the sixties and eighties, spent time in jail as did Martin Luther King, Jr. and had, in fact, argued that in a society which imprisons people unjustly, the only place for a just man was in jail. It is just a few short steps from opting out of the system to setting one's self against the system, to becoming the enemy of the system and thus an outlaw. This the sixties accepted fully, going Thoreau one step further in assuming that everybody who lives outside the law was honest, and everyone in jail was a "misdemeanor outlaw, chased an' cheated by pursuit" ("Chimes of Freedom"). At the very least, they're just as good as anyone else. As we've seen, this soft-headedness led Dylan to sympathize with the man who shot Medgar Evers (but not the man who shot Martin Luther King, Jr.), and misinterpret, or misrepresent, Rubin Carter and Joey Gallo. This soft-headedness moved American popular culture quickly from hunted heroes like Batman and Superman through imprisoned Cool Hand Luke and Randle Patrick McMurphy to a series of Mafia heroes, including The Godfather and Tony Soprano.

"As a counterpoint to his critique of the political system, Dylan is recognized to embrace the romantic counter-image of the outlaw or drifter," write Boucher and Browning (5). His songs are full of quirky characters, including outlaws from the Lone Ranger and Tonto "ridin' down the line, fixin' everybody's troubles" ("Bob Dylan's Blues"), to his own John Wesley Harding. Dylan reflects the sixties notion that whatever hope exists for America lies in citizens who are not ordinarily held up as role models in schools, church, politics, or media . . . or in the less publicized aspects of the role models we have been given. If Dylan finally has a politics, it is the politics of the outsider, the shady character, the outlaw, all of whom get lumped together in his thinking and in songs like "Chimes of Freedom": rebel, rake, prostitute, outlaw, lonesome lover. "Lookit here, buddy," ends "Bob Dylan's Blues," "You want to be like me, / Pull out your six-shooter / And rob every bank you can see." (One of the great things that *Thelma and Louise* has to tell us is that women too can develop "a knack" for things like armed robbery.) "I walked my road an sung my song / Like an arch criminal," Dylan writes in *Joan Baez in Concert, Part 2*. "The world is but a courtroom," Dylan writes in "11 Outlined Epitaphs," "but I know the defendants better 'n you."

Bob Dylan at least liked to think that he knew those defendants from growing up on the Iron Range. He saw himself, or wanted to be seen, as . . . well, if not an outlaw wanted for armed robbery, at least as an outsider ("a refugee / in mental terms an in physical terms," he puts it in "11 Outlined Epitaphs") and one more familiar with the pool hall than the library. "You can find a lot about a small town by hanging around its poolroom," he told Nat Hentoff in 1964 (McGregor: 45). He didn't say nothing about the school, or even the library.

It was this image that the November 4, 1963, *Newsweek* article on Dylan attacked, labeling him a conventional middle-class kid from a conventional middle-class family in a conventional middle-American town. To an extent the article was correct; even Dylan admitted to *Spin* in 1985, "I've been raised by people who feel that fathers, whether they're married or not, should be responsible for their children, that all sons should be taught a trade, and that parents should be punished for their children's crimes" (Engel: 75). But *Newsweek* missed "the mental terms" which made Dylan a refugee-outlaw, and it missed a lot of colorful Iron Range history.[22] *Newsweek* also missed the other side of Main Street, Hibbing, in the 1950s, which Dylan actually knew pretty well through his high school "main man" John Bucklen (strictly working-class), their black DJ friend Jim Dandy in neighboring Virginia, and "that girl," Dylan's parents' name for Echo Star Helstrom. "Bobby always went with the daughters of miners, farmers, and workers," David Zimmerman told Robert Shelton; "He just found them more interesting" (*Home*: 47). This is not the Hibbing we think of when we think "Midwest Small Town," but Hibbing, Duluth, and Virginia, Minnesota were still crazy places when Dylan was growing up, full of characters and outlaws. "I grew up in the same area as Charlie Starkweather and I remember that happening," Dylan told the *L.A. Times* in 1984; "everybody pretty much kept their mouth shut about it. Because he did have a sort of a James Dean quality to him" (Engel: 163)[23] And Dylan identified with James Dean.

Bobby Zimmerman and Echo Helstrom as Starkweather and Fugate is a bit of a stretch, even on the motorcycle, but Echo's dad was one of those backwoods Minnesota characters you can't make up. He had served in World War II, and after the war worked as a well-digger, welder, and handyman. He owned a bunch of guitars and records, and according to Dylan a bunch of guns too: deer rifles and shotguns, some long-barreled pistols. Dylan calls him "creepy" and says he had a reputation for being mean (*Chronicles*: 59). He was building his own house three miles south of town, but it never seemed to get finished. "A hide tacked on a shed from a bear he has killed seems suggestive," writes Dave Engel (177). When Dylan and Echo were dating, the house was in limbo owing to a garage fire which consumed most of the building materials. In 1968 Robert Shelton tracked down an "ailing, embittered" Matt Helstrom living in a box-like, tar-paper shanty near Maple Hill. The north end of Maple Hill Road is Finnish farm country, while the south end is wooded; today half the homes along this road are abandoned, making the place almost as ghostly as North Hibbing, and at the junction of Maple Hill Road and Townline Road is one of those country biker bars that looks the perfect hangout for a whole gang of Helstroms. Helstrom, according to Engel, did not much care for his daughter's boyfriend, and once took out after Dylan and his pal Dick Kangas with a flashlight and perhaps a shotgun. Engel quotes a letter from Dylan to Echo remembering that night he was running down the road in the rain with her ol' man's flashlight on his ass (178).

Characters like these verified songs and stories of the old days, and the whackos and weirdoes of Harry Smith's six-album compilation *Anthology of American Folk Music*. What Dylan found in this side of the North Country and in the Smith anthology — and in the Stack A Lees and Delias and Jack-a-Roes of the musical tradition he revisited in the 1990s — is described by Greil Marcus as "Smithville": "a small town whose citizens are not distinguishable by race. There are no masters and no slaves. The prison population is large, and most are part of it at one time or another. . . . God reigns here, but his rule can be refused" (*Invisible Republic*: 124, 125). Marcus recounts a series of celebrated crimes and criminals from the songs in Smith's anthology, and from a town named Kill Devil Hills, North Carolina. These Americans are not unlike some of the folks in old Hibbing and Duluth, as Marcus himself had learned by 2005, when he published *Like a Rolling Stone* (28).[24]

These are the Jesse Venturas and Al Frankens of Dylan's songs, rogue citizens who are sources of energy and vision, alternatives to the corrupt politicians, priests, educationists, businessmen, lawyers, and high-degree thieves whom Dylan blames for America gone wrong. The earliest of these is "Rambling, Gambling Willie," a 1962 Dylan song based on "Brennan on the Moor," a song about an Irish gambler sung by Dylan's Greenwich Village pals, The Clancy Brothers. Willie, Dylan tells us, "had a heart of gold" and actually supported all his 27 illegitimate children (and their mothers too). He helped the sick and the poor as well. Willie gambled from the White House to New Orleans to Cripple Creek and always won . . . until he was shot in the head while holding a hand of aces and eights.[25] The song is a cliché and something of a throwaway, and not to sound too much like some feminist or a Puritan, Willie's enthusiasms are a little suspect: too much sex, money, and travel, too little contact with the working-class poor. Too much big-time bullshit, too little real work.

Although Dylan gives his history as Kansas and Washington, the self-confessed outlaw-murderer-outsider Donald White is another such North Country outlaw. In bidding farewell to the old north woods which he once roamed, and to the crowded bars which had been his home, White paints himself as a victim of society and a man whose main crime was striving to be free. Dylan saw White, like those other residents of the other side of Main Street, Hibbing, of Smithville and Kill Devil Hills, of Brecht's songs and his own surreal sixties lyrics — all of whom have dual natures, and many of whom are simply not nice folks — as the grassroots of American democracy, in touch with a reality that is attractive because, as Paul Nelson says, it "coincides with that of this planet" (McGregor: 75). "Man cannot exist inside the gates of Eden," suggests Andrew Muir (*Troubadour*: 82); James Spiegel is more philosophical: "Perhaps part of the intuitive appeal that Dylan finds in Christian theology is its concept of original sin" (139) and the allowance Christianity makes for sinful people. It's the sin that's interesting — the shotguns and the bearskin on the wall. From a historical rather than a religious standpoint, Dylan's grudging affection for American society exists because he considers outlaws like this to be descendants of the archetypal American pioneer:

> From one point of view Daniel Boone — a genuine backwoodsman who became mythologized — was regarded as a harbinger of civilization, taming the wilderness in order to bless it with the benefits of culture and technology; from another he was seen as congenital Adamic man, fleeing the shams of civilization in order to find himself in communion with nature and a transcendent godhead, rather than with the God of a defined creed. No sooner had Daniel decided on some spot where he wanted to rest a while than some 'damned Yankee' would establish a claim a mere hundred miles away, forcing him to trek even further West. (Mellers: 19)

John Wesley Harding is an album of mythologized archetypes, almost an allegory, which finds American renewal in precisely such bad-boy figures: Harding, the outlaw who travels with a gun in every hand; the joker and the thief; Frankie Lee, the gambler whose father is deceased; the drifter who escapes when a bolt of lightning strikes the courtroom; the lonesome hobo without family or friends; the immigrant whose town is filled with blood; even the wicked messenger sent from Eli. Add to these the "Wanted Man" from *Nashville Skyline*, and Billy the Kid from the film *Pat Garrett and Billy the Kid*, in which Dylan acted and for which Dylan wrote the film score. Garrett and Billy "were symbols of a changing America in the last century," said scriptwriter Rudy Wurlitzer, "the one a roving free spirit, symbolizing the pioneer nature of the Old West, the other selling out to the Establishment for a steady job and security, representing, therefore, the solidifying respectability of the new America" (Whithouse: 23). In the background of the film looms cattle baron Jesse Chisholm, whose will is being imposed on all free spirits of the frontier, whose will Garrett bows to, whose will Billy opposes. Garrett's killing of Billy represents his final betrayal of the old West ideals of freedom and individuality, and his acquiescence to the new Power Establishment: money, class structure, inequality. Dylan's song for the film portrays Billy as beset by agents of the System: bounty hunters, old whores making advances on his spirit and his soul, businessmen from Taos who want him rubbed out, the whole Main Street crowd who don't like him to be so free. The line "Billy, you're so far away from home" suggests that old idealized American dream of freedom and independence that was lost somewhere in the dreaming: an idealized past to which Dylan would like to see the country return.

Dylan's later outlaw heroes include honest men living outside the law, disconnected free spirits, shady characters, and con artists like that genial artist figure the Jack of Hearts, who distracts Big Jim and the boys in the cabaret while the rest of his gang drills away at the bank, cleaning out the safe before waiting in the darkness by the riverbed for "one more member who had business back in town." Jack of Hearts leaves town with Big Jim stabbed and Lily hanged . . . and Rosemary and the rest of us thinking about the law, but most of all, thinkin' in admiration of the Jack of Hearts. Jack is heroic because his victims, like the respectable businessmen on Pirate Jenny's liner, deserve what they get . . . and, to an extent, because he is active and imaginative in a static and placid society.

Somewhere in the middle to late seventies, Dylan seems to have realized that there are bad outlaws as well as good outlaws. Perhaps the key song in this regard is "Black Diamond Bay," which foreshadows the damned/elect distinctions of songs like "Gotta Serve Somebody." But even during this period, Dylan follows his own orthodoxy. Joey Gallo is an okay guy. So is the outlaw-father of "One More Cup of Coffee," and the killer of "Romance in Durango." "Lenny Bruce" was a good guy; he had some problems, Dylan admits, but he never robbed any churches or cut off any babies' heads, he just showed the wise men of his day to be nothing more than fools — had insight ahead of his time. He was, in other words, a good outlaw. The "Neighborhood Bully" is a throwback to *The Basement Tapes* characters and a foreshadowing of outlaws and ethical systems to come. Like the inmates of Red Wing, Donald White, and the "Clean-Cut Kid," the Neighborhood Bully is an outlaw whom the System has created, for whom the System is responsible, and — perhaps Dylan is backing away from Christianity in his accommodation of judgment, if not the System — to whom we can look for deliverance. Bully's main problem seems to be that he's strong and proactive in a world that favors weakness and passivity, but he has just cause for his crusade, and for his revenge.

As the twentieth century melted into the twenty-first, Dylan seemed increasingly to accept the dark side of human nature and American nature. Explaining to Robert Shelton why he felt at home in America, and could create in America, and drew all his feelings from America, Dylan had once said, "America is a very violent place. . . . In America everybody's got a gun. I've got a few of them!" (*Home*: 480). "Dark Eyes," the final song in *Lyrics, 1962–1985*, seems to point in the direction of salvation from people who lurk on the periphery of American civilization, anticipating dead risen to claim overdue debts, feeling heat and flames, and seeing only dark eyes. "The system's just too damned corrupt," Dylan sings in "Band of the Hand (It's Hell Time Man!)"; blacks and whites steal each other's knives, pimps and pushers are everywhere, and the name of the game is who you know higher up. In Dylan, this message is just more of the same old same old. What's new here — or interesting, or troubling as the case may be — is Dylan's solution: "We're gonna blow up your home of Voodoo, / And watch it burn without any regret / . . . it's countdown time now / We're gonna do what the law should do." No turning the other cheek here, or even waiting for God's final judgment — just violent revenge now. The speaker in "Honest with Me" tells us, "I'm glad I fought — I only wish we'd won," and threatens to "do whatever circumstances require" (an echo of the old sixties slogan, "by all means necessary"?) in the next fight. "I know when the time is right to strike," warns the singer of the otherwise pastoral "Moonlight." "If you ever try to interfere with me or cross my path again," warns the Matt Helstrom-type backwoodsman of "Floater (Too Much to Ask)," "you do so at the peril of your own life."

In earlier songs like "Hezekiah Jones" and "Oxford Town," Dylan had pointed angry and judgmental fingers at folks who killed outside of the law. Not here. "Gonna raise me an army, some tough sons-of-bitches," Dylan sings in "Thunder on the Mountain." "If I catch my opponents ever sleepin' / I'll just slaughter them where they lie," sings the narrator of "Ain't Talkin'." Couple those dark promises with a line like "I'll drag 'em all down to hell and I'll stand 'em at the wall" ("Workingman's Blues #2") and warnings like "If it keep on raining, the levee's gonna break" ("The Levee's Gonna Break"), and you are close to being right back to Pharaoh's tribe drownded in the tide and Goliath conquered at last. Only this time the agents of change and justice are the angry victims, a rough crowd indeed.

Is this another one of Dylan's predictions that show a disconcerting track record of right-on-target? Who can say? Perhaps it's just a description of the way things are these days, in America and around the world. My young Turkish-German friend Timm Okan worries that the next generation of Berliners, who have no work and no prospect of finding work, are now carrying guns. "And where will that lead?" he asks rhetorically. Perhaps it leads where the injustice wrought by unbridled greed has always led. In an e-mail of May 4, 2009, adding a footnote to his book *Provoking Thought*, Hugh Mercer Curtler notes,

> When Imperialism exploded on the scene at the end of the nineteenth century, sweeping aside the Victorian values and any remnant of the concept of "virtue" — replacing them with bourgeoisie ideals and unfettered greed — nihilism sprang up, even among the intellectual elite, and there appeared a yearning for war: to cleanse the air and destroy the stench of decayed values and the stifling atmosphere of money for money's sake. Even the terribly bright, people like Thomas Mann, spoke out in favor of "purification" or a "chastisement" by war. Anything would be preferable to the choking air of bourgeoisie "values" and the expansion of empires.

That was their political agenda. In his recent songs, terribly bright Bob Dylan seems to suggest — or predict — this same thing. Sometimes one senses in Dylan's antipolitical jeremiads not just prophesy but hope.

Chapter 6

The Prophet and His Mission

"Native sons — adventurers, prophets, writers and musicians. They were all from the North Country. Each one followed their own vision, didn't care what the pictures showed. Each one of them would have understood what my inarticulate dreams were about. I felt like I was one of them or all of them put together."

— *Chronicles*

THE AMERICAN DREAM

Put simply, the American Dream is nothing more (or less) than a vision of freedom, equality, and material prosperity for everybody. This notion, today almost a global commonplace, is in fact a historical novelty and a proposition as yet unproved and very much in doubt, these days especially. America's best-loved president suggests his own doubts, as well as his own wonder, in lines every American schoolchild used to memorize and — probably because they are so familiar — usually failed to grasp: "our fathers brought forth on this continent a new nation, conceived in liberty and dedicated to the proposition that all men are created equal. We are now engaged in a great civil war, testing whether that nation or any nation so conceived and so dedicated, can long endure."[1] Abraham Lincoln's doubts should be every American's: what if this remarkable proposition is just an illusion and we are not all equal, democracy won't work, and no nation so conceived and dedicated can expect to survive for very long?

The American Dream, however, is that such a society is possible in the good old U. S. of A. *and* throughout the world, and that it is the moral obligation of every American to wring reality from possibility everywhere from Alabama to Iran and Africa — even Vietnam and Russia and China. The Dream — if not the questions — is what Midwesterners are taught in their school from the start by the rule. America's special mission sets this nation (and its people) apart from the rest of the world (including Canada and Mexico, whose citizens are not, alas, among the elect), but it creates impossible tensions: if all are equal, America is not special. If all are not equal, Americans are chasing a will-o'-the-wisp. This is the central American contradiction explored by German theologian Jurgen Moltmann in his essay of that title. Moltmann argues that the dream is "both necessary and impossible," and the contradiction is heightened by the inevitable moral compromises involved in bringing democracy, equal justice under the law, and material prosperity to an autocratic, unjust, impoverished world. Can the crimes against humanity incidental to invasions of Vietnam and Iraq really be morally sanctioned because the mission is "bringing democracy to the country"? Lyndon Johnson and George Bush certainly thought so. So does Jake Blues. "We're on a mission from God," he explains in *The Blues Brothers*, excusing reckless, illegal, and ill-mannered behavior of all sorts, and the trashing of one perfectly good shopping mall and a whole herd of Chicago police cars. The rest of us know better (so does Jake, really). We know that the American Dream has become an American nightmare. Thus those who would remain true to the pristine American Dream must pitch the full weight of their being against the American nightmare . . . like Norman Mailer in *An American Dream*, which Craig McGregor reports Dylan as reading on his 1966 concert tour in Australia (9).

Puritan Americans especially saw themselves as on a mission from God. They had been chosen, singled out for a great adventure, *the* test upon which the eyes of the world were fixed, by which the world might know once and for all whether God's good Eden could be re-established upon Earth. And they were not in any way humble about this business. In 1630, Governor-to-be John Winthrop had lectured a company of Pilgrims on the good ship *Arabella* concerning their mission and the special covenant which existed between them and God. Because it explains so much about what the nation became, this sermon, although severely questioned and edited by the Founding Fathers, has become a foundational text in American Studies, one quoted at length by Greil Marcus in summarizing his *Invisible Republic: Bob Dylan's Basement Tapes* (208ff.):

> Thus stands the cause between God and us. We are entered into a covenant with Him for this work. We have taken out a commission, the Lord has given us leave to draw our own Articles . . . but if we shall neglect the observation of these Articles . . .

and . . . shall fall to embrace this present world and prosecute our carnal intentions, seeking great things for ourselves and our posterity, the Lord will surely break out in wrath against us; be revenged of such a perjured people and make us know the price of a breach of such a covenant. . . . For we must consider that we shall be as a city upon a hill. The eyes of all people are upon us, so that if we shall deal falsely with our God in this work we have undertaken, and so cause Him to withdraw His present help from us, we shall be made a story and a by-word through the world. (P. Smith: 5, 6)

So you're on a mission approved by God. He's watching. In fact, the whole wide world is watching. If you screw up, you're in deep shit. In his brilliant novel *Why Are We in Vietnam?*, with an eye toward Texan Lyndon Johnson if not Texan George Bush, Norman Mailer wrote what amounts to a parody of Winthrop's sermon in adolescent D. J.'s explanation of his dad Rusty's mission in life:

If he is less great than God intended him to be, then America is in trouble. They don't breed Texans for nothing. Rusty has a great philosophy, states D. J., it is just you have to be an honest son of a bitch to make it work, for — peer into this — you're the fulcrum of the universe, right? The good Lord takes His reading off you, right? (Rusty figures — D. J. will tell you — that the Lord despising mass methods does not bother to weigh man in the aggregate or the mass; instead he stays close to a chosen few, and they ain't Hebes, Rusty hopes to tell you) so Rusty being the cat off whom the reading is read, being that fundament of mind, flesh, and being whose moves are intimate to the Lord, he got to be honest with himself if he want to be on fulcrum point, because if he think he's doing good, and the good Lord knows he's not, well, then, kiss your own sweet ass, Eustacia, Rusty is then no longer up tight with G. O. D. — Grand Old Divinity (biggest corporation of them all? Rusty often thinks not) no, you are one place, God is another, how can you serve? (116–17)

Americans, including Rusty and Jake and Elwood Blues, are God's new chosen people on an errand into the wilderness: pilgrims destined for an errand in sacred history.

The phrases "errand into the wilderness" and "errand in sacred history" come from Perry Miller's *Errand into the Wilderness* (1956) and Sacvan Bercovitch's *The American Jeremiad* (1978) respectively. In these books, the authors trace the rhetoric and mind-set of the American mission as it played out in American culture and history. The Puritans saw themselves as embarked upon the spiritual journey we discussed in Chapter 4, a one-way ride through the present wicked world with all its dangers and persecutions, to salvation at the end of the line.

The journey out of European, urban wickedness into American pastoral grace was, as Winthrop's sermon suggests, an important, even crucial step. Writes Bercovitch, "the Great Migration to America, in all its divine original beauty, was but the first stage of an errand to the end of time" (72).

It didn't take long for the American mission to get sidetracked. Long before D. J. and the Blues brothers showed up, the mission had expanded (or degenerated) into simply making a lot of money — although for a good cause. In fact many colonists coming to the New World signed on to plantation company schemes designed from the start to make money by exploiting natural resources in the usual colonial operations — the very antithesis of pastoralism. These included Puritans in Plymouth Colony, absorbed into Massachusetts Bay Company in 1630; toward the end of his history *Of Plymouth Plantation*, Governor William Bradford laments the colony's increasing wickedness and materialism, and their cost to the church: "Thus, she that had made many rich became herself poor" (334). In any event, the journey was not exactly a straight line, and it came with regular lectures warning people who had wandered off track to get right with God. These classical jeremiads followed a standard outline: listeners were reminded of God's goodness and his generous covenant with His chosen people; they were accused of neglecting their duties and falling into sin and wickedness; a terrible judgment was announced and damnation was threatened; the people were urged to shape up; and, finally, they were promised God's grace upon the end of their journey.[2]

The model for these sermons was the book of Jeremiah, with early verses like 2.7, 9, and 19: "I brought you into a plentiful land to enjoy its fruits and its good things. But when you came in you defiled my land, and made my heritage an abomination. . . . Therefore I still contend with you, says the Lord, and with your children's children I will contend. . . . Your wickedness will chasten you, and your apostasy will reprove you." Or ch. 6, v. 6: "For thus says the Lord of hosts: 'Hew down her trees; cast up a siege mound against Jerusalem. This is the city which must be punished; there is nothing but oppression within her.'" This sermon Jeremiah preached again and again to Israel, until the priests and the other prophets decided that he was an enemy of the people and deserved to be put to death. He became a "Wanted Man" in both senses of the word. After being found innocent of prophesying against Jerusalem, Jeremiah developed the idea of a "saving remnant" (the chosen of the chosen), whom God would save at the moment of judgment, when "every one shall die for his own sin" (31.30) and "the city shall be rebuilt for the Lord from the tower of Hananel to the Corner Gate" (31.38).

As American Puritans considered themselves the saving remnant, and to make sure they stayed God's chosen people, they appropriated the jeremiad for their own purposes, preaching the prophet's sermon again and again in their churches. The most famous of these is Jonathan Edwards's sermon "Sinners in the Hands of an Angry God," preached in 1741 in the midst of the Great Awakening. Edwards's text was Deuteronomy 32.35: "To me belongeth vengeance, and recompense; their foot shall slide in due time: for the day of their calamity is at hand, and the things that shall come upon them make haste." He began, "In this verse is threatened the vengeance of God on the wicked unbelieving Israelites, that were God's visible people, and lived under means of grace; and that — not withstanding all God's wonderful works that He had wrought towards that people — yet remained, as expressed [in] verse 28, void of counsel, having no understanding in them. . . ." Half an hour later, Edwards cranked up the heat:

> The God that holds you over the pit of hell, much as one holds a spider or some loathsome insect over the fire, abhors you and is dreadfully provoked. His wrath toward you burns like fire; He looks upon you as worthy of nothing else but to be cast into the fire; He is of purer eyes than to bear to have you in His sight; you are ten thousand times more abominable in His eyes than the most hateful and venomous serpent is in ours. You have offended Him infinitely more than ever a stubborn rebel did his prince; and yet it is nothing but His hand that holds you from falling into the fire every moment. . . .

Edwards wrapped it all up with the standard call to repentance: "Therefore, let every one that is out of Christ, now awake and fly from the wrath to come."

Possibly because they found themselves part of colonial plantations, Puritans whose theology was fundamentally Calvinist (that is, they were basically fatalists, believing that an all-knowing, providential God sees even before we are born who will be saved and who will be damned, so there's not much an individual could do to "earn" salvation) came up with the notion of like-minded religious souls bound together (they actually signed a written agreement) in "covenanted communities" to do God's work on earth and, if not to earn salvation, at least to show the world the way things ought to be done. Bercovitch quotes a sermon of one Urian Oake: "This our Common-wealth seems to exhibit a *little model of the Kingdome of Christ upon Earth*" (72). So the mission in the wilderness was wed to the social contract as embodied in the American village, and an essentially theological proposition became a social operation. Anxieties over personal state of grace expanded to encompass attention to the social (and then economic) well-being of the community as a whole. Here is an amendment of major significance: if Calvinism is fundamentally passive, a watchful covenanted community trying to stay on fulcrum point with G. O. D. is pro-active in an almost Victorian sense. "The covenant theology becomes, therefore, the theoretical foundation both for metaphysics and for the state and the church in New England," writes Miller (89).

How quickly theology became secularized, and how useful this secularization was! Theology merged with economic development and civic planning, enabling Puritan theology "to play a significant role in the development of what was to become modern middle-class American culture" (Bercovitch: 18). The American consensus absorbs Blacks, Indians, gays, and even feminists ("as long as that would lead them into the middle-class American way" — Bercovitch: 161) and most important, the jeremiad is skewed on the side of celebrating God's plan for America, and a renewed call for movement into a brighter tomorrow. Winthrop's lecture and Edwards's sermon become Mercer's "accentuate the positive, eliminate the negative." Bercovitch writes, "Mediating between religion and ideology, the jeremiad gave contract the sanctity of covenant, free enterprise the halo of grace, progress the assurance of the chiliad, and nationalism the grandeur of typology. In short, it wed self-interest to social perfection, and conferred on both the unique blessings of American destiny" (141).

In *As a City upon a Hill*, Page Smith quotes an 1832 speech by Henry Clay which echoes the Winthrop speech, deleting the religion: "The eyes of all civilized nations are gazing upon us," said Clay (150). Then Smith quotes an 1882 speech by President Chester Arthur which also appropriates religious terminology for secular purposes:

> The American is the ark of safety, the anointed civilizer, the only visible source of light and heat and repose to the dark and discordant and troubled World, which is heaving and groaning, and livid in convulsions all around him! He is liberty's chosen apostle. . . . Rainbows of promise and visions of grandeur crowd upon his enraptured mind. (151)

Smith corroborates Bercovitch's conclusion at the end of *The American Jeremiad*: "The American Jeremiahs obviated the separation of the world and the kingdom, and then invested the symbol of America with the attributes of the sacred" (178). God is on America's side.

As we have observed in previous discussions of politics and the journey from and toward home, Midwestern small towns easily assumed the mantle of the covenanted community. Too quickly these villages became what they set out to be an alternative to, secularizing into patently commercial enterprises that out-Levittowned post-war suburban "communities."

Loudly proclaiming the superior virtues of country life, [Midwestern towns] waged ruthless campaigns to attract railroads and industries while lusting for the forbidden riches that their spokesmen never tired of denouncing. . . . The Western towns gave homage to the ethic, but their settlement was often accompanied by the most exaggerated hopes of material success. (P. Smith: 97)

James Finley, an Ohio circuit rider of the pre-Civil War era, notes an "almost universal spirit of speculation which prevailed. . . . A money mania seemed to have seized, like an epidemic, the entire people" (P. Smith: 98).

When agrarian-pastoral turns industrial-urban, and the goal of salvation morphs into making a lot of money, and the place to which God's elect escaped begins to resemble that place from which they departed, dream becomes nightmare. But although the American mission can admit temporary failure, there can be no call to stasis, only a call to further action. The Puritan response to a falling off was always a call to repentance and renewed effort. And there were many of these, the so-called "Great Awakening" of the 1740s being but the most conspicuous example. As the mission secularized and the pastoral urbanized, the critiques continued . . . as did the journey forward. So, for example, in the late 1950s a writer and social critic like Paul Goodman (by no means a Chamber of Commerce apologist for the grand American IS) could tell his secular congregation, "We have no recourse to going back, there is nothing to go back to. If we are to have a stable and whole community in which the young can grow to manhood, we must painfully perfect the revolutionary modern tradition we have" (231). The great American destination is the one Ken Kesey painted on the Merry Pranksters' day-glo bus: F U R T H U R.

Both the American Dream as a trope and the American jeremiad as a tradition incorporate the Christian paradigm of fall, repentance, *and rebirth* . . . or corruption, recognition, and *recommitment*. It is true that the very figures in which the American Dream particularizes itself are easily recognized as deadly sins (a nod here to Christopher Ricks) — materialism, lawlessness, egotism, concupiscence, selfishness, greed, sloth — but the sins produce the humbling fall prerequisite to a reclaimed dream. No resurrection without death. No mission without corruption. So even though the Dream, if and when fleetingly actualized, quickly disintegrates, it is quickly reborn in some new journey elsewhere into another ultimately unrealizable attempt to do better and even better. The genius of the American Dream is that the prophet against a dream-turned-nightmare confirms the uncorrupted form of that dream. Because it is a dream of a people rejecting a corrupt society, of the Elect on their pilgrimage toward a new Eden/Jerusalem, *through* the world but not *of* the world, of the outlaw and cowboy and mountain man and yeoman-farmer-colonist-turned-rebel, the American Dream is actually fulfilled the very moment the dreamers become aware of the wasteland surrounding them and their own complicity in making the mess, repent of their evil, and set out again in search of grace. It is almost as if the Dream must fail to succeed — or, at the least, failure is but an opportunity for penance and renewal. In the parable of the two men who went up into the temple to pray (Luke 18.10–14), the Pharisee who thanks God for his own righteousness is, Christ implies, condemned; the tax-collector who prays for forgiveness for his sins is, Christ tells us, justified, for "he who humbles himself will be exalted." So Dylan himself, commercialized like so much of the counterculture into a "sub-cultural variant of the dominant society" (Campbell: 704) and thereby made an exit–entrance into more of the same old shit, is reborn a prophet the moment he sloughs off his role as prophet-leader to become . . . a prophet-critic. (And Dylan repeats that cycle several times in his career.)

A PROPHET NEWLY ARISEN IN THE NEW WORLD

The prophet is integral to the American Dream — the Jeremiah who points his finger at the failed American Dream, warns of the judgment to come, and calls us again to the American mission. The prophet-critic is the genuine American. Wrote Emerson of Henry Thoreau, jailbird and critic of American society, "No truer American existed." Wrote Kerouac of Dean Moriarty, "He was BEAT — the root, the soul of Beatific."

Jeremiahs should come from outside the established power clique and have moral credibility. So while Fourth of July speeches would appear to be the ideal opportunity for American jeremiads, the people who give them are usually boosters, too much inside the power structure to qualify as prophets: ministers, educators, politicians. Politicians especially are not prophets, as I mentioned in the last chapter, and even good presidents like Franklin Roosevelt and Theodore Roosevelt, or martyred presidents like Abraham Lincoln or John Kennedy, won't really work as prophet figures, and I do not think that maverick and minority President Barack Obama can be an American Jeremiah, although his speeches are full of the "populist rhetoric." George W. Bush — of the System, by the System, and for the System — is of course O U T from the git-go. A true maverick politician, like Eugene McCarthy, John Altgeld, or William Jennings Bryan, can play the role — but he must not win the election. The role better suits a minority minister like Martin Luther King, Jr., a union man like Joe Hill (whom Dylan calls "a Messianic figure" in *Chronicles*: 52), or a maverick song writer like Woody Guthrie. Cisco Houston told Robert Shelton that Guthrie was "like the biblical prophets who sang the news" (*Home*: 78). Henry Thoreau, who preached "resist much; obey little," and was therefore the truest of Americans, made a good Jeremiah:

> How does it become a man to behave toward this American government to-day? I answer that he cannot without disgrace be associated with it. I cannot for an instant recognize that political organization as my government which is the *slave's* government also. . . . Let your life be a counterfriction to stop the machine. ("Civil Disobedience," 227, 231)

Poet Walt Whitman made a good Jeremiah in *Democratic Vistas*:

> I say we had best look our times and lands searchingly in the face, like a physician diagnosing some deep disease. Never was there, perhaps, more hollowness at heart than at present, and here in the United States. Genuine belief seems to have left us. The underlying principles of the States are not honestly believ'd in, (for all this hectic glow, and these melodramatic screamings,) nor is humanity itself believ'd in. What penetrating eye does not everywhere see through the mask? The spectacle is appaling. [sic] We live in an atmosphere of hypocrisy throughout. The men believe not in the women, nor the women in the men. A scornful superciliousness rules in literature. The aim of all the *littérateurs* is to find something to make fun of. A lot of churches, sects, &c., the most dismal phantasms I know, usurp the name of religion. Conversation is a mass of badinage. From deceit in the spirit, the mother of all false deeds, the offspring is already incalculable. (369–70)

Reading a similar bill of particulars in his preface to *Growing Up Absurd* in 1960, Paul Goodman demonstrated the combination of external critique and internal affirmation of values that makes a good Jeremiah:

> [W]ith all the tidying up of background conditions that you please, our abundant society is at present simply deficient in many of the most elementary objective opportunities and worth-while goals that could make growing up possible. It is lacking in enough man's work. It is lacking in honest public speech, and people are not taken seriously. It is lacking in the opportunity to be useful. It thwarts aptitude and creates stupidity. It corrupts ingenuous patriotism. It corrupts the fine arts. It shackles science. It dampens animal ardor. It discourages the religious convictions of Justification and Vocation and it dims the sense that there is a Creation. It has no Honor. It has no Community. (12)

Pete Seeger, who was blacklisted, will work as a Jeremiah, but not Elvis Presley, the young rebel who sold out because his real goal in life had always been not to critique the system but to play Las Vegas. And, Dylan himself tells us in *Chronicles*, there's no mistaking Ricky Nelson for a shaman-prophet because "He didn't sing desperately. . . . It didn't feel like his endurance was ever being tested to the utmost" (13).

Given their understated speech patterns, their Main Street reluctance to rock the boat, and the success of their educational system in anesthetizing students with sports, proms, and cultural diversity distractions, one might expect that Minnesotans would make poor prophets. Exactly the opposite is true. American prophets hang out on the margins of society and "far from the centers of ambition" (this is a Robert Bly line), so they are usually close to nature, and on the receiving end of nature's often-stern jeremiads. That's the North Country. A disproportionate number of American cranks and prophets have come from Minnesota, including true maverick politicians like Eugene McCarthy and Paul Wellstone, poets like Robert Bly and Bill Holm, and the prophet-heroes Dylan himself identifies on the last page of *Chronicles*. In an essay in her book *Letters from the Country*, Carol Bly has her farmer-prophet in the VFW (Veterans of Foreign Wars) lounge, drinking beer and

> saying the damned things: all our leaders in Washington are a bunch of bad-language nouns, and big businessmen who have control of everything have bad-language verbed the country, and this being conned into buying presents is a lot of collective bad-language noun, and in family life — in raising kids — a human being is somehow partially bad-language past participle by raising family at all. (54, 55)

In the introduction to a selection of his antiwar poems in *Selected Poems*; her husband, Robert Bly, writes, "I had been composing for the previous six or seven years a book called *Poems for the Ascension of J. P. Morgan*; it was a book of judgment rather than of affinity, and the poems on the Vietnam War were a continuation of that series" (62). Meridel Le Sueur raged against the corrupt System, testifying against those who corrupted the pastoral dream:

> Corn has been kidnapped, raped, stolen, overproduced, hoarded, robbed, the protein invaded for profit. Hoarders, world eaters have stolen our nitrogen. The Chicago Grain Market speculates in bodies it never sees or touches. The throw of the dice, grain futures, raises the price, robs starving children, destroys small farms. The life-giving protein is invaded. Plunderers, desecrators, gamblers, burglars, speculators,

human weevils, hoarders, thieves, world eaters, enemies invade the rood with cold
insolence of buying and selling what they never loved. (*Ripening*: 258)

In an essay for the book *Growing up in Minnesota*, Le Sueur specifically tied the
North Star prophets to the Minnesota landscape: "Thousands passed through
the villages, . . . producing idiots, mystics, prophets, and inventors. . . . A Dakota
priest said to me, 'It will be from here that the prophets come'" (18, 19).

Bob Dylan is certainly one of those prophets. "Whether Dylan likes it or not
— and he clearly does not — he is a prophet for our time," writes Marcia Ford
(Marshall and Ford: xvi). "Dylan was Isaiah in a corduroy cap, calling down
the hard rain," writes Nat Hentoff (113). Ken Kesey goes Ford and Hentoff a bit
better: "a prophet like [Dylan] happens once every five hundred years or so,"
he says (Thomson and Gutman: 143). Dylan is not just Midwest prophet, but
— as Jon Landau (McGregor: 250), Steven Goldberg (McGregor: 369), Stephen
Scobie (29), and Michael Gray (*Song*: 393) all point out — a folk-prophet and a
poet-prophet on top of that. "Bob Dylan," wrote Jonathan Cott in a preface to
the *Rolling Stone* interview of January 26, 1978, "has kept alive the idea of the
poet and artist as *vates* — the visionary eye of the body politic" (Cott: 171).[3]

Like a good prophet, Dylan repeatedly denied his leadership role, most vehe-
mently in the sixties when expectations were strongest. "I'm not a shepherd,"
Dylan told *Playboy* readers in his March 1966 interview; "And I'm not about
to save anybody from fate, which I know nothing about" (Cott: 102). Besides,
if everyone is free and equal, we don't need anybody special to tell us how to
be free and special. "I was more a cowpuncher than a Pied Piper," Dylan writes
in *Chronicles* (115).

Well — maybe that's what he wanted to be: a cowpuncher-Jeremiah.
Elsewhere Dylan has been more honest about his role in American culture:
"Check on Elijah the prophet," he told the *L.A. Times* in 1983; "He could make
rain. Isaiah the prophet, even Jeremiah, see if their brethren didn't want to bust
their brains for telling it right like it is, yeah — these are my roots" (Heylin,
Shades: 354). Dylan's early jeremiads include some of his sixties protest anthems,
which are, Andy Gill writes, "in effect, secular hymns, [in which Dylan's] delivery frequently takes on a sermonizing cast" (44); *John Wesley Harding*, with an
estimated 60-plus biblical allusions, where Dylan examines his own role as a
prophet; the songs of Dylan's religious period, especially *Slow Train Coming*,
when the preaching gets stronger and the judgment more severe; and songs on
recent albums like *Modern Times*, where Dylan secularizes his sermon.

As we have seen, Dylan's early songs are colored by the opportunities
presented by *Sing Out!* and *Broadside*, a biweekly topical song publication

(originally mimeographed) established by Peter Seeger and Sis Cunningham after Seeger's return from Britain in 1961.[4] On their pages the folk prophets preached to the already converted. On the jacket of a book discussing the folk-protest singer as a cultural hero, Jerry Rodnitzky writes, "If you were a young adult in the sixties it was still possible to have a hero, and more likely than not you looked up to Pete Seeger, Bob Dylan, Joan Baez, or Phil Ochs." Inside, in a chapter titled "Protest Music as Religious Experience," he astutely observes, "it is not capricious to compare a folk concert with a revival meeting, while the journey to a folk festival was probably as close as our society has come to a religious pilgrimage" (18). "Our best protest-song writers have indeed been a cleansing force," he concludes. "They have had the revivalist's faith that to hear of evil was to hate it" (39).

Some of the "early songs" in Dylan's *Lyrics, 1962–1985* are classic American jeremiads. The corrupted landscape may be New York City, or it may be Mississippi, where the body of Emmett Till still screams its accusations. The corrupt landscape is the iron train of hatred in "Train A-Travelin'," full of crazy mixed-up souls, and kill-crazy bandits. The alternative vision of a just and honorable America is *im*plicit in both "Talkin' New York" and "The Death of Emmett Till," and *ex*plicit in the western American landscape of the closing stanza of "Let Me Die in My Footsteps," in singers like Cisco and Sonny and Leadbelly in "Song to Woody," and in the person of Jesus Christ himself, who preached of "peace and brotherhood" and got hung from a cross in "Long Ago, Far Away." Dylan himself plays the prophet-poet in these early songs, trying to "show somebody / They are travelin' wrong" in the very song he sings "I know I ain't no prophet" ("Long Time Gone").

Dylan's technique in these songs varies. In "The Death of Emmett Till," he follows a formula similar to that used by Puritan preachers and writers of topical protest songs. First he recounts Emmett Till's murder in graphic and heightened detail; then he harps for a stanza on the moral of the story; then he moves to a stanza's worth of program: if we all got together and worked hard, we could make America a better place to live. "Oxford Town" works differently: Dylan offers some very sketchy details of James Meredith's enrollment at the University of Mississippi and his own visit there, then throws away the song with "Don't even know why we come."[5] "Only a Pawn in Their Game" opens with facts, then moves to ideas that anticipate Dylan's speech at the December 13, 1963 banquet of the Emergency Civil Liberties Committee, where he admitted seeing some of himself in Lee Harvey Oswald, the man who, less than a month before, had assassinated John Kennedy. "The Lonesome Death of Hattie Carroll" is a matter-of-fact account of the murder "right out of the newspapers," according to Dylan according to Ricks (231). Dylan's flat delivery here is typical of his strongest sermons, as Clinton Heylin notes: "Dylan even seemed to emphasize the unrelenting nature of the material with the droning melodies he utilized and the monotony of his vocal delivery" (*Shades*: 90). This was apparently the way Jonathan Edwards delivered "Sinners in the Hands of an Angry God": with dramatic calmness and restraint.

Dylan's career as folk prophet was short. In *Broadside* 20, Josh Dunson paints a warm picture of Sis Cunningham, Gil Turner, Pete Seeger, Phil Ochs, Happy Traum, Dylan, and Suze Rotolo crowded into the *Broadside* office making cultural history (Rotolo even drew an illustration for "Train A-Travelin'"), but by the end of 1963 the Dylan-Rotolo relationship was in trouble, Dylan had made his Tom Paine Award speech, and he was writing a letter, published in *Broadside* 38 (January 20, 1964), apologizing for not getting over to the offices. After the blow-up at the Newport Folk Festival of July 24–26, 1964 (such a dramatic contrast to the festival of 1963, with its workshop on topical songs), came a letter from Irwin Silber in *Sing Out!* suggesting that Dylan was wasting people's time, and a long article in *Broadside* (December 20, 1964) in which Paul Wolfe crowned Phil Ochs "the most important voice in the movement, simultaneous with the renunciation of topical music by its major prophet, Bob Dylan."

Dylan had tired of message songs, even his own, and had broken with the *Broadside* crowd and with Phil Ochs.[6] He was seeing the world in a new light — more populist/New Left. Protest songs are programmatic and tend to dichotomize: they are almost allegorical in the manner of a Puritan sermon or *Pilgrim's Progress*. There is us good guys and *them* against whom the good guys battle. The singer is one of the good guys. The implication is that people might, with a certain conscious effort and the right kind of education and laws, come from there to here, banish or at least reform racism with a conviction or two in the South and a stiffer prison sentence for William Zantzinger, fix class problems with a little Farm Aid for Hollis Brown, and straighten out America with confiscatory taxes on the manufacturers of guns and missiles. The quintessential songs of this type are "The Times They Are A-Changin'" and "When the Ship Comes In." In the first, Dylan divides the country into young and old (as he had done at the Emergency Civil Liberty Committee's banquet), tells the mothers and fathers to get out of the new road (as he had also done at the banquet), and confidently predicts the victory of the new order when the present is past and the slow have become fast. In "When the Ship Comes In" Dylan, at the head of the company of righteous youth, indulges fully in the moral dichotomy of damned and elect, and looks forward to the day when the young conquer the old like David knocking off Goliath, or drown them like the God flushing Pharaoh's horsemen down the Red Sea. Like Puritan theology, this song is confident to the point of being smug: judgment is inevitable, and God, nature, and time all side with the good guys. "Clearly in 'The Times They Are A-Changin'' Dylan was using the apocalyptic myth to bring judgment upon the society which may read out its Bible but to no avail," wrote Bert Cartwright (6). Biblical typology underscores the moral distinctions, which are absolute.

By the middle sixties, Dylan was seeing things differently. "Good an' evil are but words / invented by those / that are trapped in scenes," Dylan wrote on the jacket notes to *Another Side of Bob Dylan*. In "My Back Pages," he explained things this way: preaching "Rip down all hate" is really a form of half-wracked prejudice; preaching "equality" turns a fellow into a self-ordained professor; aiming at others turns a fellow into just another soldier; in preaching one becomes just another preacher — like one's enemy. So to jeers from the Newport audience, letters in *Sing Out!*, and articles in *Broadside* (R. Serge Denisoff contributed one titled "Dylan: Hero or Villain?"), Dylan moved on.

But the prophet really didn't move on; he just rejected dichotomies, turned his back on fame and fortune and commercialism (as a good prophet must), and moved to a different kind of testimony in a way more biblical than his protest songs. Topical protests are tightly focused in subject and agenda — Phil Ochs in his early album *All the News That's Fit to Sing*, with its cover photo of Ochs reading a paper and songs on the lost U.S. nuclear sub *Thresher*, the Cuban Missile Crisis, and Medgar Evers. Jeremiads are less specific. By 1964, Dylan had realized — or re-realized — that what's wrong politically "goes much deeper than the bomb. What's wrong is how few people are free. Most people walking around are tied down to something that doesn't let them really *speak*, so they just add their confusion to the mess" (Cott: 23). What people need is not plans but explosions. Jeremiah's prophesies, Winthrop's sermons, Ginsberg's "Howl" and Adrian C. Louis's terrific "A Colossal American Copulation"[7] are more explosions than newspaper stories: jeremiads tend to be more imagistic than narrative, very open-ended and broad canvas, because the problem is not really passing the Civil Rights Act or getting out of Vietnam, it's the whole big picture.

Using imagistic techniques that he had been developing in his protest material, Dylan too opened his focus to allow an individual song to target a wide array of subjects, all subsumed under one general subject: the unfreedom of life in the land of the free, and people who think they are free but are not. "Subterranean Homesick Blues," "Ballad of a Thin Man," "Just Like Tom Thumb's Blues," "Leopard-Skin Pill-Box Hat" — "These are all protest songs," Dylan could tell jeering fans at the Royal Albert Hall concert in London,

May 27, 1966. And in the largest sense, they are. Protest is "anything that goes against the ordinary and the established," Dylan told *Playboy* in June of 1984, adding, "And who's the founder of protest? Martin Luther" (Cott: 298).

Some early songs suggested the direction he would take. That direction is not satire, although satire is an effective critique, and Dylan can do humorous social commentary, as evidenced by early talking blues like "Talking Bear Mountain Picnic Massacre Blues" and "Talkin' John Birch Paranoid Blues." The future of Dylan was foreshadowed by early songs like "Blowin' in the Wind,"[8] and "A Hard Rain's A-Gonna Fall." "A Hard Rain" — which synthesizes Dylan's themes of apocalypse, politics, and his calling as a singer — is nothing if not Dylan's self-anointing as American Jeremiah (Beebee: 32), his promise to preach and to testify against an American-Dream-turned-nightmare, his calling down 40 days and 40 nights of purgation on a perjured and unrepentant people. But this "topical protest song" is not really a topical protest song because there's no specific topic. Or, rather, as Dylan among others points out (*Scrapbook*: 27), it's a protest song about many subjects: each line, each image, suggests a new corruption. Nor are these images clichés, like the roads, seas, white doves, and cannon balls of "Blowin' in the Wind." The highway of diamonds (what *Ramparts* magazine once called "welfare for the rich," alive today in George Bush's last-minute bailout for bankers and auto executives), the talkers with broken tongues, the white ladder covered with water are brilliant and intriguing images. Dylan the prophet looks beyond politics, programs, and blueprints for social amelioration. In this land of hunger and forgotten souls, Dylan commandeers the moral high ground, promising to tell and think and speak and breathe the truth, and, like a good prophet, reflect it from the mountains so that everyone can see it, and stick by his commitment until he sinks into the ocean. But he has no solutions, no agenda.

"Subterranean Homesick Blues" is every bit as much a jeremiad as "A Hard Rain," but after a bit of soul-searching, Dylan-Jeremiah has relocated his position from the mountaintop to a hidden place underground. He is hiding like an Old Testament prophet, hunkered down like Ralph Ellison's *Invisible Man*, who fell through an open manhole fleeing a major race riot, and plunged into some basement far below the New York City streets. There he lives in secure isolation, to tell his story and rediscover himself in a room he has fitted out with a radiophonograph and 1,369 electric light bulbs. Ellison writes,

I'm an invisible man and it placed me in a hole — or showed me the hole I was in, if you will — and I reluctantly accepted the fact.... My problem was that I always tried to go in everyone's way but my own.... You go along for years knowing something is wrong, then suddenly you discover that you're as transparent as air. At first you tell yourself that it's all a dirty joke, or that it's due to the "political situation." But deep down you come to suspect that you're yourself to blame, and you stand naked and shivering before the millions of eyes who look through you unseeingly. *That* is the real soul-sickness. (572, 575)

In "Subterranean Homesick Blues," Dylan grasps what Ellison realized: the ultimate corruption in America is the control exercised by the System, which is overpoweringly strong. "Some damn odin" who "eats us up," as Illinois poet John Knoepfle puts it in "man in overalls"; "one by one by one / he holds us upside down / by our ankles and what / can we do with him / nothing I can tell you" (83).

Dylan had hinted at this position in songs like "Only a Pawn in Their Game," where he sympathized with Medgar Evers's killer on the grounds that he'd been brainwashed and controlled; and he'd suggested the solution in "The Times They Are A-Changin'" where he celebrated sons and daughters who had moved beyond their parents' conventional wisdom.[9] In "Subterranean Homesick Blues," Dylan puts it all together: cops (or mafia, or mine guards) are on the take and hassle you for breaking laws you didn't know existed, the telephone is tapped, school is a con, the only jobs are with the Army, girls are worse than the cops when it comes to messing with your mind (one line in an early typed version of this song reproduced in *Lyrics, 1962–1985* implicates preachers as well), playing things straight gets you nowhere . . . and then the System pays off in counterfeit bills. "They only want to nail you," runs a line purged from this depiction of a System wrecked beyond repair. Andy Gill claims this song "remains the most concise compendium of anti-establishment attitude Dylan ever composed" (68).

On the great electric rock albums of the middle sixties, Dylan prophesies against this amorphous but palpably corrupt system in one song after another, often — as in "Like a Rolling Stone" — in that old level, cold, Jonathan Edwards voice. The songs are musical rehearsals for the film *Masked and Anonymous*; they are postmodern paintings of America, filled with allusions biblical, cultural, and pop; they are catalogues out of Walt Whitman or Allen Ginsberg (or more properly, tales out of Dante's *Inferno*) with crowds of warped people and plenty of adjectives. Individual examples of Christopher Ricks's seven deadly sins blur into one Bosch-like portrait of a corrupt world after another. Dylan goes into very big-picture ideas: money vs. spirituality, conformity vs. freedom, phony religious organizations vs. authentic religious experience, nature vs. art, ownership vs. self-fulfillment, tumult vs. silence, breakdown of authority, breakdown of language, breakdown of rationality, and breakdown of identity (Muir, *Troubadour*: 97–111).

Racial considerations have largely disappeared, but Dylan questions the value of bourgeois culture like Cecil B. DeMille's films ("Tombstone Blues") and *Phantom of the Opera* ("Desolation Row"), and the relevance of high culture like T. S. Eliot and Ezra Pound ("Desolation Row") and Shakespeare ("Stuck Inside of Mobile"). "It's Alright, Ma (I'm Only Bleeding)" married Arthur Crudup's "It's All Right, Mama" with Arthur Koestler to make a broad philosophical point: everything is not all right in America today. "This song," Bill King wrote, "is to capitalism what Koestler's *Darkness at Noon* is to communism" (Shelton, *Home*: 276).

"What can you do about it?" we ask with John Knoepfle.

Opt out, Dylan suggests. It's just too much monkey business for you to be involved in, to borrow a line from Chuck Berry (who could preach a pretty good jeremiad of his own). Ellison's Invisible Man has been haunted all his life by the largely self-imposed demands that grew out of his early successes at school, his high school diploma, and the directive of a letter he dreams came with that diploma: "Keep This Nigger-Boy Running." He escapes this dream-nightmare not by beating the game, or fighting it, or outrunning it, but by ducking underground. This is the solution Dylan suggests. Individual freedom, Gregg Campbell points out (702), is Dylan's last refuge from the insane city and the corrupted countryside both. Get out of the "Mixed Up Confusion" and go your own way. Listen to the "Chimes of Freedom" and disengage and be free. "Strike another match, go start anew," advises Dylan in "It's All Over Now, Baby Blue." Head out on your own, no direction home, like a rolling stone. Throw away the National Bank road map for your soul and duck out into the alley with the "Tombstone Blues." Forget the books, Mr. Jones, and all the hotshot lawyers and professors . . . and while you're at it, forget about rationality and sense, because you can't figure out what's going on. Otherwise, you're gonna have to go through all of these things twice . . . or maybe three or four times.

Say it with Bob Dylan: "He who's not busy bein' born / Is busy dying." "I ain't gonna work on Maggie's Farm no more." The deaf, the blind, the mute, the single mother, the prostitute, the lonesome lover, the prisoner, and strung-out souls all across the universe need to just say no. Therein lies the only hope for America and Americans.

Even this solution dimmed as the sixties unfolded,[10] and Dylan's own take on the American disaster seems to darken from *Bringing It All Back Home* to *Highway 61 Revisited* to *Blonde on Blonde*. The earliest of these albums is filled with moments of transcendence and resolution: Dylan implies that the

hang-ups of "Subterranean Homesick Blues" (more external than psychological) or the more personal "Baby Blue" can be resolved by transcending reality
into either art ("She Belongs to Me") or an idealized self ("Love Minus Zero/No
Limit"). *Highway 61 Revisited* is more philosophically complex, and its lead cut,
"Like a Rolling Stone," makes it clear that being free is not as easy, or as much
fun, as "Maggie's Farm" implied.

   Blonde on Blonde takes Dylan to the core of the storm and, apart from
producing some of his best songs, contains some of his most complex visions.
The album abounds in songs of separation, hate, scorn, and departure which
one cannot help reading as Dylan on Dylan. The prophet is as dissatisfied
with America as ever, and the direction in which it is heading, but he seems
equally dissatisfied with himself and his own direction. "Most Likely You Go
Your Way (and I'll Go Mine)" is a lyric of separation and distances: "I just
can't do what I've done before . . . I'm gonna let you pass." "Temporary Like
Achilles" scorns the singer himself for becoming temporarily vulnerable, like a
conventional lover. "Absolutely Sweet Marie" pushes scorn of self and others to
new extremes: anyone can be like me, but fortunately not too many can be like
you. The notion is repeated in "Memphis Blues Again": nobody can hide, and
even underground your mind gets strangled up. All Dylan can do is wonder
"can this really be the end?"

JOHN WESLEY HARDING: THE
PROPHET EXAMINES HIMSELF

In 1967 Dylan liberated himself from the city, the road, rock music — and
from Bob Dylan, once again "appropriated by the music business as the trend
of the year" (Shelton, *Home*: 310), but he did not liberate himself from his job
as Jeremiah. *The Basement Tapes*, most of which were recorded in 1967, are full
of testimony: "Million Dollar Bash," "Too Much of Nothing," "Nothing Was
Delivered," and "Tears of Rage," which Scobie calls a definitive statement of the
inevitable betrayal of America's infinite idealism (221). Talk about preaching
the jeremiad! And Dylan's next album, *John Wesley Harding*, recorded in the
late fall of 1967, was both a familiar portrait of America and a thoughtful re-
examination of Dylan's own role as prophet, similar to "My Back Pages." Michael
Gilmour spends two pages of his book *Tangled Up in the Bible: Bob Dylan &
Scripture* discussing "the reluctance of some biblical prophets to fulfill the
obligations of their vocation" (27), and Dylan was always a reluctant prophet.
He spends the better part of this album looking around, before reaching the
startling decision to bring good news for a change.

John Wesley Harding threw most Dylan fans for a loop, but as unlike the three great sixties electric albums as it appears (which is very unlike — as unlike those three albums as they were to Dylan's acoustic albums), Dylan is really doing in the country mode what he had done in the rock mode: calling America to repentance. The difference is, here he's also calling himself to — well, not repent, but to abandon pride and ego. "Take off your mask," Dylan will tell us later in "When He Returns," even your prophet mask — it doesn't do any good because "He sees your deeds." You kid only yourself, and your delusion contributes to the problem.

Dylan's jeremiad begins with the fable of the Three Kings, written by Dylan for the liner of *John Wesley Harding*, and loosely based on Brecht's *The Good Woman of Setzuan* (Scaduto: 250). "There is a creeping consumption in the land," proclaims one Terry Shute; "It begins with these three fellas and it travels outward. . . . Forgiveness is not in them. The wilderness is rotten all over their foreheads." Prophet Shute, like Prophet Jeremiah and Prophet Dylan, is summarily dismissed by Frank: "Get out of here, you ragged man! Come ye no more." Then Frank reveals himself to be the key to Mr. Dylan's new album and pulls a few stunts to impress the visitors. The fable ends with the three kings sent happily on their way, and old pals Frank and Terry, like Jeremiah and the King of Zedekiah, cutting their deal. Whether we interpret this fable as Dylan's rejection of the prophet, his rejection of the three kings, his suggestion of universal complicity (and thereby a rejection of guilty/innocent dichotomies), or perhaps a little postmodernist fable against interpretation, the creeping consumption upon the land is obviously upon Dylan's mind — the consumption, his role in creating the consumption, and what to do about it all. The album's final songs radiate the forgiveness which resolves the consumption, but how did we get from here to there? Just what *is* that some way out of here?

John Wesley Harding is a vaguely linear album, a dialectic of stories or little parables in the tradition of Chaucer's *The Canterbury Tales*, Eliot's *The Waste Land*, and, I would argue, the Beatles' *Sgt. Pepper's Lonely Hearts Club Band*. It chooses a broad subject — the role of the prophet-outlaw in America today — explores a position on that subject, reaches a tentative conclusion, reacts to that conclusion with another possibility, which is in turn critiqued, modified, incorporated into the continuing discussion until the symposium arrives at a final conclusion. *John Wesley Harding* ends more like *The Canterbury Tales*, which closes with the pilgrim's entrance into Canterbury/New Jerusalem, than *Pepper's*, which ends in chaos and night. It closes with a pastoral vision that anticipates Dylan's 1997 "Red River Shore" — "go home and lead a simple life."

The album begins, however, with a series of allegories as stark as anything

Dylan had previously written. One examines the outlaw-hero myth with all its violent overtones; a second paints a system so perverse that people must apologize for desiring freedom; a third analyses martyrdom and sin; a fourth portrays human existence in the starkest, most claustrophobic terms; a fifth recounts the death attendant on twentieth century materialism. Only in the last song on the album's first side does anyone finally escape. Side one is filled with a very Judeo-Christian sense of guilt and the need for atonement, with considerable Christian imagery, and with the realization that despite his best intentions, man is inherently sinful. Only in terms of such dark realizations, however, does Dylan's final affirmation of love make any sense. "Love is all there is," Dylan tells us later, echoing, perhaps, the Beatles' "All you need is love" — but that insight came only after some real soul-searching, both in person and masked behind various personae. Unless we share the search, the resolution seems superficial. At least Dylan promises grace after the soul-searching and penance. His is a better deal than the one Jeremiah cut with Zedekiah: "If you will surrender to the princes of the king of Babylon, then your life shall be spared, and this city shall not be burned with fire" (Jeremiah 38.17).

The first cut on the album is its title song: "John Wesley Harding." The name is a curious blend of the strict Calvinist religion of John Wesley and the loose amorality of John Wesley Hardin, a post-Reconstruction-era Texas vigilante.[11] Stephen Scobie sees an allusion to Yaweh — "I am that I am" — in the letters of the outlaw's name (154), an idea which works too: Dylan operates here in the land of myth, not history (no state in the Union has a "Chaynee County, although five states have a Cherokee County, including Texas and Nebraska). The apparent contradiction between priest and outlaw, appropriate in one who assumes the mantle of Jeremiah, is explored further in such juxtaposed phrases as "friend to the poor," "trav'led with a gun in every hand," and "never known / To hurt an honest man." That phrase of Dylan's, "to live outside the law you must be honest," runs through ours heads here, and raises a few questions. How do you help people with guns? Just what sort of a stand is John Wesley Harding taking? If he's a good guy, what's he charged with? To the extent that we ask questions, Michael Gray is correct in saying that the song poses more problems than it answers. But answers emerge in the very contradictions of the outlaw's name and the tensions between what is traditionally right and just, and what is presented here as right and just. In modern America, where generosity is criminal and honesty is illegal, outlaws are wiser than judges. We are in the beatnik fifties, the protest sixties, and "beat" is the root word of "beatific." Dylan draws on the cowboy legends with lines like "all across the telegraph" and "track or chain him down," but the myth was as current in the sixties as

Daniel Ellsberg or Philip Berrigan, and as old as the Pilgrims and the Founding Fathers.

Anthony Scaduto suggests that John Wesley Harding is a projection of Dylan himself (249), and he represents a starting point for Dylan's movement toward personal salvation and national rehabilitation: when justice and morality are perverted, the generous man lives outside conventional law and faces its strictures. This is a good starting point for any American confronting the System, even today. Help the good people and carry a gun.

"As I Went Out One Morning" reverses the point of view: no longer the outlaw-hero, Dylan finds himself aligned with forces constraining freedom. The tensions of "John Wesley Harding" are again present: "fairest damsel" is juxtaposed against "chains." The damsel awaits rescue, which the singer appears to offer before feeling threatened and ordering her to depart. Her request for liberty is denied first by the narrator and then by the great libertarian Tom Paine, whose likeness was part of Dylan's Emergency Civil Liberties Committee award. (The flight will be south, not north or west, an interesting inversion reminiscent of Huck and Jim's escape to freedom down the Mississippi.) So Dylan has repositioned himself in this song, closer to slave-master Tom Paine than to outlaw-hero John Harding. This lyric turns on Dylan's ability to find a part of himself in everyone from Hollis Brown to Lee Oswald, from victim to oppressor. Tom Paine is like Simon Legree, and Dylan is like both. The repositioning frees Dylan from the self-righteousness of "John Wesley Harding" and his own earlier us–them protest songs. He recognizes himself as part of the restrictive society he formerly felt apart from, and he becomes a Jeremiah preaching against himself. This awareness prepares the physician to heal himself. Eventually.

John Wesley Harding is pervaded with sin and redemption, and associated concerns for the health of the soul. "A penitent's album," Craig McGregor has called it, "ridden with shame, guilt, and desire for atonement — Dylan's *Ash Wednesday* as surely as 'Desolation Row' was his *Waste Land*" (12). "As I Went Out One Morning" introduced sin into the album and implied the need for forgiveness, although in a kind of misdirected line: "I'm sorry for what she's done." Sin and contrition are at the core of the album's third song, "I Dreamed I Saw St. Augustine." Like Tom Paine, Dylan's saint is not a historical personage (neither St. Augustine of Hippo nor St. Augustine of England were martyred), but his name — like those of Harding and Paine — is suggestive, just as the opening lines of Dylan's song ("I dreamed I saw St. Augustine / Alive as you or me") call to mind the first lines of a popular commemoration of murdered labor organizer Joe Hill written by Alfred Hayes and Earl Robinson: "I dreamed I saw

Joe Hill last night / Alive as you or me." Augustine tears frantically through his country searching for lost souls, lamenting the death of prophets and martyrs in this modern American wasteland, and offering his own message of comfort: "know you're not alone." For his testimony, he is martyred himself, and the narrator of this dream vision finds himself among the company of those who put him to death — Paul holding the coats of those who stoned St. Stephen, as it were. The point is clear: the human condition is such that we always martyr the prophet, kill the Christ. No man can rise above his own sin; every man is implicated in every death. Dylan has moved somewhere here, from recognizing that he is *like* Lee Oswald to realizing that he *is* Lee Oswald. This is exactly the opposite of simplistic early me/you positions like "Train A-Travelin'," in which a smug Dylan asks if you ever thought that the person standing next to you (but certainly not yourself) "just might be misled."

The revelation regarding St. Augustine comes in a dream, but cannot be dismissed as only a dream because it contains a real-life truth, the measure of which is the song's closing lines: "I awoke in anger, so alone and terrified." Augustine died in the dream, and it was in the dream that he told men they are not alone, yet the narrator's recognition and terror come after the dream has ended. "This retelling of the legendary martyr-singer's tale is in part Dylan's reflection on his own democratic-prophetic vocation," writes Marqusee, and his recognition that the "true prophets of freedom (not the charlatans in the media) will always be rejected by those who fear freedom. The pathos of the song, however, lies in the admission of mutual complicity — one of the themes that ties *John Wesley Harding* together" (235).

Dylan's acceptance of what theologians would call man's inherent sin occasions a series of reactions: anger, terror, prayer, and the contrition of tears. The first is a remnant of the rage which Augustine elicited and which no doubt provoked his death ("Don't ever tell anybody that they're not free 'cause then they're gonna get real busy killin' and maimin' to prove to you that they are"); it is yet another link between the world of the dream and reality. The second is a reaction to Dylan's recognition of his own capacity for evil. The third and fourth are important theologically: recognizing his own guilt, Dylan feels the need of prayer and contrition. "The glass" may be interpreted in two ways, each of similar significance: either it is a looking glass in which Dylan sees his own reflection ("I swear I see my reflection / Some place so high above this wall" he sang in "I Shall Be Released"), or it is a window through which Dylan can see visions of what ought to be, but through which he cannot pass to realize those visions. In either case, it is the view into or through this glass which crystallizes his awareness of his own need for grace. And in either case, the glass must shatter.

In three songs, Dylan has brought us quite a distance, but the journey has just begun. Aware of his own guilt, Dylan at first despairs, then escapes from his own despondency, then expiates his guilt, and finally achieves salvation.

"All Along the Watchtower" and "The Ballad of Frankie Lee and Judas Priest" are desperate lyrics. The one bangs frantically on walls, the other describes mistaken paradises and resultant spiritual deaths. No exit. Jon Landau speaks of "experiencing" a poem and of the mood evoked by "All Along the Watchtower," but vague intangibles don't explain what's happening here. The lyric presents an imagined conversation between the joker and the thief. One represents an extension of the claustrophobic terror of the song previous, but the terror extends now in a different direction. Those businessmen so disdained in "Sad-Eyed Lady of the Lowlands" now drink his wine, the joker tells us, and plowmen dig his earth. Certainly, the joker is a man of importance ("*my* wine, *my* earth"), certainly he has power and knowledge beyond other people, but he also finds himself trapped. The thief (we're back to John Wesley Harding) responds with an assurance we might better expect of his more important (deific?) counterpart: "we've been through that," he assures the joker, "and this is not our fate." It is as if the thief and Christ have traded crosses. The closing lines of that speech, however, suggest a certain uneasiness, as if the thief realizes not only the extremities of their circumstances, but also the validity of his companion's doubts. "So let us not talk falsely now, the hour is getting late." The joker does not answer. Dylan instead directs our attention to externals: princes watching and waiting, imminent disaster in approaching wildcats, riders, storms. Apocalypse is upon us. "For the Lord said to me: 'Go, set a watchman, let him announce what he sees. When he sees riders, horsemen in pairs, riders on asses, riders on camels, let him listen diligently, very diligently.' Then he who saw cried: 'Upon a watchtower I stand, O lord'. . ." (Isa. 21.6–8). That is where Dylan leaves us hanging in this song.

"The Ballad of Frankie Lee and Judas Priest" addresses temptation and death. Judas Priest is another interesting and ambiguous conjunction of familiar names, representing, according to Wilfred Mellers, "the Established Church gone rotten" (156). ("Judas Priest" is also a useful cuss word for Americans, like my mother, who want to cuss without cussing.) Priest plays the role of tempter, and Frankie Lee (the outlaws Frankie and Johnny plus Robert E. Lee?) plays his willing victim. When Frankie needs cash, Judas pulls out a roll of tens. Frankie senses something awry and requests time to think; Judas, fearing that he will lose his catch, applies the pressure. Gullible Frankie Lee comes running, then realizes his mistake and attempts to recover (selling everything he owns while the mission bells toll his death), but he's too late. "Died of thirst," Dylan tells us, recalling Christ on the cross, although in this song Frankie Lee probably died of sexual exhaustion. The song closes with a complicitous neighbor boy and a moral Dylan appends to the tale. The two are at odds with each other. The moral is a typically Christian aphorism to the effect that one should help his neighbor; the innocuous child, so peripheral to the story's plot, is the zinger that Dylan sneaks in almost under the radar screen. "We are all guilty," he suggests, merely by virtue of being born. The point is the point of "St. Augustine" and "All Along the Watchtower": man hates and kills, even little kids, and there is no apparent way out of here.

No *apparent* way, that is. For in the last lyric of side one, Dylan in the personage of an old drifter makes his escape. "Drifter's Escape" hinges on a Kafka-esque recognition of man's inherent guilt and his inability to comprehend that guilt. "And I still do not know / What it was that I've done wrong" sounds like the accused K in Kafka's *The Trial*. Here is a recognition of weakness and a very human plea for help which frankly admits the drifter's inability to help himself. Exactly who is addressed is unclear, but probably it's not "that cursed jury" or the judge who has stepped down — the human agents of justice pretty much ignore the drifter, having only done their job. The crowd too seems eager for condemnation in the manner of the crowd that dispatched St. Augustine. Like K, the drifter is largely ignored. He is guilty and deserves to die, and that is all anyone needs to know.

But the drifter does not die. In what can only be described as a classic act of divine intervention (a bolt of lightning which strikes the courthouse out of shape), the drifter escapes while others pray. Grace overrides law and human nature, if we only let it. "Drifter's Escape" is nothing less than salvation come to one who has recognized his condition and set pride aside long enough to request help — the very message Jonathan Edwards had preached to America a quarter of a millennium before Dylan. The 1966 *Playboy* interview, for which Dylan purportedly wrote both questions and answers, contains this exchange:

> *Playboy*: You told an interviewer last year, "I've done everything I ever wanted to." If that's true, what do you have to look forward to?
> Dylan: Salvation. Just plain salvation.
> *Playboy*: Anything else?
> Dylan: Praying. (Cott: 110)

Most of the shame and guilt of *John Wesley Harding* is found on side one; atonement and grace appear on side two. "Dear Landlord" contains an understanding of self and others rarely found in Dylan's songs of the sixties. Some have suggested that the song is written to set off the line "Now each of us has his own special gift," but the second stanza seems more important. The song takes us back to Frankie Lee and Judas Priest, to "Like a Rolling Stone," to the hang-ups which plagued Dylan most of his career, and to the way in which Dylan has played the Jeremiah. Dylan is beyond all that now, ready to forgive others and — more important — to forgive himself. The tone here is light-years away from "Positively 4th Street" or "Leopard-Skin Pill-Box Hat" or "Absolutely Sweet Marie": understated, quiet, devoid of scorn and anger and bitterness. The poet accepts his subservience to a landlord who is neither humane nor understanding. Instead of bristling hostility, however, Dylan offers sympathy. Three pleas in three successive stanzas are remarkable for Bob Dylan. Unlike his sad-eyed lady, Dylan of the sixties had a pronounced tendency to argue and to judge. With the final lines of this song — "And if you don't underestimate me / I won't underestimate you" — Dylan has found his way back to Bob Dylan folksinger doing "Talkin' World War III Blues": letting us be in his dream if he can be in ours.

Where "Dear Landlord" offers sympathy, "I Am a Lonesome Hobo" offers advice. The character, a cross between the drifter and John Wesley Harding, sounds suspiciously like Dylan of "Like a Rolling Stone." Perhaps that last line is the key: this character has been too proud to beg, to submit himself to anyone except himself. His inability to trust his brother led him to his fatal doom. Now, like a rich man come back from the dead to warn his five brothers, this lonesome hobo returns from his metaphorical death to warn us all: "Stay free from petty jealousies / Live by no man's code / And hold your judgments for yourself."

"I Pity the Poor Immigrant" follows. It is the finest song on *John Wesley Harding*, tightly structured, ordering each of its stanzas in a series of parallel phrases, using rhetorical parallelisms within those phrases. The song borrows from the Bible, of course (Leviticus 26.20, 26, "Your strength shall be spent in vain. . . . Ye shall eat, and not be satisfied"), but it also reaches back to many of the album's other songs and characters: to St. Augustine with its concern for man's propensity to do evil and the glass which would not shatter there; to Frankie Lee who fell in love with wealth and feared his own death; to the joker and the thief, who could find no way out of their nightmare. The lyric's central image is carefully chosen: the immigrant, the man exiled from his native land, the stranger in a strange land. This immigrant is, in the simplest sense, a foreigner who needs Dylan's understanding; in a larger sense he is Dylan himself, who spent much of his career searching angrily for himself, hating, fearing, spending his strength in vain; in another sense, the immigrant is every modern American and especially every modern man, for we have all lost control of ourselves, fallen in love with wealth, filled our mouths with laughing and our towns with blood. Our visions, Dylan suggests, must ultimately shatter as his own visions have shattered, and the process will be painful. But it will be therapeutic as well: it will be our gladness, it will be our salvation as it was Dylan's salvation as it was Israel's salvation.[12]

"The Wicked Messenger" is a redefinition of Dylan's own role similar to that of "A Hard Rain's A-Gonna Fall," written what seems like centuries ago. This song personalizes the album just after "The Poor Immigrant" universalized it. If anything, the prophet is too hard on his former self: "his tongue it could not speak, but only flatter." But the wicked messenger has confronted a few people lately — Frankie Lee, John Wesley Harding, St. Augustine, his landlord, a certain lonesome hobo — and his heart has been opened up by a few simple words: "If you cannot bring good news, then don't bring any." Dylan has decided to bring good news (not yet the Christian gospel, but he's moving in that direction), both in the remainder of this album and in succeeding albums: the joyful affirmation of "Down Along the Cove" and "I'll Be Your Baby Tonight," of *Nashville Skyline*, of his hymn "Father of Night," of the great benediction of *Planet Waves*, "Forever Young." The good news of Dylan's early seventies albums is cast into simple tunes, simple (even trite) lyrics, clean rhymes, and the basic truth that love is ultimately all there is. The simplicity of this album's final cut offers tremendous relief after the philosophical complexities of earlier Dylan albums, after the dark apocalypse of "All Along the Watchtower," after the despair of "I Dreamed I Saw St. Augustine." The vision is as easy as the pastoral idyll, as comfortable as country music . . . which Dylan adopted for what seemed to many fans as a long period of sleep. We can almost hear Dylan singing to Dylan, as to America, "You don't have to worry anymore." In the end, prophet Jeremiah promises grace to the people.

THE PROPHET RETURNS, RETIRES, AND THEN RETURNS AGAIN

Complacency, however, may be a deadlier disease than conceit, especially for an American prophet. Thinking you have nothing to worry about proves to be the main worry. Reviews of *Nashville Skyline* were tepid, and reviews of *Self Portrait* were famously hostile: "what is this shit?" By now, Dylan fans and critics have pretty much agreed that it was not as bad as all that, but still shit, not so much for the pastoral vision as for the almost-deliberate clichés, the stripped down sound, and the careless production. *Self Portrait* is too close to self-satisfaction, with no sense of the big picture or, for that matter, America. *New Morning* has a slightly wider focus, with the imagery/allusion of "Day of the Locusts" and the hymn which ends the album, "Father of Night," but Dylan is still too passive. The problem, as members of the sixties generation discovered, is that you can retreat into your marriage, or your Minnesota acreage, or the artistic mansion in your own mind, and busy yourself with straightening out your own head (and raising your kids), but when you walk out the door and find the car stolen and somebody tossing garbage on your lawn, you realize that a fellow needs to take care of business. America needed another stern sermon. Or two. After a vacation in the wilderness, the prophet re-engaged.

On *Blood on the Tracks* Dylan opens his eyes to the stolen car and the trashed lawn. Much of what he has to say appears to be personal, but this personal is communal and unsettling. "Shelter from the Storm" is certainly a song about marriage, or at least a song about a love relationship which offered a place that was "always safe and warm" to one who was "burned out from exhaustion," but the salvation was lethal, and the relationship proved a toss-up at best, debilitating at worst. The girl, as she often does in Dylan, represents something larger — salvation become stasis — and this is a song about a sense of salvation which proves lethal, another case of the American Dream gone bad. "This is what salvation must be like after a while," Dylan had written in "Visions of Johanna." The seventies, which had first seemed a blessed relief from the chaos of the sixties, proved to be a disaster, a tomb, a decade of repression, denial, and neglect.[13] Dylan's song is a call to sleeping prophets to wake up and kick the dust off their shoes. "Eden is burning," he will warn in "Changing of the Guards"; either accept elimination or find the courage to change.

Many songs of *Blood on the Tracks*, as we noticed earlier, suggest a loss which Dylan seeks to reclaim even while sensing it cannot be reclaimed. Something in his voice rings with resignation — "All ya can do is do what you must," he sings in "Buckets of Rain" — but other songs are a little more New Left activist (doesn't Dylan-Jack-of-Hearts pull off a great con on millionaire-industrialist Big Jim in "Lily, Rosemary and the Jack of Hearts"?) and some songs ring with the old anger and commitment. "I been double-crossed now for the very last time," Dylan sings triumphantly in "Idiot Wind," a song which converts a very personal male–female relationship gone awry into a metaphor for the larger world gone sour by expanding his vision from the Grand Coulee Dam (in early versions, Mardi Gras) to the Capitol. Here is a sweep as broad as Jordan to west of the Rock of Gibraltar ("Groom's Still Waiting at the Altar"), or Mexico to Tibet ("True Love Tends to Forget"), or Valley Coast to Dylan's back yard, and Tokyo to the British Isles, which Scobie finds in an early concert version of "Caribbean Wind" (179), but not quite as wide as "Broadway to the Milky Way" ("Union Sundown"). In Dylan's description of materialism gone berserk,

we identify the seventies Yuppie Generation: Young, Urban, Professional slackers with ten-cent talents and ten-dollar egos — and budgets to match — and a
time of distorted facts, truth covered with lies, everything upside down, wheels
stopped, good become bad, bad become good, a nation that thought itself at the
top finding itself plunging toward the bottom. The prophet had returned, with
a message: get back to work. Again he was right on target.

And the prophet stayed returned for a couple of specific protest songs and
some general Bosch-like landscapes depicting the nightmare of American
materialism exported in the late twentieth century all around the world by the
yuppie jet set: "Isis," "Romance in Durango," "Changing of the Guards," and
"Where Are You Tonight? (Journey Through Dark Heat)": "a million dreams
gone . . . a landscape being raped." In "No Time to Think," Dylan's first full-scale
jeremiad since the sixties, he reads the full mid-sixties indictment:

> In death, you face life with a child and a wife
> Who sleep-walks through your dreams into walls
> You're a soldier of mercy, you're cold and you curse
> "He who cannot be trusted must fall"

Fitzgerald's bitch-goddess success (in Dylan, "suck-cess") is an empress who
attracts you while oppression makes you feel violent and strange. Judges haunt
you (must be something you did), tyrants waylay you, Babylon girls distract
you, and con men ("magicians") are everywhere. (You have to love Dylan's
offhand slam, "I'd have paid off the traitor and killed him much later, / But that's
just the way that I am.") The abstractions are all there too, all corrupted, all
phony: notoriety, society, ecstasy, hypocrisy, paradise, sacrifice, equality, liberty,
humility, nobility, loyalty, unity, and the –isms from socialism, to patriotism,
and materialism. "Distracted from distraction by distraction," was Eliot's line;
no time to choose, prepare, blink, or think is Dylan's take in 1978.

That same year he wrote, although he did not release, "Señor (Tales of Yankee
Power)," in which Dylan as American Jeremiah addresses the Lord with the
easy familiarity of the thief talking with the joker, and with some of his doubts
as well: Just where *is* this country headed? Lincoln County Road, with its suggestions of Midwestern pastoralism, or Armageddon? This is less a sermon to
slackers than a discussion with the big boss on what to do with a trainload of
hard-hearted sinners. In the prophet's dual role as a man and as God's mouth-
piece, Dylan positions himself outside the train, not among the people, at the
Lord's side. He makes an offer — "I'm ready when you are, señor" — and a
suggestion, based on Christ's plan for dealing with the money-changers in the

temple: disconnect the cables and overturn the tables. The song's closing line suggests that the Lord is far more patient with this generation of hard-hearted vipers than Dylan. The impatient question "Can you tell me what we're waiting for?" hangs in the air long after the song is finished, an accusation, a prophecy, even a wish. One sometimes suspects that American Jeremiahs are hoping as much as they are predicting, a little self-righteous, a little impatient with the Lord's patience, and that is the case here. Perhaps the album's next song is Dylan's deliberate response to "Señor": "True Love Tends to Forget."

The song foreshadows Dylan's conversion to a fundamentalist Christianity and his turn to an austere version of the jeremiad on songs of his early eighties albums. The songs of *Street-Legal* (1978) had indicated trouble in Dylan's life (when was his life anything but turbulent?) and in America as well — what he would call a "Legionnaire's Disease" infecting everything and everybody. The road offered itself as an attractive — or perhaps the only viable — alternative (again, this is a familiar motif in Dylan), but the road was taking its toll, not working its magic, on Dylan at this time. At a concert in San Diego on November 17, 1978, someone threw a silver cross at Dylan's feet as he performed on stage. He picked it up and put it in his pocket (Heylin, *Shades*: 315). Shortly thereafter, Dylan told Karen Hughes in 1980, "Jesus put his hand on me. It was a physical thing. I felt it. I felt it all over me. I felt my whole body tremble. The glory of the Lord knocked me down and picked me up" (Cott: 276). In late November performances, the woman in the topless bar in "Tangled Up in Blue" was quoting not from an Italian poet, but from the book of Matthew. (Later it became Jeremiah 31.31.) After conversations with evangelical Christian members of his band, Dylan took a three-month, four-days-a-week, 8:30 a.m.-to-noon course at the Vineyard Fellowship's School of Discipleship in Reseda, California, in the early months of 1979. He also started reading Hal Lindsey's 1970 best seller, *The Late, Great Planet Earth*, a prose jeremiad which interpreted current events in light of biblical prophesies to announce the imminent end of the world and *dies irae*. Long-time prophet and American Jeremiah Bob Dylan was baptized a Christian in February. Wow!

Robert Zimmerman of Hibbing, Minnesota, had been raised Jewish. He received a Bar Mitzvah, even though a rabbi had to be imported from Duluth for the occasion. He attended a Jewish summer camp while in high school, visited Israel at various points in his career, and at a couple points explored his Jewish heritage with some intensity, especially the ultra-orthodox sect Lubavitcher Hasidim. In 1971 he even toyed with the idea of joining a kibbutz in Israel. A. J. Weberman tried to link him with the Jewish Defense League. However, as David Boucher notes, "Dylan's enthusiasm for Judaism was short lived"

(*Dylan & Cohen*: 214), and Hibbing, where Dylan was raised, was simply not very Jewish, not as Jewish as Duluth, or Minneapolis, or New York City. Beatty and Abe Zimmerman were the only Jewish family in their Fairfield Addition in Hibbing, and Beatty went to all the neighborhood weddings, confirmations, and graduations (Shelton, *Home*: 32). Hibbing was overwhelmingly, even aggressively, Christian, especially the high school during holiday seasons. It is inaccurate to suppose, as Bert Cartwright does, that the typical youth of Dylan's Hibbing "would have been hard pressed to name the Ten Commandments of the Old Testament or the Four Gospels of the New" (1). Dylan told Rosenbaum in the March 1978 *Playboy* interview, "I've never felt Jewish. . . . I don't have much of a Jewish background."[14] In Australia in 1978, Dylan suggested that his blue eyes showed he was Cossack.

Whether "the terms of [Dylan's] imagination have always been fundamentally Christian" (8), as John Hinchey argues in his detailed study of *Slow Train Coming*, Dylan's songs, very early on, do exhibit a biblical background. Shelton reports that even in the late sixties, Dylan "kept a large Bible on a reading stand in Woodstock" (*Home*: 15), and Howard Sounes reports that when Noel Paul Stookey drove to Woodstock in the fall of 1967 to ask Dylan — no joke — about the meaning of life, Dylan's response was, "Do you ever read the Bible?" (228). The Christian narrative — "humanity's relationship to God, humanity's separation from God, the reconciliation of one with the other by means of the death and resurrection of God's Son, and His eventual return and the establishment of his Kingdom on earth" — is deeply embedded in Dylan's worldview, as Francis Beckwith (146, 147) notes because, as Dylan himself told Bill Flanagan in an interview, a biblical thread "runs through all U.S. life, whether people know it or not." The Bible is "the founding book" of the Founding Fathers, and "You can't get away from it wherever you go" (Gray, *Song*: 561). The holiday Dylan always celebrated was Christmas.[15]

There is also a lot of Christianity in American music, including folk, gospel, country, and rock-'n'-roll — more Christianity, certainly, than orthodox Judaism. John Herdman points out that what Dylan absorbed from his early musical and literary influences from Little Richard to Woody Guthrie to John Steinbeck was an ethic of social conscience "steeped in Christian mythology of a fundamentalist cast" which is at once both radical and conservative (84). The Christianity Dylan experienced at Hibbing High School (less radical, to be sure) was reinforced by the Sunday gospel shows he attended every week in New York City and by the music of the folk revival: hymns like "Amazing Grace," "Will the Circle Be Unbroken," "How Great Thou Art," "This Train," (especially relevant to "Slow Train Coming"), "I Shall Not Be Moved," and "I Saw the

Light," a song specifically mentioned by Dylan in 1997 (Gates: 64) as a musical source of his religion. American folk music is full of black hymns like "Wade in the Water," "Them Bones," and "Swing Low, Sweet Chariot." Religious songs even made the pop charts. Hank Williams sang and wrote religious songs, like "I Saw the Light." Elvis Presley and Johnny Cash sang religious songs.[16] Aretha Franklin sang religious songs. Joan Baez sang religious songs. Willie Nelson sang religious songs. Dylan sang "Gospel Plow" on his first album. Even in his Dinkytown days, Clinton Heylin reports, Dylan was adapting spirituals like "Every Time I feel the Spirit" (*Revolution*: 30). And while "Dylan's apocalyptic visions . . . represent a strain rarely found in Guthrie or in the Anglo-American tradition" (Beebee: 22), the folk music tradition was a repository of hope beyond apocalypse, a crucial notion in Dylan's thinking.

Suggestions of an austere strain of Christianity amenable to a hard version of the jeremiad can be found as early in Dylan's own songs as "Long Ago, Far Away" (1962) and "House Carpenter," "Child Ballad 243," a song he recorded in March 1962 for his second album, in which a mother who runs off with a demon lover is told, "Those are the hills of heaven, that we will never know," and "those are the hills of hell fire where you and I shall unite." "The imagery on [*The Times They Are A-Changin'*] goes back to the grand myth, Christianity," observes Jon Landau (McGregor: 252). The first line of "Quinn the Eskimo" probably references Noah. But these songs are not just incidental allusions and appropriate uses of Christian imagery. Some are sermons calling for repentance: "You're gonna hear out a voice say, 'Shoulda listened when you heard the word down there'" ("I'd Hate to Be You on That Dreadful Day," 1964). Some are sermons on the death of Christ:

> Ev'ry day, ev'ry night, see the sign on the cross just layin' up on top of the hill. Yes, we thought it might have disappeared long ago, but I'm here to tell you, friends, that I'm afraid it's lying there still. Yes, just a little time is all you need, you might say, but I don't know 'bout that any more, because the bird [sic] is here and you might want to enter it, but, of course, the door might be closed. I just would like to tell you one time, if I don't see you again, that the thing is, that the sign on the cross is the thing you might need the most. ("Sign on the Cross," 1971)

The tropes which Dylan most often played — prophet, pastoral, social critic — all came with a Christian flavoring, and as John Herdman notes (105), Dylan had a habit of identifying himself with Christ from early in his career: "I said, 'You know they refused Jesus, too' / He said, 'You're not Him'" ("Bob Dylan's 115th Dream"), "She . . . took my crown of thorns" and "they gambled for my clothes" ("Shelter from the Storm"). Michael Gray sees Dylan as offering parallel after parallel between himself and Christ: "In retrospect, it is as if Dylan eventually converts to Christianity because of the way he has identified with Christ and understood his struggles through his own" (*Song*: 210, 211).

Still, nothing in earlier Dylan had prepared his fans for what was to come. By April of 1979, a few short months after his baptism, Dylan had the songs of *Slow Train Coming* ready; he recorded the album in May and in November 1979 began a promotional tour in which he sang only Christian songs. After *Saved* was released in June 1980 — with a quote from Jeremiah on the album sleeve: "Behold, the days come, saith the Lord, that I will make a new covenant with the house of Israel, and with the house of Judah" — Dylan began a similar tour. These tours sounded like the Sunday gospel shows Dylan had attended in New York City, and mixed music with personal testimony beyond the songs themselves. John Bauldie's *Wanted Man* reprints several of these "extraordinary Bob Dylan sermons from these shows" (130–4):

> How many people are aware that we're living in the end times right now? How many people are aware of that? Anybody wanna know? Anybody interested to know that we're living in the end times? How many people do know that? Well we are. We're living in the end times. That's right.

In March 1981 Dylan began writing the songs on *Shot of Love*, and in June he began a tour on which he included some older non-evangelical songs. The album appeared in August 1982. November 1983 brought *Infidels*; June 1985 brought *Empire Burlesque*. "Blind Willie McTell," one of the masterpieces of this period and of Dylan's career, circulated as a bootleg. The prophet was busy 24-7.

The first song of *Slow Train Coming* lays everything out in black and white: "it may be the devil or it may be the Lord / But you're gonna have to serve somebody." Take your choice. Dancer, gambler, ambassador or heavyweight champion of the world, you have to serve somebody. Rock star, business man, doctor or thief, you have to serve somebody. Construction worker, landlord, preacher, city councilman, barber, you have to serve somebody. Who's that somebody gonna be? Where are you gonna stand — with the good guys or the bad guys, serving the Lord or serving Satan? This song is exactly the opposite of "Dear Landlord," with its "if you won't underestimate me, / I won't underestimate you." It is vaguely self-righteous, in that we know that rock star Dylan sees himself as serving the Lord, but Dylan does not assert himself, and the humor of the next-to-last stanza — a parody of Bill Saluga's comic routine[17] and an admission, finally, that "I am Zimmerman" — moderates a very stern lecture.

This sermon is followed on the album by "I Believe in You," a declaration of faith which again dichotomizes into I and They: "They don't want me around / 'Cause I believe in you." Dylan identifies himself with the outlawed prophet (and with Christ), but this song too is buffered by admissions of vulnerability in requests that the Lord keep Dylan from drifting, changing his heart, rejoining the crowd. The line "a thousand miles from home" takes us back mentally to "Song to Woody," and reviews in a second the remarkable journey of Dylan's long career since that song, with its various loves, schemes, journeys, and plans. What an incredible trip life is! What a moving song "I Believe in You" really is!

Dichotomies continue, and jeremiads. In "Precious Angel" Dylan sings, "Ya either got faith or ya got unbelief and there ain't no neutral ground." The darkness is coming; it will fall from on high; men will beg God to kill them; hope that your forefathers, who lived and died under the Law, have found mercy in their bone-filled graves. The song is good theology, and a harsh sermon. So is "Gonna Change My Way of Thinking": "He said, 'He who is not for Me is against Me' / Just so you know where He's coming from." "When You Gonna Wake Up?" seems particularly judgmental: you had better start thinking about what God wants, because He didn't put you here just to satisfy your own whimsical desires. In the liner notes to *The Bootleg Series Volumes 1–3*, John Bauldie described "Foot of Pride" as "an extraordinary series of images" followed by "condemnation of those false prophets who misuse religion and faith, abuse trust, hoodwink the gullible, all in the pursuit of earthly riches." He concludes,

> Dylan never painted as convincing a picture of the fallen world, of a 20th century Babylon, as he does in this song; neither has be been so overtly wrathful in his abhorrence of the corrupters and the corrupted, nor as confident that eternal judgment is to be meted out at last beyond this world, and that for the wicked, the dividers of the word of truth, vengeance will be terrible, swift and sure. (60)

Then there's "Trouble in Mind": "The truth is far from you, so you know you got to lie." And "Dead Man, Dead Man": "Satan got you by the heel, there's a bird's nest in your hair." And "When He Returns": "How long can you falsify and deny what is real? / How long can you hate yourself for the weakness you conceal?"). And "Are You Ready":

> Are you ready to meet Jesus?
> Are you where you ought to be?
> Will He know you when He sees you,
> Or will he say, 'Depart from me?' . . .

When destruction cometh swiftly
And there's no time to say fare-thee-well
Have you decided whether you want to be
In heaven or in hell? . . .
Are you ready for the judgment?"

In Tempe, Arizona, in 1979, Dylan told his audience, "there's only two kinds of people: there's saved people and there's lost people."

While "Gotta Serve Somebody" gave Dylan his first top-30 single in six years, college students and critics alike attacked the songs and the sermons with more vehemence than they had unleashed on *New Morning* and *Self Portrait*. The media were especially hostile, painting audience reaction at concerts as worse than it really was, as they had done in the U.K. tour of 1965 (Heylin, *Shades*: 332). Craig Scobie accused Dylan of "poor writing," because he had mortgaged songs to the "constraints of a religious orthodoxy with a strongly formative rhetorical code" (169), namely the Bible and biblical commentators and preachers, but other factors were at play. One is that, compared to many older songs when Dylan was also complaining about the general fucked-uppedness of America and the world, he here implies that *you* might be the cause. It's no longer "*they* stone you when you're trying' to be so good"; it's not Maggie's Ma, or Pa, or Maggie herself; it's not "look out, kid, *they* keep it all hid"; it's not Isis, or Sara, or a partner or a landlord . . . suddenly it's *you* doin' it. One way of interpreting "Blind Willie McTell," as somebody has pointed out, is that man sits on the sidelines (or in the St. James Hotel), looking out the window, and there's nothing he can do about power and greed and corruptible seed; *another* way of looking at that song is that man condemns his own land in choosing the fairgrounds over the fields, opting to be a plantation owner, strutting her feathers like a gypsy maiden, dressing up like a squire, and turning away from the truth-tellers and the prophets like blues singer Blind Willie McTell. Strong accusations like these make a person uncomfortable. Of course if you saw yourself as one of the friends who was forsaking Dylan, or one of the "so-called friends [who] have fallen under a spell" in "Precious Angel," or one of the influencing "fools" of "Gonna Change My Way of Thinking," or one of the disgusting earthly companions of "Slow Train" . . . in that case, you were probably not happy with Dylan the Prophet and his message. Dylan, as always, was ahead of his time. In American culture today we get a very twisted view of human failures: they can be the fault of external conditions (sociological determinism), they can be the fault of a bad self-image (psychological determinism), or they can be the fault of bad genes (biological determinism), but rarely in our schools do we teach that success is the result of hard work and problems are the inevitable result of our own bad choices. We teach a kind of secular version of deterministic divine providence in the Calvinist or Augustinian sense, but we downplay the role of free will and free choice, and subsequent judgment. The results we see daily in schools, business, government, courts, and the media: "Who can I blame? There must be somebody I can blame."

Joel Slevin's "Bob Dylan's God-Awful Gospel!" in the *San Francisco Chronicle* closed with the accusation that Dylan was "no longer asking hard questions" and had opted "for the soothing soporific which the simple 'truths' of his brand of Christianity provides" (Heylin, *Shades*: 332). Like, when is he gonna wake up? Dylan was doing exactly the opposite.

One of the best of these lyrics is in fact "When You Gonna Wake Up?" which will stand as an American jeremiad with "Stuck Inside of Mobile" and "Desolation Row." Counterfeit philosophers have indeed polluted thinking and teaching; the jails are indeed filled to overflowing; the rich do feed on the poor, old men and women daily embarrass themselves by trying to dress and act like teenagers (have you caught Hugh Hefner in *The Girls Next Door*?); gangsters run the political system (as I write, it's the governor of Illinois; before that, it was the senator from Alaska; before that . . .); television is full of new age gurus guiding the populace to soft, new age spiritualism. Or listen to "Slow Train": "All that foreign oil controlling American soil" — did you see *Fahrenheit 9–11*?

Or listen to "Man of Peace" and think of the Bush's pretext for invading Iraq: "I hear that sometimes Satan comes as a man of peace." Listen to "Union Sundown" and then walk into a Wal-mart. Listen to "The Groom's Still Waiting at the Altar," with its cities on fire and fighting on the border. "Caribbean Wind," with its apocalyptic fury and "distant ships of liberty . . . bringing everything that's near to me nearer to the fire." These songs, worthy of Jonathan Winthrop, were exactly what America needed to hear. What made listeners uncomfortable was their own complicity; what made leftists uncomfortable was Dylan's suggestion that each individual is not a law unto himself ("Trouble in Mind"); what troubled them all was the suggestion that God, not man, is in control. And Dylan's overt Christian testimony. That above all else. American liberals seem to think that all Christians are Ronald Reagan/George Bush neocons. They forget that Martin Luther was a monk and Martin Luther King, Jr., was a Christian minister. They have trouble seeing Christ as a man of the people (as per Guthrie's song "Jesus Christ"), or seeing Christian social ministry as a progressive force.

Dylan tempers his sermon in the songs of *Saved*, focusing more on grace and gratitude than on judgment and wrath, and admitting in songs like "Solid

Rock" to some doubt and uncertainty. "I'm hangin' on," he sings in the album's strongest song, but barely — a bit desperately. "I am ready, hope I'm ready," he sings in "Are You Ready?" Although this song warns in no uncertain terms of Armageddon, judgment, and a terrible swift sword, the word "hope" is a significant qualifier — Dylan is not 100 percent sure of himself. The lyrics of *Shot of Love* show a retreat from Evangelical Christianity as well, including the title song, which is anything but pious or smug, and shows Dylan, for just an instant, considering a prudent, not-so-Christian, pre-emptive strike on an approaching enemy

As the 1980s unwound, Dylan would mute — although not lose — the specifically Christian element in his songs; he would also backburner the on-stage sermons, and he would change his concert play list. "License to Kill," on *Infidels*, retains the jeremiad's view of fallen America, the country which rules the earth and landed on the moon and thinks it can do whatever it pleases, but avoids specifically Christian content. The abstract and infinitely less threatening "they" are again to blame: "*they* take him and they teach him and *they* groom him for life / And *they* set him on a path where he's bound to get ill" ("License to Kill"). "*They* made a killer out of him" ("Clean-Cut Kid"). It's (once again) the fault of the System, which tells you that what's up is down, what isn't is, turns your head inside out, and then wonders why you're a "disgruntled employee." Dylan had been here before, with "twenty years of schoolin' and they put you on the day shift." And he will be here again in "Sweetheart Like You": "Steal a little and they throw you in jail / Steal a lot and they make you king."

Oh Mercy (1989) is full of committed testimony and social critique, but these jeremiads lack righteous anger. Dylan's Christianity is obvious in references to the Good Shepherd and the Sermon on the Mount, but it's the Christianity of self-examination and humble service, not angry judgment. Songs like "Political World" are abstract enough to make us wish for the days of topical protest songs, and "Ring Them Bells" obscures distinctions between cities and valleys, heathens and believers, right and wrong, as if Dylan is too tired to draw distinctions. Everybody suffers from the "Disease of Conceit"; everybody is out looking (in vain) for "Dignity." Everything and everyone is broken, including the very open-ended "broken words never meant to be spoken." Some songs toward the end of this album suggest self-doubt, reassessment, or exhaustion. "Most of the Time" his head is on straight, but how about the rest of the time? Asking "What Good Am I?" if I'm disengaged like all the rest implies that you've been disengaged like the rest. In these songs, as in "Trust Yourself," Dylan replicates his sixties retreat from crusades: you're on your own in this land of wolves and thieves, as you always were; don't be disappointed when others let you down, don't put your hope in others, don't look for answers where there aren't any, don't trust anyone except yourself. Not God, not Bob Dylan — trust yourself.

Self-reliance, the greatest Emersonian virtue, is basically antisocial. Self-reliant people, like Thoreau, are often hermits and happy to be recluses. Elizabeth Brake writes, "Emerson suggests that society threatens selfhood: 'the voices which we hear in solitude . . . grow faint and inaudible as we enter into the world'" (Porter and Vernezze: 84). "I feel nothing for their game," Dylan sings in "Dark Eyes," not even sweet revenge. In the song, Dylan retreats again to his own Walden Pond, with a reference to Thoreau in "I can hear another drum beating for the dead that rise."

Possibly Dylan is a prophet who takes occasional time off to attend to personal matters or just celebrate the Christmas holiday; possibly he's setting an example which the rest of us would do well to follow. In either case, he's often not there. Clinton Heylin identifies at least three lost years in Dylan's career — 1968, 1972, and 1982 (*Shades*: 352). Stephen Scobie identifies two "time outs" (24). One was the early 1970s, of which Mick Farren quipped, "It was clear Bob wasn't going to lead us to the Promised Land. The Prophet had quit" (Blake: 122). A second "period of drift" came in the 1980s, when Dylan's songs seemed elegiac to the point of conceding defeat. Scobie credits Dylan with performance commitment, if not writing commitment, in the 1990s, but in February of 1991, when Dylan sang "Masters of War" while receiving a Lifetime Achievement Award at the Grammy Festival (in the midst of the first Gulf War), the fire was extinguished: his voice was so murky and his delivery so incoherent the song and its message were nearly indecipherable. Scattered lines in songs of the early nineties suggest that Dylan's general view of America had not changed ("They said it was the land of milk and honey / Now they say it's the land of money" in "Unbelievable"; "the world's being slaughtered and it's such a bloody disgrace" in "Cat's in the Well"), but clearly the prophet was ailing.

Time Out of Mind (1997) found Dylan wandering incoherently through the dead streets, plowed under after having lost everything and a little bit more, his sense of humanity "gone down the drain," content to try to relive his dreams in the isolation of his mind. "My ship's been split to splinters and it's sinking fast," he sang in "Mississippi," a song released on *Love and Theft* but written in 1997. The songs of *Time Out of Mind* are haunting, compelling, filled with ideas, but the prophet is on a coffee break, nursing his age and unrequited loves. The sign on the window reads "Nobody Home." Come back again next album, next millennium. I might have something for you then.

And Dylan did come back, from the grave as it were, to repeat the past, including on *Love and Theft* (2001) some low-key sermons against politicians who have been sucking the blood out of genius ("Summer Days"), a warning against the rising waters of relativism and social injustice ("High Water [for Charley Patton]"), and a call for Americans to look up and seek the Maker before Gabriel blows his horn. Somewhere between the 1985 edition of Dylan's printed lyrics and the 2001 edition, the words to "If You See Her, Say Hello" changed remarkably, from "She still lives inside of me, we've never been apart" to "I got to find someone to take her place," from "If she's passing back this way, I'm not that hard to find" to "If She's passing back this way, and I sure hope she don't / Tell her she can look me up. I'll either be here or I won't." The prophet is no longer tangled up in blue memory. With *Modern Times* (2006), Dylan seemed fully awake, as befits a true prophet in the reign of George Bush, and ready to overturn some tables, disconnect a lot of cables. "Feel like my soul is beginning to expand," he sings on the album's first cut. Awakened by the ruckus in the alley, he's ready to forget himself, see what other people need. This mission includes testimony, but it also includes raising an army and raising hell. "Shame on your greed," shouts preacher Dylan; "shame on your wicked schemes," offering no apologies for being less than an angel, because he's already confessed and sees no need to confess again. In "Workingman's Blues #2," confronting the alternatives of hanging back or fighting on the front line, he opts for fighting, as we've mentioned. "Some people still sleepin'," he warns in "The Levee's Gonna Break," but "some people are wide awake." The sixties are back.

On October 25, 2005, Robert Bly sat down to dinner and conversation after a reading he had given at the college where I teach. Bly, like Henry Thoreau and Bob Dylan, has written a lot about nature, but also like Bob Dylan he qualifies as a Midwest prophet. Bly and Dylan spent some time together in Moscow in July 1985 at the Twelfth World's Festival of Youth and Students, and Bly had a few things to say about that event and how he saw Dylan and himself as pretty much on the same page. At his reading, Bly had expressed bewilderment at the passivity of the present generation of American college students, and at supper the poet-prophet, approaching his eightieth birthday, wondered aloud about the rest of us. "Why is nobody saying anything?" he asked. "Why are the old ones saying nothing? What have we got to lose?"

That seems to be the question Dylan raises in his own life and some of his recent songs. "Why are the old ones silent? What have they got to lose?" This is not quite the anger and sense of mission of the young Bob Dylan, or even what we got in the 1980s Dylan, but it is a commitment. It is also a legitimate response to the System's arrogant tyrannies, the very response suggested by Henry Thoreau when he wrote, "Let your life be a counterfriction to stop the machine." If you can't engage, follow that other road suggested by many sixties activists: step outside the game and freak the whole thing out. Quit buying and start stealing (these days it's called "dumpster diving"). Stop working — or at least stop consuming — and start playing. Fold, spindle, and mutilate. Do it in the road. You can do this, even when you're a full professor of English, even when you're a famous American poet, even when you're Bob Dylan. What have you got to lose? In this sense Dylan remains true like ice, like fire. He fulfills in the twenty-first century the commitment he made way back in 1963 to "tell it and think it and speak it and breathe it, / And reflect it from the mountain so all souls can see it, / And . . . stand on the mountain until I start sinkin', / And . . . know [his] song well before [he] starts singin.'"

Because it's a hard, it's a hard, it's a hard, it's a hard, it's a hard rain's begun to fall.

"Ain't Talkin'":
A Postscript

I n April of 2009, Bob Dylan released *Together Through Life*, a collection of love songs and anti-love songs that continues to move Dylan in a direction apparent in earlier twenty-first century albums, and one compatible with or influenced by his Theme Time Radio Hour show, namely urban blues, swing, and Tin Pan Alley pop of the pre-Cold War period. It is as if Dylan has returned to his youth, when Guy Lombardo toured the eastern Midwest, and swing bands played nightly on the stage in the 600-seat dining room of the Oaks Night Club in Minnesota City, and Lawrence Welk roamed the western Midwest from North Dakota to Yankton, South Dakota (playing, a local old-timer swears, at least one barn dance in southwestern Minnesota). The collection as a whole is focused and honest, and in the U.K., *Together Through Life* helped Dylan set a record for longest time between two #1 albums. Ardent Dylan supporters swore the album belongs in the Dylan Top Ten; sympathetic reviewers used trowels and brushes to excavate existential and apocalyptic significances from lines like "I love you pretty baby, you're the only love I've ever known" and "life is hard without you near me." The reaction of the general public seems to have been, "It's a good beat and you can dance to it. I give it an 89." The album's final song, "It's All Good," is a typical Dylan jeremiad with more irony than anger, closer to "Summer Days" than "A Hard Rain's A-Gonna Fall." Dark words undercut a bright tune and refrain: lying politicians, cheating women, crying widows, bleeding orphans, cold-blooded killers on the loose, crumbling neighborhoods, and the old amorphous "they" who tear you down brick by brick. Dylan's point seems pretty clear to me, although many listeners apparently missed the sarcasm, and lost the message in the squishy cliché (put in the mouth of "them") that Dylan uses as a refrain line: "all good, it's all good." This is the very "It's all good" that Del Bressen's father-in-law mumbles in departing a Wood Lake, Minnesota, family gathering in the spring of 2009, dismissing an evening's worth of troubling thoughts. "All is well," Dylan's so-called friends had told him in "Precious Angel"; now "It's all good." Right — let's all come together now to accentuate the positive, eliminate the negative.

But even with that powerful last song, the love laments of *Together Through Life* cannot compete with the "apocalyptic visions" Joe Levy found in *Modern Times* in his *Rolling Stone* review of 2006. *Modern Times* was a milestone Dylan album — maybe not a great album, but possibly Dylan's last major work. The year before *Together Through Life*, Dylan had released volume 8 in the Bootleg Series, *Tell Tale Signs*, filled with dynamite if dated material; the year before that he had released yet another (unnecessary) greatest hits collection; and the year before that — 2006 — he had released *Modern Times*, which won him a Grammy Award, gave him his first Billboard #1 album since 1976, and sold over ten million copies. For nearly four years, then, *Modern Times* stood as Dylan's most current collection of all-new material . . . and since all songs but one on *Together Through Life* were co-written with Robert Hunter, *Modern Times* still stands as Dylan's most recent solo statement. The album is more profoundly religious than any album since the Christian albums, philosophically complex, musically rich, and as dark as anything Dylan had ever produced, including *Time Out of Mind*. Its final song — "Ain't Talkin'" — is a penetrating analysis of America today, its significance underscored by repeated performance on tour. It's a State of the Union speech, not really a jeremiad. Although women lurk mysteriously in the lyrics, this is no love song, no "I love you pretty baby, you're the only love I've ever known." "Ain't Talkin'" is a masterpiece which rewards detailed examination and makes a good recapitulation of this book's themes.

Dylan has given us two significantly different versions of "Ain't Talkin'," one on *Tell Tale Signs* and another on *Modern Times*, which head in directions not always congruent, especially in what they have to say about women. But both versions open and close with the "mystic garden" which is central to our understanding of Dylan's song. The singer is walking through the garden when the song begins, on his way to somewhere either in the garden or beyond the garden. But Dylan also says that he has been walking through cities of the plague, and in the *Tell Tale Signs* version he needs to see a doctor "in this town." So perhaps the walking takes place outside of the garden, through the "weary world of woe." In this case, the garden is both a *terminus a quo* and a *terminus ad quem* for the song's journey, a kind of Garden of Eden to counterbalance the corrupt cities. Dylan plays both the Pilgrimage of Life and the Garden of Eden motifs here. In the middle of the garden sits a cool, crystal fountain borrowed from "Wild Mountain Thyme," an Irish ballad Dylan was performing as early as May 1961, when it was recorded on the Minneapolis Party Tape, along with "Bonnie, Why'd You Cut My Hair?" That song is Old-World pastoralism the likes of which Midwesterners long ago outgrew: in early summer when the trees are just leafing out, a lad invites a lassie to join him in gathering the wild mountain thyme and the purple heather. He promises to build a tower "by yon clear crystal fountain" upon which he will pile all the flowers of the mountain, just for the girl he loves. And if she won't come with him, by golly, some other lassie surely will. Despite the phallic tower (absent from Dylan's song), the female fountain gives Dylan's mystic garden an Edenic quality, which is reinforced in Dylan's song by the melody: simple in the extreme (his vocal range is not what it once was) and suggesting the ancient pentatonic scale. Moreover, this garden comes *sans* technology, which makes it even more Romantic: the speaker is walking, not riding a motorcycle or a hopped-up Mustang Ford. In the last stanza of the *Modern Times* version, this pastoralism is reinforced by overtones of Christ's post-resurrection appearance to Mary in the garden (John 20), when Mary mistakes Jesus for the gardener and inquires after her risen Lord.[1]

On the other hand, the garden is where the speaker got hit from behind, and this Eden is as full of overripe decay as Dylan's ancient, rheumy voice and the song's hypnotic tune (in G♯ minor on *Modern Times*, in B♭ minor in *Tell Tale Signs*). In spite of the fountain in both versions, and the presence of a "Queen of Love" in the *Tell Tale Signs* version, the blistering summer sun has left flowers wounded on their vines. The mules are sick, the horse is blind in the *Modern Times* version. The wrecked garden suggests a wrecked world, and the wounded flowers are one with the wrecked singer, all worn down by weeping. The gardener mentioned in the *Modern Times* version, who might heal both the garden and the singer, is absent, and in his place are one very high maintenance lady and at least one assailant who creeps up behind and strikes when you're not looking. And, of course, one rural curmudgeon-narrator and his band of loyal companions. Let's call him the 2006 archetypal Appalachian hillbilly.

The mule and horse suggest a type long gone, something out of nineteenth century America, and the walking cane — along with the line "one extra hour" — suggests an older 2006 archetypal American hillbilly. He is more a latter-day Matt Helstrom or some character out of *Deliverance* than the Wandering Jew some critics have made him out to be. His nature is defined in part by Dylan's borrowings from old folk songs, which are a mixed lot indeed. "This weary world of woe" comes from the anonymous ballad "Poor Wayfaring Stranger," first published in Anania Davisson's *Kentucky Highway* (1816), and recorded by a host of modern singers including Emmy Lou Harris, Burl Ives, Dolly Parton, and Joan Baez on *David's Album*. The song is melancholy narrative of the Christian journey through a world of woe toward a bright land without toil or danger. While this particular allusion reinforces the biblical overtones of the mystic garden, other lines do not. The line "eatin' hog-eyed grease in hog-eyed town" is an obscene reference to "Hog-Eye Man" ("hog-eye" meant "vagina"), a song of the Civil War era about a Negro backdoor man (or a roustabout) who hangs around the steamboat wharves looking for handouts and sex on the side, which he is remarkably successful in finding. "Walkin' with a toothache in my heel" is borrowed from an Ozark Mountains version of the nineteenth century song "Old Dan Tucker," popularized in 1843 by the blackface troupe Virginia Minstrels. The song is innocent enough, and the line was familiar to most American kids in the 1950s, although both my sister and I remember it as having melded, at least around Buffalo, New York, with the jump-rope song "Not Last Night but the Night Before" into something a little less innocent:

> Not last night, but the night before
> Three little niggers were at my door.
> I went down to let them in,
> And what do you think they began to sing?
>
> "My old man was the funniest man.
> He washed his face in a frying pan,
> Combed his hair with a wagon wheel,
> And died with a toothache in his heel."

If this is the version of "Old Dan Tucker" to which Dylan alludes, his Appalachian hillbilly becomes a funny old man who is also a racist. The line "hand me down my walking cane" appears in some versions of "Hog-Eye Man," but it also titles a song about a wayward son, drunk and just out of jail, contemplating his final journey into eternity and judgment. It has both obscene and religious connotations. Dylan's refrain lines, "Ain't talkin', just walkin' . . . Heart burnin', still yearnin'" come from a not particularly obscene bluegrass song, "Highway Of Regret," the lament of a jilted lover for a girl now departed. Dylan's solitary wanderer is of a very mixed lineage.

He is also a curious mix of innocence and experience. He was once a good man, who tried — or so he says — to love his neighbor and do good unto others. Even now, though worn out from tears of contrition (or commiseration), he is "still yearning" for grace, and hopeful of healing prayer from "the mother."

That's one side of the story. The other side is that being a good Christian is not easy for an Average Joe in this fallen world, and of late things "ain't goin' well." In fact, this guy has fallen off the Christian wagon after being mugged from behind physically, or perhaps metaphorically by the wealth and power which attack him later in the *Modern Times* version. He does not seem cursed, like the biblical Cain or the Wandering Jew; he did not "kill a man back there," as did the man cast out from paradise in "Spirit on the Water," also on *Modern Times*. But there does seem to be some "evil spirit" dwelling in his soul; he is one of those rebel outlaws we have seen in one Dylan song after another. In the *Tell Tale Signs* version of this song, the man is a low-level convict, beginning to crack after years of "public service" for crimes unspecified ("public service" is a common sentence in the States these days, at least in Minnesota — criminals "Sentenced to Serve" save the state incarceration expenses and the cost of hiring workers by paying their debt to society by cleaning up trash in roadside ditches or painting the county museum). Perhaps because he's just old and crotchety, perhaps because he's justifiably bitter, this walker lacks the good-natured glad-handedness of outlaws like Gamblin' Willie, John Wesley Harding, and the Jack of Hearts. He seems dark, perhaps demented, and dangerous — almost a Montana Freeman. Whatever he says about prayers from the mother, he has abandoned New Testament charity and prayer, and even the Old Testament altars where Cain offered a sacrifice to the Lord. Some listeners have found this song further evidence of a transition, begun in "Caribbean Wind," to "a more Old Testament understanding of divine judgment, unleavened by the Christian idea of divine forgiveness" (Day, "Dylan's Judgment": 91), but this world seems pre-Hebraic, almost Anglo-Saxon.

So this man goes about his business — Caliban set loose in the garden of Dylan's *Tempest*. While giving the appearance of an average stranger minding his own business as he wanders through town, he is secretly bent on revenge. Dylan repeats the idea in four separate lines: "I'll burn that bridge before you can cross," "There'll be no mercy for you once you've lost," "I'll just slaughter them where they lie," and "I'll revenge my father's death before I die." We are in Smithville, or, as one critic suggested, a Raymond Chandler novel. Or a biker bar outside of Hibbing. Like the curmudgeons found in such places, this guy seems to direct his imagined revenge indiscriminately: his target is certainly whoever or whatever it was that whacked him from behind, but it's also vaguer "opponents" in one line, and "you" — including, I suppose, us listeners — in another.

This character is not as fanciful as we might want to think. We have seen plenty of them in Minnesota, and they did not all disappear with Charlie

Starkweather and Matt Helstrom. Several of Howard Mohr's characters in *How to Talk Minnesotan* are close to, if not already over, the edge. Like "Bob," of Deadwood Falls (read Redwood Falls), who started out blowing up tree stumps with dynamite, then moved on to restoring a B-17 he bought down in Arizona. In 1963 he opened Bob's B-17 Park. "If Bob's in a good mood — it's hard to tell one mood from the other with him — he'll let you sit in the top gun turret and push the pedals and rotate the bubble and take aim," writes Mohr.

> He'll even talk to you from the cockpit. "Bogey at two o'clock," he'll tell you over the intercom. . . . And the only thing that worries me is that one of these days he may put a runway in front of that B-17 with the Cat, fire up all four engines, and take off for parts unknown without so much as a good-bye. But that's Bob for you. (148)

We get the picture.

Then there was James Jenkins and his 18-year-old son Steven Jenkins. Having lost their farm to the Ruthton (Minnesota) Bank in a foreclosure in 1980, the pair returned to Ruthton in 1983, posing as perspective buyers, lured bankers Rudy Blythe and Deems Thulin out to the farm site, and blew them both away with a rifle. An off-duty sheriff's deputy was on the scene within minutes, and another deputy spotted them near the town of Luverne, but in the fog and dirt roads of rural Minnesota, they eluded a police dragnet and made their way south to Texas, where the father ended up dead (a "suicide" his son claimed), and Steven was finally arrested, returned to Minnesota, tried, convicted, sentenced. The story was famous enough to reach Illinois poet Dave Etter, who used it as the basis of his poem "Failing." The case created quite a stir throughout the region, both when it happened and throughout the trial (see Joseph Amato, *When Father and Son Conspire*). If Bob Dylan heard this story — and it's hard to imagine he did not, hanging out on his Minnesota farm in the 1980s — it might be one source of the character on this song, and of the idea of slaughtering opponents where they lie.[2]

In the course of the long trial, Steve Jenkins became something of a hero to poor Minnesota farm kids, especially the young girls, who saw in him a kind of tough-guy heartthrob-hero. The Jenkins duo and Dylan's hillbilly claim a degree of empathy, if not legitimacy, from the world around them, a world of wealth and power which preaches prayer while whacking you on the back of the head, tells you to sing while you slave and then fines you every time you slam the door. In this song, the gross injustices of this weary world of woe make a mockery of Christian charity. Prayer, tears, loving your neighbor, and doing good unto others do not work, Dylan tells us. Withdrawal into contemplation?

The world tears your mind from contemplation with "speculation," and jumps on you when you're down. "Speculation" is a well-chosen word, suggesting the unearned rewards of grain elevator owners and mining company executives, the Le Sueur "plunderers, desecrators, gamblers, burglars, speculators, human weevils, hoarders, thieves, world eaters" on the commodities exchange, or, to seize on more current examples which come immediately to mind, the Ponzi schemers and the CEOs who collected millions for wrecking the American banking system. "Speculation" is a rich man's pastime; speculation is what goes on in the cities of the plague, although in this song the countryside is also ruined pastoral which affords no restoration, only the protection of its amplitudes.

So far the song, powerful as it is, sounds vaguely familiar. America is overwhelmed with corruption spreading from city to countryside; the suffering is unending; the overdue bill on a long history of injustice and class exploitation portends some imminent, well-deserved apocalypse. People say the world is round, Dylan reminds us in this song, implying with Meridel Le Sueur that "your shit is going to fall on your own head." It's an old story that each generation needs to relearn for itself. Dylan's many borrowings from and echoes of earlier songs and writers enhance the story's timelessness. And the relentless walking, heightened by Dylan's weary but determined voice and the song's cadences and accompaniment, smack of that "compulsive walking" Michael Gray mentioned in connection with journeys of lost hope and abandonment.

At the end of Chapter 5, we noted a dark justice-as-revenge creeping into turn-of-the-millennium Dylan songs, which we took as a return to early sixties songs like "When the Ship Comes In." Usually, in Dylan judgment and retribution come from either nature, in the form of a hard rain about to fall or a river about to rise, or from God, in the form of a Judgment Day that you'd better prepare yourself for. Justice is built into the system: God or nature test every aspect of your human nature, then pay you tit for tat . . . and in recompense, "You won't get anything you don't deserve" ("Born in Time"). In "Ain't Talkin'," however, the judgment — and the payback — will be delivered by humans of dubious character, namely the speaker and his band of loyal companions. A band of companions is highly unusual in post-"When the Ship Comes In" Dylan, who reflects his native state in rejecting organizations of any sort. You don't find Montana Freemen in Minnesota. Rhoda Gilman writes, "The phenomenon of 'organized' militias has been largely absent from Minnesota, but its seedbed can be seen in rampant individualism, in hostility to wilderness preserves, in attacks upon resource conservation, and in the mystique of the hunter. No question in Minnesota politics stirs more fury than gun control" (26). This song gives us John Wesley Harding returned with a gun in every hand

and a band of outlaws, Blind Willie McTell at the head of a vigilante committee sabotaging the internet cables, chainsawing billboards, and "monkeywrenching" everything in the system. Among the posse, I see Matt Helstrom and certain rural curmudgeons out here along the Minnesota River where I live. Enough is enough, they tell you ("The hour has come to do or die," Dylan sings in "Tell Ol' Bill"). Get them before they get you — they started it, anyway. Burn the bridges, slaughter them where they lie. Or as Dylan suggested in "Thunder on the Mountain" (the opening cut on *Modern Times*), retreat to the North Country to live outside of the System and recruit an army of tough sons of bitches from Red Wing and elsewhere.

While the organized militia is new, the idea of retribution takes us back to early Dylan, with Pirate Jenny throwing death sentences at her befuddled abusers, or Dylan standing over the grave of the masters of war to make sure that they're dead. After several periods of disengagement and Christian patience, Dylan began to return to this harsh vengeance in several songs of the early twentieth century: "Cry a While," "Honest with Me," "Floater (Too Much to Ask)." Like the Freeman of "Ain't Talkin'," the union man of "Cry a While" had gone to the church house, walked the extra mile, cried to the Lord, and tried to be meek and mild, but in this song he threatens, "I might need a good lawyer, could be your funeral, my trial, . . . now it's your turn, you can cry awhile." The curmudgeon of "Floater (Too Much to Ask)" threatens to shoot trespassers, warning us all, "I'm not quite as cool or forgiving as I sound." Ordinarily, we call people like this "terrorists," whether they come from outside the country (the Trade Center Towers and Pentagon, 2001), from among our high school students (Columbine, 1999), from the adult American populace (James and Steve Jenkins, or Timothy McVeigh in Oklahoma City, 1995), or from inside the U.S. government (Waco, Texas, 1993). In Dylan's song and world, however, they're not terrorists, because Dylan takes a different perspective. In "Shot of Love" (1981) Dylan had written,

> Why would I want to take your life?
> You've only murdered my father, raped his wife
> Tattooed my babies with a poison pen
> Mocked my God, humiliated my friends

Back then, Dylan would have sought to turn the other cheek; now justifiable homicide — carrying the dead man's shield — is a basis for honor and fame. This is indeed a "faith long abandoned," as Dylan tells us in the *Modern Times* version.

Further, this dark agent of retribution suggests that the rest of us will one day be grateful to him for handling our dirty work or protecting us ("Someday you'll be glad to have me around"), and also that he and his band just might receive "heavenly aid." The Montana Freeman, following some ancient code of fame and honor, becomes an agent of both human and divine justice in his unannounced execution without arraignment or trial. We normally associate the Pilgrimage of Life trope which Dylan uses in his refrain — "walkin' through this weary world of woe" — with the Christian allegory of life as a journey, and thus with Christian justice, but the gardener — Christ — is gone, and with him the gospel of forgiveness, and that kind of heavenly aid. Dylan has discovered a new kind of journey, the journey of revenge. Is this really what Americans seek? Are we really going to be glad to have him around?

In a poem titled "The Quaker Graveyard at Nantucket," which received a lot of air play in the sixties, Robert Lowell analyzes American materialism and militarism reaching back to the Puritan times. Over the course of the poem he works his way back to the medieval Shrine of Our Lady, in Walsingham, England. Readers of the recent historical novel *Her Majesty's Spymaster* might recognize the name: Sir Francis Walsingham, Queen Elizabeth's combination C.I.A.-Special Operations officer, was a tight-lipped, pious Puritan of the highest order. In the statue of St. Mary, Walsingham, Lowell finds

> no comeliness
> At all or charm in that expressionless
> Face with it heavy eyelids. As before,
> This face, for centuries a memory,
> *Non est species, neque decor,*
> Expressionless, expresses God: it goes
> Past castled Sion.

(13)

This Mary, Lowell writes, seems almost pre-Christian. She "knows what God knows, / Not Calvary's cross nor crib at Bethlehem." She is precisely the kind of deity who might lend heavenly aid in Dylan's song. And Lowell concludes his critique of American materialism with a sense of pre-Christian, eye-for-an-eye vengeance similar to that found in Dylan's "Ain't Talkin'": the waves of the Atlantic lumbering in for the kill, and a dark prophecy of a new divine dispensation — "The Lord survives the rainbow of His will."

Our Lady of Walsingham may be relevant to Dylan's song in another way. Dylan's use of the father in both versions of this song ("avenge my father's death and then step back"), and the presence of various forms of the feminine in both versions (especially the Queen of Love in the *Tell Tale Signs* version) open up a whole nother can of worms, namely the eternal war between women and men, the matter of just what masculine and feminine connote, and the direction American culture has taken roughly since the mid-seventies in relation to the father and the mother. Dylan's song suggests not only that "the father" — and what he represents — is dead, but that his death deserves some avenging. The feminine is still alive and present — in the mother from whom prayer is requested, the owner of those loving breasts, the "you" who has to be purged from the speaker's miserable brain (are these all the same person? the same set of values?), and, in the earlier version, in the Queen of Love. So in "Ain't Talkin'," especially the earlier version of the song, Dylan addresses the very current subject of gender issues from a perspective that is bound to be controversial . . . which may be the reason Dylan backed off his earlier version. (But since when has Dylan ducked controversy?)

In the general consciousness, "female" represents healing, soft love, closeness, forgiveness and the social niceties, and mothering bordering on smothering (just add the "s"). This is the kind of woman who might pray for a wayward son, upon whose "loving breast" a fellow might throw himself, as Dylan suggests in the *Tell Tale Signs* version. "Father" represents discipline of the back-of-the-fist or ruler-across-the-knuckles variety, hard love which may seem to be no love, distance bordering on absence (add an "r" and you get "farther"), and . . . well, what does Bill Kloefkorn say, the attraction of going somewhere dark to do something forbidden is damned near irresistible to the average American male. The father in Dylan's earlier song was, among other things, "Father of Night," the "Father of loneliness and pain." Maybe these values are overgeneralizations, maybe they are socially constructed, maybe they have biological or genetic origins, but that's what we think when we think "male" and "female." Most gender studies programs — while identifying males and females biologically — explain the differences in terms of social conditioning. Camille Paglia prefers the biological explanation:

> Maleness at its hormonal extreme is an angry, ruthless density of self, motivated by a principle of "attack". . . . Femaleness at its hormonal extreme is first an acute sensitivity of response, literally thin-skinned (a hormonal effect in women), and secondly a stability, composure, and self-containment, a slowness approaching the sultry. Biologically, the male is impelled toward restless movement; his moral danger is brutishness. Biologically, the female is impelled toward waiting, *expectancy*; her moral danger is stasis. (108)

A lot of recent social theory and practice suggests that the male is an "evil spirit" dwelling deep in the human heart, and encourages us to bury it just as deep as Freud will allow.[3] "Yes," it tells young boys, "get rid of your aggressions. Do kill your father." Perhaps, however, we need some of this hardness and aggression, men and women both. Robert Bly called the more positive side of this male *Iron John*, and wrote a best seller on the suppression of maleness in late twentieth century America and the problems it has created: "The waste and violence of the Vietnam War made men question whether they knew what an adult male really was. If manhood meant Vietnam, did they want any part of it?" So we got what Bly calls the seventies male: "more thoughtful, more gentle. . . . It seemed like a nice arrangement for a while, but we've lived with it long enough now to see that it isn't working out" (2, 3). The old father has been lost, Bly says, and needs to be recovered, especially by young men, who cannot progress beyond adolescence without making contract with this Iron John. In our times, he suggests, many women — various embodiments of the mother, who protest their powerlessness but in fact control everything — block access to Iron John in a deliberate attempt to prevent male growth.[4] Boys need to get these women out of their miserable brains, as Dylan suggests in both versions of his song.

As Bly notes, the general social and intellectual movement in America during the seventies, eighties, and nineties was from hard male to soft male or female-male, from testosterone to estrogen, from aggression to social niceties. This transition was abetted by social programs in what we might call "victimology," designed to identify victims, compensate those victims (or their heirs, or other members of the persecuted group, or even just spokespeople for the group), and "make sure this never happens again." In the case of gender, we are talking about academic feminists and the regulations they imposed on behavior, first in regard to "date rape" and "harassment" (terms which lumped together a wide "continuum" of behaviors, from the despicable to the innocuous, in order to apply penalties appropriate for one extreme to violations on the middle and light end of the continuum), and more recently in "guidelines" intended to discourage "bullying" and encourage a "civil society." Dylan has been involved with more than his fair share of women, and while the rock road tour is not exactly high school or office society, these notions cut close to home. Even in the middle sixties, Dylan was addressing the neo-Victorian sexual repressions evident in this agenda with characters like the hysterical bride of "Tombstone Blues," the twelfth daughter of "Highway 61 Revisited," Ophelia of "Desolation Row" (already an old maid on her twenty-second birthday), the prick-tease Ruthie of "Stuck Inside of Mobile," the ding-dong in the leopard-skin pill-box hat, and "Baby" (Edie Sedgwick?) who makes love like a woman, but breaks like a little girl. A fat lot of good it did: the general trend of the eighties and nineties, Paglia points out, was to privilege values hormonally or sociologically associated with the female, and discourage values associated with maleness wherever they appear. The sexual revolution and free speech were repealed, the discredited doctrine of *in loco parentis* was reasserted, and the old dean of women, dismissed by sixties males and females alike, reappeared in the person of the harassment officer, charged by law with enforcing Victorian codes of decorum and politeness. Daphne Patai says it all in the title of her 1998 book, *Heterophobia: Sexual Harassment and the Future of Feminism*. So does Christina Hoff Sommers in her book, *The War Against Boys* (2000). Of course Paglia, Sommers, and Patai are precisely the women authors who most upset feminists who read only a certain kind of women author, and are most unhappy with Bob Dylan lines from "You're No Good" (the first song on Dylan's first album) to "Hell's my wife's hometown" on Dylan's most recent album: "Can't recall a useful thing you ever did for me" ("Dirge"), "I think women rule the world, and that no man has ever done anything that a woman either hasn't allowed him to do or encouraged him to do" (Cott: 306), "Can you cook and sew, make flowers grow?" ("Is Your Love in Vain?), "This woman so crazy I swear I ain't gonna touch another one for years" ("Rollin' and Tumblin'"), "There ain't no limit to the amount of trouble women bring" ("Sugar Baby"), "I'm gonna wring your neck / When all else fails, I'll make it a matter of self-respect" ("Someday Baby") — brilliant, using an argument against those who invented it. These feminists respond to Paglia and Sommers with — and I am quoting one now — "They're brainwashed," "They're not really women," and "We've got to burn those books." Dylan is just a chauvinist. And they're mean: they sneak up from behind and hit people when they're not looking. They can get you investigated, sued, or fired. Ask Bill Clinton.

Despite the critiques of Bly and Paglia (and others), this antimale view has come to predominate, especially in our schools and courts . . . and in a society overpopulated with lawyers who are happy to prove, for a fee, that organizations and individuals with money have acted threateningly, or hatefully, or negligently in the matter of more and more criminalized behavior. Paul Hodson was about 15 years behind the times and 180 degrees wrong when he wrote in 1989,

> Our culture hands privileges to White heterosexual men — the attention of school teachers, the right to walk the streets noisily at night and the power to define the world. These privileges are created by oppressing Black people, women and gay men. By taking advantage of them, we contribute to and benefit from other people's oppression. (187)

But every action has its reaction, and as Paglia notes, human behavior is human behavior and "no legislation or grievance committee can change these eternal facts" (108). Programs promoting "civil society" (code for Victorian "virtue") have produced mainly outrage over civil financiers who steal billions of dollars and an increasingly "hormonal" (for want of a better word) behavior in both males and females (Paglia may be partially wrong in saying it's all genetic), who rebel against "niceness" and seek the Iron John and Iron Jane inside themselves. On the lighter end, this search for hard maleness produces boys obsessed with smacking the shit out of the baseball and slam-dunking the basketball, and girl volleyball players looking to six-pack (knock out) an opponent or two. On a more troubling level, it produces Fight Club boys blasting gangsta-rap from trucks with glass-pack mufflers, and Girls Gone Wild. The far-end danger to American society is precisely what Dylan suggests in this song: citizens young and old will react to overregulation in one direction by going over the edge in the opposite direction, recovering a code long abandoned, avenging the death of that father side, glorifying the mobster in films and on television, ratcheting up gratuitous violence from Iraq to high schools to American college campuses. The character in "Ain't Talkin'" is in one sense the fifties male returned, in reaction to females like the Queen of Love, who have not accepted the peace treaty Dylan offered in 1975 in "Oh, Sister":

Oh, sister, when I come to lie in your arms
You should not treat me like a stranger.
Our Father would not like the way that you act
And you must realize the danger.

Both versions of "Ain't Talkin'" mention "a gal I left behind," who is still troubling "my miserable brain," perhaps a vision of the female or of America Dylan would like to reclaim. The *Tell Tale Signs* version of the song deletes the "miserable brain" reference while adding a desire to "throw myself upon your loving breast." This version also contains that Queen of Love, who parades across the garden grass on the first day of a grand and glorious autumn. One of the many borrowings/allusions in this song is a reference to Ovid's *The Poems of Exile*,[5] and at first glance, the Queen of Love appears to represent something Ovidian, or some form of salvation through love, if not sex. The fact that this is a pleasant autumn might suggest that Dylan sees himself redeemed in his twilight years by some Queen of Wands, or maybe even a homecoming queen, some feminine principle with a loving breast. But this Queen of Love has no loving breasts. She is far from erotic or, for that matter, nurturing. She comes across as a Dean Quigley from Hibbing High School: distant and impassive in the manner of neo-Victorian feminists who, as Paglia says, would like to purge *eros* right out of American life. "None dare call her anything but 'Madam,'" Dylan notes wryly, and he's not talking about the manager of a whorehouse. "Dare" is the operative word; "No one flirts with her or even makes a pass." (A pass might be construed as sexual harassment.) The Queen of Love is not even, given the song's vaguely religious overtones, a Mary in the Italian Renaissance tradition of comely young Mothers of God breast-feeding baby Jesus in full view of churchgoers. (Paglia, raised Italian-Catholic, often comments on the Protestant dismissal of these sensuous Marys, on Protestantism's general suppression of the body, and on feminists' fetish with abstract words and fear of the physical body.) Dylan's Queen of Love may represent the impassive early medieval Marys, like Our Lady of Walsingham, which seem pre-Christian: fully clothed, they stare inscrutably straight ahead, baby Jesus planted firmly on the lap, looking also inscrutable and timeless. Neither beautiful nor comely, this Mary is not a girl in whom one might get interested, not the kind of feminine whom one would solicit for help with prayer or anything else. She is the feminine sought by one element of late twentieth century American society, and old Puritan Lowell had indeed predicted in the last line of his poem that "the world shall come to Walsingham." The feminine in Dylan's song, like the feminine in Lowell's poem, produces no fun and no faith, no salvation, no grace. There are no altars along the road, perhaps because this Queen of Love is not worth praying to. Dylan's walker directs his energies *against* this Queen, toward revenging — if not recovering — his marginalized father. Maybe the queen is one of those whom the walker looks forward to slaughtering . . . with his band of followers and with heavenly aid.

Dylan's walker is a tough cookie, restless and riled up and anything but civil. Some time ago Jurgen Moltmann wrote that only the oppressed and the restless people in this "land of the free" are interested in renewal, and that "America can expect its renewal from them" (64). These do not have to be men — they can be women like Caril Ann Fugate, Bonnie Parker, or Thelma and Louise. (Or Paglia, Sommers, and the good-looking, hard-hitting, self-confident volleyball players.) They are the characters I discussed at the close of Chapter 5, where I also suggested — echoing Greil Marcus — that Dylan looks to them for whatever hope he sees for America. Perhaps Dylan is right: what he presents in this song is a recognizable and even reasonable response to protracted annoyance and abuse in a time when the apparatus of justice is inaccessible to the common man. Homicides and random murders typically increase in times of social or economic trauma, as they have over the past decades, and I cannot tell you the number of people who, in reference to Bernard Madoff, have said, "Off the record, maybe somebody should just shoot him." Still, the America foreseen in Dylan's "Ain't Talkin'" is a kind of last insane outpost which marks the end of the world, the Do Lung bridge in *Apocalypse Now*. We hope against hope that this song will not chart America's future as "The Levee's Gonna Break" predicted Hurricane Katrina, and "High Water" predicted the attack on the World Trade Center, one day after that song's release in 2001. We hope that Dylan is not that good a prophet.

Or maybe we should hope Dylan will be right again. For all the ominous prophecies in "Ain't Talkin'," we notice that in the last stanza of the *Modern Times* version, the walker is "still yearning" and still walking, headed up the road, around the bend, "clean out of sight." The song ends in pilgrimage, not revenge. And if we listen carefully, we notice that after the dark descriptions, threats, and predictions, there at the very, very, very end of this song, in the subtle, almost-slips-by-you, quiet, final resolution of minor key signature to an affirmative major chord at the end of the performance, there as the music is dying out, the suggestion, just the smallest, slightest suggestion, of hope. "A moonbeam" Alex Ross called it in the *New Yorker*. It is exactly the opposite of the final piano chord which closes *Sgt. Pepper's Lonely Hearts Club Band*, and Dylan's message here is exactly the opposite of what the Beatles told us on that album. That understated promise of grace — so tentative and remote, yet in its way so firm and unambiguous — seems truer to American reality than the more blatant yet possibly ironic "It's All Good," and makes "Ain't Talkin'" the better song.

Endnotes

Notes to Introduction: Bob Dylan and the Midwest

1   Further — not to sound like some North Country academic in a backwoods check shirt — let me suggest that there might be a lot less to postmodernism than meets the eye; perhaps we have been played by commodifiers, textbook hustlers, multinational corporations, and a media-fueled, global lifestyle which, for its own enormous profit, wrecks people, places, local economies and the environment.

2   Interestingly, the original concept behind postmodern *Sgt. Pepper's Lonely Hearts Club Band*, arguably the Beatles' greatest album and — with the possible exception of Dylan's *Blonde on Blonde* — in my opinion rock's greatest album, was a retrospective on the group's early Liverpool days. Liverpool disappeared when "Penny Lane" and "Strawberry Fields" were released as singles, but *Pepper's* retains a retro theme: "It was twenty years ago today Sgt. Pepper taught the band to play. . . ."

3   In a chapter titled "Grass Roots," Wilfred Mellers early on examined Dylan's literary and musical roots, but except to note that the mythology of the Bible "permeates the American Midwest" (112), he ignored the influence of Dylan's true place entirely. Robert Shelton's *No Direction Home* surveys academic work on Dylan through 1986 (228–38), and Elizabeth Thomson and David Gutman provide another overview of scholarship in their introduction and bibliography in *The Dylan Companion* (1990). For a later overview of literary influences and critical interpretations, see Chapter 8 of Michael Gray's *Song & Dance Man III*, titled "Well I Investigated All the Books in the Library." See also Neil Corcoran's *"Do You, Mr Jones?" Bob Dylan with the Poets and Professors*, which contains not a single essay written by an American professor outside of Princeton ("Day of the Locusts") University.

4   Eight years after the publication of *Jokerman*, Aidan Day concluded a paper titled "Dylan's Judgment" by recanting the interpretation of "Jokerman" that he had taken in his book. Instead of viewing the song as "a celebration of a kind of postmodern groundlessness," Day said he has come to view "the consistent anticipation, in various guises, of final catastrophe, social and personal, as the matrix of Dylan's lyrical

imagination" (98), something he had picked up in his youth and figured very early in his career in the description of deserted North Hibbing he gives in "11 Outlined Epitaphs" (99–100).

Notes to Chapter 1: Dylan's Songs of the North Country

1   We all defer to the East. Western South Dakota looks with envious eyes east-river toward Sioux Falls and across the state line; western Minnesota bows to the Twin Cities, just as western Wisconsin bows east to Milwaukee, outstate Illinois to Chicago, the Midwest in general to the East Coast, residents of Buffalo, New York, to the Manhattan crowd. Americans defer to the British, and workers of Manchester to the bankers of London. The flipside of deference, however, is hostility and suspicion. Andy Gill notes that the suspicion of New York expressed in early songs like "Talkin' New York" seems "rather unfair" for someone who was "virtually from the moment of his arrival" the golden boy of the folk scene (13). I would suggest that Dylan's attitude was a legacy of his origins.

2   "I was with the carnival off and on for six years," he told Cynthia Gooding in a 1962 radio interview (Cott: 3); "When I was thirteen, I was traveling with a carnival through upper Minnesota and North and South Dakota, and I got picked up again," he told Nat Hentoff (Cott: 24).

3   The cynical argument that Dylan was selling his protest material receives some support from conversations like that reported in Gill (61): "'Hey, news can sell, right?' he claimed, cynically. 'You know me. I knew people would buy that kind of shit, right?'" An old acquaintance claimed that when Dylan returned to Dinkytown, Minnesota, from New York in December, 1961, he talked cynically "about how he was styling the language into a certain image that he was acting back there in New York, building a character that will sell. Those were the words that he used, 'building a character that would sell'" (Scaduto: 108); Dylan denied having said any such thing. In a fascinating but equally cynical essay in *The Journal of American Culture*, Richard E. Hishmeh suggests that a few years later, multinational corporate entertainment conglomerates were using a "fully integrated and elaborate marketing strategy" (395) to promote the friendship of Bob Dylan and Allen Ginsberg at a time when Dylan had reached artistic stagnation and Ginsberg's most influential work was behind him.

4   Here are three passages on the subject from three of my favorite Midwest writers. All sound like Dylan's "North Country Blues":

> For most people, business is poor. Nearby cities have siphoned off all but a neighborhood trade. Except for feed and grain and farm supplies, you stand a chance to sell only what one runs out to buy. Chevrolet has quit, and Frigidaire. A locker plant has left its afterimage. The lumberyard has been, so far, six months about its going. Gas stations change hands clumsily, a restaurant becomes available, a grocery store closes. . . . Everywhere, in this manner, the past speaks, and it mostly speaks of failure. The empty stores, the old signs and dusty fixtures,

the debris in alleys, the flaking paint and rusty gutters, the heavy locks and sagging boards: they say the same disagreeable things.

— William Gass, "In the Heart of the Heart of the Country," 1968 (189)

Birds fly in the broken windows
of the hotel in Argyle.
Their wings are the cobwebs
of abandoned lead mines.

Across the street at Skelly's
the screen door bangs against the bricks
and the card games last all day.

Another beer truck comes to town,
chased by a dog on three legs.
Batman lies drunk in the weeds.

— Dave Etter, "Two Beers in Argyle, Wisconsin," 1966 (*Selected Poems*: 19)

The mayor of Lake Wobegon, Clint Bunsen, peers out from the grease pit under a black Ford pickup. His brother Clarence, wiping the showroom glass (BUNSEN MOTORS — FORD — NEW & USED — SALES & SERVICE) with an old blue shirt, knocks on the window. The showroom is empty. The boy follows the chunk [of pavement] a few doors north to Ralph's window, which displays the mournful cardboard pig, his body marked with the names of cuts. An old man sits on Ralph's bench, white hair as fine as spun glass poking out under his green feed cap, his grizzled chin on his skinny chest, snoozing, the afternoon sun reaching under the faded brown canvas awning up to his belt.

— Garrison Keillor, *Lake Wobegon Days*, 1985 (2)

5   A couple years ago I interviewed a Minnesota farmer whose family lost its land to a bank foreclosure in the mid-thirties, only to be relocated on the same farm during World War II by the federal government, which had picked up the mortgage after the bank failed. The government needed farmers on the land producing crops for the war effort, and sold him the place for a song.

6   Ten thousand dollars in 1963 was a good year's salary. Harry Bell, my high school baseball coach, told us in the late fifties that "to be really comfortable, a guy supporting a family of four needs to earn $10,000 a year." "That is a ton of money," thought the kid who used to walk the streets picking up discarded Coke bottles for the 2-cent deposit, and on trash days collected discarded newspapers to take to the recycling center; "How can I ever make $10,000 a year?" But my parents' house, which had cost them only $17,000, was in 1963 worth perhaps $24,000. Gasoline was 30 cents a gallon. Burger, fries, and a Coke at the local McDonald's was 45 cents. As I write this, those prices have multiplied by a factor of ten, and a person supporting a family of four probably needs, to be comfortable, $100,000 a year. By the time they reach my age, my students will need to bring home $1,000,000 a year. Each fall I tell my freshmen this story.

7   Both Highway 61 and Route 66 have more currency than U.S. 51, which runs from Ironwood, Wisconsin, and also to New Orleans. Dylan had mentioned Highway 51 on his first album in the song "Highway 51 Blues," one of his less noteworthy compositions: a rewrite of a Curtis Jones original which changes the melody, deletes Curtis's mention of buses, but retains "up Wisconsin way." The original song traced one route taken by southern blacks on their northern migration (thus singer Dylan's request to be buried "out on the Highway 51"), but Dylan's real intent in this song is claiming to know Highway 51 "like I know the back of my hand" . . . and sending a message to whichever gal he was intent on lovin' at the time. But Dylan was not from Wisconsin, and he was not migrating north or south: the song lacks the legitimacy of "Girl of the North Country."

8   An online posting about a decade ago made the lumberjacks, along with other elements of the song, a homosexual reference (possibly their interpretation was influenced by Monty Python's "I'm a Lumberjack"), and the song about the outing of a closet queer, but to my knowledge Fitzgerald has not been accused of being a latent homosexual. Yet.

9   Like so many of us, Dylan sometimes exemplifies the vice he critiques, as in "When the Ship Comes In": "*They*'ll raise their hands." Or "Clean-Cut Kid": "*they* made a killer out of him." Or "It's All Good": "if *they* could *they* would" (my italics). Tor Egil Førland argues that Bob Dylan and Joe McCarthy actually share a Midwest tradition of "representing the little man against the vast, apparently impersonal system hurting ordinary people" (350), although they part company in assigning blame: "McCarthy is the more specific, pointing his finger at communists — real or, more probably, imagined. Dylan is vaguer. His culprits are the somewhat less helpful 'they'" (351).

10 In understanding Dylan's displeasure with what schools taught, it might help to remember that following World War II, the school orthodoxy across America quickly turned pro-German and anti-Russian, while in Dylan's particular place Russians and Lithuanians — who were, in the 1950s, unwilling members of the Soviet Union — outnumbered Germans. In *Chronicles*, Dylan expresses his personal reservations about the Cold War in an amusing recollection of the "duck-and-cover" training we all received at school: "We were also told that the Russians could be parachuting from planes over our town at any time. These were the same Russians that my uncles had fought alongside only a few years earlier. Now they had become monsters who were coming to slit our throats and incinerate us. It seemed peculiar (29)."

11 For an essay titled "Times of War," written shortly after the 9/11 attacks, Aaron Brown interviewed Bill Schleppegrell, Sr., retired German teacher at Hibbing High School and a World War II POW, and his son Bill, Jr., who served in Vietnam until he decided the war was evil and risked court-martial (and loss of friends) to become a conscientious objector. Brown teaches at the Community College in Hibbing, where some of his students are returning Iraq War veterans. Concluding his interview, Brown decides that "Not everyone who knows war agrees about what it means or whether it should be waged. I could probably have found an equally honorable Iron Range family that supports the war in Iraq. That same family might have supported the war in Vietnam. But I am left pondering the grim statistic that most of the iron our parents,

grandparents, or great-grandparents mined during the early 1940s or the late 1960s is buried somewhere in Europe or Southeast Asia. (114)"

His own position, while guarded, is not difficult to figure out.

12   He then directed Cott to describe the little New England village they were passing through. From what Cott got down (pine trees, ducks, Garrison Street, Stroudwater Baptist Church, clothes hanging on the line) the town sounds a lot like the small towns of Dylan's Iron Range youth: Silica, Pengily, Forbes, Calumet, Buhl, Nashwauk, Zim. "It's real special," Dylan told Cott. "You don't see this in New York City." When Cott suggested they'll never see the place again, Dylan responded, "Oh, I bet we come back" (Cott: 256–7).

13   I am being commonsensical and perhaps anti-intellectual here. Michael Gray tracks (no pun intended) a string of musical references in his *Song & Dance Man III* (742ff.), and Steven Heine suggests a Blues-Beats connection in Dylan's railroad imagery (64). Bryan Cheyette structures a whole essay on Dylan's many journeys, primarily by train, both real and imagined, literal and spiritual, using "the schema of Wolfgang Schivelbusch, the cultural historian of train travel, who has suggested that 'the railroad knows only points of departure and destination'" (221).

14   In truth, education everywhere in America during the 1950s was mortgaged to this middle-class, middlebrow agenda, but other communities lacked Hibbing's leftist history and were more attuned to middle-class values wrapped in lofty rhetoric.

15   In this regard, Hibbing High in the 1950s was not far from programs of "cultural diversity" in the 1990s. Thus is was, is now, and ever shall be. On this subject Camille Paglia is not far from Bob Dylan:

We can move tender, safe, clean, hand-holding gays and lesbians to the center — but not, of course, pederasts, prostitutes, strippers, pornographers, or sadomasochists. And if we're going to learn from the marginalized, what about drug dealers, moon-shiners, Elvis impersonators, string collectors, Mafiosi, foot fetishists, serial murders, cannibals, Satanists, and the Ku Klux Klan. I'm sure they'll all have a lot to say. (31)

16   This is possibly a reference to Dick Kangas, who, according to Dave Engel (155) performed "All Shook Up" at the spring talent show. But Engel gives no date for the performance, which might have been the "sensational novelty number which at the moment is top secret" mentioned in the April 5, 1957 issue of the *Hibbing Hi-Times*.

17   Hibbing in general paid Bob Dylan little attention when he was Bob Zimmerman, and not much attention after he became famous. As late as August 17, 1988, reporter Roger Worthington could write, "There's a sign outside Hibbing that tells you this is the hometown of Governor Rudy Perpich. This is also the town singer-songwriter Bob Dylan grew up in. But no signs mention him. The Hibbing city library has no special collection or files devoted to Dylan or his music. Nor does the town's museum. Nor does the town's newspaper" (B1).

In fairness to Hibbing, the Hibbing Public Library now has a Bob Dylan Collection containing, among other items, newspaper articles from both the *Duluth News Tribune* and the *Hibbing Daily Tribune* dating to as early as 1962.

18   Dylan himself suggested these connections in the *Playboy* interview of March, 1978: "Well, in the winter, everything was still, nothing moved. Eight months of that. You

can put that together. You can have some amazing hallucinogenic experiences doing nothing but looking out your window. There is also the summer, when it gets hot and sticky and the air is very metallic. There is a lot of Indian spirit. The earth there is unusual, filled with ore. So there is something happening that is hard to define. There is a magnetic attraction there. Maybe thousands and thousands of years ago, some planet bumped into the land there. There is a great spiritual quality throughout the Midwest. Very subtle, very strong, and that is where I grew up" (Cott: 202).

Dylan may have a point: in *Minnesota on the Map*, David Lanegran says that around Hibbing the highly magnetic ore actually deflected the compasses of the surveyors, causing odd angles in property lines and roads, visible on the Hibbing City plat map.

Notes to Chapter 2: *"And the Language That He Used"*

1   Robert Shelton thought young Bob Dylan sounded not like an Iron Range miner or a Woody Guthrie Oakie, but like "a Southern field hand" (*Home*: 190), and in a hatchet job of May 31, 1963, *Time* magazine described his accent as belonging "to a jive Nebraskan, or maybe a Brooklyn Hillbilly."

2   "Post-vocalic /r/ is maintained by all the Iron Range informants and all the other Minnesota informants as well," Gary Underwood states unequivocally (62). I suspect it was the combined influence of blues singers and New Yorkers that killed Dylan's "r". Dylan satirizes the New York missing "r" by spelling "parking meters" as "pawking metaws" in the lyrics of "Subterranean Homesick Blues" on the placards he holds in the famous first scene of *dont look back*, using "woikas" for "workers" in *Tarantula* (131), and in a handwritten prose poem on page 501 of *Lyrics, 1962–1985*: "see how small the woild is aftah all." A close listening to the early albums, to early tapes, and to the songs on Bootleg Series 1–3, shows that Dylan dropped his r's early on when singing blues songs, and r's began to disappear from other material as early as 1964, not from the demos or the folk songs on disc one of the Bootleg Series, but from the hipper urban songs on disc two. In this respect, New York urban reinforced rural blues because of their shared dialectal feature. "He came back [from New York] with a different accent," Dave Whitaker remembers of Dylan; "He spoke differently" (35).

3   "Only one Iron Range informant (#9) uses the A-/ə-/ prefix to present participles," notes Gary Underwood; "This prefix is also infrequent among other Minnesota informants" (50). Remembering Dylan during his year at the University of Minnesota, Bonnie Beecher said, "He was talking in the strangest Woody Guthrie-Oklahoma accent." She remembers Dylan deliberately refusing to treat a bronchial cough because he thought the rougher his voice sounded, the more he'd sound like Guthrie (Bauldie, *Wanted Man*: 23, 25). Dylan may also have borrowed from Guthrie — or from the southern radio stations he listened to as a youth — the pronunciation of "the" to rhyme with "thee," as well as "can't" to rhyme with "ain't" (as in "kaint do nobody harm" in "Do, Re, Mi"). Dylan did not borrow the "r" inserted into "wash" to make "warsh," which enters the Midwest dialect below the Iowa line, but is rare in the North Country. Guthrie usually goes with "just," not "jist," as in "I Ain't Got No Home, I'm just a

ramblin' man." Guthrie often transforms the "ow" at the end of "fellow" into "er" to make "feller," something else Dylan does not borrow. Guthrie often uses "knowed" as the preterit of "know," a usage occasionally borrowed by Dylan. Minnesotans — and Dylan — share with Guthrie a number of dialectal features, including a fondness for double negatives, the frequent use of the adjective "old" (as in "good old boys") and "come" as a past tense of "came," "done" as a past tense of "do." Then again, Clinton Heylin quotes Bonnie Beecher as saying Dylan brought the Guthrie accent back from *Colorado*, along with "a cowboy hat and boots" (*Shades*: 43), so possibly Guthrie is not alone responsible for Dylan's "Guthrie" sound.

4   In this obviously offhand comment, Dylan was wise beyond his years in distinguishing between the dialect of Minnesota and North Dakota and the dialect of the rest of the Upper Midwest. *The Linguistic Atlas of the Upper Midwest* records consistent and significant distinctions between Minnesota-North Dakota and the rest of the Upper Midwest in matters of pronunciation, usage, and vocabulary. Where differences exist, Dylan's speech, vocabulary, and usage consistently reflect Minnesota-North Dakota preferences over Upper Midwest choices.

5   While the interviews on which the *Atlas* is based are dated, Craig Carver reports in 1989 that the preferences of subregional "northern" speech have not changed much in the last half century (137).

6   It goes without saying, of course, that the long "e" in British "been" (the equivalent of "bean") is in American English the word "Ben," which in the Midwest usually becomes pronounced "bin," as in "Seems like I *bin* down this way before" ("Señor") or "the one I've *bin* looking for" ("Tight Connection to My Heart").

7   For example, "I will not go" in "Let Me Die in My Footsteps," "thrown in like bandits" in "Walls of Red Wing," "ocean" and "whole" on the demo tape of "When the Ship Comes In," "stone," "don't," "no tellin'," "don't criticize," and "old road" in the demo tape of "The Times They Are A-Changin'."

8   For example, "my stones won't take" ("Million Dollar Bash"), "show me" and "know me" ("Emotionally Yours"), "down the road" and "go in now" ("Sugar Baby"), "floats by" ("Tell Ol' Bill"), and "Go home and lead a quiet life" ("Red River Shore"). The long o's in "bones" and "grindstones" are one of the many features which give "Tweedle Dee & Tweedle Dum" a Minnesota flavor. The same is true of the o's of "coat," "note," and "quote" in "The Man in the Long Black Coat," which work with the generally dead, backwoods sound of "old dance hall by the outskirts of town" to suggest some dilapidated shack in one of the ghost towns in the woods around Hibbing.

9   Dylan sings "winda" in "look out your winda fair" ("All Over You"), "look out your winda and I'll be gone" ("Don't Think Twice, It's Alright"), "from the winda I watched" ("North Country Blues"), "rain falls 'round my winda" ("I Can't Escape from You"), "stand at the winda" ("Dignity"), and "Down over the winda" ("Floater [Too Much to Ask]"). However, he sings "window" in "Maggie's Farm," "Desolation Row," "Love Minus Zero/No Limit," "It Ain't Me, Babe," "Ballad in Plain D," "The Ballad of Frankie Lee and Judas Priest," and "Beyond Here Lies Nothin'."

10 The diphthong can also be heard in "you must *say* that I'm young" in "Masters of War"; in "you *say* you're lookin' for someone" in "It Ain't Me, Babe"; in "I heard the drifter

say" in "Drifter's Escape"; and "I wish there was somethin' you would do or *say*" in "Don't Think Twice, It's Alright."

11 A similar glide sometimes intrudes between an "r" and an "l" in words like "girl": [gərəl], as in the line "Oh every girl that ever I touched" in "Restless Farewell" or "queen of my flesh, girl" in "Precious Angel." The glide does not appear in "girl by the whirlpool" in "Subterranean Homesick Blues," or "lovely girl" in "As I Went Out One Morning."

12 These pronunciations and spellings are rampant in the Midwest ("ya shoulda been there") and thus in Mohr's *How to Talk Minnesotan*: "ain't gonna be cheap" (5), "kinda thick" (26), "that's gonna be $2.33" (35), "kinda what I thought" (96), "coulda told them" (112). In Keillor's *Lake Wobegon Days* we find "gonna" (110, 135), "gotta" (144, 182, 317), "oughta" (147, 335), "mighta" (241), "dontcha" (285), "whatcha" (317, 335), and "kinda" (335).

13 Compare Dylan's song "Whatcha Gonna Do," and "Whatcha wanna go and do that for?" in "Tell me, Momma," and "whaja thinka that Monet painting?" in *Tarantula* (123).

14 The "yer" spelling reappears in every refrain, but not the title, of "You're Gonna Make Me Lonesome When You Go" (in *Lyrics: 1962–2001*). This strong Midwest "fur" instead of "for" can be heard in the speech of Minnesotan Tony Glover during his interviews in *No Direction Home*.

15 On page xiii of the 1988 *Wanted Man* edition of his book *Stolen Moments*, Clinton Heylin reproduces a facsimile of the lyrics to "Temporary Like Achilles" which actually spell the line "kneelin' neath your ceilin'" as "kneelin' neath your ceiling."

16 Then again, most Minnesotans are not filling notes in a song, or slipping in an unaccented syllable between two accented syllables to flesh out the meter. Many, many participles in Dylan's songs, even from his early Guthrie period, come without the a- prefix. Comparing those with the places Dylan *does* use the a- prefix suggests that Dylan uses the prefix mostly when he needs a short syllable. In the line "I'm a-goin' back out 'fore the rain starts a-fallin'" ("A Hard Rain's A-Gonna Fall") the a- prefixes in conjunction with the lost first syllable of "before" produce a line of perfect anapestic tetrameter). In the line "the wind keeps a-blowin' me" ("Bob Dylan's Blues"), it nudges the line toward iambic tetrameter. In "I was a-scared to move" and "I was just a-runnin'" ("Bob Dylan's New Orleans Rag") the a- prefixes set up lines of perfect iambic and trochaic trimeter. On the other hand, "Last Thoughts on Woody Guthrie" is a free-verse poem which has no meter; it is full of participles without that prefix, with and without the final "g": "laggin'," "losin'," "doing," "givin'," "slipping," "holdin'," etc. Only once, in the next-to-last stanza of this poem, Dylan slips the prefix in: "for this lamp that's a-burnin'." Dylan also attaches that a- prefix to words that are not participles when he needs to fill space or make a line of iambic tetrameter, as in "An' I been out a-ramblin' round" ("I Was Young When I Left Home").

17 On very early bootleg tapes, Dylan usually pronounces his r's, but he lost many of his medial and final r's early, and as he grew older, things only got worse. Early records suggest to me that Dylan was consciously trying to lose the "r" (in imitation of either blues singers or New Yorkers), but it slipped back into his speech when he lost concentration. In the rhyming sequence "bark," "mark," "spark," and "dark" of "It's Alright,

Ma" the first and fourth words are pretty crisp, while the second and third are a little light in the "r" department. Later, he killed the letter almost entirely. In terms of this important linguistic feature, Dylan sounds like a New Yawkah, with this exception: Dylan loses his "r" more after a front vowel than after a back vowel, where he retains it. This makes a certain sense, in that "r" is a back-of-the-mouth sound. So it's just plain harder to pronounce (and sing) the first r's in "harder" and "clearer" than the first "r" in "further."

18   I suspect that in experiments like lowercase letters, missing apostrophes (except *its* for *it's*, which is probably a typo), and streamlined spellings, Dylan was following e. e. cummings (whom we all read in high school, and whom Dylan alludes to in *Tarantula* — 52, 76, 84) and just trying to be hip, avant-garde, and inscrutable: *thru* for *through*, *dont* for *don't*, *i* for *I*, *&* for *and*, *theyre* for *they're*, and so forth. In eccentric spellings which reflect pronunciation, however, I suspect that Dylan saw himself following the lead of Mark Twain, John Steinbeck, and especially Woody Guthrie. In *Bound for Glory*, Guthrie is actually quite masterful at making spelling convey dialect, especially in places where he has a boxcar full of hobos speaking several different accents:

> "Say, stud! Who daya t'ink youse are? Dat bottle was mine, see?" . . .
> "Go git it." I looked him straight in the eye.
> "Whattaya tryin' ta pull?"
> "Well, since yer so interested, I'll jest tell ya. See, I might wanta lay down after while an' git a little sleep. I don't wanta wake up with my feet blistered. 'Cause then, dam yer hide, I'd hafta throw ya outta this door!"
> "We was gonna use dat gas ta start a fire ta cook wid." (23)

19   Dylan admits to having had a tough time getting Faulkner (*Chronicles*: 37), and he says this about Joyce: "I couldn't make hide nor hair of it. James Joyce seemed like the most arrogant man who ever lived, had both his eyes wide open and great faculty of speech, but what he say, I knew not what" (*Chronicles*: 130). *Tarantula* seems to be faux-Joyce, but by *Chronicles*, Dylan had settled into his own Midwestern prose which sounds very much like Hemingway: "I was ecstatic. At least it was a place to stay out of the cold. This was good" (10).

20   Another tape made by Bonnie Beecher on December 22, 1961, and used as the basis for the *Rare Batch of Little White Wonder* bootlegs, shows the same mixture of borrowed and native Minnesotan sounds. Borrowed from elsewhere are the "mah" for "my" and "ah" for "I" in "California," "Who You Really Are," "Baby, Please Don't Go," "Candy Man," etc.; the various missing r's in "sure," "morning," "dark," "hard," "sister," etc.; the diphthonged vowels in "Only a Hobo"; and of course "salty dawg." And of course "a-dyin" and "blowed" in "Poor Lazarus." From the Minnesota side, the "jist" that sneaks into the last line of "California" and the "git" of "Poor Lazarus"; the long "o" vowels in "California," "Man of Constant Sorrow," "Only a Hobo," "Emmett Till," and "Poor Lazarus"; the "r" still present in "borderline" in "Angelina" and in "hard" in "Farewell Angelina," and in "hard," "born," and "barn" in "Emmett Till"; the various pure "I" first-person pronouns.

21　This "r" being present, incidentally, is one of the more noticeable features of Dylan's natural voice in the Oscar Brand interview of October 1961 and the Cynthia Gooding interview of January 1962. Dylan is heavy into playing Woody Guthrie, with a heavy hillbilly accent and plenty of glides and diphthongs.

22　Neil Smith, a New Orleans friend, tells me that anybody native to New Orleans would say "shrimp boat" or just "boat" (even though neither fits the meter of the song).

Notes to Chapter 3: Bob Dylan and the Pastoral Tradition

1　That ideal, Marx admits, blurred in the nineteenth century, as dreams of escape from an increasingly technological and commercial European culture to a fresh, green landscape in America morphed into "various utopian schemes for making America the site of a new beginning for Western society" (3). Those schemes inevitably turned America technological and commercial, a transformation which accelerated in the twentieth century. In this period American pastoral literature, romantic or realistic, also lost ground in the academic world, because, as William Barillas notes (12ff.), it is too tied to physical reality for postmodernist cultural theoreticians, who are more inclined to invent reality than discover reality. In 1964, Marx wondered in print, "What possible bearing can the urge to idealize a simple, rural environment have upon the lives men lead in an intricately organized, urban, industrial, nuclear-armed society?" (5). Forty years later, in *Working the Garden*, William Conlogue was wondering in print how agriculture could be relevant to matters of race, gender, and class (4).

2　Barillas identifies Jeffersonianism as the first stage of what he calls "midwestern pastoralism" because Jefferson links nature to production, a combination which Barillas sees as characteristic of the Midwest (25).

3　William Conlogue, an unabashed apologist for agribusiness as a legitimate expression of American pastoralism, locates the source of that work ethic further in the past than Luther and Calvin. Citing L. P. Wilkinson, he traces the link between work and pastoralism to Virgil's *Georgics* (in contrast to his *Eclogues*, where most pastoralists begin), a poem whose whole moral fabric rests on the yeoman who must work for himself (8). Humans, he goes on to argue, must accept the fact that they are not only in nature, but must manage nature (9), and they had better not duck their god-given responsibilities. "By 1870 at least, many farmers understood themselves to be businessmen rather than Jeffersonian yeomen," Conlogue claims (12).

4　Sigmund Freud, who suggested that the repressions associated with civilization actually had detrimental effects on human psychology, was used by Minnesotan Sigurd Olson in his campaign for preserving American wilderness. Olson argued that a few brief centuries could not undo millennia of human history, that psychologically man is still in tune with water, woods, and fields, that separating man from wilderness caused mental problems which could be undone only by renewed contact with wilderness (Nash: 265). Minnesota's Quetico-Superior country, a hundred miles northeast of Hibbing, achieved national notoriety in the 1940s and 1950s as Olson and Ernest Oberholtzer campaigned to ban aircraft over the region at an altitude below 4,000 feet — thereby terminating the fly-in resort industry.

5   In a postmodernist piece titled "In the Heart of the Heart of the Country," philosopher-writer William Gass dismissed this notion as "a lie of old poetry. The modern husbandman uses chemicals from cylinders and sacks, spike-ball-and-claw machines, metal sheds, and cost accounting. Nature in the old sense does not matter. It does not exist. Our farmer's only mystical attachment is to parity" (194).

6   Scott Russell Sanders expands the claims: "Because of its resources and history, and in spite of its home-grown critics, the Midwest would eventually become in our mythology something of an agrarian theme park, a repository for values that Americans wish to preserve but not live by: hard work, honesty, frugality, simplicity, integrity, neighborliness, egalitarianism, politeness, and decency. There is enough truth in that list of Heartland virtues for the impression to have survived into our own time" (39).

7   Unfortunately, the new world Newman chooses is the Old World, France. He should have headed out to The Territory, although he had already done that: that's where he had made his fortune to begin with. Perhaps Newman could have imitated Bob Dylan, pulled his cap over his eyes, and headed out for the western skies. But Henry James had been born in New York.

8   Marcus goes on to argue, with some degree of plausibility, that one reason for the tremendous public reaction against Dylan when he went electric was that he was in effect denying the pastoral myth: "As he stood on the stage he was seen to affirm the claims of the city over the country, and capital over labor" (*Invisible Republic*: 30).

9   Sixties pastoralism was popular enough for Howard Mohr, who got his start writing for *A Prairie Home Companion*, to satirize it in several sections of his book *How to Talk Minnesotan*, including the "Minnesota Prairie Poet League" and "Living Off the Land": "My brother farms out in southwestern Minnesota, and since 1968, he has had five different tenants in an old farmhouse at a building site he owns on what he calls 'Mortgage Hill.' The renters were all young people who wanted to live off the land. My brother had no objection to somebody trying to live off the land. He'd been trying it himself for years. Three of the tenants lasted less than a month" (127).

10 "Grass," Whitman suggested in Section 6 of *Leaves of Grass*, is "the handkerchief of the Lord, / A scented gift and remembrance designedly dropt, / Bearing the owner's name someway in the corners, that we may see and remark, and say *Whose?*" The smallest sprout, he goes on to say, "shows there is really no death . . . And to die is different from what anyone supposed, and luckier." Carl Sandburg's poem "Grass" was very popular in the fifties, much read and recited:

> Pile the bodies high at Austerlitz and Waterloo.
> Shovel them under and let me work —
>   I am the grass; I cover all.
>
> And pile them high at Gettysburg
> And pile them high at Ypres and Verdun.
> Shovel them under and let me work.

Two years, ten years, and passengers ask the conductor:
   What place is this?
   Where are we now?

   I am the grass.
   Let me work.

11   Michael Gray finds Dylan's pastoralism sometimes falsified, "not real," a "conceit,"
     and sees this escape to the Black Hills of Dakota as "Dylan rushing off to Doris Day"
     (*Song*: 175), but the Black Hills are precisely where a boy from small-town Minnesota
     might go to cure a heavy infection of Princeton bullshit. It is also possible that the song
     of the Princeton locusts is not an analogue to the buzz of the academics, but nature's
     response and antidote to their sterile noise.

12   This is one of the very few instances where Dylan politicizes nature, although nature
     can certainly be politicized. William Jennings Bryan did just that in his "Cross of Gold"
     speech, and eco-environmentalists like Wendell Berry and Ed Abbey spin a whole
     politics out of nature.

13   These associations came out of Dylan's childhood, reinforced by his experience just
     before writing the poem: "I just returned from a trip to the West," he told Robert Shelton
     in 1962, "and I had forgotten how quiet and pleasant life there was" (*Home*: 148).

14   In 2006, David Rovics released a CD of twenty-first century topical protest songs titled
     Halliburton Boardroom Massacre. The photo of Rovics on the CD shows him playing
     a guitar carrying the slogan "This Machine Kills CEOs."

15   Dylan may consciously allude to Frost's line in his own line "the woods are dark" in
     "Tell Ol' Bill."

16   Caddy devotes most of *The Color of Mesabi Bones* to the social ramifications of Iron
     Range life, the way the landscape colors human behavior. His first collection of poems,
     Eating the Sting, focuses more on the natural landscape, both its lighter and darker
     aspects. In his preface to the book, John Rezmerski (with a reference to Bob Dylan,
     no less) notes that "Caddy has no nature nostalgia, no inclination to settle for pop
     sublimity. His encounters are as likely to be with voles and fledgling kingfishers and
     stray dogs as with bears and hawks" (9) . . . as in "Bottomland," where Caddy finds
     nothing but debris from the flood, yellow scum, patches of oil, dead carp, and yellow
     algae (46).

17   *Giants in the Earth* ends with Per Hansa, not his wife, dying. Against his better judg-
     ment but at his wife's insistence, he sets out in a blizzard to fetch a minister for a dying
     friend. He never returns. The following spring his corpse is found, clad in snowshoes
     and winter coat, propped as if resting against a hay stack along the James River, eyes
     set toward the West.

18   Jonathan Cott, in the January, 1978, *Rolling Stone* interview, bounces a quote off of
     Dylan which Dylan finds "fantastic" and "true, exactly": "I am everything that was,
     that is, that shall be. . . . Nor has any mortal ever been able to discover what lies under
     my veil" (183). But Dylan does not need Isis to recover his female side. As Annette
     Kolodny notes, American pastoral literature "hailed the essential femininity of the

terrain in a way European pastoral never had" (6), and earth as fertility goddess fits right into the American pastoral mode of thinking.

Notes to Chapter 4: Going Out/Coming Back

1 Earlier American on-the-road stories celebrated the highway as an adventure fraught with dangers, including deserved deaths (*The Wizard of Oz*), but the hero(es) survived and matured (in *2001: A Space Odyssey*, Dave Bowman is literally reborn). However, many recent on-the-road flicks end in the death of the heroes, from *Easy Rider* (1969) to *Vanishing Point* (1971), and *Dirty Mary, Crazy Larry* (1974) through *Thelma and Louise* (1991). Recently, the on-the-road flick merged with the horror-suspense flick to produce mainly murder and mayhem on the road: *The Hitcher* (1986/2007), *Kalifornia* (1993), *Natural Born Killers* (1994), *The Doom Generation* (1995), *Joy Ride* (2001). I'm not sure what this says about the country or the generation.

2 The reason for their absence puzzles Sanders. "It's too easy to say that writers always migrate to publishing centers, where dollars and reputations are to be made," he speculates; "Midwestern writers have not been so much lured elsewhere, I suspect, as driven out, by a combination of puritanical religion, utilitarian economics, and anti-intellectualism" (25). That theory might explain Bob Dylan, as well as F. Scott Fitzgerald, Sinclair Lewis, and Tim O'Brien. Sanders himself returned. Having escaped the Midwest to college in New England and graduate school in Great Britain, there to write "steadily and badly, in tortured sentences" (151), he found himself weighing, upon completing his degree, two job offers, one in the U.K. and one at the University of Indiana. "By choosing to settle in the Midwest, far from the mythical cutting edge and actual publishing houses, I made another unfashionable decision," he writes; "every young writer I knew in my wandering years wished to live in London or Paris, New York or Boston, San Francisco or Los Angeles. My friends asked me what on earth I would do way out there in Indiana. Whom would I talk with? How would I keep my mind alive" (161). At least Sanders had the University of Indiana.

3 Tennyson tells us that age, past successes, power, and acclaim are no excuses for retirement when there is work to be done:

> It little profits that an idle king,
> By this still hearth, among these barren crags,
> Matched with an aged wife, I mete and dole
> Unequal laws unto a savage race,
> That hoard, and sleep, and feed, and know not me.
> I cannot rest from travel; I will drink
> Life to the lees. . . .
>   Come, my friends,
> 'Tis not too late to seek a newer world.
> Push off, and sitting well in order smite
> The sounding furrows. . . .

Though much is taken, much abides; and though
We are not now that strength which in old days
Moved earth and heaven, that which we are, we are —
One equal temper of heroic hearts,
Made weak by time and fate, but strong in will
To strive, to seek, to find, and not to yield.

"As long as you got your health, you keep your job," says one of the Old Ones in Zimmy's Restaurant in Hibbing.

4   I spent 1989–91 at the University of Łódz in Poland, on a Fulbright Fellowship, lecturing on American culture and literature. In that country just awakening from four decades of Soviet sleep, I was reminded repeatedly that a car on the open road is America's most compelling symbol. In the fall of 1989, for example, Polish colleague Agnieszka Salska mused aloud, "I'm not sure the old symbols work in Poland these days. The red star and the cross both seem to have lost their power."

"Same in America," I answered. "The flag doesn't mean much anymore."

"Oh, David," she sighed, "the symbol of America is not the stars and stripes. It's the automobile and the open highway."

The following spring, well into a two-day conference on "The American Dream, Past and Present," a student asked a panel of scholars, "You've been talking for two days now about The American Dream — what is the American Dream?"

"Well humph and harrumph," the scholars mumbled in their mineral water, "that's a very complicated subject, hard to explain in a few words, subtle, full of nuances. . . ."

"Not at all," objected another member of the audience; "The American Dream is simple: you're driving down the road at 200 kilometers an hour, your girl friend beside you, with the radio playing rock-'n'-roll at top volume, throwing empty beer cans out the window behind you."

5   Another poem that was quite popular in the fifties and sixties was Archibald MacLeish's "You, Andrew Marvell," which tracks the decline of civilization westward out of Persia, through Syria and Lebanon, through Sicily and Spain, and across the Atlantic, where the poet, lying face-down beneath an American noontime sun feels "how swift how secretly / The shadow of the night comes on" (25). Probably, Dylan knew this poem. He certainly knew MacLeish. In *Chronicles* (107), he calls MacLeish "Poet Laureate of America — one of them. Carl Sandburg, poet of the prairie and the city, and Robert Frost, the poet of dark meditations[,] were the others. MacLeish was the poet of night stones and the quick earth. These three, the Yeats, Browning and Shelley of the New World, were gigantic figures, had defined the landscape of twentieth century America. They put everything in perspective. Even if you didn't know their poems, you knew their names" (107). MacLeish was also a good guy. Whether Dylan knew it or not, as Librarian of Congress, he was in part responsible for preserving the photographic archives of Depression-era rural suffering assembled by Roy Stryker's Farm Security Administration: by accepting them for the Library of Congress, MacLeish saved them from the dustbin of history, to which conservative Republicans repeatedly attempted to consign them.

6   However, as we shall see in Chapter 5, these writers are repudiating only one side of Main Street, only one half of the rural Midwestern experience. William Barillas notes that writers like Masters, Lewis, and Anderson, far from rejecting the Midwestern pastoral myth, make it central to their thought, as an ideal against which the actual conditions of life needed to be measured (52).

7   Keillor himself stayed in the Twin Cities, when he was not in Denmark or gallivanting around the globe. Robert Bly moved off the farm in Madison to a place in Moose Lake, and finally to St. Paul as well. After the turn of the millennium, Bill Holm cut himself to half-time at the university and split his year between Minneota, Minnesota, and Iceland.

8   L. Frank Baum, author of *The Wizard of Oz*, was a Midwest populist from way back, and both the book and the film versions (more the book than the film) reflect that populism. First — and relevant to Dylan because of Baum's emphasis on the work ethic — is the kind of girl Dorothy is. In one of his Aberdeen newspaper editorials, Baum wrote in 1890,

> Too many ladies of the Atlantic states sit with idly folded arms or listlessly dallying with fancy work, whose sire is at his wits end to supply the necessities for his family, because it is still considered a disgrace for young ladies to engage in any kind of regular occupation, and even a married woman loses her social status by engaging in business or following any pursuit that brings her monetary returns. . . . What a vast difference between these undesirable damsels and our brave, helpful western Girls! . . . Here a woman delights in being useful; a young lady's highest ambition is to become a bread-winner. And they do. . . . They have more energy and vitality than those of the east and . . . there is no nonsense or self pride in their constitutions and they cannot brook idleness when they see before them work to be done which is eminently fitted to their hands. (*Annotated*: 13)

The Wizard of Oz also reflects the social and political situations in the East and the Midwest around the time Baum was writing. Baum's Great Plains are every bit as gray and bleak as Cather's Nebraska in *O Pioneers!*, but this is still the Promised Land. Like other writers of what was called "the Chicago Renaissance," Baum idealized the Midwestern farmer, however poor he might have been. Oz is an essentially prosperous pastoral landscape, despite having been dominated by the Wicked Witches of the East and West. Those witches are in fact the enemies of the Wizard of Oz who, as many people have pointed out, came from Omaha, birthplace of William Jennings Bryan, "The Prairie Populist." The city in this book is a comfortable scam with a superiority complex and a distaste for hard work (a quality enhanced in the film). This hard metropolis is where "the Yellow Brick Road" leads a person: off the farm, away from nature, into the city, which is the color of paper money and where the streets are paved with the gold of $20 coins. One interpretation of OZ is that it's NY with a one-letter spelling shift: N becomes O, Y becomes Z (*Annotated*: 43). Another interpretation has OZ the abbreviation for "ounces," as in ounces of silver and ounces of gold. In this regard, one detail of the book (lost in the movie) is very significant: Dorothy's protective silver slippers. Baum was a free silver man from his Aberdeen days. On the

Yellow Brick Road and in her encounters with the Wicked Witch, Dorothy is protected by silver, which the populists thought would be their weapon against exploitation by eastern bankers. (The film, incidentally, changed silver to red because the makers thought red would show up better in Technicolor . . . or because they were of the bankers' party.) The Woodman's gold and silver ax at the end of the novel represents an acknowledgment and rewarding of labor in the populist-socialist tradition. See Henry M. Littlefield's article "*The Wizard of Oz*: Parable on Populism."

9   In its non-pastoral heyday, the Midwest was the seat of most American agricultural and industrial production; a tornado of energy, and a source of real prosperity for the working class — not for bankers or entertainers, of course, but for the real workers on farm and in the factory. Farm and factory work both required a large labor force, so the region was populous in a manner that judged people by what they brought to the table beyond appetite and attitude. Prosperous settlements sprang up everywhere, with nice buildings — not too grand or up-scale like Boston or Philadelphia, but solid practical architecture that would appeal to blue-collar people devoted to school, church, and work. Red frame barn out of a Sears catalogue. House with porch and garden and a leaded glass window or two. White church with steeple and bell. Train depot, small hotel, bank with marble pillars on either side of the door.

     And then, before the Midwest could develop real elegance or history, it was over. Not immediately, but all too quickly. Agricultural production continued — continues — but machines reduced the number of workers dramatically (what most strikes someone viewing the film versions of Steinbeck's *Of Mice and Men* and Will Weaver's *Sweet Land* is the number of workers required to bring in a harvest in the old days). Farms consolidated and small towns dried up. Churches and schools closed. Barns emptied and sagged. As we noted in Chapter 1, that process, masked by the Dust Bowl, actually began shortly after World War I and continued through the post-World War II period, when the rest of America was recovering. Towns and cities also felt the squeeze, as industrial production first automated — costing millions of workers their jobs — and then disappeared as production was outsourced abroad. I remember looking at the empty factory buildings of International Harvester when I came to Springfield, Ohio, in 1961, sensing that something had died there without really comprehending the full story. Where population will support renovation, the warehouses and schools are rehabbed into condos or assisted-living centers; some barns and churches even become homes (or methamphetamine labs). But usually the population is not there, and buildings just sit empty and abandoned and accusatory, until they are burned or bulldozed. Even the buildings that remain — Hibbing High School or the St. James Hotel — speak the same sentence: "Imagine what I was back in the day."

10   The line echoes Dylan's earlier "I'm a stranger here and nobody sees me 'cept you" ("Nobody 'Cept You," 1973), but the specific reference is to Robert Heinlein's novel *Stranger in a Strange Land*. Gregg M. Campbell had used precisely the same phrase (and reference?) in his 1974 essay "Bob Dylan and the Pastoral Apocalypse": "Robert Zimmerman was thus a stranger in a strange land, who, like so many other strangers, created a mask, a fictive persona — Bob Dylan — to shield what was most essential in himself" (697). Campbell sees Dylan as an outsider-prophet, and ties the pastoralism

we discussed in Chapter 3 to the apocalyptic vision we will discuss in Chapter 6: "The poets and prophets of the counter-culture believed that new truths, or rather, old and timeless truths had been revealed to them, and they expressed this vision in their apocalyptic music. But the apocalyptic tradition has deep roots in the Indo-European and Judeo-Christian imagination, and there are at least three identifiable variants of this tradition — the black or cataclysmic, the red or revolutionary, and the green or pastoral" (698).

11   One last personal anecdote. At one point in the late seventies, I took my family to the U.K., rented a car and headed north out of London to the upper edges of Scotland. The U.K. was relatively cheap in those days, but my salary was modest, especially with a family of four, and we ate carefully. In some very small town north of Inverness, we found a pub that served a steak and French fries dinner that was tasty, and cheap. We dined there three days running. By the third night, we knew the waiter on sight, and he knew us well enough to ask, with burning eyes, a question that had been bothering him for a couple days:

"So yerrr Amerrrikans, arrre ye?"

"Yes, Americans."

"Have ye everrr rrread a book called . . . *On the RRRoad*???!!"

12   This is, by the way, as much a literary fiction as Keillor's Lake Wobegon youth: Kerouac had already collected episodes, visions, and pearls with his service in the Merchant Marine, but these adventures are not part of his novel, and a reader of *On the Road* does not know this. And since they have probably not read Kerouac's first novel, *The Town and the City*, those readers also do not know that at one time New York City (and the Beats he hung with) represented for Kerouac an escape from/contrast to the environment in which he had grown up in Lowell, Massachusetts. Kerouac was always escaping, always in the process of going out. When he could not go out anymore, he died.

13   Minnesota Census figures for St. Louis County: 1930: 204,596; 1940: 206,917; 1950: 206,062; 1960: 231,588; 1980: 222,229; 1990: 198,213; 2000: 200,528. Minnesota Census figures for Hibbing: 1920: 15,699; 1930: 15,666; 1940: 16,385; 1950: 16,276; 1960: 17,731. The city of Eveleth, 15 miles east of Hibbing, was harder hit: 1930: 7,484; 1940: 6,884; 1950: 5,872 (Milinovich: 36).

14   In a November 1961 interview with Columbia Records' head of publicity Billy James, Dylan claimed he rode a freight train into New York. In *Chronicles*, Dylan comes clean in a passage worthy of Jack Kerouac: "I hadn't come in on a freight train at all. What I did was come across the country from the Midwest in a four-door sedan, '57 Impala — straight out of Chicago, clearing the hell out of there — racing all the way through the smoky towns, winding roads, green fields covered with snow, onward, eastbound through the state lines, Ohio, Indiana, Pennsylvania, a twenty-four-hour ride, dozing most of the way in the backseat, making small talk" (8). The only problem is Dylan did not apparently ride a '57 Impala from Chicago to the City, and Heylin reports him singing all the way until the driver told him to "shut the fuck up" (*Stolen Moments*: 12). That kind of disinformation, which circulated widely in the early sixties, provoked the *Newsweek* expose of November 4, 1963, which knocked Dylan seriously off stride.

Luckily for him, the Kennedy assassination on November 22 knocked everybody off stride, and erased the Dylan story from the public consciousness.

15 A small irony, or a very subtle allusion, is at work here, insofar as Davies's poem is about coal mining towns in South Wales. Seeger's note to this song on the jacket of *Pete Seeger's Greatest Hits* mentions Davies participating in a general strike in 1926, then clearing out to become a schoolteacher in London. Later Seeger visited Rhymney: "Like many mining towns, it is a mile long and a hundred yards wide. The other towns [mentioned in the poem] are also in South Wales, except for Wye, which is a more prosperous farming valley to the east." Gray (*Song & Dance Man*: 643) says that Dylan performed the song in 1961, and Marcus discusses Dylan's recording of it on *The Basement Tapes* (*Invisible Republic*: 73, 239–40).

16 Dylan will return to the idea of being a thousand miles from his home in subsequent songs — songs of experience on the road as it were — and never do we hear that same simple excitement. In 1962 Dylan recorded "He Was a Friend of Mine," about a friend who "never done no wrong," "never harmed no one," and died on the road "a thousand miles from home." In 1964 a Bob Dylan ready to leave his girl looked with resignation and regret back into a room once full of love and found himself and his former love "just one too many mornings / An' a thousand miles behind." In 1979 a weathered and wizened Dylan, forsaken by fans and derided by friends because he "don't be like they'd like [him] to," walked out on his own "a thousand miles from home," to declare his faith even though "the earth may shake me," even though "my friends forsake me." There is more desperation (or determination) than excitement here, and just a tinge of regret. And there's plenty of desperation in "Don't Fall Apart on Me Tonight" (1983): streets full of vipers, hope gone, no place safe, yesterday nothing but a memory, nowhere to go, and "The only place open is a thousand miles away and I can't take you there."

17 "If the mother was the central, loving, inspiring, life-giving figure in the home, and the town was an extension of the home, mother and town merged in the depths of the psyche. The yearning for the security and the love of the mother was part of and fused with the search for the meaning of the town" (217).

18 Michael Gray notes that Meredith, 35 years later, was working for Republican Senator Jesse Helms of North Carolina, whose politics were slightly to the right of the American Nazi Party (*Song*: 785). The world is filled with ironies.

19 Apparently, road weariness hits performers a little sooner than it hits the rest of us. The Beatles reached their moment of awareness on August 28, 1966. Tony Barrow, the Beatles' press officer, remembers the Fab Four hunkered down in a locker room of Dodger Stadium on the group's penultimate tour gig, waiting in terrified silence for cops to clear "the hysterically boisterous crowd" which made escape impossible. The silence, he says, was broken finally by Ringo asking in a small voice (echoing scenes in *A Hard Day's Night*), "Can I please go home to my mummy now, can I please?" "Silently to ourselves we repeated Ringo's heartfelt plea," writes Barrow; "We wanted to go home now" (215). John, George, and Ringo had been voicing reservations for weeks; finally Paul joined the other three: "I've fucking had it up to here too," he announced (Miles: 295). By the middle sixties, Dylan had also fucking had it up to here. He was burned out, partly from the New York scene, partly from life on the road, and partly from

inane interviews and press conferences like those in Great Britain (*dont look back*) or the one in at TV station KQED in San Francisco (see *No Direction Home* the film, or *No Direction Home* the book, 284–91). The film *No Direction Home* closes with the equivalent of the Beatles in Dodger Stadium: a totally wiped out Dylan, thinking perhaps of Buddy Holly, tells his manager that he doesn't want to go to Italy, doesn't want to tour anymore, he's afraid he might die in a plane wreck in Sicily somewhere. Last line of the film is, "I don't know — I just want to go home."

20 In *The Great Gatsby*, Fitzgerald's hero and narrator both try unsuccessfully to attach their lost Midwest home to Long Island; the one dies, and the other returns from the corruption of New York to a Minnesota which, although sophisticated and far from the "lost Swede towns" of the western part of the state, still offers more possibility for sanity and salvation.

21 This realization very much foreshadows Grandma's advice of "Going, Going, Gone" — "Boy, go and follow your heart / And you'll be fine at the end of the line" — and the advice of the girl in "Red River Shore" — "Go home and lead a quiet life" — which road-weary Dylan says was true to him and true to life.

22 Nick Hawthorne devotes an entire article attempting to localize this meeting between Elvis and Dylan in time and place. Given the schedules of Presley's gig in Las Vegas and Dylan's presences in Minnesota, he is largely unsuccessful. He admits finally that he cannot find a time for the two of them to have crossed paths, but — against his own evidence — holds out for an actual meeting because so much of the rest of *New Morning* is based on fact: "Day of the Locusts," the personal life reflected in "If Not for You" and "Time Passes Slowly," the Christmas decorations which inspired "Three Angels."

23 Steven Goldberg might have the appropriate response to Greil Marcus in his essay "Bob Dylan and the Poetry of Salvation": "To a man who yearns for meaning, the thought that life is merely playing out directions imprinted before birth, or given in childhood, or decreed by an alien society, is intolerable unless it is part of a master plan"; to a mystic, however, "the mystical truth that 'life is pain' is not in the slightest nihilistic, but an acknowledgment that all the separate joys that this world has to offer contain the basic pain of our seeming separation from the One"; on the other hand, "a man who sees his life as satisfactorily defined by the terms of his society will have no need to roam that border area which, while it does hold his salvation, also threatens him with madness" (43, 44).

24 In his song Dylan is more hopeful, however, than Betty Carter's "Tell Him I Said Hello," which Andrew Muir offers as a possible source (*Troubadour*: 145):

> Do I love him? Don't say "yes" or "no"
> If he should ask, but he won't, I know
> 'Cos it's all over and forgotten
> Just tell him I said hello . . . hello

25 "Mississippi" suggests that Dylan crossed the river (in the song north to south; in his own life, west to east) to be with a girl who represents the bad system but is also

an interesting distraction from troubles. For a Minnesotan mindful of the Civil War, of course, Mississippi has very negative connotations (fully operative in a song like "Oxford Town"), and let it be noted that in this past election Mississippi gave John McCain 684,000 votes to Barack Obama's 517,000. While Mississippi is not a state we associate with the city (that's more New York — east from Minnesota), it is not a place you'd want to stay too long, no matter how interesting the girl is. In other words, Mississippi is any dangerous Elsewhere which is seductive but ultimately eats you up to the point where you can't go anywhere. Dylan is drawn to the South, Michael Gray notes analyzing "Angelina" (*Song*: 432–5), but he is wary. Better just stay away.

26 The past haunted Dylan in Hibbing, in cemeteries and ghost towns and the ravaged landscape. "You're talking to a person that feels like he's walking around in the ruins of Pompeii all the time," Dylan told Mikal Gilmore in 2001; "it's always been that way" (Cott: 425). But the past also haunted Dylan in records and books. *Chronicles* contains an extended appreciation of the Vestry Street apartment of Ray Gooch and Chloe Kiel, where he stayed "off and on longer than anywhere" when he first arrived in New York City. It was their library which most appealed to him: "The place had an overpowering presence of literature and you couldn't help but lose your passion for dumbness," Dylan writes (35). Dylan rambles on for a couple pages listing the writers he read, from Thucydides through Dante and Milton to Faulkner and Pushkin. Reading, he says, annihilates time, expands present to past and future: "It's like nothing has changed from his time to mine" (36).

27 "I'm only about twenty minutes ahead, so I won't get far," Dylan told John Lennon (Marcus, *Dustbin*: 82).

28 Annie Dillard is good on the differences between modernism and postmodernism: "on a very gloomy day one could say this: that contemporary modernism accurately puts its finger upon, and claims, every quality of modernist fiction that is not essential. It throws out the baby and proclaims the bath. Joyce wrote parodies and made puns and allusions on his way to elaborating a full and deep fictional world called Dublin. Now people write little parodies full of puns and allusions. Kafka wrote fiction rooted in profound cultural criticism and in metaphysical and theological longing; along the way he had a character turn into a cockroach. Some contemporary writing has jettisoned the rest and kept the cockroach for a laugh. Joyce and Woolf bade their characters think on the page to deepen the characters, not to flatten the world solipsistically. Proust and Faulkner fiddled with time to create an artful simulacrum of our experience of time and also our knowledge of the world; now some contemporary writing may fiddle with time to keep us awake, the way television commercials splice scenes to keep us awake, or they made fiddle with time to distract us from the absence of narration, or even just to fiddle. The wit that was perhaps incidental in Joyce has become an end in itself. In short, modernist writers expanded fictional techniques in the service of traditional ends — one could say on this putative very gloomy day — and those ends have been lost" (*Living*: 63–4).

29 Howard Sounes reports that Warhol gave Dylan one of his Elvis silk screens, which Dylan and Neuwirth hauled back to Woodstock on the roof of Dylan's station wagon. "Once Bob got the artwork home," Sounes writes, "he made it clear that he loathed

it . . . by hanging it upside down and putting it in a cupboard" (199). Eventually, he traded it to Sally and Albert Grossman for a sofa. (Sally Grossman sold it at auction in 1988 for $720,000, so the joke was on Dylan. Or perhaps on the buyer.)

30   Robert Shelton's editor, Gabrielle Goodchild, offers a three-page explication of *Tarantula* in *No Direction Home* (236–8).

31   Allen Ginsberg's explanation of the film is quoted by Clinton Heylin in a chapter of *Bob Dylan: Behind the Shades* titled "Everything Went from Bad to Worse": "You'd have to study it like *Finnegans Wake*, or Cézanne, to discern the texture, the composition of the tapestry. He shot about 110 hours of film, or more, and he looked at all the scenes. Then he put all the scenes on index cards, according to some preconceptions he had when he was directing the shooting. Namely, themes: God, rock and roll, art, poetry, marriage, women, sex, Bob Dylan, poets, death — maybe eighteen or twenty thematic preoccupations. Then he also put on index cards all the different characters, as well as the scenes. He also marked on index cards the dominant color — blue or red . . . and certain other images that go through the movie, like the rose and the hat, and Indians — American Indians — so that he finally had a cross-file of all that. And then he went through it all again and began composing it, thematically, weaving these specific compositional references in and out. So it's compositional, and the idea was not to have a plot, but to have a composition of those themes. So you notice the movie begins with a rose and a hat — masculine and feminine. The rose is like a 'traveling vagina' — those are his words. The hat is masculine — crowns. The rose . . . travels from hand to hand. . . . It's a painter's film, and was composed like that" (294). Larry David Smith spends 16 pages of *Writing Dylan* on the film. I find it as unintelligible as Laurence Lieberman's explication of John Ashbery's "Self-Portrait in a Convex Mirror" in his book *Unassigned Frequencies*.

Notes to Chapter 5: Bob Dylan's Prairie Populism

1   These guys were real crooks, as anyone who has read Frank Norris's *The Pit* knows. The first chapter of Robert Morlan's nonfiction book on the Nonpartisan League is also an eye-opener, although too far removed from Bob Dylan for lengthy exploration here. Among other revealing items, Morlan passes along this report from one Duluth grain elevator in 1906 (13):

	Bushels Received	Bushels Shipped
No. 1 *Northern*	99,711.40	196,288.30
No. 2	141,455.10	467,764.00
No. 3	2,047.20	213,549.30
No. 4	201,267.20	None
No grade	116,021.10	None
Rejected	59,742.30	None

2   Something as simple — and necessary — as fencing could be burdensome to a farmer just getting started. In his book *The Great Plains*, Walter Prescott Webb points out that while homesteaders could acquire land for a mere song, the price of fencing that land was almost ruinously expensive, at least before the invention of barbed wire in the 1870s. He quotes a U.S. Department of Agriculture report from 1871 which figures the cost of fencing, necessary to protect crops from grazing cattle, at one dollar per rod, making the cost of 640 acres (one square mile) $1,280, or $2 per acre; of 160 acres (the quarter section promised each homesteader free in the Homestead Act of 1862) at $640, or $4 per acre; and of 40 acres at $320, or $8 per acre. "Thus," the report concludes, "the fencing system is one of differential mortgages, the poor man in this case being burdened with an extra mortgage of $6 per acre which his richer neighbor is not compelled to bear." Barbed wire had reduced the cost of this particular "improvement" to almost nothing when the Nonpartisan League began its campaign to make improvements tax-exempt, but by then farmers were dealing with the "improvements" of threshing machines and tractors. And compared to the price of a 1912 Minneapolis or Case 65, the cost of fencing was small potatoes.

3   Just before American entered World War I, Le Sueur had in fact written a letter to Haywood speculating that "This damned war business is going to make it mighty hard to do good . . . radical work of any kind, but I think the fight should be now centered against spy bills and conscription" (Chrislock: 173).

4   Supporting Burnquist was the "Independent Voters Association" and its anti-League publication named *The Red Flame*, devoted to exposing the "blind, unreasoning, radical SOCIALISM that has stolen into North Dakota" (Morlan: 267), with attendant dangers of anarchy, free love, and bolshevism. Among other attacks on Townley and the Nonpartisan League was a booklet authored by one Jerry Dempster Bacon: *Warning to the Farmer Against Townleyism as Exploited in North Dakota: An Expose and Inside Story of the Methods, Personnel and Menace of the Most Remarkable Phenomenon of Fifty Years in American Political History* (Grand Forks, 1918). This screed was reprinted, along with the League's *General Handbook*, in a 1975 by Arno Press under the title *The National Nonpartisan League Debate*.

5   Speaking of strange characters coming off the Iron Range, how about DFL state representative Tom Rukavina, from district 05A (Hibbing and Virginia), a graduate of the University of Minnesota at Duluth? In 2009, when the University of Minnesota requested a license permitting the sale of alcohol in the luxury boxes of its new football stadium, Rukavina and other state DFLers introduced a bill to require beer sales *throughout* the stadium or nowhere at all, on the populist ground that selling alcohol only in the high-priced seats discriminated against the working-class fans.

6   The fact that the Midwest's ascendency in American Literature coincided with the rise of realism plays a role here, since realism lends itself to political art more than do Romanticism, modernism, or postmodernism. Or one could argue that their Midwest pastoralism turned Midwest modernists against Main Street, and into politically conscious socialist realists. David Holman explains the relationship this way: "Realism — the 'democratic' mode — is appropriate for the region the midwest writer depicts because the history of the Midwest and its inhabitants is inextricably entangled with

populist idealism. . . . Implicit in the idea of the Midwest is the belief that it is a region that holds the promise of Jacksonian democracy" (51).

7   Usually he read "Under the Lion's Paw," the defining story of Midwest Populism, antedating Frank Norris's story "A Deal in Wheat" by a decade: a Kansas homesteader, whose crops have been destroyed four years running by grasshoppers, returns east to Wisconsin, where he signs a three-year contract for a run-down farm at 10 percent annual interest on the contract price of $2,500. After he, his wife, and their nine-year-old son work like fiends to pay their rent and improve the farm, the owner doubles the purchase price, and thus the rent:

> "This farm is worth five thousand and five hundred dollars," said Butler in a careless but decided voice.
>
> "*What!*" almost shrieked the astounded Haskins. "What's that? Five thousand. Why, that's double what you offered it for three years ago."
>
> "Of course; and it's worth it. It was all run down then; now it's in good shape. You've laid out fifteen hundred dollars in improvements according to your own story."
>
> "But *you* had nothin' t' do about that. It's my work an' my money."
>
> "You bet it was; but it's my land." (*Main-Travelled Roads*: 153)

Haskins goes after Butler with a pitchfork. Then again, in light of the long-range debt carried by most Midwest farmers these days, it is nothing short of stupefying to learn that Butler's original offer of a quarter down and three years' time to pay the balance was a reasonable offer, something a farmer might conceivably manage in 1890.

8   In a 1965 interview with Paul Robbins of the *L.A. Free Press*, Dylan, at the height of his first postmodern period, inventoried high school English material: "You go to school, man, and what kind of poetry do you read? You read Robert Frost's 'The Two Roads,' you read T. S. Eliot — you read all that bullshit. . . . And then, on top of it, they throw Shakespeare at some kid who can't read Shakespeare in high school, right? Who digs reading *Hamlet*, man? All they give you is *Ivanhoe, Silas Marner, Tale of Two Cities*" (Cott: 39–40). Screeds like this lead Clinton Heylin to undervalue literary influences and while overvaluing the world of pop, postmodernism, and painting: "Despite displays of literary ambition, one must be wary (as others have not been) of reading too much into Dylan's name-dropping of literary sources in midsixties songs, a list of which would imply an awfully well-read twenty-four-year-old university dropout" (*Revolution*: 249). In his work Dylan references Eliot's *The Waste Land*, Frost's "The Road not Taken" (the untrodden path in "I and I"), and *King Lear* (whose famous admonition "Nothing will come of nothing" is taken by several critics to be the source of "Too much of nothing" . . . unless we are making too much of "nothing") in ways that show he understood them very well. Marqusee reads "Say hello to Valerie, say hello to Vivien" ("Too Much of Nothing") as a reference to Eliot's two wives in a poem which bears traces of Eliot's content (217), and on his English tour of 1965, Dylan changed "Abraham Lincoln said that" in "Talkin' World War III Blues" to "T. S. Eliot said that" (Corcoran: 3), a very clever joke which would have been understood by Dylan's audience at the time.

What exactly Bob Dylan read in high school — what he was assigned to read, what he actually read, what was in the textbooks for him to read — is an intriguing question. The Hibbing High School library long ago deep-sixed textbooks used in those middle fifties classes, but Hibbing High School was well-heeled and probably current in its American Literature anthologies. Odds are that the class used either Ghodes and Hart's *America's Literature* (Holt, Rinehart and Winston, 1955) or Blair, Hornberger and Stewart's *The Literature of the United States* (Scott, Foresman, 1957). Both presented the standard fifties canon. For the record, these canonical authors are John Smith, William Bradford, Roger Williams, Edward Taylor, Cotton Mather, William Byrd, Jonathan Edwards, Benjamin Franklin ("The Way to Wealth"), John Woolman, Jean de Crèvecoeur, Thomas Paine, Thomas Jefferson, Philip Freneau, Washington Irving, William Cullen Bryant, Ralph Waldo Emerson ("Self-Reliance"), Nathaniel Hawthorne, Henry Wadsworth Longfellow ("A Psalm of Life"), John Greenleaf Whittier, Edgar Allan Poe, Oliver Wendell Holmes, Henry Thoreau, James Russell Lowell, Herman Melville, Walt Whitman, Emily Dickinson, Mark Twain, Bret Harte, William Deans Howells, Henry Adams, Sidney Lanier, Henry James, Stephen Crane, Edwin Arlington Robinson, Theodore Dreiser, Robert Frost, Willa Cather, Carl Sandburg, Sinclair Lewis, Eugene O'Neill, T. S. Eliot, William Faulkner, Ernest Hemingway, and Thomas Wolfe. Here endeth American Literature in the 1950s.

The fact that only *The Literature of the United States* contains Eliot's *The Waste Land* and John Steinbeck stories, and the fact that one editor of that collection (Theodore Hornberger) taught at the University of Minnesota, makes *The Literature of the United States* the likely candidate. It is the richer anthology, and contains some idiosyncratic features consonant with Dylan's conceptions of "literature" and writers. In addition to Steinbeck, it contains a broader range of social critics, like Vachel Lindsay, H. L. Mencken, Sherwood Anderson, F. Scott Fitzgerald, Sinclair Lewis, Finley Peter Dunne, Hamlin Garland, and Bret Harte; two interesting groupings of "Literary Comedians" (including Artemus Ward and John Billings) and "Southwestern Yarnspinners" (including Davey Crockett, George Washington Harris, and Thomas Bangs Thorpe); and a running series of American songs offered as a legitimate form of American Literature: "Singers of the Revolution," "Singers of the West," "Civil War Singers," "Spirituals," "Cowboy Songs," songs of the railroad, slums, and pioneer homestead.

Dylan also read outside of the classroom. "He read every book there was," his proud mother told Robert Shelton (*Home*: 41); "he was in the library a lot." Echo Helstrom told Robert Shelton that Bob was always reading something by Steinbeck (51). On the other hand, Dinkytown acquaintances Harry Weber and Harvey Abrams both told Shelton that Dylan read little if at all (67, 69). However, Carla Rotolo says that in New York Dylan "read voraciously" (Shelton, *Home*: 134). In *Tarantula*, he references *Silas Marner*, *King Lear*, *Hamlet*, *Romeo and Juliet*, *Ivanhoe*, *The Great Gatsby*, *The Catcher in the Rye*, Hemingway, e e cummings, and *The Waste Land*. In his biography *No Direction Home*, Shelton has Dylan inventorying poets: "people like Carl Sandburg, T. S. Eliot, Stephen Spender, and Rupert Brooke. Hey, name them — Edna St. Vincent Millay and Robert Louis Stevenson and Edgar Allen Poe and Robert Lowell" (353). Ohio poet and artist Kenneth Patchen, whose *Journal of Albion Moonlight* Shelton sees as the real inspiration for *Tarantula*, was a favorite of Tony Glover, Dylan's Minneapolis friend.

In an essay titled "Playing Time," Nicholas Roe lists alphabetically the numerous writers, works, and literary traditions with which Dylan's songs have been linked, with varying degrees of proof (he misses Patchen): "W. H. Auden, James Baldwin, William Blake, The Bible, Bertolt Brecht, André Breton, Robert Browning, William Burroughs, Lord Byron, Albert Camus, Joseph Conrad, Gregory Corso, Hart Crane, Leonardo Da Vinci, Charles Dickens, John Donne, T. S. Eliot, William Faulkner, F. Scott Fitzgerald, the French symbolists, Allen Ginsberg, the Gothic novel, Robert Graves, Greek tragedy, Arthur Hallam, *Hamlet*, Ernest Hemingway, Herman Hesse, Geoffrey Hill, Homer, James Joyce, Carl Jung, Franz Kafka, Jack Kerouac, Arthur Koestler, F. R. Leavis, Louis MacNiece, Norman Mailer, Andrew Marvell, John Milton, Friedrich Nietzsche, Thomas Pynchon, John Crowe Ransom, Arthur Rimbaud, Christina Rossetti, Carl Sandburg, Scandinavian epics, Scottish ballads, William Shakespeare, John Skelton, John Steinbeck, Dylan Thomas, Henry David Thoreau, twelfth-century troubadours, François Villon, Walt Whitman, W. B. Yeats, and Yevgeny Yevtushenko" (85).

This is an impressive list, although the names are familiar to a male of my geography and generation. Looking at it with an eye to what has become of the literature curriculum at my own Midwestern American university in these politically correct times, I am struck by how tied to time and place that list is. English majors today know neither poet-singers, nor Byron and Milton, Fitzgerald and Hemingway and Kerouac. Not to mention the Bible. And in even their "diversity literature" classes today's students are unlikely to encounter the likes of Christina Rossetti, James Baldwin, or François Villon.

9 Thomas McGrath is virtually unread these days, but in the middle of the twentieth century he was better known. Michael Anania once told me a story of talking poetry in a Chicago cab with Allan Swallow, publisher of Swallow Press, back in the late fifties or early sixties. When he heard the words "poet" and "poetry," the cabbie piped up, "Poetry, eh? Well there's only one goddam poet in this country worth a shit, and that's Tom McGrath."

10 The flow of Italians into the Iron Range crested in 1907; the flow of Slavs, Czechs, Serbs, Slovenes, Jews, Russians, Balts, and Finns crested in 1913. Still, 75 percent of Duluth's population was foreign-born in the early 1900s (Engel: 15). Over 40 nationalities were represented in Hibbing's population, and Old Hibbing had at least four different Lutheran churches tied to four different ethnic groups: Swedish, Finnish, German, and American. Today a glass case outside of the Hibbing High School library showcases dolls in ethnic costumes to commemorate Hibbing's cultural diversity.

11 Dylan is among these Jeffersonians. "In the home of the brave, Jefferson's turnin' over in his grave," Dylan sings in "Slow Train"; "We carried you in our arms / On Independence Day," he sings in "Tears of Rage." Craig Scobie finds the Christian lyrics of *Slow Train Coming* a "return to the themes of social critique so prominent in the early 1960s," but from a "communally based position" in contrast with his more individualistic/anarchistic hard rock songs. He finds them dangerous in being

too closely associated with the language of born-again Christianity, uncomfortably right wing. "On the whole, however," he decides, reversing himself slightly, "Dylan's position might be described more accurately as populist than as reactionary" (170–1). Of course prairie populists can seem reactionary: Bob Dylan's favorite politician (*Chronicles*: 283) was the man for whom both Bill Holm and I cast our first-ever votes for President of the United States: Barry Goldwater.

12   The problem, he suggests in another song from *The Basement Tapes*, is that after all the plans and promises, "Nothing Was Delivered." The time for accounting has arrived, and the sooner you come up with answers, the sooner you can go.

13   Some elements of this speech sound typically Midwest egalitarian populist: "There's no black and white, left and right to me anymore; there's up and down, and down is very close to the ground." What got Dylan in trouble were his remarks on class — "I was on the [August 28, 1963] March on Washington up on the platform and I looked around at all the Negroes there and I didn't see any Negroes that looked like none of my friends. My friends don't wear *suits*" (Shelton, *Home*: 200).

14   Dylan might not be as much of an anachronism as Førland thinks. Introducing an issue of *Dædalus*, the journal of the American Academy of Arts and Sciences, focused entirely on *Minnesota: A Different America?* editor Stephen R. Graubard says that the idea for the special issue came from an awareness among European intellectuals that the America they were getting from the media was very much New York and Washington and L.A., but very little the Midwest and South, and their sense that America outside those metropolitan areas "had turned inward" upon itself somewhere around 1990 (v). Ten years later, in the midst of national hysteria after 9–11, a colleague who will remain anonymous expressed what amounts to a 40-years-later version of Dylan's isolationism: "There aren't enough airplanes in the world to take out every corn field in Southwest Minnesota." Pressed for elaboration, he gave me a 40-years-later version of Dylan's Iron Range antipathy for the military-industrial complex headquartered "out East": "What do they expect when they headquarter American economic imperialism in the symbolic 'World Trade Center' — really the 'World Exploitation Center' — and American military imperialism in the Pentagon? Of course some pissed third-world radicals are going to take a shot at buildings like that."

15   Bill Holm claimed Senator Eugene McCarthy refused to sing "God bless America" because he did not feel America should be singled out for blessing over any other place on earth. If this is true, McCarthy was a true prairie populist. If it's not, Holm is being prairie populist.

16   However, Zantzinger was apparently an asshole after all. Mark Edmundson reported in 1997, "After serving his six months for the death of Hattie Carroll, it turns out Zantzinger eventually came into a handsome inheritance and went on to be a respected real-estate owner in southern Maryland. Then in 1991 he was exposed by the local press as a slumlord who charged poor black families exorbitant rents to live in wooden shacks with no running water or toilets. The properties, a reporter discovered, didn't even belong to him — he'd lost them for nonpayment of taxes five years before. Zantzinger's well-placed friends spoke up for him ('the nicest guy you'd ever want

to meet,' said a member of the state legislature), but he was sentenced to 18 months in jail" (53).

17   *Rolling Stone* (July 9, 1970) did an amusing story on Dylan at Princeton, beginning "Yes, it's true, Bob Dylan accepted an honorary degree from Princeton University," and continuing "All during the ceremony, Dave Crosby was licking a half-orange and looking greatly amused," before closing, "After the ceremony, Dylan left the stage, took off his robe and, with his party, got into a waiting car and drove on down the road" (Thomson and Gutman: 134–6).

18   The retribution foreseen in "When the Ship Comes In" owes something to Berthold Brecht's song "Pirate Jenny," to which Suze Rotollo introduced Dylan in 1963 when she worked as assistant to the stage manager for an off-Broadway production of a play called *Brecht on Brecht.* "The song is a tale of the toil and trouble of a hotel maid constantly ordered about by everyone," Rotolo recalls in *A Freewheelin' Time;* "She sings her song of revenge as the Pirate Jenny on a great ship, the Black Freighter, where all her tormentors are taken prisoner. One by one, she sends them to their death. The hour of her ship had come in" (234). Dylan mentions Brecht briefly in "11 Outlined Epitaphs," and discusses "Pirate Jenny" at some length in *Chronicles.* What first drew him into the song, he admits, was the sound of the freighter itself, which called up instant memories of ships in Duluth with their great foghorns in the dark. Then he forgot about the foghorn and focused on the story of the scrubbing maid and the gentlemen she had served, now brought before her for judgment: "the gentlemen are chained up and brought to her and she's asked if they should be killed now or later. It's up to her. The old scrubbing lady's eyes light up at the end of the song. The ship is shooting guns from its bow and the gentlemen are wiping the laughs off their faces. The ship is still turning around in the harbor. The old lady says, 'Kill 'em right now, that'll learn 'em.' What did the gentlemen do to deserve such a fate? The song doesn't say. . . . It's a nasty song, sung by an evil fiend, and when she's done singing, there's not a word to say. It leaves you breathless" (275).

19   Summarizing an essay on American idealism in Bob Dylan and the folk protest movement, James Dunlap writes, "Bob Dylan's approach to folk music initially appeared compatible with the political outlook of the older left-wing sponsors of *Sing Out!* and *Broadside* magazines. However, with pre-World War II attitudes, such sponsors generally viewed folk music as a way to understand or promote the common beliefs and aspirations of entire social groups. Dylan, by contrast, often used songs to focus on the feelings of unique individuals" (549).

20   A band member on the 1990 tour told Howard Sounes that Dylan was not much for fancy motels either: "Bob has this penchant for staying out of town in little motels. . . . We were stuck in some really out of the way places" (393). Robert Shelton tells a relevant anecdote of attending a black gospel festival in New York with Dylan back in 1962: "There were two fascinating women at the gospel show; Dylan was taken with one and appalled by the ostentatious life-style of the other. Mavis Staples and Bob hit it off like lightning smacking an Iowa barn. Pop Staples smiled benevolently at the obvious attraction. After all, isn't God love? But God is also righteous anger, and when the late 'Queen of Gospel,' Mahalia Jackson, got out of her fancy limousine with

flowing capes and courtiers keeping her long skirts out of the mud, Dylan ranted in my ear that that wasn't his idea of what gospel music was all about" ("Change": 15).

21 Aaron Brown's column, reprinted in his book *Overburden*, says it all and says it well: "Hibbing's most famous son just released an autobiography. It was big news — on the cover of *Newsweek*, touted in *Rolling Stone*. These are national magazines. Near as I can tell, only a couple dozen copies of his book were sold in our town. This column is the first time Bob Dylan's *Chronicles, Vol. 1* has been mentioned in this, our hometown newspaper. The book came out twelve days ago. Such is the quirky mystique of Bob Dylan in Hibbing" (103).

22 According to Paul Henry Landis, "The original census forms for the [Minnesota] State Census list fifty-three Virginia women as 'demi-monde' and three as 'prostitutes.' Thirteen Hibbing women were listed as 'sports.' Many men were also of questionable character, nineteen being listed as gamblers in this first census of Virginia" (20). Later in his book Landis writes, "Prostitutes in those days, according to informants, did not seclude themselves from public view in daylight on the streets. There was no shame in their vocation, for a considerable part of the female population could be labeled *demimonde*. Prostitutes were not respected by all but were, apparently tolerated" (66). Landis passes along the recollections of an old logger: "But the old days when we came down from the woods were glorious ones. For the first week we always owned the town. The constable and sheriff either had business about that time in some neighboring town or locked themselves up in their houses. The wild dissipation we indulged in and the amount of villainous whiskey we consumed would kill anyone except one possessed with a constitution such as a winter's campaign in the woods insures" (69).

23 Charles Starkweather and his under-aged girlfriend Caril (sic) Ann Fugate murdered 11 people in Nebraska and Wyoming in 1958, including, early on, her family. The story was famous across America, and the pair became kind of folk heroes, a modern Bonnie and Clyde. The story inspired a number of films including *Starkweather, Murder in the Heartland*, and *Natural Born Killers*. Dylan mentions Charlie Starkweather briefly in *Tarantula* (8), and Bruce Springsteen's song "Nebraska" was originally "Starkweather."

24 In the *Rolling Stone* interview of December 22, 2001, Dylan says that Marcus makes "way too much" of the influence Smith's *Anthology* had on him (Cott: 423), "that's not what everybody was listening to," but song after song in Dylan's oeuvre reflects one song or another in the *Anthology*. David Boucher's list of borrowings from songs in the collection runs nearly a page in *Dylan & Cohen: Poets of Rock and Roll* (126).

25 Dylan gives Rambling, Gambling Willie's real name as Will O'Conley, but aces backed with eights is the "dead man's hand" held by Wild Bill Hickok when he was shot in the back of the head by Crooked Nose McCall on August 2, 1876, in Deadwood Gulch, the Black Hills, South Dakota. One has to believe Dylan heard the legend his summer in Colorado, in 1960.

Notes to Chapter 6: The Prophet and His Mission

1   In *Chronicles*, Dylan recalls his fascination with Lincoln and the Civil War during his first year in New York City, when he started reading articles in microfilmed newspapers from 1855 to 1865 in the Public Library: *Chicago Tribune, Brooklyn Daily Times, Pennsylvania Freeman, Memphis Daily Eagle, Savannah Daily Herald, Cincinnati Enquirer.* Slavery, he notes, was only one concern of the period, along with reform, gambling, crime, child labor, temperance, loyalty oaths, and religious revivals. Lincoln, he says, shows up in the late 1850s, caricatured as a baboon or giraffe. "After a while you become aware of nothing but a culture of feeling," he writes, "of black days, of schism, evil for evil, the common destiny of the human being getting thrown off course" (85). Dylan draws parallels between America in the 1850s and America in the 1950s, and concludes, "Back there, America was put on the cross, died and was resurrected. There was nothing synthetic about it. The god-awful truth of that would be the all-encompassing template behind everything that I would write" (86).

2   In analyzing *The American Jeremiad*, Sacvan Bercovitch extends Perry Miller's book *Errand into the Wilderness*, building on Miller's description, and pointing out a crucial distinction in the American version. "The traditional mode," he writes, "the European jeremiad, was a lament over the ways of the world. It decried the sins of 'the people' — a community, a nation, a civilization, mankind in general — and warned of God's wrath to follow" (7). Thus the name of the trope; thus Christ purges the money changers from the temple ("It was written, 'My house shall be called a house of prayer,' but you make it a den of robbers"; Matthew 21.13) and dismisses the Pharisees and Sadducees as "a brood of vipers" (Matthew 3.7). But the from the start, American preachers sounded a different note, revising the message of the jeremiad, not to minimize the threat of divine retribution, but to temper the threat by suggesting that God's punishments were corrective, not destructive. God's punishments confirmed His promise (8).

3   The prophet naturally identifies with the figure of Christ and expects to suffer rejection and suffering himself. Not only is Dylan a poet-prophet, some people have seen him as Christ returned to earth. Anthony Scaduto quotes an Australian actress who met Dylan in the 1960s to the effect that "I came to believe that Dylan was Christ revisited. I felt that everything fitted, without being Christian-religious or anything" (238). Robert Shelton quotes a letter in *Melody Maker*, 1970, captioned "Dylan is the New Christ": "Bob Dylan (and not, as previously reported, Jesus of Nazareth) is the living Messiah to today's young people. . . . You can learn more about life from Dylan than from 10 Jesuses" (*Home*: 199). The connection between Dylan-prophet and Christ is implicit in several Dylan songs, and explicit in "Yonder Comes Sin": "Jeremiah preached repentance / To those who would turn from hell / But the critics gave him bad reviews / Even threw him to the bottom of the well."

4   Shelton has Dylan "one of a half dozen regulars" at *Broadside* meetings in 1962" (*Home*: 140), perhaps because Broadside crew was "intimate and human" in contrast to the stolid Old Left-wing politicos at *Sing Out!* (141). For the record, *Broadside* magazine considered the following songs close enough to "topical protest" material to publish them between 1962 and 1965: "Talkin' John Birch Paranoid Blues," "Let Me Die in

My Footsteps," "Blowin' in the Wind," "Ain't Gonna Grieve," "The Death of Emmett Till," "Oxford Town," "Paths of Victory," "Masters of War," "Train A-Travelin'," "Don't Think Twice, It's All Right," "Ballad of Hollis Brown," "John Brown," "Only a Hobo," "Farewell," "With God on Our Side," "Who Killed Davey Moore?" "A Hard Rain's A-Gonna Fall," "Only a Pawn in Their Game," "The Times They Are A-Changin'," "The Lonesome Death of Hattie Carroll," and "It's All Right, Ma (I'm Only Bleeding)," described by Ralph Gleason as a "bitter attack on the American Dream" (McGregor: 190). The songs were published lyrics only, sometimes with illustrations, in the manner of a poem, or the songs of *Lyrics: 1962–2001*.

5   According to Clinton Heylin, Dylan's one-take performance for John Hammond at Columbia Studio A on December 6, 1962, elicited a stunned, "Don't tell me that's all" (*Stolen Moments*: 35).

6   *Broadside* 48 lists Dylan as a contributing editor, a practice which continues until *Broadside* 58, when Dylan's name disappears. Dylan did, however, help Phil Ochs out with his Friends of Chile benefit concert at Felt Forum on May 9, 1974. He did occasionally perform his early protest songs, most often "The Lonesome Death of Hattie Carroll" and most notably "Ballad of Hollis Brown" at the Live Aid concert of 1985. And Dylan would write and record other topical protest songs throughout his career. But when *Broadside* 116 (November–December 1971) printed "George Jackson," public reaction focused more on Dylan's motives for writing the song than on what happened to Jackson in the California jail. Dylan's remarks to Robert Shelton in 1986, 20 years after he lay down the weary tune of topical protest, are the voice of a Jeremiah still mindful of his mission: "We agreed that America was in trouble again, that the masters of war were still in power. Dylan did not say how, or if, he might remount the barricades. Yet, when he said to me, 'They're not going to get away with it,' there was a steely resolve in his voice" (*Home*: 18).

7   "A Colossal American Copulation" was written by Adrian C. Louis, whose office is between mine and Bill Holm's at Southwest Minnesota State University:

> They say there's a promise
> coming down that dusty road.
> They say there's a promise coming
> down that dusty road, but I don't see it.
> So, fuck the bluebird of happiness.
> Fuck the men who keep their dogs chained.
> Fuck the men who molest their daughters.
> Ditto the men who wrap their dicks
> in the Bible and then claim the right
> to speak for female reproductive organs.
> Likewise the men who hunt coyotes.
> And the whining farmers who get paid
> for not growing corn and wheat.
> The same to the *National Enquirer*.
> Also Madonna (Santa Evita, indeed).

Yes, add the gutless Tower of Babel
that they call the United Nations . . .

Fuck a duck!
And the '60s and all that righteous reefer.
Fuck James Dean and his red jacket.
John Wayne and the gelding
American horse he rode in on.
The IRA and their songs and bombs.
All the Gila monsters in Arizona.
Bob Dylan for leading me astray
for three misty, moping decades.
My gall bladder for exploding.
Fuck *The Wasteland* by T. S. Eliot
and all those useless allusions.
Fuck war in every form and all other clichés.
Fuck, no, double-fuck the Vietnam War.
Every cruel act I ever committed.
Every random act of kindness. . . .

(*Ceremonies of the Damned*: 58, 59)

8   Dylan's unconscious or conscious "source" for "Blowin' in the Wind," most people now agree, was a passage in Guthrie's *Bound for Glory* about the futility of telling the story of the lower classes: "Limp papers whipped and beat upwards, rose into the air and fell head over heels, curving over backwards and sideways, over and over, loose sheets of newspaper with pictures of people and stories of people printed somewhere on them, turning loops in the air. And it was blow little paper blow! Twist and turn and stay up as long as you can, and when you come down, come down on a penthouse porch, come down so easy so's not to hurt yourself. . . . But keep on trying to tell your message, and keep on trying to be a picture of a man, because without that story and without that message printed on you there, you wouldn't be much. Remember, it's just maybe someday, some time, somebody will pick you up and look at your picture and read your message" (295). In an interview with Gil Turner, Dylan provided the bridge when asked about the origins and meaning of his song: "I still say it's in the wind and just like a restless piece of paper — it's got to come down some time. But the only trouble is that no-one picks up the answer when it comes down so not too many people get to see and know it . . . and then it flies away again" (Muir, *Troubadour*: 9).

9   Thoreau wrote, "Age is no better, hardly so well qualified for an instructor as youth, for it has not profited so much as it has lost. One may almost doubt if the wisest man has learned any thing of absolute value by living. Practically, the old have no very important advice to give the young, their own experience has been so partial, and their lives have been such miserable failures, for private reasons, as they must believe. . . . I have lived some thirty years on this planet, and I have yet to hear the first syllable of valuable or even earnest advice from my seniors. They have told me nothing, and

probably cannot tell me any thing, to the purpose" (5). This was, of course, the source of the sixties slogan "Don't trust anyone over 30," although now old sixties types are suspicious of anyone *under* 30.

10 In one of the more memorable scenes in the very memorable 1969 film *Easy Rider*, biker Billy and alcoholic lawyer George Hanson (Jack Nicholson) discuss freedom in America:

> George: You know, this used to be a hell of a good country. I can't understand what's gone wrong with it.
> Billy: Huh. Man, everybody got chicken, that's what happened, man. Hey, we can't even get into like, uh, second-rate hotel, I mean, a second-rate motel. You dig? They think we're gonna cut their throat or something, man. They're scared, man.
> George: Oh, they're not scared of you. They're scared of what you represent to 'em.
> Billy: Hey man. All we represent to them, man, is somebody needs a haircut.
> George: Oh no. What you represent to them is freedom.
> Billy: What the hell's wrong with freedom? That's what it's all about.
> George: Oh yeah, that's right, that's what it's all about, all right. But talkin' about it and bein' it — that's two different things. I mean, it's real hard to be free when you are bought and sold in the marketplace. 'Course, don't ever tell anybody that they're not free 'cause then they're gonna get real busy killin' and maimin' to prove to you that they are. Oh yeah, they're gonna talk to you, and talk to you, and talk to you about individual freedom, but they see a free individual, it's gonna scare 'em.
> Billy: Mmmm, well, that don't make 'em runnin' scared.
> George: No, it makes 'em dangerous.

11 Andy Gill claims Hardin killed 30 people, none of whom deserved to die; other sources say 40. Gill writes, "Born the son of a Methodist preacher on the 26 May 1853, Hardin lived a life of gambling, roaming and killing, with several notches on his gun-handles before he reached the age of 21, largely as a result of the hair-trigger temper for which he was famed. Again contrary to Dylan's interpretation, he was not immune to the occasional foolish move, the most serious being when he attracted the attentions of the Texas Rangers by killing a deputy sheriff of Brown County, Texas. Hardin was tracked down and captured in Pensacola, Florida in July 1877, and sentenced to 25 years in jail the following year. He was released with a full pardon in 1894, having spent his time in prison learning law. Upon his release he became a lawyer, and it was while prosecuting a case in El Paso, Texas, that, on August 19, 1895, he himself was finally killed, shot in the back of the head by one John Selman, a local constable, in an echo of the death of Jesse James mentioned by Dylan in 'Outlaw Blues'" (127). "John Wesley Harding" also owes something to Woody Guthrie's portrait of Pretty Boy Floyd.

12 Those of us who grew up in the sixties thought the glass shattered with Vietnam. Bush and Bush, however, managed to forget Vietnam long enough to invent Iran and Iraq, so that the glass could shatter twice. In 2008 retired military officer and historian Andrew Bacevich published his own jeremiad titled *The Limits of Power: The End of American Exceptionalism*, which traces the decline of the world's strongest and richest power

from the end of World War II to the present, citing as its cause the nation's growing arrogance, from Kennedy to Bush.

13   The Rolling Stones concluded their retrospective 1978 album *Some Girls* with a declaration of bankruptcy: "What a mess, this town's in tatters. . . . My brain's been battered." In the final chapter of *A Generation in Motion: Popular Music and Culture in the Sixties*, I described the seventies as "virtually uninhabitable" (221). My friend John Nemo, who had grown up in Minnesota and later became Dean of the College St. Thomas in St. Paul, actually threw a party on December 31, 1979, to celebrate the end of the decade. But you can catch a few episodes of *That 70's Show* and decide for yourself. One thing is certain: the currently popular concept of a monolithic "baby boomer" generation does us a great disservice in lumping together those who achieved adolescence in the difficult and turbulent sixties and those who spent their teens and early twenties in the comfortable, placid seventies. Those are two schools of very different fish.

14   On the 1965 tour of Britain, Shelton reports, "A reporter for the *Jewish Chronicle* asked [Dylan]: 'Are you Jewish?' He replied: 'No, I am not, but some of my best friends are'" (*Home*: 291). If Dylan didn't feel especially Jewish when he was in Hibbing, perhaps the reason is that the Agudath Achim Synagogue at 2320 second Avenue West was actually the old Swedish Evangelical Emanuel Lutheran Church from North Hibbing, bought from Oliver Mining Company and moved to South Hibbing. The building lost its steeple, but it retained its basic shape and the four arched church windows on either side. Steven Heine's *Bargainin' for Salvation* contains a recent photo of the building (36). Most of the time it had no rabbi. Or perhaps the influence of Blessed Sacrament Roman Catholic Church, a huge building which sat one block down the road from Dylan's house, constituted a larger, more immediate presence than Agudath Achim on the far side of town.

15   Michael Gray sometimes distinguishes between what is Midwest in Dylan and what is biblical (*Song*: 160), but in fact there is plenty of overlap: what James Spiegel (138) labels "the compatibalist approach" to religion (finding room within God's providence for human freedom and responsibility) is basically a Midwest reconciliation of the need to work for one's own survival with a recognition of how much our survival is circumscribed by the whims of God's nature. Perhaps this is one reason the Midwest ethos is, on its surface, Protestant-Christian.

16   On December 4, 1956, Elvis Presley, Carl Perkins, Jerry Lee Lewis, and Johnny Cash found themselves in an impromptu jam session in the Sun Records Studio. Somebody hit the "record" button on Sam Phillips's tape machine, giving posterity the gift now known as the *Million Dollar Quartet*, released officially in February 1990. The recording was brilliant in its talent and spontaneity — it was later made into a musical — and a revelation: with no preparation or thought, these four founders of rock-'n'-roll sang one gospel song after another: "Just a Little Talk with Jesus," "Jesus Walked that Lonesome Valley," "I Shall not Be Moved," "Peace in the Valley," "Farther Along," "Blessed Jesus (Hold My Hand)," "As We Travel Along the Jericho Road." They knew the words, and they knew the harmonies. These songs were their roots.

17   "Ya doesn't have ta call me Johnson," the routine begins. ("Johnson" was a slang term

for penis; cf. the film *PCU* in which one of the male band members suggests the band name itself "My Johnson is Twelve Inches" and one of the female band members says, "Interesting, but not relevant"). "You can call me Ray, or you can call me Jay, or you can call me Johnny, or you can call me Sonny, or you can call me Ray Jay, or you can call me RJ . . . but ya doesn't hafta call me Johnson."

Notes to "Ain't Talkin'": A Postscript

1   Dylan's song "In the Garden," where the garden is clearly the Garden of Gethsemane, may offer a useful gloss on the garden of "Ain't Talkin'."

2   We may look and listen beyond Minnesota for these curmudgeons. On August 5, 2009, I overheard a conversation in an Uptown Chicago diner on Lawrence, just off the Lake (a couple of blocks from where Studs Terkel used to live) which sounded like something straight out of Bob Dylan: a jeremiad of mixed lamentations and threats: "The end is in sight, brother." "Tell it, brother." "I know the times we're livin' in. Revelations is here. Women going with women, men going with men, children going against their parents." "I hear, brother." "My dad had him a job workin' in the post office. I came home from high school, told him my shoes were square. I wanted them new ones. He says, 'Go get yourself a job. $8 an hour, that's $64 a day. You want more, come back tomorrow.' Now some kid come up and try to take your money. Not from this old boy. He gonna try the wrong guy. You reap what you sow. I'll lay him out. Ain't gonna need no cop, either." "Amen, brother." "He mess with me, he be tryin' the wrong guy."

3   Robert Shelton suggests that Dylan may have seen his manager Albert Grossman as a substitute father whom he "had never known" (Sounes: 233) and sought, consciously or unconsciously, to kill in the 1970s (145). Is Dylan now seeing Abe and Albert and the father values in a new light? Dylan's comments on his father in *Chronicles* seem also conciliatory: "My father had his own way of looking at things. To him life was hard work. He came from a generation of different values, heroes and music, and wasn't so sure that the truth would set anybody free. He was pragmatic and always had a word of cryptic advice" (226).

4   Bly grew up on a Minnesota farm, and the pastoral tradition especially plays male against female in fashion not especially complimentary to men: the organic female land is raped by inorganic male machines, be they tractors or ore shovels; men obsessed with making a lot of money exploit nurturing women; the proper relationship between humans and landscape, emblemized by marriage, is destroyed, as are the marriages themselves. Men appear to have all the power and to abuse that power, but in her maternal amplitude the female land absorbs men's violence and replenishes herself while the men either disappear or degenerate into alcoholics or village characters.

5   The eleventh stanza of Dylan's song comes almost entirely from Ovid, picking up almost verbatim Ovid's "loyal and much loved companions," "who approve, and share, your code," and "I practice terms long abandoned." Dylan borrowed at least three other lines from Ovid in the rest of "Ain't Talkin'," and more in other songs on the album.

(Also on the album he borrowed from other poets.) These allusions seem less central to the song than the others I've discussed at greater length. For a detailed list, see Cliff Fell, "An Avid Follower of Ovid." In connection with Dylan and Ovid, we remember that in 1957, Robert Allen Zimmerman was a member of the Hibbing High School Latin Club.

References

Allen, Harold. *Minor Dialect Areas of the Upper Midwest*. Tuscaloosa: University of Alabama Press, 1958.

——*The Linguistic Atlas of the Upper Midwest*. 3 vols. Minneapolis: University of Minnesota Press, 1973–76.

Amato, Joseph. *When Father and Son Conspire*. Ames: Iowa State University Press, 1988.

American Tongues. Dir. Louis Alvarez and Andrew Kolker. Video cassette. New York: Center for New American Media, 1987.

Anderson, Chester G., ed. *Growing Up in Minnesota*. Minneapolis: University of Minnesota Press, 1976.

Anderson, Sherwood. *Winesburg, Ohio*. Ed. Malcolm Cowley. New York: Viking, 1958.

——*Letters of Sherwood Anderson*. Ed. Howard Mumford Jones. Boston: Little, Brown and Company, 1953.

Bacevich, Andrew. *The Limits of Power: The End of American Exceptionalism*. New York: Henry Holt and Company, 2008.

Baez, Joan. *Daybreak: An Autobiography*. New York: Dial Press, 1968.

Barillas, William. *The Midwestern Pastoral*. Athens: Ohio University Press, 2006.

Barrow, Tony. *John, Paul, George, Ringo & Me: The Real Beatles Story*. New York: Thunder's Mouth Press, 2005.

Bauldie, John. *Bob Dylan: The Bootleg Series, Volumes 1–3*. (Booklet Notes.) Columbia CD C3K 47382, 1991.

——*Wanted Man: In Search of Bob Dylan*. New York: Citadel Press, 1991.

Baum, L. Frank. *The Annotated Wizard of Oz*. Ed. Michael Patrick Hern. New York: Norton, 2000.

Beckwith, Francis. "Busy Being Born Again: Bob Dylan's Christian Philosophy." Porter and Vernezze 145–55.

Beebee, Thomas O. "Ballad of the Apocalypse: Another Look at Bob Dylan's 'Hard Rain.'" *Text and Performance Quarterly* 11.1 (1991): 18–34.

Bercovitch, Sacvan. *The American Jeremiad*. Madison: University of Wisconsin Press, 1978.

Berry, Wendell. *The Unsettling of America: Culture and Agriculture*. New York: Avon Books, 1978.

341

Beverley, Robert. *The History and Present State of Virginia.* (In Four Parts). London: Printed for R. Parker, 1705.

Blair, Walter, Theodore Hornberger, and Randall Stewart, eds. *The Literature of the United States.* Chicago: Scott, Foresman and Company, 1957.

Blake, Mark, ed. *Dylan: Visions, Portraits & Back Pages.* New York: DK Publishing, 2005.

Blegen, Theodore C. *Minnesota: A History of the State.* Minneapolis: University of Minnesota Press, 1963.

Bly, Carol. *Letters from the Country.* New York: Penguin, 1982.

Bly, Robert. *Iron John: A Book About Men.* Reading, Massachusetts: Addison-Wesley, 1990.

——*Selected Poems.* New York: Harper & Row, 1986.

——"Being a Lutheran Boy-God in Minnesota." Chester Anderson 205–22.

Boucher, David. *Dylan & Cohen: Poets of Rock and Roll.* New York: Continuum, 2004.

Boucher, David and Gary Browning, eds. *The Political Art of Bob Dylan.* Hampshire, UK: Palgrave MacMillan, 2004.

Bradford, William. *Of Plymouth Plantation: 1620–1647.* Ed. Samuel Eliot Morison. New York: Alfred A. Knopf, 1987.

Bradshaw, Michael. *Regions and Regionalism in the United States.* Jackson: University of Mississippi Press, 1988.

Bream, Jon. "Bob Dylan: Expect the Unexpected When He Performs." *The Minneapolis Star* 27 October 1978: C2.

Bromfield, Louis. *The Farm.* New York: Harper, 1933.

Brown, Aaron. *Overburden: Modern Life on the Iron Range.* Duluth, Minnesota: Red Step Press, 2008.

Brown, Richard. "Highway 61 and Other American States of Mind." Corcoran 193–220.

Buechsel, Mark Peter. *The American Pastoral Revisited.* Unpublished manuscript submitted to Kent State University Press, 2008.

Caddy, John. *The Color of Mesabi Bones.* Minneapolis: Milkweed Editions, 1989.

——*Eating the Sting.* Minneapolis: Milkweed Editions, 1986.

Campbell, Gregg M. "Bob Dylan and the Pastoral Apocalypse." *Journal of Popular Culture* 8.4 (1974): 696–707.

Campbell, Joseph and Bill Moyers. *The Power of Myth.* New York: Doubleday, 1988.

Capel, Maurice. "The Blessing of the Damned." Thomson and Gutman 102–16.

Carpenter, D. A. "Living in the Land of Nod: Dylan's Vision of America." *Judas!* 18 (July 2006): 3–35.

Cartwright, Bert. *The Bible in the Lyrics of Bob Dylan.* Bury, Lancashire: Wanted Man, 1985.

Carver, Craig. *American Regional Dialects.* Ann Arbor: University of Michigan Press, 1989.

Cassidy, Frederick. ed. *Dictionary of American Regional English.* Cambridge, Massachusetts: Belknap Press of Harvard University Press, 1985–96.

——*Dictionary of American Regional English.* Cambridge, Massachusetts: Belknap Press of Harvard University Press, 1985.

Cather, Willa. *My Ántonia.* Boston: Houghton Mifflin, 1918.

——*O Pioneers!* Boston: Houghton Mifflin, 1913.

Cheyette, Bryan. "On the 'D' Train: Bob Dylan's Conversions." Corcoran 221–52.

Child, Ben. "Raised in the Country, Working in the Town: Temporal and Spatial Modernisms in Bob Dylan's *Love and Theft.*" *Popular Music and Society* 32.2 (May 2009): 199–210.

Ching, Barbara and Gerald W. Creed, eds. *Knowing Your Place: Rural Identity and Cultural Hierarchy*. New York: Routledge, 1997.

Chrislock, Carl H. *The Progressive Era in Minnesota, 1899–1918*. St. Paul: Minnesota Historical Society Press, 1971.

Clemens, Samuel Langhorn. *Adventures of Huckleberry Finn*. Ed. Sculley Bradley. New York: W. W. Norton, 1961.

Coffino, Michael A. "Genre, Narrative and Judgment: Legal and Protest Song Stories in Two Criminal Cases." *Judas!* 13 (April 2005): 4–26.

Cohen, John and Happy Traum. "Conversations with Bob Dylan." McGregor 264–92.

Cohen, Scott. "'Don't Ask Me Nothin' About Nothin' I Might Just Tell You the Truth: Bob Dylan Revisited," *Spin* December 1985.

Conlogue, William. *Working the Garden*. Chapel Hill: University of North Carolina Press, 2001.

Corcoran, Neil, ed. *"Do You, Mr Jones?": Bob Dylan with the Poets and Professors*. London: Chatto & Windus, 2002.

Corn, David. "Jerusalem Calling." *Nation* 4 November 2002: 20–2.

Cott, Jonathan, ed. *Bob Dylan: The Essential Interviews*. New York: Wenner Media, 2006.

de Crèvecoeur, J. Hector St. John. *Letters from an American Farmer and Sketches of 18th-Century America*. Ed. Albert E. Stone. New York: Penguin, 1981.

Crowe, Cameron. "Liner Notes and Text," *Biograph* (LP). New York: Columbia Records, 1985.

Curtler, Hugh Mercer. *Provoking Thought*. Gainesville: Florida Academic Press, 2009.

Dangel, Leo. *Home from the Field*. Granite Falls, Minnesota: Spoon River Poetry Press, 1997.

Day, Aidan."Dylan's Judgment." *American Studies in Scandinavia* 39.1 (2007): 84–101.

——*Jokerman: Reading the Lyrics of Bob Dylan*. Oxford: Basil Blackwell, 1988.

De Somogyi, Nick. *Jokerman and Thieves: Bob Dylan and the Ballad Tradition*. Bury, Lancashire: Wanted Man, 1986.

DeMott, Robert, ed. *Conversations with Jim Harrison*. Jackson: University of Mississippi Press, 2002.

Dempster, Jerry. *The National Nonpartisan League Debate*. New York: Arno Press, 1975.

Diddle, Gavin. "Robert Hilburn Interview: West Berlin, 13–6–84." *Talkin' Bob Dylan*. Gavin Diddle, 1984. 26–30.

Dillard, Annie. *An American Childhood*. New York: Harper & Row, 1987.

——*Living by Fiction*. New York: Harper & Row, 1982.

Dreiser, Theodore. *Sister Carrie*. New York: Norton, 1970.

Dunlap, James. "Through the Eyes of Tom Joad: Patterns of American Idealism, Bob Dylan, and the Folk Protest Movement." *Popular Music and Society* 29.5 (December 2006): 549–73.

Dylan, Bob. *The Bob Dylan Scrapbook, 1956–1966*. New York: Simon & Schuster, 2005.

——*Lyrics: 1962-2001*. New York: Simon & Schuster, 2004.

——*Chronicles, Volume One*. New York: Simon & Schuster, 2004.

——*Lyrics, 1962-1985*. New York: Knopf, 1985.

——"Jacket Notes," *Planet Waves* (LP). New York: Asylum Records, 1974.

——*Tarantula*. New York: Macmillan, 1971.

——"Three Kings" (Jacket Notes), *John Wesley Harding* (LP). New York: Columbia CS 9604, 1968.

——"Jacket Notes," *Bringing It All Back Home* (LP). New York: Columbia CL 2328, 1965.

——"11 Outlined Epitaphs" (Jacket and Liner Notes), *The Times They Are A-Changin'* (LP). New York: Columbia CS 8905, 1964.

——"Some other kinds of songs" (Jacket Notes), *Another Side of Bob Dylan* (LP). New York: Columbia CS 8993, 1964.

——"Jacket Notes," *Joan Baez in Concert, Part 2* (LP). New York: Vanguard, VSD-2123, 1963.

Edmundson, Mark. "Tangled Up in Truth." *Civilization* October–November 1997: 50–55.

Eliot, T. S. *The Complete Poems and Plays, 1909–1950*. New York: Harcourt, Brace & World, 1962.

——"Tradition and the Individual Talent." *The Sacred Wood: Essays on Poetry and Criticism*. New York: Barnes & Noble, 1960.

Ellison, Ralph. *Invisible Man*. New York: Random House, 1952.

Emerson, Ralph Waldo. "The Young American." *Works*. Vol. 1. Cambridge, Massachusetts: Riverside Press, 1983.

—— "Nature." *The Works of Ralph Waldo Emerson*. Vol. 1. Boston: Houghton, Mifflin and Company, 1855.

Engel, Dave. *Just Like Bob Zimmerman's Blues: Dylan in Minnesota*. Mesabi, Wisconsin: River City Memoirs, 1997.

Ervin, Jean, ed. *The Minnesota Experience: An Anthology*. Minneapolis: The Adams Press, 1979.

Etter, Dave. *Alliance, Illinois*. Peoria, Illinois: Spoon River Poetry Press, 1983; reprinted Evanston, Illinois: Northwestern University Press, 2005.

——*Selected Poems*. Peoria, Illinois: Spoon River Poetry Press, 1987.

Fell, Cliff. "An Avid Follower of Ovid." *Nelson Mail* 7 October 2006: 22.

Fitzgerald, F. Scott. "The Rich Boy." *Babylon Revisited & Other Stories*, New York: Charles Scribner's Sons, 1960.

——*The Crack-Up*. (Originally published *Esquire*, February 1936.) New York: New Directions, 1945.

——*The Great Gatsby*. New York: Charles Scribner's Sons, 1925.

Ford, Mark. "Trust Yourself: Emerson and Dylan." Corcoran 127–42.

Førland, Tor Egil. "Bringing It All Back Home: Or, Another Side of Bob Dylan: Midwestern Isolationist." *Journal of American Studies* 26.3 (1992): 337–55.

Franklin, Wayne and Michael Steiner, eds. *Mapping American Culture*. Iowa City: University of Iowa Press, 1992.

Frazer, James George. *The Golden Bough*. New York: Macmillan, 1951.

Frazer, Timothy C., ed. *"Heartland" English: Variety and Transition in the American Midwest*. Tuscaloosa: University of Alabama Press, 1993.

Furtak, Rick Anthony. "'I Used to Care, But Things Have Changed': Passion and the Absurd in Dylan's Later Work." Porter and Vernezze 16–28.

Gamble, Andrew. "The Drifter's Escape." *The Political Art of Bob Dylan*. Boucher and Browning 12–34.

Garland, Hamlin. *A Son of the Middle Border*. Lincoln: University of Nebraska Press, 1979.

——*Main-Travelled Roads*. New York: New American Library, 1962.

——*The Mystery of the Buried Crosses: A Narrative of Psychic Exploration*. New York: Dutton, 1939.

Gass, William H. *On Being Blue*. Boston: David Godine, 1997.

——*In the Heart of the Heart of the Country and Other Stories*. New York: Harper & Row, 1968.

Gates, David. "Dylan Revisited." *Newsweek* 6 October 1997: 62–8.

Gibb, Trev. "The Midnight Train: The Mystic World of 'Standing in the Doorway.'" *Judas!* 10 (July 2004): 6–12.

Gill, Andy. *Don't Think Twice, It's All Right: Bob Dylan, The Early Years*. New York: Thunder's Mouth Press, 1998.

Gill, Andy and Kevin Odegard. *A Simple Twist of Fate: Bob Dylan and the Making of Blood on the Tracks*. Cambridge, Massachusetts: Da Capo, 2004.

Gilman, Rhoda. "The History and Peopling of Minnesota: Its Culture." Graubard 1–30.

Gilmour, Michael J. *Tangled Up in the Bible: Bob Dylan & Scripture*. New York: Continuum, 2004.

Gohdes, Clarence and James D. Hart, eds. *America's Literature*. New York: Holt, Rinehart and Winston, 1955.

Goldberg, Steven. "Bob Dylan and the Poetry of Salvation." *Saturday Review* 30 May 1970: 43–6, 67.

Goodman, Paul. *Growing Up Absurd*. New York: Random House, 1960.

Graubard, Stephen R., ed. *Minnesota: A Different America?* Special issue of *Dædalus: Journal of the American Academy of Arts and Sciences* 129.3 (Summer 2000).

Gray, Michael. *The Bob Dylan Encyclopedia*. New York: Continuum, 2006.

——*Song and Dance Man III*. New York: Continuum, 2000.

Gruchow, Paul. *Grass Roots*. Minneapolis: Milkweed Editions, 1995.

——*Journal of a Prairie Year*. Minneapolis: University of Minnesota Press, 1985.

Guthrie, Woody. *Bound for Glory*. New York: New American Library, 1970.

Hajdu, David. *Positively 4th Street: The Lives and Times of Joan Baez, Bob Dylan, Mimi Baez Fariña and Richard Fariña*. New York: Farrar, Straus and Giroux, 2001.

Hanratty, Pádraig. "Time Is an Enemy." *Judas!* 11 (October 2004): 50–66.

Harrison, Jim. *Legends of the Fall*. New York: Dell Publishing, 1979.

Hawthorne, Nick. "The Gypsy Trail." *Judas!* 9 (April 2004): 21–35.

Haynes, John Earl. *Dubious Alliance: The Making of Minnesota's DFL Party*. Minneapolis: University of Minnesota Press, 1984.

Haynes, Robin. *Geographical Images and Mental Images*. London: Macmillan, 1981.

Heine, Steven. *Bargainin' for Salvation: Bob Dylan, A Zen Master?* New York: Continuum, 2009.

Hentoff, Nat. "Dylan: The Times Are A-Changin' Again." *Knockin' on Dylan's Door: On the Road in '74*. New York: Pocket Books, 1974. 113–18.

Herdman, John. *Voice without Restraint*. Edinburgh: Paul Harris, 1982.

Herman, Lewis Helmar and Marguerite Shalett Herman. *American Dialects: A Manual for Actors, Directors, and Writers*. New York: Theatre Arts Books, 1947.

Herr, Cheryl Temple. *Critical Regionalism and Cultural Studies: from Ireland to the American Midwest*. Gainesville: University of Florida Press, 1996.

Heylin, Clinton. *Revolution in the Air*. Chicago: Chicago Review Press, 2009.

——*Bob Dylan: A Life in Stolen Moments*. New York: Schirmer Books, 1996.

——*Bob Dylan: Behind the Shades*. New York: Summit Books, 1991.

——*Bob Dylan: Stolen Moments*. Romford, Essex: Wanted Man Publications, 1988.

——*Rain Unravelled Tales: (The Nightingale's Code Examined) — A Rumorography*, 3rd edition. Juarez: Ashes and Sand, 1985.

Heynen, Jim. *Being Youngest*. New York: Henry Holt and Company, 1997.

Hilfer, Anthony Channell. *The Revolt from the Village: 1915-1930*. Chapel Hill: University of North Carolina Press, 1969.

Hinchey, John. "Planet Waves: 'Not Too Far Off.'" *Judas!* 12 (January 2005): 3–23.

——"*New Morning* and Beyond: Biding Time, Biting His Tongue." *Judas!* 9 (April 2004): 3–18.

——*Bob Dylan's Slow Train*. Bury, Lancashire: Wanted Man, 1983.

Hishmeh, Richard E. "Marketing Genius: The Friendship of Allen Ginsberg and Bob Dylan." *The Journal of American Culture* 29.4 (2006): 395–405.

Hodson, Paul. "Bob Dylan's Stories About Men." Thomson and Gutman 183–9.

Holm, Bill. *Landscape of Ghosts*. Stillwater, Minnesota: Voyageur Press, 1993.

—— *The Dead Get By with Everything*. Minneapolis, Minnesota: Milkweed Editions, 1990.

——*The Music of Failure*. Marshall, Minnesota: Plains Press, 1986.

Holm, Bill and Doug Ohman. *Cabins of Minnesota*. St. Paul: Minnesota Historical Society Press, 2007.

Holman, David Marion. *A Certain Slant of Light: Regionalism and the Form of Southern and Midwest Fiction*. Baton Rouge: Louisiana State University Press, 1995.

Jesperson, Otto. *A Modern English Grammar on Historical Principles*. 7 vols. Heidelberg: C. Winter, 1909–40.

Johnson, Jeffrey. *"They Are All Red Out Here": Socialist Politics in the Pacific Northwest, 1895–1925*. Norman: University of Oklahoma Press, 2008.

Jung, Carl. *The Portable Jung*. Ed. Joseph Campbell. New York: Viking, 1971.

Kangas, Carolyn. Personal Interview. Hibbing, Minnesota, 4 September 2008.

Keillor, Garrison. *Lake Wobegon Days*. New York: Viking, 1985.

Kerouac, Jack. *On the Road*. New York: Viking, 1959.

——*The Town and the City*. San Diego: Harcourt Brace, 1950.

Kloefkorn, William. *Breathing in the Fullness of Time*. Lincoln: University of Nebraska Press, 2009.

Knoepfle, John. *poems from the sangamon*. Champaign: University of Illinois Press, 1985.

Kolodny, Annette. *The Lay of the Land: Metaphor as Experience and History in American Life and Letters*. Chapel Hill: University of North Carolina Press, 1975.

Kowalewski, Michael. "Contemporary Regionalism." *A Companion to the Regional Literatures of America*. Ed. Charles L. Crowe. Malden, Massachusetts: Blackwell, 2003.

Krause, Herbert. *The Thresher*. Indianapolis: Bobbs-Merrill Co., 1946.

Krein, Kevin and Abigail Levin, "Just Like a Woman: Dylan, Authenticity, and the Second Sex." Porter and Vernezze 53–65.

Kunstler, James. *The Geography of Nowhere: The Rise and Decline of America's Man-Made Landscape*. New York: Free Press, 1993.

Landis, Paul Henry. *Three Iron Mining Towns*. New York: Arno Press, 1970.

Lanegran, David A. *Minnesota on the Map*. St. Paul: Minnesota Historical Society Press, 2008.

——"Minnesota: Nature's Playground." Graubard 81–100.

Lawrence, D. H. *Studies in Classic American Literature*. Eds Ezra Greenspan, Lindeth Vasey and John Worthen. Cambridge: Cambridge University Press, 1923.

Le Sueur, Meridel. *Crusaders: The Radical Legacy of Marian and Arthur Le Sueur*. St. Paul: Minnesota Historical Society Press, 1984.

——*Ripening: Selected Works*. New York: The Feminist Press, 1982.

——"The Ancient People and the Newly Come." Chester Anderson 17–46.

——*My People Are My Home*. Film. Minneapolis, Minnesota: Twin Cities Women's Film Collective, 1976.

Lerner, Laurence. *The Uses of Nostalgia: Studies in Pastoral Poetry*. New York: Schocken, 1972.

Lewis, Sinclair. *Main Street*. New York: New American Library, 1961.

Lieberman, Laurence. *Unassigned Frequencies: American Poetry in Review, 1964–1977*. Champaign, Illinois: University of Illinois Press, 1977.

Lillie, Ronald George. *The Industrial Workers of the World and the Strike of Iron Ore Miners of Minnesota in 1916*. Thesis. Bemidji State University, August 1976. Print.

Lindsay, Vachel. *The Poetry of Vachel Lindsay, Complete & with Lindsay's Drawings*. Ed. Dennis Camp. 3 vols. Peoria, Illinois: Spoon River Poetry Press, 1984, 1985, 1986.

——*Vachel Lindsay Reading The Congo, Chinese Nightingale, and Other Poems*. Sound Recording (LP). New York: Caedmon TC1041, 1941.

Lindsey, Hal and Carole C. Carlson. *The Late, Great Planet Earth*. Grand Rapids, Michigan: Zondervan, 1970.

Lisa, David Carter. *"We Never Forget": I.W.W. Support for Finnish Draft Resisters on the Minnesota Iron Range During World War I*. Ph.D. Diss. Syracuse University, August 1988. Print.

Littlefield, Henry M. *"The Wizard of Oz*: Parable on Populism." *American Quarterly* 16 (Spring 1964): 47–58.

Louis, Adrian C. *Ceremonies of the Damned*. Las Vegas: University of Nevada Press, 1997.

Lowell, Robert. *Lord Weary's Castle*. New York: Harcourt, Brace & World, 1944.

Lundin, Roger. *The Culture of Interpretation: Christian Faith and the Postmodern World*. Grand Rapids, Michigan: William B. Eerdmans Publishing Company, 1993.

Lynan, John. *The Pastoral Art of Robert Frost*. New Haven: Yale University Press, 1960.

Lyotard, Jean-François. *The Postmodern Condition: A Report on Knowledge*. Trans. Geoff Bennington and Brian Massumi. Minneapolis: University of Minnesota Press, 1984.

McGrath, Thomas. *Letter to an Imaginary Friend, Parts I & II*. Chicago: The Swallow Press, 1962.

McGregor, Craig, ed. *Bob Dylan: A Retrospective*. New York: Morrow, 1972.

MacLeish, Archibald. *The Human Season: Selected Poems 1926–1972*. Boston: Houghton Mifflin, 1972.

Mailer, Norman. *The Armies of the Night*. New York: Signet, 1968.

——*Why Are We in Vietnam?* New York: G. P. Putnam's Sons, 1968.

Marcus, Greil. *Like a Rolling Stone: Bob Dylan at the Crossroads*. New York: Public Affairs, 2005.

——*Invisible Republic: Bob Dylan's Basement Tapes*. New York: Henry Holt, 1997.

——*The Dustbin of History*. Cambridge, Massachusetts: Harvard University Press, 1995.

——"Amazing Chutzpah." Thomson and Gutman 237–40.

Marqusee, Mike. *Chimes of Freedom: The Politics of Bob Dylan's Art*. New York: The New Press, 2003.

Marshall, Scott M. and Marcia Ford. *Restless Pilgrim: The Spiritual Journey of Bob Dylan*. Lake Mary, Florida: Relevant Books, 2002.

Marx, Leo. *The Machine in the Garden: Technology and the Pastoral Ideal in America*. New York: Oxford University Press, 1964.

Mellers, Wilfred. *A Darker Shade of Pale: A Backdrop to Bob Dylan*. London: Faber and Faber, 1984.

Meyrowitz, Joshua. *No Sense of Place: The Impact of Electronic Media on Social Behaviour*. New York: Oxford University Press, 1985.

Miles, Barry. *Paul McCartney: Many Years from Now*. New York: Henry Holt and
    Company, 1997.
Milinovich, Joseph. *The History of Old North Hibbing*. Thesis. University of North
    Dakota, 7 August 1957. Print.
Miller, Arthur. *The Portable Arthur Miller*. Ed. Harold Clurman. New York: Viking,
    1971.
Miller, Curtis. "Organized Labor: A Look Back." *Duluth: Sketches of the Past*. Eds Ryck
    Lydecker and Lawrence J. Sommer. Duluth, Minnesota: American Revolution
    Bicentennial Commission, 1976. 209–19.
Miller, Perry. *Errand into the Wilderness*. Boston: Harvard University, 1956.
Minnesota Department of Agriculture. *Minnesota Farm Financial Survey: 1985*. St.
    Paul, Minnesota: Minnesota Dept. of Agriculture, 90 West Plato Blvd., 3 February
    1986.
Mohr, Howard. *How to Talk Minnesotan*. New York: Penguin, 1987.
Moltmann, Jurgen. "American Contradictions." *Center* November–December 1976:
    59–65.
Morlan, Robert L. *Political Prairie Fire: The Nonpartisan League, 1915–1922*.
    Minneapolis: University of Minnesota Press, 1955.
Morris, Robin. "A Place That You Can Call Home." *Popular Music and Society* 32.2
    (May 2009): 167–77.
Moyers, Bill. "Poet at Large: A Conversation with Robert Bly." *Bill Moyers' Journal*
    403 (19 February 1979). Video cassette. New York: Educational Broadcasting
    Corporation, 1979.
Muir, Andrew. "Lies that Truth Is Black and White." *Judas!* 11 (October 2004): 33–49.
——*Troubadour: Early & Late Songs of Bob Dylan*. Bluntisham, Cambridgeshire:
    Woodstock Publications, 2003.
Nash, Roderick Frazier. *Wilderness and the American Mind*. 4th edition. New Haven:
    Yale University Press, 2001.
Nass, David, ed. *Holiday: Minnesotans Remember the Farmers' Holiday Association*.
    Marshall, Minnesota: Plains Press, 1984.
Nelson, Paul. "Bob Dylan: Another View." McGregor 104–7.
Norris, Frank. *The Pit*. New York: Doubleday, Page & Co., 1903.
Paglia, Camille. *Sex, Art, and American Culture*. New York: Vintage, 1992.
Parker, Kathleen. "Mainstream Media Need to Get Outside Their Bubble." *National
    Review*. Reprinted in *Wilmar Tribune*, 16 October, 2008, 4.
Patai, Daphne. *Heterophobia: Sexual Harassment and the Future of Feminism*. Lanham,
    Maryland: Rowman & Littlefield Publishers, 1998
Pichaske, David. *Rooted: Seven Midwest Writers of Place*. Iowa City: University of Iowa
    Press, 2006.
——*A Generation in Motion: Popular Music and Culture in the Sixties*. New York:
    Schirmer Books, 1979.
Polizzotti, Mark. *Highway 61 Revisited*. New York: Continuum, 2006.
Porter, Carl J. and Peter Vernezze, eds. *Bob Dylan and Philosophy*. Chicago: Open
    Court, 2006.
Ricks, Christopher. *Dylan's Visions of Sin*. New York: HarperCollins, 2004.
Riesman, David. *The Lonely Crowd*. New York: Doubleday, 1953.
Riley, Tim. *Hard Rain: A Dylan Commentary*. New York: Alfred Knopf, 1992.
Rodnitzky, Jerome L. *Minstrels of the Dawn: The Folk-Protest Singer as a Cultural Hero*.
    Chicago: Nelson-Hall, 1976.
Roe, Nicholas. "Playing Time." Corcoran 81–104.

Rölvaag, Ole. *Giants in the Earth*. New York: Harper & Row, 1955.

Ross, Alex. "Final Theme." *New Yorker* 18 September 2006.

Rotolo, Suze. *A Freewheelin' Time*. New York: Broadway Books, 2008.

Salisbury, Harrison E. "The Victorian City in the Midwest." Chester Anderson 49–75.

Sandburg, Carl. *Harvest Poems, 1910–1960*. New York: Harcourt Brace, 1960.

——*The American Songbag*. New York: Harcourt, Brace & Company, 1927.

Sanders, Scott Russell. *Writing from the Center*. Bloomington: University of Indiana Press, 1995.

Scaduto, Anthony. *Bob Dylan: An Intimate Biography*. New York: Grosset & Dunlap, 1971.

Schorer, Mark. *Sinclair Lewis: An American Life*. New York: McGraw-Hill, 1961.

Scobie, Stephen. "Always Other Voices," *Judas!* 12 (January 2005): 32–44.

——"The Stephen Scobie Interview," *Judas!* 9 (April 2004): 37–56.

——*Alias: Bob Dylan Revisited*. Calgary, Canada: Red Deer Press, 2003.

Seeger, Pete. *Pete Seeger's Greatest Hits* (LP). Columbia Stereo Record CS 9416, 1987.

Seventy-Fifth Anniversary Committee. *Hibbing Minnesota 1893–1968 Diamond Jubilee Days*. Hibbing: NP, 1968.

Shelton, Robert. *No Direction Home: The Life and Music of Bob Dylan*. New York: William Morrow, 1986.

——"I Can Change, I Swear." *Conclusions on the Wall: New Essays on Bob Dylan*. Ed. Elizabeth Thomson. Prestwich, Manchester: Thin Man, 1980. 7–19.

——"Bob Dylan: A Distinctive Folk-Song Stylist." McGregor 17–18.

Shepard, Sam. *Rolling Thunder Logbook*. New York: Penguin, 1978.

Shimkin, Jonathan. "'it then must be time for you to rest & learn new songs:' Bob Dylan's 'Mr. Tambourine Man.'" *Judas!* 8 (January 2004): 58–66.

Shortridge, James. *The Middle West: Its Meaning in American Culture*. Lawrence: University of Kansas Press, 1989.

Silber, Irwin. "Topical Song: Polarisation Sets In." McGregor 102–3.

Sinclair, Upton. *The Jungle*. New York: Doubleday, Jabber & Co., 1906.

Smaby, Alpha. *Political Upheaval: Minnesota and the Vietnam Anti-War Protests*. Minneapolis, Minnesota: Dillon Press, 1987.

Smart, Nick. "Nothing but Affection for All Those Who've Sailed with Me: Bob Dylan from Place to Place." *Popular Music and Society* 32.2 (May 2009): 179–97.

Smith, Anthony Neil. *Yellow Medicine*. Madison, Wisconsin: Bleak House Books, 2008.

Smith, Larry David. *Writing Dylan: The Songs of a Lonesome Traveler*. Westport, Connecticut: Praeger, 2005.

Smith, Page. *As a City upon a Hill: The Town in American History*. New York: Alfred A. Knopf, 1966.

Snow, Craig Robert. *Folksinger and Beat Poet: The Prophetic Vision of Bob Dylan*. Diss. Purdue University, August 1987. Print.

Sommers, Christina Hoff. *The War Against Boys: How Misguided Feminism Is Harming Our Young Men*. New York: Touchstone, 2000.

Sounes, Howard. *Down the Highway: The Life of Bob Dylan*. New York: Grove Press, 2001.

Spiegel, James S. "With God (and Socrates and Augustine) on Our Side." Porter and Vernezze 124–33.

Spitz, Bob. *Dylan: A Biography*. New York: Norton, 1989.

Stegner, Wallace. "Wilderness Letter, December 3, 1960." *The Sound of Mountain Water*. New York: Doubleday, 1969. 145–53.

——*Wolf Willow*. New York: Macmillan, 1962.

Steinbeck, John. *The Grapes of Wrath*. New York: Viking, 1939.

Stern, David Alan. *Speaking without an Accent: Mid-West Farm*. Audio cassette and booklet. Los Angeles: Dialect Accent Specialists, Inc., 1982.

Sutter, Barton. *My Father's War and Other Stories*. New York: Viking, 1991.

Thompson, Toby. *Positively Main Street: An Unorthodox View of Bob Dylan*. New York: Coward-McCann, 1971.

Thomson, Elizabeth and David Gutman, eds., *The Dylan Companion*. London: Macmillan, 1990.

Thoreau, Henry David. *Walden and Civil Disobedience*. Ed. Owen Thomas. New York: W. W. Norton, 1966.

de Tocqueville, Alexis. *De la démocratie en Amerique* (1835/1840) — *Democracy in America*. 2 vols (1835, 1840). English language versions: Tocqueville, *Democracy in America*. Trans. and Eds., Harvey C. Mansfield and Delba Winthrop, University of Chicago Press, 2000; Tocqueville, *Democracy in America*. Trans. Arthur Goldhammer, Ed. Olivier Zunz, New York: The Library of America, 2004.

Trager, Oliver. *Keys to the Rain: The Definitive Bob Dylan Encyclopedia*. New York: Billboard Books, 2004.

Turner, Frederick Jackson. *The Frontier in American History*. New York: Henry, Holt, 1920.

Underwood, Gary N. *The Dialect of the Mesabi Range*. Publications of the American Dialect Society, 67. University, Alabama: University of Alabama Press, 1981.

Van Hees, Martin. "The Free Will in Bob Dylan." Porter and Vernezze 115–23.

Webb, Walter Prescott. *The Great Plains*. New York: Grosset & Dunlap, 1931.

Weber, Max. *The Protestant Ethic and the Spirit of Capitalism*. Trans. Talcott Parsons. New York: Scribner's, 1958.

Welles, Chris. "Bob Dylan: Angry Folk Singer." *Life*, April 1964: 110–14.

West, Nathanael. *The Day of the Locust*. New York: Random House, 1939.

Whitaker, Dave. "Brief Encounters." *Telegraph* 26 (Spring 1987): 33–5.

Whithouse, Chris. "Alias," *Telegraph* 19 (Spring 1985): 23.

Whitman, Walt. *Prose Works 1892*. Ed. Floyd Stovall. 2 vols. New York: New York University Press, 1964.

Whyte, William. *The Organization Man*. New York: Simon & Schuster, 1956.

Wiener, Barbara, producer. "The Iron Range: A People's History." Video cassette. Minneapolis: KTCA Productions, 1994.

Williams, Paul. *Bob Dylan: Performing Artist, The Middle Years*. Lancaster, Pennsylvania: Underwood-Miller, 1992.

Worthington, Roger. "No Sign of Dylan Legacy in Hibbing." *Duluth News-Tribune* 17 August 1988: B1.

Zeller, Brad. "The Walls of Red Wing." *City Pages*, 3 December 2003. citypages.com. 7 August 2009.

Index